Merry Christmas From the Old Country Priest

2011

MORE MEMORIES of an Old Country Priest

Memories of an Old Country Priest

MORE MEMORIES of an Old Country Priest

Monsignor
Francis J. Weber

Saint Francis Historical Society
Mission Hills, California
Anno Domini MMXI

Anno Domini MMXI

The author gratefully acknowledges the
dedicated interest of the Ernest and Helen Chagon
Trust in the publication of this book.

Printed by BookMasters, Inc.
of Ashland, Ohio

Jacket Design by Terry Ruscin

ISBN 0-9678477-7-X

Frontice Piece: The reproduction of the "Old Country Priest" is made from a wooden engraving taken from the archives of McLaughlin Brothers of New York in the 1860s. It is used here through the kindness of the late Regis Graden.

Table of Contents

Preface

This book expands and completes the "memories" published by the author in 2000. Unlike his earlier, more formalized studies, this is a "personalized" reflection of ministry in the Catholic Church in Southern California over the last half century by someone who has served on the curial staff of three cardinals since 1962.

Few diocesan priests in the history of California have had a comparable influence upon our understanding of Catholic California as the writer through his many, many publications. The Archdiocese of Los Angeles made a very wise decision when it allowed him to develop his talents as an historian, archivist, bookman, critic, and history professor, in addition to his pastoral duties at San Fernando Mission.

His career and influence remind me of two other notable diocesan priest scholars, namely, Msgr. John Ryan and Msgr. John Tracy Ellis of the Catholic University of America, where Msgr. Weber did his graduate work.

As far as the development of my own talents is concerned, I would point to the late Father William Monihan, SJ, librarian at the University of San Francisco, and to Msgr. Weber as individuals from whom I have absorbed something of my own ethos.

Congratulations for that day, fifty years ago, on the feast of St. Catherine of Siena, when the late great James Francis Cardinal McIntyre, seated before the high altar of the venerable St. Vibiana's Cathedral anointed his hands with oil and welcomed him, into the priesthood of Jesus Christ, according to the order of Melchisedech.

April 30, 2009

Kevin Starr

The writer wishes to thank Bill Loughlin of Glendale for reading and correcting the page galleys of this book, and Kevin Feeney of Palmdale for formatting and putting the manuscript into its final corrected version.

1
Introduction

Who would have thought or dreamed, a decade ago, that this haggard, bedraggled and antiquated cleric would be granted another ten years on planet earth? Had that notion seemed even remotely likely, given my precarious health, *Memories of an Old Country Priest* would have borne the imprint of 2010 instead of 2000.

Somewhere I recall reading that there are three queries that traditionally determine whether a person's memories are worth remembering, much less publishing.

a) does anyone really care;
b) would they make a useful contribution;
c) are they interesting and well-written.

In my case, the most optimistic response to all three queries would be "maybe". Though the earlier volume never reached the *New York Times* 'best sellers' list, several reviewers and a fair number of casual readers were kind and charitable in their responses.

Longevity has never been a characteristic of the Webers. The only one to live into her nineties was my grandmother, Rose, a "Meier" who married into the Weber family in the early part of the 20th century.

My major professor at Catholic University was not a great fan of autobiographies. In one of his books, Msgr. John Tracy Ellis quoted the late Humphrey Carpenter who stated that "Autobiography is probably the most respectable form of lying. No one expects the whole truth in any case, how could it be revealed, since the person we know least is likely to be ourself? The worst autobiographies are those that fail to take account of the deceptive nature of the genre; the best are those that exploit it."

In any event, here is a sequel to "Memories" which may well be just another bleep on somebody's computer.

Hope you like it.

2

Memories I, *Reception and Reviews*

The first volume of the memoir, *Memories of an Old Country Priest,* appeared in 2000. Judging by the reviews, it was well received. Paul G. Fox, writing in the *Mooresville / Decatur Times* applauded the "illustrated autobiographical summary" quoting my rationalization for the book, namely that I was "one of the majority who has always enjoyed being a priest. I have welcomed the challenges of ministry and I have never experienced an image problem. Maybe it is time to tell the world how priesthood looks from the inside by someone who never wanted to be anything else." During a subsequent visit to my birthplace Valley Mills, Paul hosted a gathering of a dozen or so classmates from Decatur Central to a delightful luncheon. Another reviewer claimed that "though the book is detail ridden, and highly readable, if the monsignor were to re-write the phonebook, it would probably become a best seller."

On October 4, 2000, I was invited to speak at the Zamorano Club about the book. The substance of those remarks is reproduced.

> A few years ago, I wrote a series of essays about some of the prominent churchmen I had known over the years. The idea for that project was inspired by John Tracy Ellis' book on *Catholic Bishops: A Memoir* which was to have been a chapter in his never completed autobiography. In 1997, while doing research at the Archival Center for the Archdiocese of Los Angeles, one of our researchers read and liked the manuscript, suggesting that it be further enlarged to encompass the other people and events of my life.
>
> Later, a local historian from Indianapolis, asked me to reflect on my early childhood days in the Hoosier state. That request brought about the realization that as the last male of the Weber line, my demise will close forever a chapter that only I could provide.

A MAN WHO NEEDS NO INTRODUCTION

MONSIGNOR FRANCIS J. WEBER
WILL TELL OF HIS MEMORIES

AT THE

ZAMORANO CLUB

OUR FIRST MEETING OF THE FALL SEASON

WEDNESDAY, OCTOBER 4, 2000

McCORMICK & SCHMICK'S RESTAURANT
111 NORTH LOS ROBLES
PASADENA, CALIFORNIA

SHERRY AT SIX-THIRTY, DINNER AT SEVEN

R.S.V.P. (213)538-0364
LUNCHEON AT THE HUNTINGTON
ON THE THIRD WEDNESDAY OF THE MONTH.

When I first confided to my sister that I was thinking of publishing my memories, her response was as immediate as it was disconcerting: "Whatever for? Who would read them? How positively presumptuous!" After mentally deciding against giving her a review copy, I explained that her elder brother was an exception to the widespread (and, I think, erroneous) image of the contemporary priest conjured up by certain omniscient sociologists and loquacious journalists. I am one of the majority who has always enjoyed being a priest, I have welcomed the challenges of ministry

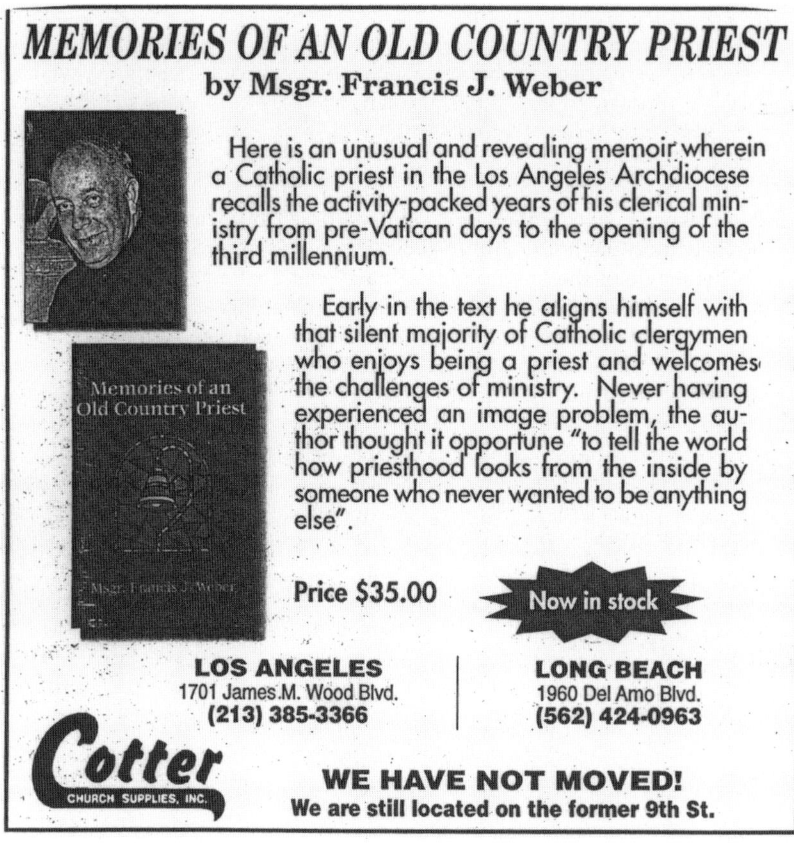

and I have never experienced an image problem. Maybe it was time to tell the world how priesthood looks from the inside.

As to the derivation of the title for this book, *Memories of an Old Country Priest*, may I point out that, by definition, an autobiography is "the story of one's life written by himself." Unhappily, I never kept a journal or diary and, for that reason, I felt that another term, such as "memories" would more accurately describe this book. There was much that I had forgotten or could not document and other events seemed too trivial, ambiguous and/or unimportant to include. Through the kindness of Regis Graden, my Christmas card for 1993 had featured a reproduction of an "old country priest" from a wood engraving taken from the archives of McLoughlin Brothers of New York City in the 1860s. [That title was all the more appealing since a version of it was used by George Bernanos in his famous book, *Diary of a Country Priest*, issued in the 1950s.]

With some few exceptions, the book was been written totally in my own words. In certain areas, I resurrected thoughts and comments spoken or published in earlier contexts and that factor will explain the evolution of grammatical style that has occurred over these many years.

Never having been in therapy, I didn't feel any special compulsion to dwell on my own imperfections, though surely they are legionary. Rather, the emphasis in these memories is simply that of recalling certain events and relating them to my own life as it has unfolded since 1933. And, finally, to assuage the allegations spoken or thought by certain observers, this book was not compiled on "company time," but was put together in the early morning hours, from 3 to 5 o'clock over most of two years.

This is one of the few volumes I have ever written that has no footnotes. That *lacuna* in no way diminishes the reliability of the book. While most of the factual data is verifiable from outside sources, I am personally the ultimate authority for everything else. And I must tell you that it's far more difficult to manufacture and sustain a lie than it is to tell the truth.

Perhaps a true story will illustrate this point. When I was a teenage seminarian, my pastor drafted me to take an elderly man in the parish to the barber every Saturday morning. The distinguished gentleman had been legal counsel for the Santa Fe Railway and he insisted that we drive downtown to a barber whose shop was in the old Santa Fe building. In those days, I had few funds and my wealthy rider never once even offered to pay for the gasoline. One day, I told him that I had read in the paper that his barber had died, "So, let's go over to Western Avenue to a barber that I know." He was agreeable. After he climbed into the chair, he confided that his own barber had died during the week. To which, the new barber responded: "Oh, that's not true, I had breakfast with him this morning." After that I decided that lying just complicated a person's life and wasn't something I wanted to pursue.

If I counted correctly, there are 167 photographs in the book, an amazing number for someone who never made any attempt to save pictures. As a matter of fact, I've never liked my photographs probably because they are so life-like. A number of people helped to assemble the illustrations. I actually took three or four myself and thereby confirmed that being a photographer is totally beyond my limited competence.

The dust jacket for this book was designed and executed by the talented Terry Ruscin of San Diego. Ruscin's recently published, coffee-table book on the California Missions is nothing short of a masterpiece. One lady told me that I could have my book back after she read it, but she wanted to keep the jacket. From that point of view, this book resembles a beautifully prepared Christmas gift whose wrapping far surpasses its content.

I learned some valuable lessons while putting these memories into narrative form. To begin with, a person's memory, especially about himself, can be and very often is amazingly fallible, inconsistent and inaccurate. For that reason, probably more research went into this volume than to any other that I have written over the years. Nothing was included without verification.

Secondly, the chronology of events in a person's memory-bank tends to blur with the passage of time. Names occasionally get distorted, especially if the same family name recurs at different times over the years.

Thirdly, it is exceedingly difficult and may even be impossible to look at one's own personal life impartially. Recognizing that factor is probably a first step in taking the necessary precautions toward keeping a balance in recalling controversial or two-sided events.

Finally, there is a strange and unrealistic tendency to look backward *romantically.* Places, events and people in one's rear vision mirror tend to be bigger, happier and more pleasant than indeed they were and are. When I revisited the tiny village of my birth and early youth, the buildings were smaller, the events less memorable and the people less impressive. I am not sure why the past appears so attractive. Though I write about the events of earlier years I wouldn't care to live then.

While publishing one's memories can intimidate others, even churchmen, I rather thought that, at age sixty-seven, I posed no threat to anyone. In fact I wrote at an age when one is supposed to tread carefully in order to avoid stumbling on the way out. I have already lived beyond the life expectancy rate when my father was a child.

For many years, Gladys Posakony, a lovely and patient lady in San Buenaventura, read my manuscripts and corrected my galleys. She gave me a lot of advice about this particular treatise, most of which I followed. On a number of occasions, she suggested that this event be minimized or that person's name be deleted. In addition to keeping me out of libel suits, she helped me to retain the external appearance of being kind and charitable.

Memories of an Old Country Priest is the largest, thickest and heaviest among the 154 books and monographs I have written, compiled, edited, translated and/or published over the years. It wasn't meant to be so mammoth and for that I feel a little apologetic.

For the most part, the book is laid out chronologically. While some events and a lot of people stand out more prominently than others, I attempted to place everything in perspective and that involved omitting a lot of details that seemed important at the time, but less so after the passage of years. Interestingly, the unpleasantries of former times have a short shelf-life and, they appear far less vital and crucial once the scar tissue has been given time to heal.

Though it's a little early for serious book reviews, there has been a lot of mostly favorably coverage in the local newspapers. In a Catholic magazine, distributed nationally, another reviewer said that "So inclusive is this book that its author anticipates in considerable detail his own funeral, even to the point of providing a suggested homily for that occasion. His grave is selected with a marker already in place containing all the wording except the date of his demise. When asked about this, the monsignor replied: "If such a distinguished southlander as Arabella Huntington could have her birthdate purposefully mistaken on her sarcophagus, imagine what some curial bureaucrat could do to the simple tombstone of an old country priest."

As to whether I have any regrets, the answer is "yes." Almost daily in the months since the book appeared, I recall events and people that somehow eluded me during the two years the book was in progress. And some of them were significant. Maybe that's why so many autobiographers, like Harris Newmark, felt compelled to issue expanded accounts and updates. While I would hope to avoid such a temptation, I make no

promises. If I were to live another decade or so, there might be a supplement. Father Andrew Greeley wrote his autobiography some years ago and then, just at the end of the century, he released a second volume, this one entitled: *Furthermore!*

Working on a project such as this enforces the realization that we are all standing on the shoulders of our predecessors. What we have become is due, in great measure, to a confluence of events over which we had little or no personal control. Let me give you some examples: (a) had not my parents had the good sense to relocate to California after World War II, I would probably be driving a school bus on the back roads of Marion county, Indiana; (b) had not an elderly nun practically kidnapped me into the seminary, I would likely be an antiquarian clerk at Caravan bookstore next door to the Biltmore Hotel; (c) had not an archbishop sent me off to graduate studies in history, I might be pastor of a large parish in beautiful, downtown Burbank.

Now, these scenarios and others too numerous to mention are not, of themselves, bad, unattractive or disconcerting. But I believe that God has a master plan for everyone and our challenge is to recognize that master plan and try, as best we can, to keep out of His way as we try to live it to the fullest.

Would I advise others to write their "memories?" Yes, for several reasons: Parents owe it to their offspring, scholars owe it to their profession and politicians owe it to their constituents. In my own case, preparing this book was a reverse learning process. As the project moved along, the pattern of my life began making better sense and the Lord's hand became increasingly clear.

Several members of the Zamorano Club have written their autobiographies including Ward Ritchie and Lawrence Clark Powell. Another friend, Raymond Wood, has penned a humongous 5,701 page tome entitled *No Candidate for Sainthood.* While those who read the latter book might feel inclined to endorse its title, it surely is the most bluntly honest set of memoirs I have ever read. The Wood volume tells all, something which is fairly uncharacteristic of most autobiographies. But I am not sure that everything should be revealed. After all, even Saint Paul said that "certain things are better left unsaid."

* * * * * *

Several months later, I gave the following address to the Los Angeles Corral of the Westerners:

Last October, I spoke to the Zamorano Club about my recent autobiography, why it was written, how it was put together, who might read it, and what the general reaction was. Here I would like to mention some items that were omitted. The reason is that books are often more remembered for what they omit than for what they contain. A classical example of this is the anthology of James Whitcomb Riley's works published by the Bobbs-Merrill company. Throughout Riley's life, the publisher refused to acknowledge or even mention "The Passing of the Backhouse." This poem was considered unworthy of Riley, yet it remains today one of his most memorable writings.

Among the subjects that were omitted in *Memories of an Old Country Priest,* I would like to mention three:

There is no sex or account of any sexual encounters in the book. Despite what one reads in the newspapers, hears on the radio, or watches on television, I can testify that few priests have had any experiential association with the 6th and 9th commandments beyond what they have studied in theological manuals or heard in the confessional.

So, how does someone like Father Andrew Greeley write such steamy novels? I do not know him personally, but he obviously is a man with a vivid imagination and, at the same time, a person who verbalizes extremely well. He reminds me of James Ohio Pattie, who wrote extensively about inoculating the California natives in sixteen missions against smallpox with a rare serum he brought from Kentucky. Very likely he never even came to California or visited a single mission. But surely he was a talented prevaricator whose factional account has been published frequently since 1831. One of the readers who reviewed the manuscript of my book had the effrontery to suggest that anything I would need to say about sex could be contained in a "miniature" book.

The second subject omitted is the confessional. Probably more time is devoted by the average priest to the Sacrament of Penance than to any other single activity. As to why that subject was not so much as mentioned, keep in mind that the sacramental seal is inviolable, and it must be kept that way even in the face of a death threat. The confessor is bound to avoid betraying the penitent for any reason whatsoever. Nor may he use any knowledge acquired in confession to the detriment or even the betterment of the penitent. Most people are surprised to know that the hearing of confessions is about the most boring of all priestly duties, especially when it involves listening to the antics of a class of youngsters, an experience which someone described as being slowly plucked to death by a flock of geese. One of my favorite anecdotes involves a youngster who was told to recite three Hail Mary's for his penance. "Sorry, Father," he said. "I can't do that. I know only one."

And, finally, very little if any attention was devoted in the book to personal failures, of which there were many over almost seventy years. It seemed to me, that the telling of one's story should emphasize what actually happened over what did not happen. I have tried not to allow failures to discourage me, and, in fact, I once wrote an editorial pointing out that the great people in human annals are invariably those who persevere in whatever pursuit they undertake. They do not allow themselves to be crushed by failure, daunted by setbacks, or crestfallen by disappointments. I then pointed out that Babe Ruth is remembered for his home runs. His fans were not told that he struck out at bat no fewer than 1,330 times! Admiral Perry tried to reach the North Pole seven times

Prominent Visitors

to the

California Missions

Compiled with Critical Introductions

by

Msgr. Francis J. Weber

before he was finally successful. Thomas Edison experimented with 1,660 different materials before perfecting carbon for the electric light bulb. And Oscar Hammerstein had five Broadway disasters before "Oklahoma," which ran for 269 weeks and grossed $7,000,000 on an investment of $83,000.

I have dealt with and known a lot of people over the past forty-plus years, and they range from the very rich to the extremely poor, from the highly educated to the totally unschooled, from the very talented to the barely literate. For none of them was life a bowl of cherries. I mention this because among the cherries in my life there have been a fair percentage of pits, or failures, to which I shall briefly allude there. The meaning of the term "failure" used in this context is extended to include projects and dreams that were aborted, never left the tarmac, or otherwise did not materialize. In my admittedly biased opinion, any one of them would have added immeasurably to what little claim I have to immortality.

For many years, I dreamed of inaugurating a western Catholic historical journal that would have specialized in persons, places, and events along the Pacific Slope. In my files are half-a-hundred refusals from foundations and other funding agencies. I envisioned that such a journal would have needed to be at least partially subsidized for at least five years. I was greatly encouraged when the late Dr. Norton Stern began his *Western States Jewish Historical Quarterly* in 1968. Dr. Stern was most supportive of my aspirations, and we spent long hours in his Santa Monica office strategizing how my journal would meet the challenges he had so successfully met and resolved. The Stern journal continues its publication and is now in its thirty-second volume. Even in retrospect, I believe that such a journal would have been viable.

There were other disappointments, not the least of which was a volume to be entitled *Prominent Visitors to the California Missions*, which Grant Dahlstrom agreed to print between other projects in 1975. Unhappily, that tome never got beyond a draft of the title page because Grant got busy with more lucrative commissions. The text, finally released sixteen years later, was surely less elegantly printed than would have been the case with Grant Dahlstrom.

Father Steve Avella reviewed *Memories Of An Old Country Priest* for the *Catholic Historical Review* in these words:

The one thing that is confusing about Monsignor Francis Weber's interesting memoir is the title *Old Country Priest*. In fact by his own account, Weber is anything but a rural pastor. By contrast, he has spent the totality of his priestly ministry in one of the most heavily urbanized Catholic communities in the United States: The Archdiocese of Los Angeles. Here the lines between development and hinterland had been erased long before the Weber family migrated westward in the 1940s.

One is struck by how typical the Webers were of the thousands who came to California after World War II. Like so many other Californians they migrated from the snowy Midwest to find work and new opportunity in the Golden State. The elder Weber went to work for a family-owned business, the Ritz Plumbing Company, which provided a good wage and a respectable middle-class existence. Young "Frankie" was able to supplement his meager allowance with earnings from a *Los Angeles Times* paper route. Fortune smiled on the ambitious lad, for among his grateful customers was Buffie Chandler, one of the owners of the paper, and Archbishop James Francis McIntyre. During his high school and college years he worked for the Pierce Brothers Funeral Home, where he happened to meet the legendary Catholic benefactress, Estelle Doheny. These early contacts paid off. McIntyre would advance his clerical career, and Doheny's subsequent foundation bestowed some money for historical research.

The core of this narrative is about the priesthood. Weber writes the book as one "who has always enjoyed being a priest" and with a desire "to tell the world how priesthood looks from the inside by someone who never wanted to be anything else." His vocation to the priesthood developed under the watchful tutelage of the nuns and priests of St. Brendan's parish on Third and Van Ness. In 1946 he entered Los Angeles College, the preparatory seminary of the Archdiocese of Los Angeles. He was ordained to the priesthood in 1959 by his former paper-route customer, James Francis Cardinal McIntyre.

THE REVEREND MONSIGNOR JOHN TRACY ELLIS

Weber's career as a priest of the Archdiocese of Los Angeles was in many respects typical of clergy elsewhere: daily and Sunday Mass, "door" duty, sick calls, confessions, counseling and convert instructions. But his priestly ministry also had a distinctively Southern California twist. At St. Victor's parish in West Hollywood he came into frequent contact with a handful of Hollywood stars who sought spiritual ministry. He gave convert instructions to the second wife of the legendary Jimmy "The Schnozz" Durante, and was an occasional meal-time guest of Loretta Young. He shared the rectory with the famous Monsignor John Joseph Devlin, who had devised the codes of the Legion of Decency. Among the other luminaries that passed through Weber's life were figures as diverse as historians Will and Ariel Durant and the bubbly blonde comedian, Goldie Hawn.

In 1961 McIntyre sent Weber to The Catholic University of America, where he worked with John Tracy Ellis. At Ellis' insistence, he wrote extensively on Los Angeles subjects—areas of historiographical interest that remained outside the scope of the "mainstream" of American Catholic historiography. Weber's published corpus includes substantial studies on all the bishops/archbishops of Los Angeles. In imitation of Ellis' work on Gibbons, Weber penned two hefty volumes on Cardinal McIntyre that appeared in 1997.

But before he could write, Weber had to do the hard task of assembling archival records. Given a small space in a cramped chancery annex at 9th and Green Street, he single-handedly rescued many documents from oblivion (at one point hiding some of them in his long suffering father's garage). He parlayed his rising prestige as a local historian to press for more and more room and resources. Any archivist reading this account will readily recognize the bleak conditions under which Weber had to work: the abrupt treatment by "busy" chancery officials, the bemused disdain that priests "in the field" felt for the curators of musty documents, and the occasional impression that bishops gave in to a particular request for time, money, or space to get a pesky priest "off their neck." Fortunately for California Catholic history, Weber never gave up, and subsequent historians will be forever indebted to his collection policies and to the voluminous body of books and articles that he produced.

Weber took a major role in popularizing the Catholic history of the Golden State through a successful column on bits and pieces of historical data that ran in the Los Angeles *Tidings*. Weber also collected memorabilia for a first-rate historical museum connected to the archival center built with a substantial grant from the Daniel Donohue foundation in 1981 at Mission San Fernando. He even helped to transfer the bodies of deceased California prelates, such as San Francisco Archbishop Joseph Sadoc Alemany, to their rightful resting places with their people.

Weber made contacts with the Jesuit historian John B. McGloin, the Franciscan Maynard Geiger, the Vincentian Newman Eberhardt, and a graduate school classmate, James Gaffey; he became a close friend of Doyce Nunis of the University of Southern California. Like his mentor Ellis, he has generously encouraged the works of younger scholars. His love for the Church and his own grasp of the sources have occasionally found him wading into controversial subjects such as those surrounding the beatification of Fray Junípero Serra and Cardinal McIntyre's conflicts with the Sisters of the Immaculate Heart of Mary.

Weber's work in historical studies gave him a bird's eye view of many of the important figures in Los Angeles Catholic life. His characterizations of them are worth the price of the book. For example, he paints an accurate and balanced picture of Cardinals McIntyre and Manning's most trusted subaltern, Monsignor Benjamin Hawkes. His depiction of the eloquent, yet always guarded, Timothy Manning is always on target.

Weber's autobiography, fortunately, does not contain an epilogue noting his parting. He is still very much alive as this review is being written. Students of California Catholic history, historians of clerical culture, and those interested in the evolution of the field of American Catholic history will derive a great deal from this well-written and entertaining memoir.

Another reviewer, whose name I can not recall had this to say:

Here is an unusual and revealing memoir wherein a Catholic priest in the Los Angeles archdiocese recalls the activity-packed years of his clerical ministry from pre-Vatican days to the opening of the third millennium.

Early in the text he aligns himself with that silent majority of Catholic clergymen who enjoys being a priest and welcomes the challenges of ministry. Never having experienced an image problem, the author thought it opportune "to tell the world how priesthood looks from the inside by someone who never wanted to be anything else."

Having never been in therapy, he didn't feel any special compulsion to dwell on his own imperfections which he admits are legionary. Rather he concentrated on recalling a myriad of events, relating them to his own life as it has unfolded since 1933. As he looked backward, he found that the pattern of his life began making better sense and the Lord's hand became increasingly clear. The more he delved into his past, the more obvious it became that he had been God's pawn and for that he offers no apologies.

Though the book is detail-ridden, it is highly readable. A reviewer of a recent Weber book aptly declared that if the monsignor were to re-write the phonebook, it would probably become a best seller. Once again, the author reveals himself as a masterful storyteller who has successfully mirrored in himself the pageantry of American Catholic life.

Though he claims never to have kept a diary, there appears to be little of interest missing in this book of "memories." For perhaps the only time in his busy historical life, the author has published a volume without footnotes. He alone is the authority for what he has written.

While admitting to periods of discouragement and times when he was "denounced, calumniated, compromised, criticized and misjudged," sometimes even by his fellow clerics, Weber says that "happily the scars of those un-pleasantries have healed" and today he is far too conscious of his own inadequacies to worry about or recall the unkindness of others.

Of the thirty chapters, epilogue and four appendices in this book, none is more fascinating than the section on "Questions and Answers" in which the author reveals his innermost thoughts on a host of relevant subjects. While admitting with Saint Paul that, "certain things are better left unsaid," he openly and candidly expresses his views about Vatican Council II, the bishopric and the caliber of the nation's hierarchy. He reveals his favorite of the many books he has written translated, edited or published, his "regrets" and personal aspirations, his prayer-life, the ten best books he has read over the past half century and copious other insights into the life of a busy and widely respected California clergyman.

Throughout the pages of this remarkable memoir, the author could be classified as an amateur artist, at least in the context of Henry Thoreau who once observed that, "it is something to be able to paint a picture, or to carve a statue and so to make a few objects beautiful. But it is far more glorious to carve and paint the atmosphere in which we work, to effect the quality of the day. This is the highest of the arts."

Finally, the Cardinal weighed in on June 20, 2000.

Thanks so very much for dropping off a copy of your new and fascinating book *Memories of an Old Country Priest.*

I was so taken by the book that I actually paged through it upon receiving it. During the summer I hope to have the opportunity to read it much more thoroughly.

Since I will be on vacation some days during July, I will not return it to you to get your signature on the book itself, but will wait until after vacation is over.

As you might imagine, I read with great interest the sections on the four Archbishops of Los Angeles, and I was delighted—and a bit relieved! - to find that the Fourth Archbishop came out OK!

3
Personal Chronicle

In the mid-1990's I sponsored a fellowship at the Huntington Library in memory of my beloved parents. Among the awardees have been Susan Cogan, Steve Hackel and Nicole Roci. Usually the recipient would call me while in San Marino doing research. Here is how the Fellowship is publicized each year.

Serra Contest

One of the most pleasant of my many blessings was the day I first met William H. Hannon who at the time was President of the Fritz Burns Foundation. In subsequent years he channeled yearly subsidies to the Old Mission for restorative purposes.

FRANCIS J. WEBER RESEARCH FELLOWSHIP
IN ROMAN CATHOLIC HISTORY

The Huntington is pleased to announce a new fellowship, the Francis J. Weber Research Fellowship in Roman Catholic History. The fellowship, to be awarded annually, carries a stipend of $1,800 for one month. The recipient of the fellowship is expected to be in continuous residence at the Huntington and to participate in its intellectual life.

The Huntington is an independent research center with holdings in British and American history, as well as literature, art history, and the history of science. The Library collections range chronologically from the ninth to the twentieth centuries and include a half-million rare books and ephemera, 600,000 photographs, and 3.5 million manuscripts, supported by a half-million reference works.

Applications are accepted between October 1 and December 15. For more details, please contact the Committee on Fellowships.

THE HUNTINGTON
1151 Oxford Road, San Marino, CA 91108
Phone: (626) 405-2194 e-mail: cpowell@huntington.org

In 1992, Bill decided to inaugurate a Memorial Scholarship Contest for the Catholic Schools in the Archdiocese. He asked Sister Cecelia Louise Moore (or CL as we knew her) and me to serve as judges for the annual competition. Together we came up with the guidelines for the contest, which are still operational for the forty or so schools that participate each year. When CL died, I carried on as judge for the contest, which continues as one of the many outreaches of the William A. Hannon Foundation.

Santa Cruz Island

Early in 1967, I stumbled across a letter in the Chancery Archives for the Archdiocese of Los Angeles from Father Charles Philipps asking permission "to say Mass in the Private Chapel of Santa Cruz Island" where he planned to spend his annual vacation. Further research unearthed the "Delphine A. Caire Memorandum" which had been dictated later to give "an accurate description of the building (chapel) and of the events clustered around it." Brazenly, I wrote to Dr. Carey Stanton, asking if I might celebrate the Eucharist in the chapel.

The letter, which I had addressed to the "Santa Cruz Island Corporation" in Los Angeles, went unanswered for several months. One day, November 27 to be exact, a phone call came to the seminary where I was teaching, for the "Reverend Weber" from a man who would identify himself only as "a concerned Episcopalian." When I finally came on the line, there ensued a rather testy monologue, which concluded with a dozen or so questions such as why did I want to say Mass on "his" island, how did I get his address and who told me to write?

It took about half an hour to calm him down. Apparently my answers were acceptable because he eventually said: "All right, you may come on May 3rd, the titular feastday of the island . . . it'll cost you $100 for the air fare." When I asked if I could bring along two priest associates to share the fare, he blurted out: "Three priests at once. I don't know if I can handle that . . . okay, I am not a Roman Catholic, but I make all the

rules. The Mass has to be in Latin." Then he noted that there were about a dozen *braceros* working on the island and they would constitute the congregation. "Oh, by the way, they'll want to go to confession. Lord knows they need it."

When we arrived at the air station in Oxnard early on the morning of the appointed day, the pilot was full of his own observations: "How did you get permission? He discourages visitors and never, never does he

Tiny chapel on Santa Cruz Island.

Mariana and Santa Cruz

(Homily delivered to the Dominican Sisters at Anaheim on June 22, 1973)

A freckle-faced nine year old girl who speaks English only sparingly, asked me to bring you this little flower. It is her way of expressing gratitude for the inconvenience of changing your schedule today so I could offer Mass for her and a handful of people who reside far out to sea.

Mariana lives on Santa Cruz, one of the five channel islands off the California coast. She has been to Mass five times in as many years, yet she probably knows as much about her faith as do the students of this school with all their book-learning.

That little girl has never played with or even seen another youngster. Probably, in her sheltered world, she pictures herself as something of a unique creature among God's people.

Her faith is at once simple and majestic for Mariana is something of a priestess. Each Sunday morning, she walks across the meadow to an ancient stone church, where she lights the candles, adorns the altar with freshly-cut flowers and then rings the bell for weekly prayer.

For the last two years, Mariana has led the small community in worship—first singing, then reciting the rosary and finally blessing one another with holy water. It's a primitive kind of Christianity but one which surely pleases God immensely.

And so you can imagine how she looks forward to the annual visit of the priest. She scrubs the church floor, washes down the walls and arranges everything for the liturgy.

It's a glorious day for everyone, especially Mariana, when Christ, for whom Santa Cruz Island is named, comes each year.

Everyone goes to confession and then hurries off to the church there to pray in what is surely one of the last remaining vestiges from California's provincial era.

Just before we climbed aboard our tiny plane to leave, Mariana gave me this flower from the altar with instructions to give it to those "nice ladies who let you bring the Lord to my island."

Those of us who struggle to observe the vows of poverty, chastity and obedience are edified at the ease and joy with which little Mariana fulfills those counsels.

She lives alone with God's flowers, an abandoned church and a world full of adults. But Mariana is supremely happy because she knows God and speaks with HIM, perhaps more intimately than anyone of us here today.

And if Mariana touches your heart, could anyone feel sorry for a soul so closeto God? She has what the human race clamors for—peace of heart and soul.

In her primitive way of life, Christ is still, and prayerfully always will be teacher, priest and king.

Carey Stanton standing on his future grave in the cemetery of Santa Cruz Island.

let them go by air." On and on until the three of us began wondering what kind of a monster this Dr. Stanton was. After crossing the twenty-two mile channel, we flew over the east end of the island to the coast side and on to what looked like a firebreak. "There she is, Fathers, that's Santa Cruz International." It was quite a thrill landing the two motor plane, but the pilot did so with nary a bump.

We needn't have worried about our host. His chemistry and mine matched perfectly and Carey Stanton and I became instant friends until the day of his untimely death. That night, after returning to the airport, I pulled out my wallet, only to hear the pleasant news that we had been "the guests of Dr. Stanton." Later, when I called to thank him, he decreed that the visitation would be repeated annually, on the 3rd of May. And so it has been these many years.

My first meeting as a member of the Board for the Santa Cruz Island Foundation, to which I had been elected one of the seven board members, was held on September 15, 2000 aboard the Ocean Channel Cat, which spent three hours cruising around the Santa Barbara channel. Among the pleasantries associated with serving on the board of the Santa Cruz Island Foundation is the friendship developed over the

Joseph Walsh, a member of the Eagles, invited the Old Country Priest, to attend his concert at Staples Center on November 14, 2005.

years with Joe Walsh, one of the Eagles. On November 14, 2005, I was invited to attend a concert by the Eagles labeled as "The California Tour" at the Staples Center. The Eagles have sold over 120 million albums worldwide and have distributed more albums that any other recording artists (1972-2005).

Joe Walsh has won 14 Grammy awards. The Eagles were inducted into the Rock and Roll Hall of Fame in 1998. Their greatest hits have been certified by the RIAA as the best selling album of all time, with 27 million units sold in the USA.

We were picked up at 5:00 p.m. by a stretch Cadillac and taken to Staples Center where we entered a tunnel into a basement area to be met by "Smokey" Wendell. After partaking of a scrumptious meal, Marla Daily, David Watts and I were taken to Joe Walsh's private dressing room for a half hour visit—then to the Stadium (12,000 screaming people) for a three-hour concert, which was dreadfully loud.

Among the many songs written by the Eagles, over their thirty-four years of musical stardom is "Hotel California" which was written when the group was searching for and founding themselves in the clubs of Hollywood, at dawn in the desert, at midnight on Mulholland, in tiny apartments in Echo Park and living rooms in Laurel Canyon. Surely it was a novel and impressive experience for an avid client of Gregorian Chant. As I mentioned in a note to Joe Walsh, "my association with your music needs some fine tuning."

Oscar Lewis Award

I was honored in 2000 with the bestowal of the Oscar Lewis Award by the Book Club of California. Here are my remarks given at San Francisco on February 28th.

> The distinction of receiving the Oscar Lewis Award is one I highly cherish. I spoke with Mr. Lewis on several occasions and esteemed him as an outstanding bibliophile. I feel very honored to have my name associated with him.
>
> I have been a member of the Book Club since 1969 when Dorothy Whitnah wrote to say that "at the last meeting of the Board for the Directors of the Book Club of California, your name was presented and I have the pleasure of informing you that you were unanimously elected to membership."
>
> As far back as the 1950s, I had been an avid reader of the Club's quarterly. My late and good friend, Lucille V. Miller, had written an extensive treatment of the Estelle Doheny Collection for the summer issue of 1955, which she shared with me while I was still a student at Saint John's Seminary, Camarillo.

The Book Club of California
by direction of its governing board
honors
MSGR. FRANCIS J. WEBER
with the
Oscar Lewis Award
for outstanding contributions
in the field
of Western History
February 28, 2000

PRESIDENT, THE BOOK CLUB OF CALIFORNIA

One of the first articles I wrote for the newsletter appeared thirty-one years ago and was entitled "Cornerstone of Western Americana," an essay on the biography of Fray Junípero Serra written by Francisco Palou. I am happy to report that in the library of the Archival Center at Mission Hills we have a full run of the Club's quarterly, as well as a complete collection of the annual keepsakes.

Most writers would give three toes on their right foot for the privilege of having a manuscript published by the Book Club of California.

I won that privilege in 1972 and then had it snatched away when the widely-respected artist, Mallette Dean, died before completing the artwork which was to adorn the book. His work was about half finished, but his estate decided against allowing any further issuance of his works. By that time the publication schedule of the Book Club was out of kilter and the project was dropped.

I felt like a cardinal *in petto* who outlives the pope who appointed him. There was a happy ending insofar as Saul Marks took over the book and produced a lovely volume which won several awards for composition. The book appeared under the title, *Andrew Garriga's Compendium of Herbs & Remedies used by the Indians & Spanish Californians.*

Anyway, all else aside, I want to thank the members of the Awards Committee and the Book Club itself for this great honor. I love you all.

Valley Mills 2001

In 2001, I visited the small village in Indiana where I was raised and while there I was treated to a luncheon reunion of my grammar school of Decatur Central classmates. Included in the group pictures printed in the local newspapers were Dick Gavan, Jim Emmert, Jo Pierson Thompson, Pauline Giran, Murray Mills, Rosemary Jessup Swift, Mary Edwards Hibler and Alice Milhouse Emmert. A photograph at the gathering appeared in a local newspaper.

Papers of Msgr. Francis J. Weber

1. General Correspondence, 1961 - 2000.
   Letters filed chronologically in 6 file drawers;
2. Historical Materials, 1952 - 2000.
   One file on each of the writings of FJW. Contains correspondence, research data and at least one copy of each article in 27 file drawers;
3. Books, 1961 - 2000.
   One copy each of all monographs and books written, edited, translated, compiled and/or published.
4. Miniature Books, 1969 - 2000.
   One copy of each of the 112 miniature books;
5. Writings of Francis J. Weber, xeroxed, 1952 - 2000.
   This collection of 34 bound volumes also contains several hundred book reviews by FJW.
6. Pictorial scrapbooks, 1933-2000, 8 volumes.

Personal Papers

In the 1990s, I consigned my extensive miniature book collection to the Huntington Library. While I miss the little jewels, I rest assured that they are receiving T.L.C. from my favorite library in all the world. So it stood to reason that I would entrust my own personal papers to the Huntington. I was elated to hear from William P. Frank that the papers were a significant addition to new collections, not to mention that they seem to be as well organized as any one has.

Earlier I had discussed the matter with Father Michael Engh, S.J. Rector of the Jesuit Community at Loyola Marymount University. He wrote saying that "if for any reason you change your mind, or if the selected depository cannot handle the collection for whatever reason, please recheck us."

I did suggest that these materials remain closed for the duration of my lifetime. The actual transfer took place on September 3, 2000. Here is an overall inventory of what was contained in the gift.

Apostolate of Catholic Relics

Though it functioned informally for several years, the Apostolate of Catholic Relics was incorporated by the State of California on January 1, 2002 as a non-profit organization tax exempt, public benefit corporation founded by Thomas Serafin and dedicated to the cause and devotion of authenticated relics. At the time of its inauguration I was designated as the Spiritual Moderator.

Since its inauguration the Apostolate has sponsored dozens of relic pilgrimages through the United States, including the "*Tilma of Tepeyac*" tour which extended to no less than twenty-two archdioceses and dioceses. That relic is now on permanent exhibit at the Cathedral of our Lady of the Angeles in Los Angeles.

My account of the *tilma* appeared in *The Tidings* issue of December 5, 2003.

Following a triumphant tour of cities and villages throughout the United States, a tiny piece of San Juan Diego's *tilma* will soon arrive in California's southland for permanent enthronement in the Cathedral of Our Lady of the Angels.

During the past six months, members of the Apostolate for Holy Relics have accompanied the famed Mexican relic to twenty-one (arch) dioceses where it was venerated by upwards of 100,000 spiritual clients of Our Lady of Guadalupe.

It was in February of 2003 that Roger Cardinal Mahony authorized that the tiny piece of *tilma,* the only known such relic outside Mexico, be removed from the archives of the Archdiocese of Los Angeles for the nationwide tour.

That devotion to Our Lady of Guadalupe is deeply rooted among Catholics outside Mexico City's *Distrito Federal* became evident when thousands from such diverse places as Salt Lake City and Washington State came to view and venerate the *tilma.*

The story of how the precious relic found its way to what is now the largest city in the world bearing the patronage of the Blessed Mother is a remarkable chapter in California's Catholic heritage.

In October of 1941 the Apostolic Delegate to Mexico invited Archbishop John J. Cantwell to make a pilgrimage to the National Shrine of

Our Lady of Guadalupe. The southland prelate was anxious to comply for many reasons, mostly because "a visit by our people to the City of Mexico would be a gracious compliment to the hierarchy and Catholics of a country that has sent so many of its children to California".

Photographs by Librado Romero/The New York Times

ardinal Edward M. Egan, left, led a ceremony onoring a piece of St. Juan Diego's cloak. The relic ill hang on a statue of Our Lady of Guadalupe at St. Patrick's Cathedral through tomorrow. Nuns from the Institute of the Incarnate Word were among about 100 people who went to the ceremony.

Members of the M & M Club (Mass & McDonalds) meet on Saturdays for breakfast.

A Solemn Pontifical Mass was celebrated at the shrine on October 12th. It was a gala event, attended by a military delegation representing the President of Mexico. The entire diplomatic corps turned out to welcome the archbishop and his party.

Speaking over the National Broadcasting System from Mexico, Cantwell observed that "the missions built in California are our title deeds to show to the newcomers that we of the Old Church are in California by right of inheritance." He concluded by praying that "the traditions that made Mexico distinguished and honorable in the past may be perpetuated in a fuller measure in years to come, and that the glory of days gone by may be surpassed" by the pledge of the future. The visit marked a thawing in the delicate relations then existing between Church and State in Mexico. From all indications, the event was favorably received in all quarters.

Following Cantwell's return to Los Angeles, Archbishop Luis Maria Martinez of Mexico City proposed to the Canons of the National Basilica that a most appropriate way of commemorating the visit would be to present a relic of Juan Diego's *tilma* to the Archbishop of Los Angeles. He pointed out that, even then, Los Angeles boasted a larger Mexican population than any city in the world outside of the Distrito Federal.

The Canons agreed with the proposal and delegated a "Father Gomez" to personally bring a small rectangular piece of the famed *tilma*, encased in a silver reliquary, to Los Angeles.

Cantwell was understandably pleased with the gesture and received the relic with great devotion. Very likely it marked the first (and last) time a piece of the *tilma* had ever left Mexican soil.

The archbishop entrusted the relic to Father Fidencio Ezparza, a Mexican-born priest from Guadalajara who had long been active among the southland's Hispanic community.

Late in 1981, forty years after the historic trek to Mexico by Cantwell, Timothy Cardinal Manning headed another pilgrimage to the National Shrine. Upon Manning's return to Los Angeles, Msgr. Esparza confided the relic to His Eminence for safe-keeping. It was then placed on display in the Historical Museum attached to the Archival Center.

The relic, one of the four snippets detached from the original *tilma*, is draped over an artistic 17th century statue of Our Lady of Guadalupe. And it is highly significant that it be preserved in such surroundings. For beneath the *tilma* of Our Lady, Fray Francisco Garcia Diego y Moreno received Episcopal ordination as the first bishop of *Ambas Californias*, on Oct. 4, 1840.

Larry Stammer of the *Los Angeles Times* wrote an interesting article on December 10, 2003 which we quote here:

A small piece of the cloak of St. Juan Diego—on which Catholics believe an image of Our Lady of Guadalupe miraculously appeared—was permanently enshrined at the Cathedral of Our Lady of the Angels on Tuesday amid prayers and the veneration of several hundred faithful.

Known as the *Tilma of Tepeyac*, the half-inch fragment was cut from the cloak on which Roman Catholics believe the image of Mary was miraculously created by the Virgin when she appeared to a poor Indian convert,

Ordo Militaris et Hospitalaris
Sancti Lazari Hierosolemi

Magnum Monasterium Americanum
his litteris notum facit quod

The Very Reverend Monsignor Francis J. Weber

admissus est in

Ordinem Militarem et Hospitalarem
Sancti Lazari Hierosolemi

in qualitate Capellani ✠ ChLJ

numero 98GPA002 dato II die mensis Februarii, MCMXCVIII

VICE CANCELLARIUS

MAGNUS PRIOR

The Old Country Priest was made a Knight of the Military Order of Saint Lazarus in 1987.

Juan Diego Cuauhtlatoatzin, as he stood on the hill of Tepeyac in Mexico in 1531.

On Tuesday night, the relic was placed in its permanent home in a cathedral chapel by Cardinal Roger M, Mahony during a celebratory Mass. The beige fragment of coarse burlap-like material called *ayate* is contained in a sealed glass pendant that hangs on a necklace on a 17th century statue of the Virgin.

Father Benedict Groeschel at Retreat for the Confraternity of Catholic Clergy on September 10, 2003.

Thought to be the only such Juan Diego relic outside Mexico, it has become a powerful symbol of faith for millions of Latino Catholics and others. Juan Diego was canonized last year by Pope John Paul II before 10,000 worshipers in Mexico City's Basilica of Guadalupe, becoming the church's first indigenous American saint.

"It's the only miracle imprint that we know of in any form other than possibly the Shroud of Turin," Mahony said Tuesday before the Mass that celebrated the Feast Day of St. Juan Diego. "The fact that it was actually done here, in the Western Hemisphere, in Mexico, speaks volumes of the importance of the devotional life of the people."

During a recently completed 21-city tour, an estimated 140,000 people turned out to view and venerate the relic. In San Antonio, for example, 25,000 people stood in line for as long as five hours to venerate the relic, tour coordinator Andrew Walther said Tuesday. Its last stop was at New York's St. Patrick's Cathedral several days ago.

"It's been phenomenal," said Walther, vice president of the Los Angeles-based Apostolate for Holy Relics, a nonprofit corporation for educating the public about saints and encouraging devotion and veneration. "We've had people come back to the church after 15 to 20 years. We've had people say it

Los Angeles Times photo for March 13, 2001.

changed their lives. We've had people drive across three states to see it," Walther said.

Rosalinda Alcantara, 45, traveled to the downtown Los Angeles cathedral from Pico Rivera for Tuesday's ceremony. "It's a miracle to see this here in the U.S. It's going to mean a lot to the Latino people here because of Our Lady of Guadalupe. That is the mother of God to us." Tuesday's observance was part of a weeklong celebration of the feast days of the Virgin of Guadalupe and St. Juan Diego.

Mahony said it was significant that Mary had appeared to Juan Diego, a Chichimeca Indian convert. "He was not part of the Spanish reign or leadership, just an ordinary person, and he was chosen to carry this message," Mahony said.

According to church legend, a dark-skinned Mary appeared from heaven and asked Juan Diego to inform the local bishop that she wanted a chapel built for her people. Unconvinced, the Spanish bishop asked for a sign. Mary appeared again and directed Juan Diego to gather roses, even though they were out of season, and place them in his *tilma* or cloak.

When he opened the cloak for the bishop, the roses—long associated with Mary in Catholic piety—fell out. Emblazoned on the cloth was Mary's image, which is recognized worldwide today as Our Lady of Guadalupe, the patron saint of Mexico. The cloak from which the snippet was taken remains at the National Shrine in Mexico City that bears her name.

The relic was given to the Los Angeles archdiocese in 1941 by the then archbishop of Mexico City. Since 1981, the relic had been at a museum at the San Fernando Mission, until the recent tour. Before that, it had been entrusted to the late Father Fidencio Ezparza, a Mexican-born priest in Los Angeles.

Mahony said it was appropriate that a relic tied to Mary would find a permanent home in the cathedral named after her. A small piece of the cloak of St. Juan Diego—on which Catholics believe an image of Our Lady of Guadalupe miraculously appeared—was permanently enshrined at the Cathedral of Our Lady of the Angels on Tuesday amid prayers and the veneration of several hundred faithful.

John Dart wrote about the relics at the Archival Center in a feature article for the *Los Angeles Times:*

Mission Hills Relics of the saints—purported pieces of their bones, flesh or clothing or reputed artifacts from Jesus' life have had a long history of veneration in the Roman Catholic Church, although they are religiously out of fashion today.

But despite broad skepticism in Catholicism about the historical validity of many relics, the San Fernando Mission archival center has opened its first public exhibit of some 300 that had been in storage for years at the 200-year-old mission. The exhibits are open Monday and Thursday from 1 to 3 p.m.

One item is an alleged fragment from the cross on which Jesus was crucified. Scoffers in church circles say that if you could assemble all the claimed pieces of Jesus' cross, you could rebuild Noah's Ark. Devotees scoff right back, saying that the typically tiny slivers would collectively form only a small block of wood.

Playing a key role in restoring, mounting, framing and cataloging the relics was Thomas Serafin, a Catholic parishioner in San Marino who has amassed his own collection of relics—about 800 articles he described as the largest such collection on the West Coast.

A professional photographer in Los Angeles, Serafin said he displays his collection at churches and retreat houses in hopes of reviving veneration of the saints.

His collection includes another three "documented pieces" of the cross of Jesus, he said. According to Serafin, a French researcher in the late 19th century tried to catalog all known fragments of Christ's cross and came up with an amount that would total about a third of a cross.

While admitting the church "is a little bit leery about relics prior to the 5th century," Serafin says his collection includes a fragment from Jesus' crown of thorns, a bone of John the Baptist, a piece from the table of the Last Supper, and fragments from the veil of the Virgin Mary and the cloak of her husband, Joseph.

Those are some of the exact objects that have been cited as historically dubious by many embarrassed critics within the Catholic Church, especially following the period of extravagant buying and selling of relics in the Middle Ages.

Protestant reformer "Martin Luther ridiculed the church in the 16th century for some of the more fanciful items—a thorn from the crown of thorns and a twig from the burning bush of Moses—things that are more mythical than real." said Father Thomas Rausch, who chairs the theological studies department at Loyola Marymount University.

During the opening sessions of the Second Vatican Council in 1962 Rausch said, a prelate from Spain, Bishop Garcia Martinez, rose to ask how much longer the church was going to venerate relics of the Virgin Mary's milk and veil, St. Joseph's sandals, and the like. Before the bishop was cut off by the moderator, he asked that "these things be reverently buried and heard of no more." according to a book on Vatican II by Xavier Rynne.

At the same time, Rausch noted that few Catholics today become upset over what little attention there is paid to relics because many of them have come to tolerate so-called "popular religion" practiced by different Catholic cultures. "It is purely a matter of personal devotion," he said.

Echoing Rausch was Msgr. Francis J. Weber, the Los Angeles Archdiocese archivist based at the San Fernando Mission who said. "People are not obliged to accept this if they don't want to."

Despite Serafin's assertion that he has documentation for all his relics, Weber said Friday that "All the saints we have for the last 300 or 400 years are authenticated, but the documentation wasn't all that good before then." Much depends on how much credibility a believer attaches to Church tradition, a strong force in the Catholic faith, the priest said.

One relic on display at the mission does have good credentials—a bone fragment from the body of *Fray* Junípero Serra. The mission pioneer whose body was exhumed for a third time at the Carmel Mission in 1984

Blessing of American Trans Air Lockheed L-1011 on March 23, 1994 at LAX.

in connection with the campaign to win sainthood for him. Serra, who was a Franciscan priest, has now been beatified, one step from Vatican approval as a saint.

"Veneration of relics is one of those aspects of Catholic faith that is not greatly emphasized presently," said Weber. But he praised Serafin for "rescuing relics from places where they weren't appreciated,"

Indeed, many Catholics have hidden their relics away, Serafin complained. "I know of a Carmelite convent that actually has a trunk of relics stored in their vestibule, not being venerated, not on display, nothing." Serafin said. "Recently I spoke at a church in Pasadena that has relics in a drawer."

Other times, members of religious orders have approached him and requested his aid in making relics presentable for display.

Church law—an aftermath of the Protestant Reformation - prohibits Catholics from buying or selling relics. "I chastised someone on a computer web site who is trying to sell a couple of relics for $5,000 apiece" Serafin said.

However, Serafin added that he will "donate" money to acquire a relic, by paying for the presumed value of the locket or case that contains the relic.

"A lot of these didn't come free," said Serafin, motioning to a display of some of his relics. Some acquisitions come from trading duplicate relics with other owners who have more than one piece of physical remains or clothing from the same saint, he said.

For the first three years of collecting and taking his exhibit to churches, Serafin refused to accept donations. He started accepting contributions after his "collection got larger and required me to spend more money to move it around," he said.

One year he took his relics to seventeen churches on his free time. It is often children who draw adults over to his exhibits, he admitted. "The kids come over and are fascinated when they learn they are looking at a bone or a piece of a heart," he said.

"I'm not in this for the money: I'm doing this because I love the saints and their stories of sacrifice."

On December 10, 2005, I sent the following letter to Cardinal Mahony:

As you are aware, over the past six months the Apostolate of Holy Relics sponsored the national tour of the *Tilma* which involved no fewer than twenty-one (arch)dioceses. Upwards of 150,000 people were able to see and venerate the relic in areas hosted by such ecclesial luminaries as Cardinals Maida, McCarrick, Egan and numerous other prelates.

Happily there were no discordant or unpleasant occurrences and the Archdiocese of Los Angeles was widely applauded in the press, on radio and television and in personal statements by the media for its kindness in allowing others to share in our bounty.

> I feel that it would be opportune to bring the Apostolate of Holy Relics under the umbrella of the Archdiocese of Los Angeles. The four young men who comprise its leadership are Thomas Seraphin, (President) Andrew Walther, (Vice President), Michael Gibson, LLD (Secretary) and Al Corso CPA (Treasurer). I have served as chaplain or moderator.
>
> Granting some sort of official recognition to the Apostolate of Holy Relics would involve no expenditure of funds. Members have raised whatever monies were needed for their transportation and lodging.
>
> If the Apostolate were given some sort of recognition as an "organization" or "ministry", I would volunteer to serve as your appointed moderator and, in that capacity, I would endeavor to keep the group on a course in keeping with traditional Catholic values.
>
> Attached is their mission statement. I have recommended that the membership be expanded to include at least one woman. Yearly or so, I would see that you receive a report of the Apostolate's activities. The members of the Apostolate would be most receptive to such an official overture.

Happily the Cardinal agreed to my proposal.

In the February 11, 2008 issue of *Newsweek Magazine*, Lisa Miller reported on an interview with Thomas Serafin:

> There's always strange stuff for sale on eBay. Does anybody really need elk antlers? But some of the strangest is in a category called "Collectibles: Christianity," subcategory "Relics." Relics, to put it crassly, are souvenirs of a holy life: a snippet of cassock, a shred of a shroud, anything that once belonged to or came in contact with a saint. To many Christians, especially Roman Catholics, relics are sacred objects of veneration. They have healing powers: they remind believers of God's promise that in his kingdom, everything broken will become whole again. Some of the relics thought to have the most power are bits of saints' flesh, bone and hair, which have been authenticated by the Church. To put it very crassly, these are tiny antique body parts, usually in pretty little frames. Relics this precious are not intended to be owned by individuals, but worshipped by the whole Christian community.
>
> On eBay last week you could buy strands of hair, allegedly from the head of Saint Therese of Lisieux, the patron saint of the Air Force. Bids started at $40. Or you could buy what looks like a fragment of bone supposedly from Saint Philomena, a 13-year old Christian girl who, according to legend, was flogged, drowned and finally beheaded for her refusal to marry the Roman Emperor Diocletian. Bidding started at $49.99. Or if you wanted to splurge, you could purchase a "splendid, rare, antique" reliquary containing bone fragments of six different saints from a dealer in Belgium. Starting price: $625. All these items appear to violate eBay's policies prohibiting the sale of human remains. If they're real they also violate the Roman Catholic canon, which states "it is absolutely forbidden to sell sacred relics."

To skeptics and curiosity seekers, the gray market in relics is perhaps nothing more than an excellent if slightly ghoulish example of the cultural dissonances that can occur when religious impulses clash with capitalistic ones. To the Catholic faithful, however, it is an abomination. Tom Serafin is the manager of a photography studio in Los Angeles, a Catholic layperson who has made it his lifelong mission to badger eBay into removing holy relics from its site. Last month he called for yet another boycott of eBay. "As a dad and a Catholic, I just wonder where the heck is the accountability?" he says. "We have a team of 2,000 people working around the clock to identify and remove prohibited items," responds an eBay spokeswoman via email. "With nearly 7 million new items being listed every day, we may not immediately identify infringing items, but if concerned individuals bring them to our attention we will promptly take action." On his Web site, Serafin keeps a list of objects he believes violate eBay's policies.

Serafin sees it as his job to protect the world's holy relics from profiteering entrepreneurs. To that end, he collects relics himself, which he procures not with cash but through relentless letter writing, begging and the promise of safe haven. After 17 years, he has collected 1,200 relics, which he keeps in two large safes in his house and sometimes takes on tour. Later this month he is taking his prized possessions, eight relics from the Passion (including what he believes to be a piece of the True Cross and a shard from the crown of thorns) to Manila, where the archbishop is expecting 1.5 million people to come venerate them. The sale of relics on eBay may just be another small sign of our society's lust for material satisfaction, but the ire it provokes is deep and old. Is it really possible to purchase a piece of God's grace and mystery with a credit card? Or, are such gifts given by God alone? These are the questions that prompted Luther to nail his memo to the church door in 1517; it is certainly too much to expect the folks at eBay to have to answer them.

Memories of Earlier Years

On October 25, 2002, a reporter for *The Tidings* wrote an essay under the title of "Memories of a Summer Mortician."

"I needed a job." That's why some 50 years ago the young seminarian signed up to work in a mortuary and continued the unusual labor for eight summers. Today he is the renowned author, historian and archivist for the Archdiocese of Los Angeles—Monsignor Francis J. Weber.

Now the director of San Fernando Rey de España Mission in Mission Hills, the erudite writer recently recalled many of the strange, mundane and everyday routine duties of his summer work.

Charles T. Powers, then president of Pierce Brothers, offered the aspiring seminarian a job as the teenager's father was a personal friend and the youth needed funds to support his education in the college seminary.

The history of Pierce Brothers is another chapter in the illustrious story of Los Angeles. According to Msgr. Weber's account, William and Fred were the first to arrive of the family, and they opened a livery stable in 1880 that evolved into a mortuary. By 1924, with the addition of other relatives, the family had built their landmark establishment on West Washington Blvd., the first full-service funeral home in L.A.

When young Francis joined the enterprise in the 1950s, the company had the largest chain in the United States, with 16 funeral homes just in Los Angeles.

"I was hired as a limousine driver mainly," Msgr. Weber recalled, "but I held every position except that of embalmer. I was on duty over 80 hours a week and several times drew night duty at an outlying place." During those eight years in the funeral profession, he estimated that he probably drove hearses, limousines, call cars and floral trucks a total of more than 100,000 miles.

Some of the vehicles he drove were classic Cadillacs and Chryslers. One of the vintage automobiles was dubbed "Wrinkles," a Buick hearse with a hand-carved wooden exterior, which often stuck in second gear, stopping the whole procession while the drive shaft had to be manually released. Besides the many Catholic churches where he "rolled in a casket," Francis also serviced Santa Sophia Greek Orthodox Cathedral. "I got to know more about [their] *Trisagion* services than most parishioners," he said with a knowing smile.

Famous people and personalities were also part of the mortuary experience as all "ultimately fall victim to the universal democracy of death," Msgr. Weber observed. Some of the most notable persons who the seminarian "picked up" or drove during their final procession were Stan Laurel, the comedian, and Mrs. Harry Chandler, whose husband owned the *Los Angeles Times*.

But his most interesting summer experience while assigned to the motor fleet was the day Francis was dispatched to an address in Beverly Hills and drove a Lincoln Zephyr to a Spanish style, stucco mansion on Beverly Drive, surrounded by several acres of palm trees and gardens. Only then was he told they were picking up the earthly remains of none other than William Randolph Hearst.

"He had died" alone that morning and the 'removal' was made hurriedly," Msgr. Weber reported, "and though once a robust man, Hearst had wasted away to a bony 125 pounds. By the time I had maneuvered the car out of the driveway, several dozen newspaper reporters were already standing around."

Another notable personage he met, but on a much happier occasion, was the Countess Estelle Doheny. On his lunch break, Francis would often drive a few blocks to Chester Place and venture to eat in the spacious gardens despite the sentry's warnings. One day, he bravely stopped Mrs. Doheny during her walk, explained he was a seminarian and asked if he could eat his lunch inside the park. "Of course," she told him, and sometime later even sent a box of pastry goodies "for the young man who comes each day to lunch." Msgr. Weber has numerous other anecdotes, some quite humorous. For example, one morning he led a funeral procession of 27 cars into a dead-end street. But his memories of dedicated fellow workers and friends are among his fondest.

The Weber collection of Presidential Signatures is on file in the library at Azusa Pacific College.

"I was and remain edified by the commitment most morticians have to their work and their public," he pointed out. "It was also a very valuable learning experience to work with people facing the loss of a loved one. They were generally appreciative of any acts of kindness."

Burying the dead, Msgr. Weber reminded, is also a corporal work of mercy.

Visitors

On June 18, 2003, the Fellowship of American Bibliophilc Societies visited Southern California. I had been a delegate of the Zamorano Club at the organizational meeting of FABS in New York City a decade earlier.

During a bus trip to the William Andrews Clark Memorial Library and then on to the Getty Museum, I used the bus's intercom to give some historical background on the *Puebla Nuestra Señora de Los Angeles*. The FABS were pleased and later reported on it in their newsletter as "a trip to remember."

Azusa Pacific College

When I told my associate about my interest in Azusa Pacific College, he asked: "Why?" That's a fair question. After all, we have here in the Archdiocese of Los Angeles three Catholic universities none of which really excites me.

But I am very interested in Thomas Aquinas College and Azusa Pacific College, for slightly differing reasons. Thomas Aquinas College is not under the umbrella of the archdiocese. It is independently organized and operated. As you may know, students there follow the "Great Books" tract, but they are unabashedly Catholic.

But I also like what I see here at Azusa Pacific College. As a Christian, I am exceedingly pleased and impressed by, of all things, their stationery. There, in unmistaken letters are the words: "God First." I am also impressed by the fact that people here pray and they do it in public. I sense that the Lord likes that.

Anyway, it's a pleasure to have watched this institution from its early days, from college to university. I have observed the great influence Tom Andrews has exerted there and Tom is, in my opinion, a quality man in every respect and a person I admire greatly.

Following is a short talk I gave when I entrusted my presidential signatures to the existing "Weber Collection" at Azusa Pacific College.

> In my own defense, I would like to say that the presentation of this set of presidential signatures was not a *post hoc ergo propter hoc* decision. It was only after hearing about this day of recognition that I decided to make this gift.
>
> When one reaches 70, he should, in my humble opinion, begin disposing of things and that is my rationale for this gift.
>
> I recall when Charles De Gaulle was elected President of France, a reporter asked him if he was going to be another Napoleon. He laughed and said that no right-minded person in his 70s lusts after position, fame, power or riches. At that moment, he said, it's time to pass on those ambitions to the young.
>
> De Gaulle was a Catholic and his attitude has impressed me. I spent 40 years on a measly priest's salary, putting together this collection. It was fun, challenging and satisfying.
>
> But now it is time to give back and none better to give to than a Christian institution which trains young people for the future.

Chapel for TAC

March 7th, 2009 was a special day in my limited horizon for that was the day when Our Lady of the Holy Trinity Chapel at Thomas Aquinas Chapel was dedicated by Roger Cardinal Mahony.

It was my privilege to have served on the initial board for erecting the chapel a decade earlier at a meeting with Drs. Thomas Dillon and Peter De Luca at the California Club in Los Angeles. A small group of supporters met with Duncan Streit, the architect from Notre Dame.

Though I had long been a supporter of the college, it wasn't clear to me why I was asked to attend. However, during the meeting, Dr. Dillon expressed some anxiety about getting the overall plan for the chapel approved by the cardinal. It was my suggestion to put Sir Daniel Donohue on the committee, knowing that the cardinal would likely not object to anything sanctioned by Sir Daniel. Not only was my suggestion followed, but Sir Daniel and the board of the Dan Murphy Foundation eventually pledged $12 million dollars for the chapel which I believe is one of the most architecturally correct, artistically attractive and liturgically designed chapels in all of California.

The artistic chapel of the Holy Trinity at Thomas Aquinas College was dedicated in 2009.

Knee Replacement

In order to replace a badly disintegrated right knee joint with man-made parts, the old country priest underwent total knee replacement surgery at Holy Cross Hospital in Mission Hills on November 8, 2004.

The pinkie newsletter, of December 3rd reported this to the faith community of San Fernando Mission:

> "You may have wondered why the old country priest has not been on deck for the last few weeks. Well, he was one of the 250,000 Americans this year to have had what is known as a total knee replacement.
>
> Only performed since 1968, this operation is one of the greatest advances in orthopedic surgery in the 20th century. In my case, seventy plus years of normal use had caused the cartilage covering the end of the thighbone to crack and wear away. (I would like to impress people that it was due to constant prayer on my knees, but that wouldn't be altogether accurate.)
>
> The two-hour operation resulted in a total knee replacement with a newly installed artificial joint. The goal was to correctly size and match the implant to my anatomy, so I can be able to regain mobility and normal alignment.
>
> There is still some pain because the surrounding muscles are weak from inactivity and the tissues are healing. Most people are able to be up and around in six weeks. That is surely my goal. And I hope you will miss me. If all goes well, I should be back on my antiquated knees well before Christmas.
>
> So, now you know where I've been and why. It's been a learning experience for which I am very grateful. My physician does only knees and hips. If you ever need such surgery, I would highly recommend Dr. Ramin Ganjianpour.
>
> While replacing the knee with an artificial device made of plastic and titanium, the doctors noted an accelerated heartbeat that they wanted to check out. Thus what was supposed to be only a three-day hospital stay, turned into ten.
>
> A number of tests were conducted and eventually it was decided that a look inside the heart was needed. This is called a Left Heart Catherization, or Coronary Arteriography.
>
> During that procedure, a catheter was inserted into an artery and guided through the body using x-rays and TV screens until it reached the heart. The catheter is then moved around inside the heart to allow physicians to see how well the heart is working. The process took about two hours.
>
> In the case of the old country priest, the doctors were satisfied with just looking around. While there was 40% blockage to the left anterior descending artery, neither coronary artery angioplasty (cleaning out the buildup of plaque in an artery with a balloon) nor coronary artery stinting (installation of a wire mesh screen to keep an artery open) was required. The blockage can be treated with medication and diet.

Readers may wonder how much such a procedure cost. Ultimately, I was able to translate the gibberish from Blue Cross, which spelled it out as follows:

Pre-Op	
Surgeons / Lab Tests / Visits	$2,294.25
Surgery / Hospital	
Doctors / Testing / Supplies / Room Fees / Assistants / Heart Procedures	$135,964.15
After-Care	
Physical Therapy / Blood Tests /	$3,917.38
	$142,175.78
Insurance Paid:	**$14,932.97**

The Balance was written off by our Insurance Plan.

Myths and Mythology

On September 16, 2004 I was invited to give a paper on the "Myths and Mythology of the California Missions" at an International Symposium on "The Franciscan Presence in the Borderlands of North America" that was held at the De Falco Retreat Center in Amarillo, Texas. The talk was an elaborated version of an earlier work that appeared in the *Branding Iron* of the Los Angeles Corral Westerners.

Police Station

On April 30, 2005, I was asked to give the invocation for the dedication of the new police station in Mission Hills, the first such addition in Los Angeles in a greater quarter century. The new station represents an area totaling twenty-eight square mile with a population of 202,000 people.

Heavenly Father,

As we inaugurate this magnificent police facility located within the shadow of historic San Fernando Mission, we ask You to watch over and guide the actions of those dedicated to serving and protecting Your people in this northern area of San Fernando Valley.

O Lord, as we welcome the presence of the police in this portion of Your vineyard, we ask that You bless their work and reward their diligence in looking after the welfare our people especially the poor, homeless, alienated and confused.

Those joined with us at this moment need to recall St. Augustine's admonition that for a nation or a community to prosper and be happy, it is necessary that justice be the queen, charity the law and eternity the goal in all we say and do.

We conclude this benediction in the words of the Old Testament's Book of Numbers:

The Lord make His face to shine upon us and be gracious.
The Lord lift up His countenance and give us His peace,
as we continue our trek along *El Camino Real* to the
heaven and haven we all desire

Rose K. Weber

In mid 2005, my brother-in-law, John Castagna asked me to write the preface for a compilation he was preparing in memory of my fraternal grandmother:

When Rose Katherine Meier (1880-1971) married into the Weber family, in the early years of the 20th century, her spouse, George, was one of nine siblings in a prominent family that had the makings of dynasty. Now, a century or just three generations later, I am the last of the living Webers.

Rose K. Weber, my grandmother, was quite a charming and talented woman. Had she been gifted with an advanced education, there is no doubt that she would have left a substantial mark among her contemporaries. As it was, those of us who knew and loved her have a host of happy and impressive memories of a lady who lived a remarkably full life here on planet earth.

According to Rose, the Webers had migrated to the United States in the closing years of the Otto Edward Leopold von Bismark regime, ostensibly to escape the political wrath of the local German politicians.

She further claimed that the family was descended from the great composer, Karl Maria Frederich von Weber. If so, the only musical talent that surfaced in my generation was vested in my sister, Mary Alice, who can play the piano and organ with reasonable alacrity.

The Webers had lived in and around Indianapolis since the early days of the century. Shortly after the armistice was signed ending World War I, my grandfather, George A. Weber, a traveling salesman from Cincinnati, decided to open a grocery store in Valley Mills, a small rural village seven miles southwest of the "city".

The present village of Valley Mills was laid out and plotted under the name of Northport on March 21, 1839. Seventeen years later Joseph Sanders referred to the area as Fremont. Located in a small valley, the current name derives from Abner Mills, an early postmaster.

In one of the early mug-books, Valley Mills was described as having" one commodious school house of four rooms," along with a post office, a

My IBM typewriter was acquired in 1951 and was the first such machine issued by IBM. It is still in operation.

general store and a blacksmith shop. In 1917, Valley Mills became part of Decatur Township, which was erected in 1822 and named for the naval hero in the War of 1812.

The initial issue of *Joy and Gloom*, official newspaper for Valley Mills High School, advertised that George Weber was proprietor of a store where "groceries, candy and school supplies" were available. Moved several times, the store's second location was at Watson's Corner. Alongside the store, which later burned down, was a small house where the elder Webers resided. Early in the 1930s, the family moved to a more commodious home on High School Road. Not long after, the store was moved a half mile west to a brick building erected by Joseph Seerley in 1935 on Highway 67.

The rationale for this "memoir" was the death of Clara Weber Swanson, just after childbirth on November 8, 1930 and the subsequent upbringing of her son, George Sigfried Swanson (1930-1997). There were three contenders for guardianship of George: Otto Swanson (a streetcar operator and grandfather), Emma Pfafflin (a housewife and distant cousin) and Clifford Cox (the family physician). George's Father, Harry Swanson, apparently emotionally unable for the chore, unhappily died a few months later, on New Year's Day in 1933.

Never one to follow legal necessities, Rose short-circuited the whole question of guardianship by moving to California where she and her other daughter, Rosemary, made a comfortable home for grandson, George, who thrived and grew into manhood in the environs of Hollywood.

This memoir, a compilation of two separate diaries and a heavily annotated "baby book," has been carefully transcribed and edited by John Castagna the husband of my sister, Mary Alice (Weber). He also arranged the entries chronologically so as to make the overall text read more meaningfully.

So here we have a delightful piece of Americana which the extended family and others may enjoy and esteem.

Venerable Typewriter

In my monthly "Pinkie letter" of March 4, 2005 to those who attend San Fernando Mission, I mentioned one of my secrets:

Some months ago, a local reporter stopped to ask some questions about the history of San Fernando Mission. In the course of the interview, he looked at my IBM typewriter and asked why I kept that old "antique" in my office.

He was dismayed when I told him that the typewriter was anything but an "antique". I acquired the machine in 1953 (it was originally manufactured in 1948 and was the first electric typewriter issued by IBM). During the ensuing years practically everything I have written was pounded out on that "antique" machine.

I recall that when I purchased the machine, over fifty years ago, it was quite pricey. I had been given some money at the time with the suggestion that I use it to update my rather dingy lifestyle. Today, it is becoming ever more difficult to have the machine fixed, since few of the companies even carry parts anymore. Happily the Martinelli family of San Fernando still fixes it when keys are broken or some other catastrophe occurs.

This very letter is being typed on my "antique" and I make no apologies for being a tad "old fashioned" in that area. Oh, we do have a computer, but I much prefer to pound out my work on my old friend. Also,

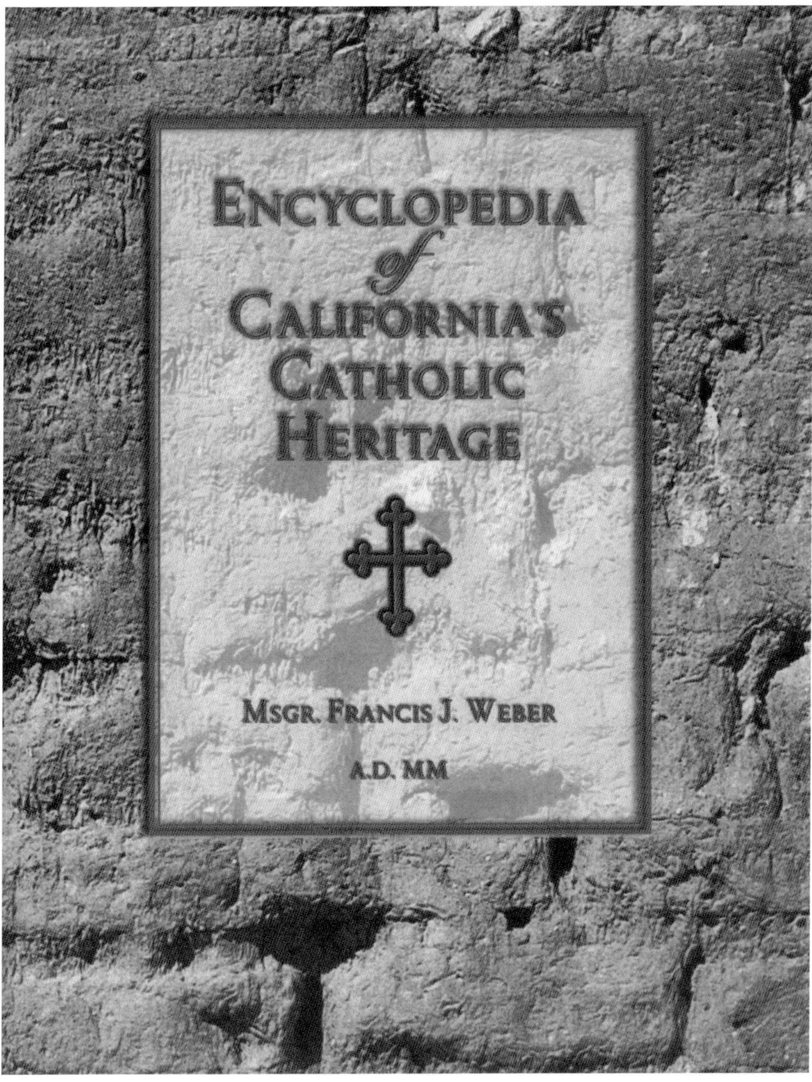

having a typewriter like that seems more appropriate for someone who has spent most of his priesthood at one or other of the California missions.

An Unexpected Blessing

In my earlier "Memories," I discussed my "termination" as a columnist for *The Tidings*, the Catholic newspaper for the Archdiocese of Los Angeles, after an uninterrupted weekly "run" of thirty-two years. The documentation for that unpleasant incident, which came abruptly and without any prior notifications, has been placed in my papers at the Huntington Library in San Marino should anyone ever wish to pursue the matter.

It goes without saying that I was upset about the action because it appeared to be an interference with my role as official historian for the Catholic Church in Southern California. In retrospect, however, the "firing" was a profound blessing because it allowed the redirecting of a goodly portion of my time and energies to other writings, which very likely would never have materialized. Examples would be the *Encyclopedia of California's Catholic Heritage, A History of the Archdiocese of Los Angeles* and *Catholic Heroes of Southern California*, to mention but a few of the publications issued since 1995 and my departure from *The Tidings*.

In 1997, in mentioning a note from a friend to the effect that when God closes one door, He opens another," I replied that perhaps "we will see our readers again in another context, on a different occasion." Indeed that occurred! The whole scenario was a further hint about the wisdom of staying out of God's way in our lives.

Obiter Dicta

I subsequently discovered a survey taken among readers a year or so before the column was dropped substantiating that it was the most widely read feature in the newspaper. Then, in January of 1996 a second survey prepared by Business Communications eventually reached the Archival Center. Therein were reprinted a number of readers comments, such as the following:

1) "Strongly dislike that you discontinued Msgr. Weber's column. His columns let us know where we've been and why we are as we are today."
2) "Bring back Msgr. Francis J. Weber's column. We need "His Story" for history, traditions, *etc.* in Archdiocese. What happened to Fr. Charles Miller's column?"

3) "*The Tidings* no longer covers local events and Los Angeles based happenings. Instead, national events take precedence, even our local columnist, Fr. Weber is gone, replaced by purchased stories from bigger diocese and national writers. What do they know about the church in L.A. and its people?
4) "I liked the old *Tidings*. I like news of the entire Church—World—USA and California and local. I miss Msgr. Weber's and the old question and answer before Fr. Coiro the Franciscan took over the slot."
5) "Enjoyed Fr. Gregory's and Fr. Miller's articles: I can't put my finger on it, but that's because it isn't there! I miss the articles by Father Greg Coiro and Father Francis Weber."
6) "We miss several of the previous columnists and prefer not hearing about Conrad this was a big disappointment. Where is Fr. Miller and Fr Weber?"
7) "We miss the historical articles on California by Father Weber. That was an interesting and nice column for us - could you bring it back occasionally? Also like the questions put to the priest column. Please keep up the good work on an excellent Catholic newspaper."
8) "You made a severe mistake in dropping Msgr. Weber. He is a world-class authority, extremely charitable and educates clearly on our Catholic Heritage."

Clearly the column was not dropped because of new readership. There were other factors at work which no one has yet stepped forward to explain. Too bad. The Church can be a tough task matter.

An Unpublished Manuscript

Several years ago, a friend introduced me at an historical gathering as a priest who had never had an unpublished thought. We were running late, so I didn't make any effort then to correct the record. Actually there was an entire book-sized manuscript on the subject that went unpublished many years ago. And here's the story.

> During my first years at Saint John's Seminary in Camarillo, I was greatly enamored with the Estelle Doheny Collection and used every opportunity to learn about and personally explore its treasures. It wasn't easy because students had no regular access, except on Visitor's Day and then only with guests by a pre-arranged appointment.
>
> There were a few chosen ones who functioned as guides, but even their access was severely limited. I never became a guide, probably because in those days, "preferences" of students were generally disregarded or totally ignored.

Very Reverend James W. Richardson, C.M.
Rector – St. John's Seminary.

But I did have friends on the "work crew" who occasionally smuggled me into the collection while they changed light-bulbs, mopped the floors or ran the vacuum cleaners. I gradually became pretty well versed about the books, manuscripts and works of art that Carrie Estelle Doheny had entrusted to the seminary.

One of my close friends, Ronald Royer, was an accomplished photographer and he was able to supply me with a goodly number of color prints of items in the collection. In my "indiference periods," I compiled in longhand a descriptive history of the Estelle Doheny Collection. I typed it, illustrated it with Ronnie's photographs then had it bound and boxed in red leather. Originally I didn't have any intention of having it published. It was just a fun project.

One day, in the fall of 1955, I stumbled across an advertisement from one of the vanity presses in the Homiletic and Pastoral Review which said: "If you have a publishable manuscript, send it to us for an objective appraisal."

I answered the ad and a few weeks later, to my utter dismay, a letter came back offering to publish the book, at no expense to me, if I would assign the royalties to the publisher.

It all sounded reasonable, especially when they said that I would get ten copies of the finished book *gratis*. So I sent for the manuscript and innocently made an appointment to show it to the rector, Father James W. Richardson, C.M. That encounter proved to be most unpleasant. He was absolutely furious, to say the least.

He accused me of being deceptive, insubordinate, presumptuous and proud. I was probably all those things at different times, but not with my manuscript. I do recall, however, nodding assent to his accusations, knowing that my entire future probably hinged on appearing repentant. He dismissed me, saying only that I would hear from him soon. "Soon" dragged on for five months, during which time I wondered if there were any openings in the antiquarian book trade.

About ten days prior to the closing of school, in May of 1956, the rector posted a list of people he wanted to see. My name was the last one on the list. The three fellows immediately ahead of me were "clipped" from orders as I could easily hear from my place in the hallway.

When my turn came, I fully expected the worst. But this time, he was in total control of himself. He didn't raise his voice or even act displeased. He simply delivered a carefully prepared statement that went something like this:

"The inappropriate suggestion that your manuscript be published has been discussed with the faculty, Mrs. Doheny and the Cardinal Archbishop. It was their unanimous decision that you put this whole notion out of your mind forever. Is that clear?"

"Yes," I muttered. He shoved the manuscript at me and indicated that I could leave. It was a victory, insofar as he didn't clip me from orders, which I fully expected.

Several years later, when Lucille W. Miller, Mrs. Doheny's secretary and personal librarian, came on staff as curator for the Estelle Doheny Collection, I decided to give her my ill-fated manuscript. Her response was as surprising as it was informative: "It is just too bad that Mrs. Doheny could not have seen this book. She would have loved it."

When I told her the scenario, she categorically denied that the manuscript had ever been presented to Mrs. Doheny. And I later discovered that the matter was never discussed with James Francis Cardinal McIntyre.

The rector had lied to me - and from that moment on I never had any respect for the man. His decision was based on his concern that the book would bring to Camarillo "throngs of people who would walk on the grass and pick the flowers."

I felt better when I realized that my unpublished manuscript was among the first recorded victims of ecological concern!

Recognition

Early in November of 2009, Msgr. Craig Cox, Rector of Saint John's Seminary, called to tell me that I had been named as one of that years' "distinguished alumni." While appreciating of the honor, I declined.

A few days later I sent Msgr. Cox, the following letter:

> May I thank you for the gracious phone call. I am grateful that you are open to my wishes about refusing the honor you mentioned.
>
> When I was appointed to Saint Victor's parish in West Hollywood, my pastor, Msgr. John J. Devlin, gave me a piece of advice which has served me well over the ensuing fifty years: "Always fly under the radar." That I have endeavored to do.
>
> Though he gave the credit to then Bishop John J. Cantwell, Devlin was the *de facto* founder of the Legion of Decency which was one of the most successful outreaches of the Catholic Church in the United States during the last century. I have his papers in the archives and they clearly indicate how he was the most effective Catholic voice in the Motion Picture Industry of the time. And he did it by "flying under the radar." He met very few of the moguls but they all knew who he was and what he would allow.

Forty-eight years in the same ministry.

> Anyway, I mention this to explain my own outlook: work hard, say your prayers, avoid the limelite and "fly under the radar."
>
> Thanks for your understanding.

The final communication on this scenario was received from Cox in December:

> Thank you for your letter of November 24. I shared with our Selection Committee your wish to decline being named as one of next year's distinguished alumni. They were disappointed to hear the news of your desire to "fly under the radar" but obviously very respectful of your choice—even though they (and I) wished you had decided otherwise.
>
> As background, the Committee has been seeking honorees that would manifest a variety of different gifts and of different ways of serving the Church. They believe you have done tremendous service, service with national impact, both as archivist and in your many books and articles, in a particular way in your many articles in *The Tidings*. Thus, their original selection, while certainly motivated by a desire to recognize your own contributions, was also motivated by the desire to emphasize the

President Jon R. Wallace and the
Azusa Pacific University Board of Trustees
cordially invite you to join them
to honor

Msgr. Francis J. Weber

as he receives the degree
Honorary Doctor of Humane Letters

Friday, April 30, 2010

11:30 a.m.
Lunch
President's Dining Room
East Campus

Kindly respond to Rachel Lopez at (626) 812-3075 by Friday, April 23.

importance of history in our Church and the importance of those "behind-the-scenes" kinds of service that too often are overlooked.

Let me take the opportunity of this letter to thank you for the support you have given St. John's Seminary, as well as to thank you for your efforts that have made the Archives of this Archdiocese something of which we can all truly be proud.

As I head for the finish line of my service in the ministry, I think often of Msgr. John J. Devlin and the sterling advice he gave this once young levite.

Staff Recognition Day

Some years ago, the Department of Human Resources at the Archdiocesan Catholic Center established a bi-annual Staff Recognition Day to honor those who had worked at the curial office for a significant number of years. The *gran dame* of those faithful laborers was the late Ethel Bissert who clocked in a total of sixty three years in the Cantwell—McIntyre—Manning and Mahony eras.

The Old Country Priest was honored for forty-eight years (since 1962) as archivist on February 10, 2010. In addition to a service pen with three diamond splinters, the Cardinal sent a personal letter, which cited "dedicated and faithful service to the mission of the Church in Los Angeles which had touched the lives of many in our archdiocesan community"

Finally

My association with Azusa Pacific University goes back to 1975 when I deposited a significant assortment of American ecclesial history (about 1500 volumes) in the Special Collections of the library. During ensuing years, I have maintained a pleasant relationship with professor Thomas Andrews who presides over that phase of the library. My own collection of Presidential signatures was added later. And, just recently I was able to give them a copy of Fray Francisco Palou's *Relacion Historica*.

On February 10, 2010, the following letter arrived from Dr. John R. Wallace, the president of the University with a totally unexpected honor for the Old Country priest.

> The Azusa Pacific University community deeply appreciates the prominent role you continue to play in helping to shape our special collections. I was thrilled to learn of your recent offer to donate your personal copy of Palou's *Life of Serra* to APU, and recall with fondness, my elation when being informed of your remarkable donation of the Presidential Signatures Collection as a fairly new president. It is an honor for this

Azusa Pacific University

Upon recommendation of the Faculty and by the authority of the Board of Trustees confers upon

Msgr. Francis J. Weber

the degree of

Doctor of Humane Letters

Honoris Causa

with all the rights and privileges thereunto pertaining. In witness of this the signatures of the appropriate officers and the seal of Azusa Pacific University are hereunto affixed this thirtieth day of April, two thousand and ten.

President of the University

Chairman of the Board of Trustees

Dr. Francis J. Weber received a Doctorate of Humane Letters from Azusa Pacific University on April 30, 2010.

university to house the Msgr. Francis J. Weber Collection within our rare books and treasures.

In recognition of your life of dedicated Christian service; accomplishments as author, editor, and archivist; and more than 35 years of interest and direct involvement in the growth and development of our special collections at Azusa Pacific University, the Board of Trustees voted unanimously at the January meeting to confer upon you the honorary degree,

CONFERRING

THE

DOCTOR OF HUMANE LETTERS

DEGREE

upon

MSGR. FRANCIS J. WEBER

APRIL 30, 2010

On the occasion of the conferral of a degree on the Old Country Priest, the commendation was reprinted in a miniature book by the Parker Press in a limited edition of fifty copies.

Doctor of Humane letters. The awarding of an honorary degree remains one of higher education's most significant accolades. Congratulations!

In my response I noted that President Wallace had "brought a bright light to a dark and dreary rainy afternoon." Here was my note:

> While not known for my humility, I have over many years endeavored to avoid the limelight, especially when I see so many others more worthy of attention.
>
> I would greatly prefer that the presentation could be very low key. Maybe I could come, fetch the parchment and, with the exception of a photo op for your local university family, fade back into the obscurity of my daily lifestyle.

The ceremony was scheduled for April 30th. At that time I made the following observations:

> I would like to thank President Wallace, Dr. Thomas Andrews, board of directors, faculty members, students and friends of Azusa Pacific University for inviting me here today to accept this valued token of their kindness to an old country priest.
>
> This day is special to me for another reason, namely for being the 51st anniversary of my ordination to the priesthood.
>
> My affinity towards all facets of the educational field comes naturally. You might recall that when Our Lord commissioned his apostles, he told

them to teach the Gospel to everyone and only then did he instruct them to baptize. In other words, teaching **precedes** the commission to administer the sacraments. Teaching, or preaching as we know it, is the premier obligation of the Christian apostolate.

The stationery of this university puts everything in context perfect by proclaiming God on its very stationery. Beyond that, everything else falls into place.

4
San Fernando Mission Chronicle

Though the Old Mission is not and was never a canonical parish, it has witnessed and been a part of all the major movements that have affected the Catholic Church in the United States since 1797. Especially has that been true in this post-conciliar era.

It is astonishing how much has occurred here at San Fernando, Rey de España, in just the last decade. In my humble opinion, the seventeenth of the California Missions has become the centerfold of *El Camino Real*. It is not surprising that our new illustrated book on the mission has become such a popular publication in the Gift Shop. A cursory glance at

Though not a canonical parish, San Fernando Mission has eighteen altar servers.

Whenever needed, Geraldine McGrath brings her choir from the next door parish of Saint John Baptist de La Salle.

the Mission chronicle surely indicates a varied, interesting and relevant history in itself.

Sacraments

The *Catechism of the Catholic Church* defines sacraments as "being instituted by Christ and entrusted to the Church as efficacious signs of grace perceptible to the senses. Through it the divine life is bestowed upon the recipients."

As are all worship communities, San Fernando Mission is concerned with the distribution of the sacraments, especially baptisms, marriages and funerals. The Old Mission is unique in its role as a non-parochial entity. In the performance of baptisms over the last ten years at the Old Mission, several permanent deacons have assisted, the most popular of whom was the late Reverend Jack Coplen.

Baptism is the first and most significant of the sacraments and we are always pleased to have the opportunity of sharing our facilities with newcomers. Some day, I plan to count up the total number of such sacraments administered here over the past two hundred years. It should prove to be quite impressive. Since 2000, there have been 848 **(through 2009)** Baptisms at San Fernando Mission. This is just one of the many ways that this venerable establishment continues its sacramental outreach first inaugurated in Alta California by Fray Junípero Serra in 1769. Probably few missions, even those which are active parishes, can surpass our quantity.

Among the reasons people have given for coming to the seventeenth of the California missions is the neatness, brightness and availability of our historical treasures. Every year people from all over the world swarm through the Old Mission.

The Fritz B. Burns Foundation makes a gift of $50,000 to the San Fernando Mission. From left: Kenneth Skinner, Trustee; Msgr. Francis J. Weber, Joseph Rawlinson, Trustee; William H. Hannon, Chairman of the Board.

We have a wedding coordinator who schedules and otherwise arranges marriages for those who wish to exchange their vows at the Old Mission. Since 2000, there have been **928 (through 2009)** weddings at San Fernando, Rey de España, most of them witnessed by priests from local parishes.

A long tradition has made the Old Mission a popular place to celebrate the Mass of Resurrection for deceased Catholics. The largest

The Old Country Priest greets guests at a worship service in the chapel at San Fernando Mission.

percentage of our funerals, are for those who will be interred next door in San Fernando Mission Cemetery.

It has always been my objective to have the liturgies performed well and according to approved guidelines. Every few years, I review some of the directives with our people. The following was read at the Masses on October 19, 2008.

In the interest of proper liturgical decorum, we occasionally need to reiterate some of the procedures followed here at San Fernando Mission. All of these are part of the official directives provided by the American Conference of Catholic Bishops.

Whether it be for the excellence of the homily, the smoothness of the liturgy or the quality of the music, applause after Mass is NOT appropriate. The Liturgy is not a performance;

The holding of hands with a child, parent or friend during the recitation or singing of the Our Father is NOT an approved gesture;

At the Kiss of Peace, only one's immediate neighbor should be greeted. Especially to be avoided is crossing the aisle to greet an acquaintance. A smile, handshake and / or the words "Peace with you" is an appropriate greeting;

It is the recipient's choice to either kneel or stand to receive Holy Communion. Here at the Old Mission, standing is the *preferred* posture; the proper response to "Body of Christ" before receiving Holy Communion is "Amen" and it should be audible;

At the reception of Holy Communion, those who wish to receive in the hand must NOT have anything else in their clutch, whether it be a baby, rosary, handkerchief, prayer book or whatever;

Non-Catholics who approach the railing at the time of Holy Communion are most welcome. They are invited to fold their hands over their breast for a blessing. This directive also applies to youngsters who have not made their first Holy Communion;

* * * * * *

And, please, do not visit with friends before or after Mass *inside* the church. Many people find that practice an obstacle to their private prayer;

There is no provision for cell phones in the liturgical directives. Here at the Old Mission, we have a policy that if a cell phone goes off during a service, the offender is exhorted to double his or her offering that day;

Finally, clothing at Holy Mass should be appropriate for the solemnity of the occasion. For example, short trousers for men and profound cleavage for women violate good taste. San Fernando Mission has adequate heat in the winter and cool air in the summer to allow for maximum comfort.

Canonically, San Fernando Mission is not a parish, but a public oratory. *Quinceañeras* are allowed because of an age old custom. For this as in other ceremonies, the pastor or associate pastor of the family is generally asked to celebrate the Mass.

Art Ballin

The human element has to be our first consideration. On December 27, 2003 we buried Art Ballin (1919-2002), a wonderful man, who had been associated with San Fernando Mission and Queen of Angels Seminary

Roberta Johnson

since 1944. Art had been trained by the W.P.A. as a tile maker. Mark Harrington hired him when the restorers were rebuilding the east and west wings of the mission after World War II.

Art stayed on and eventually became the *factotum* for both of our institutions. He actually lived here on the grounds for over a quarter

century. Art served as engineer for the seminary until his retirement. After that, he uninterruptedly occupied the same pew at the 9:00 o'clock Mass every Sunday. Always an extremely gracious person, I first knew him when I was appointed to teach at the seminary in 1962.

Art had three sons, all of whom attended the funeral. Charleen Bennett and Sylvia Dianna provided the music. Art knew and appreciated their musical talents. I have lots of pleasant memories about Art. We have a number of photos in which he is prominent among the restorers of the 1940s. Surely we are all indebted to him.

Roberta Johnson

On February 1, 2001, we buried Roberta Johnson (1904-2001) who became the first full-time secretary here at the Old Mission in the 1980s. She lived on to almost a hundred years, in the course of which she embraced our holy faith. May she rest in peace! Here's the homily preached in the church:

> For almost a century, Roberta Johnson was busy about many things. In the last twenty years of her life, she watched after those of us here in Mission Hills.
>
> Our gratitude today, as we consign her earthly remains to the soil whence it came, is that of a friend and fellow traveler along the pathway to eternity.
>
> This good woman, spoken about in the Book of Ruth, was a mother, a spouse and a giant in the wilderness.
>
> She could have invented—and maybe did—the woman's liberation movement. She didn't need Jesse Jackson to tell her what womanhood was all about. Taking a backseat to no one, she moved among contemporary society as a natural leader who charted the course. Her projects were always finished on time and her results more often than not were successful.

Today is not the time to regale you with "Roberta stories." She was bigger than those anyway. Her shadow fell on the landscape like the night overtaking the day.

Here at Mission Hills, she found the Lord and was baptized a Catholic. Had she not been in her eighties then, she would have revamped the whole image of Christendom.

Leonardo da Vinci spoke wisely when he said: "Just as a well-filled day gives joy to sleep so too does a well spent life give joy to death."

Understandably, every healthy person loves life and hopes it will be as long and joyous as possible. This seems to be what da Vinci means by a "well-spent life." For the person who uses life well, death seems spontaneously, without the least pretense, to come not as the destruction, but as the fulfillment of life.

Though we are saddened by her death, we are ever more inspired by her life. Her favorite poem says it all:

On the wings of death and sorrow
God sends us new hope for tomorrow
And in His mercy and His grace
The lonely days that stretch ahead
And know our loved one is not dead
But only sleeping and out of our sight
And we'll meet in that land
Where there is no night

Tridentine Mass

The Tridentine Mass was re-inaugurated at San Fernando Mission on May 5, 1985, in virtue of a special indult (*Quattuor abhinc annos*) given by Pope John Paul II on October 3, 1984 and confirmed by the Holy Father's apostolic Letter, *Ecclesia Dei*, July 2, 1988.

During the early years the Tridentine Mass was celebrated on the first Sunday of the month at 12 noon. It was well attended, with numbers reaching 300 and upwards. A feature story in the *Daily News* for February 4, 2006 tells how Geraldine McGrath's choir from Saint John the Baptist parish was drawing people from as far away as Bakersfield, San Pedro and Santa Barbara. However times began to change and on December 3, 2006, we announced that the Tridentine Mass would no longer be offered at the Old Mission:

> Without a single deviation from our scheduled services, the monthly Tridentine Mass has been offered at San Fernando Mission since May 5, 1985. What was begun, at the behest of Timothy Cardinal Manning, has stretched over twenty-three years.
>
> Though there are ancillary reasons for discontinuing this Mass, the primary rationale is "age". Three Masses on the first Sunday are just too much for the old country priest.

One of the half dozen angels at San Fernando Mission that were originally on outside tombs at Calvary Cemetery.

After engaging in much discussion and exploring several alternative proposals, we have concluded there is no reasonable or workable option. Latin has not been taught in our seminaries for thirty or so years and none of the older priests is able or willing to take on the challenge.

Bob Tall at the installation of the new organ for the Church at San Fernando Mission.

Our numbers have diminished considerably over the years. There were 89 people in October as opposed to upwards of 350 in the earlier years. There are only about a half dozen who have been with us since the beginning.

We are hoping that many of our communicants, especially those living in the area, will decide to attend our other two Sunday Masses, at 9 or 10:30 a.m.

We are extremely grateful to Gerry McGrath and her wonderful choir members who have provided quality Gregorian Chant since

> 1985. Our servers, all of whom have learned the Latin responses, have been outstanding. Surely we will retain a host of happy and spiritual memories of these eventful years.

Surprisingly there was little negative reaction. A whole new generation of Catholics had come along with no memories of the past. In a way that was unfortunate.

Air Conditioning

As part of the preparation for the papal visit in 1987, we had the church air-conditioned. Unfortunately the system was under powered, and so, twenty years later, we began a drive to have the whole operation updated, at a cost of $14,500 which was and is a lot of money hereabouts.

New Organ

On November 2, 2000, we sent out a letter to our "pinkie" list that I consider one of the most important:

> Sometimes even old men dream dreams and here is a graphic example. Upon returning to San Fernando Mission in January of 1980 (after being away for eight years), several things distressed me, chief of which was the antiquated *Petite Ensemble* built by the George Kilgen & Son Company.
>
> Identified as #5408, it had been manufactured for *Nuestra Señora de la Soledad* Church in 1935. In 1947, it was acquired for the chapel of Los Angeles College, the minor seminary for the Archdiocese of Los Angeles. The student organist then was Joseph Sartoris, who is now our senior auxiliary bishop.
>
> When the seminary moved to Mission Hills in 1954, the *Petite Ensemble* came too. It was installed in the loft of the Mission Church where it provided whatever music there was over the succeeding years.
>
> During the 1971 Sylmar earthquake, the choir loft and the *Petite Ensemble* collapsed into the body of the church. Almost miraculously, the harmonium was fitted back together and has continued in operation for another three decades. It will remain in the choir loft for the use of visiting organists.
>
> In May of 1983, Dr. John Shipper, who lived across the park on Brand Boulevard, gave us a two manual Model 645 Conn electronic organ from his home which he was selling. Manufactured for theatrical use in Madison, Indiana, that two-manual instrument will now be retired.
>
> In their will, Ernest and Helen Chacon left the Old Mission a substantial sum of money to be used "exclusively for a new organ." In the years since their demise, the bequest has been gaining interest in the

3 Manual Rogers 950 Organ, installed in 2000.

Archdiocesan money market. And now, with some meager funds squirreled away over these many years, we have brought the old country priest's "dream" of a glorious new pipe organ to fruition.

Then in one of our bulletins, we reproduced the specifics of the new Organ:

This 3-manual, Rodgers 950, digital console, interfaced with two wind-blown pipe ranks will be placed in the choir loft. Among its many features are rosewood keyboards; toe stud bolster, orchestra solo division and RSS sound expansion and reverberation system. The two pipe ranks will be a 4'Octave, 61 pipes and a 4'Nachthorn, 61 pipes. The pipes will be installed on the back wall of the choir loft area, one on each side of the stained glass window.

There are 76 speaking stops (representing 92 ranks) on the Rodgers 950 divided into 8 audio channels. Speakers for the digital sounds will be incorporated into the pipe layout area. The finish will be dark oak #88 to

san fernando mission

Msgr. Francis J. Weber – Director
Kevin Feeney – Curator and Business Manager

15151 San Fernando Mission Blvd.
Mission Hills, California 91345
(818) 361-0186

Richard Doyle,
Grant Irwin, George Eiser
John Vaverka and Roberto Delgado
Extraordinary Ministers

Sunday Masses offered at 9:00 and 10:30 a.m.
Daily Mass in the Serra Chapel at 7:25 a.m.
Baptisms and Weddings by appointment.

MINISTRIES AFFILIATED WITH SAN FERNANDO VALLEY'S MOTHER CHURCH

REGIONAL PASTORAL OFFICE Bishop Gerald Wilkerson, Episcopal Vicar	15101 San Fernando Mission Blvd.	EMpire 1-6009
OLD MISSION OFFICE Ana Carrera, Secretary Open Weekdays from 8:30 to 4:30 pm	15151 San Fernando Mission Blvd.	EMpire 1-0186
ALEMANY HIGH SCHOOL Frank Ferry, Principal	11111 No. Alemany Drive	EMpire 5-3925
SAN FERNANDO MISSION CEMETERY Rosalie Castillo, Superintendent	11160 Stranwood Ave.	EMpire 1-7387
PROVIDENCE-HOLY CROSS HOSPITAL Michael Madden, President	15031 Rinaldi Street	EMpire 5-8051
ARCHDIOCESAN ARCHIVAL CENTER Msgr. Francis J. Weber, Archivist Kevin Feeney, Adjunct Archivist	15151 San Fernando Mission Blvd.	EMpire 5-1501
CATHEDRAL ARCHIVES Sr. Joanne Wittenberg, S.N.D., Archivist	15151 San Fernando Mission Blvd.	EMpire 8-0312
RELIGIOUS EDUCATION OFFICE Lynn Lang	Post Office Box 7608 EMpire 5-5123 San Fernando, Calif. 91346	
MISSION HISTORICAL MUSEUM Open daily 9:00 am to 4:30 pm	15151 San Fernando Mission Blvd.	EMpire 1-0186
ARCHIVAL HISTORICAL MUSEUM Open Monday and Thursday Afternoons, 1 o'clock to 3.	15151 San Fernando Mission Blvd.	EMpire 5-1501
OLD MISSION GIFT SHOP Monica Mejorado, Manager Open daily 9:00 am to 5:00 pm	15151 San Fernando Mission Blvd.	EMpire 1-0186

match the interior of the church. The console contains the latest Rodgers digital sounds and MDI equipment, including a 6-track record and playback system.

The pipe chests will be attached to the system and the pipes affixed to the chests. This support system will also house the blower, computer interface, reservoirs, wind lines and all other pipe related equipment.

When we dedicated the organ on October 1, 2000, I made the following remarks:

> During the five and a half years that I was pastor of San Buenaventura Mission, I took Holy Communion each week to Ernest and Helen Chacon. They lived in the keys of Ventura and by then they had become shut-ins.
>
> Shortly after I returned to San Fernando in 1981, Helen died and we buried her from this church. When Ernest approached me about leaving a bequest to the Old Mission, I told him that we really did need a new pipe organ and he made provisions in his will to that effect.
>
> It's been fifteen years since Ernest died and finally the sum of money he left us grew into enough to buy a pipe organ ($80,000). How fitting it is that we inaugurate this Rogers 950 Pipe Organ by dedicating our initial program to Ernest and Helen.
>
> Saint Benedict used to say that he who sings prays twice. In the history of liturgical development, the organ has played a major role since the earliest centuries.
>
> The people of the Old Testament used music to worship the Lord—as we do today. In today's readings for the Divine Office or Breviary, David the Great King verbalized how the people of his time worshipped. Here is what he said:
>
> "Of all the instruments the organ has always been paramount because it can take the place of so many other instruments."
>
> "Especially is that true today when electronics have enhanced the organ to an ever greater extent."
>
> Robert Tall, the talented and generous organist for this concert, has chosen ten pieces which demonstrate the versatility of our magnificent new pipe organ. His pedigree is spelled out in the program today—I would place him among the greatest living organists in the world and so would anyone who hears him.
>
> Please hold your applause until the end of the concert. Then we will meet Robert Tall in the garden area.

Visitors

The Old Mission averages 35,000 visitors each year. In August of 2000, the Democratic National Convention chose San Fernando Mission as one of the historic sites which delegates could select for an outing during their sojourn in Los Angeles.

I found these people very congenial and interesting, much unlike what I had expected. My lapel pin, with the words PRO LIFE, was much in evidence as I circulated among the delegates. They surely knew that this Angeleno didn't tolerate and would not vote for candidates who campaigned for abortion. All in all, it was a pleasant day. And, to make matters all the better, we were given a modest stipend for hosting the event. It wasn't that much, but every dollar helps in keeping *ye olde Mision* afloat.

The old Guard's Bell was re-built after the Northridge Earthquake.

Servers

For a non-parish, the Old Mission has an especially distinguished corps of altar servers. In February of 2002, we raised almost $3000 for cassocks and surplices for our eighteen acolytes. Often visitors want to be photographed with them.

Opus Dei

Over the years we have endeavored to achieve the maximum use of our facilities. For example, *Opus Dei* uses the Serra Chapel and Cantwell Hall several times each week. We are always happy to cooperate with their apostolate which the Holy Fathers have so highly praised.

Bulletins—Pinkies

Not only is our mission the only one in Los Angeles, but it is the city's most memorable Catholic foundation for many reasons, chief of which is its religious significance. Our proximity to this wonderful mission should not lessen appreciation for this historic foundation.

Each month since my arrival at the Old Mission, in January of 1981, we have sent out a "pinkie" envelope to friends asking assistance for restoration and maintenance of this historic foundation. By March of 2008, we mailed 327 monthly letters.

My over-riding sentiment is that of gratitude for the marvelous way people have responded to the needs of the Old Mission. Though we are not a canonical parish, our material needs are manifold and our supporters have responded munificently.

With their assistance and numerous grants received over the years, we now boast of being the most attractive of all the California missions. Our exhibits are second to none, the grounds are beautifully maintained and the entire facility measures up to the dictates of OSHA.

The locals get all the credit. As it says on the masthead of our weekly bulletin, I am only the "administrator." Even if I were to claim all the credit, no one would believe it.

The weekly bulletin at San Fernando Mission reached 1,500 issues by December of 2005. Happily the Paluch Company has provided these bulletins at no charge to the Old Mission.

Parking Lot

We started an "Asphalt Fund" in 2001 to help defray the cost of repairing the front parking lot. Here's a copy of the appeal letter.

> It is indeed an ambitious project that will cost $35,365. Please mark your Pinkie ASPHALT DRIVE if you would like it to be credited to that purpose.
>
> We are getting ready for the summer rush here at the Old Mission. The majority of our tourists come in the warmer months. And they are all most interesting people who journey to California from all parts of the globe. Without exception, they are impressed by the exhibits and grounds here at the seventeenth of the foundations along *El Camino Real.*

The master-gate was replaced after several generations of service to the Old Mission.

The historic fountain was originally patterned after the one in Brand Park.

New Gates

In November of 2002, we had new wrought iron gates placed at the two entrances to San Fernando Mission.

A gracious donor offered to pay half if we would install new gates, so we could hardly pass up that challenge. Far from defacing our property, the new gates really enhance 15151 San Fernando Mission Boulevard.

Wrought iron is expensive, but it's really the only way to go. These gates cost quite a bit, but this is one more example of how we utilize the funds given us every month in the "Pinkie" envelope. It's no exaggeration to say that ours is the "Flagship" among the California missions. Not only is that true historically, but also artistically. Our aim is to keep that reputation as we move further along the road to Eternal Life.

Two years later we had to rebuild the two massive doors at the front of the Mission compound. One of the rotating hinges was failing, thus giving the gate only about 30% swinging capability in either direction. Guestimating that those doors were last fixed in the 1930s, we had to replace both ground rotator hinges, re-hang the gates in a newly fabricated steel frame and install a new (and larger) pass-thru doorway.

We had several bids for the overall cost which amounted to $10,660. In the meanwhile workers erected a temporary wooden wall, with a door, so we could secure the grounds while the project was underway.

Iron Gates

In Mid 2003, we had wrought iron gates installed on the front porch of the *convento.* Fashioned to match the wrought iron window-ware of the building, the new gates were necessary for security purposes and traffic control. We had a homeless man living on the front porch for several years. Despite a series of stern warnings and expulsions, he kept returning. Now he won't be able to penetrate the area. His presence posed several threats, one of which was the danger of fire from smoking and hand-held burners.

Also there was a traffic problem. On Saturdays and other occasions, wedding parties would hop over the chains to take photographs. Invariably they left behind water bottles, cigarette stubs and all sorts of related junk. Signs served no purpose and we couldn't afford to have a guard on duty. The gates were the only answer to a problem that plagued us for many years. It was the last area of the compound over which we lacked real control.

Fountain

Among the "hidden" expenses here at the Old Mission is our historic fountain, which operates daily from about 8 o'clock in the morning until five in the afternoon. Once or twice a year, the motor goes on the blink and the whole process comes to a thundering halt. For several weeks in August, 2006, only a trickle of water was moving through the pipes. That meant that the motor needed attention. Our annual "pump replacement" that year came off on schedule.

There had been "running water" in the fountain for about eighty years. The system used re-circulated water, which was pumped through the system by an elaborate machine hidden in the bushes. A series of filters and other complicated devices kept the water running fairly smoothly.

The fountain is an attraction to visitors who generally have their photograph taken there while on tour. The earliest photograph that I have seen dates to 1921. Estimates are that the water, electricity and pump cost about $250 a year to operate, which averages out to less than a dollar a day. Long ago we figured that was a small cost for keeping the "image" of San Fernando Mission intact.

Plumbing

You may recall that in the winter of 2004, during the series of rainstorms that befell this area of the Lord's vineyard, the appearance of "Lake San Fernando" made it virtually impossible to get into our church without wading through several inches of standing water.

Although that year's especially inclement weather made access to the church a formidable challenge, and probably wouldn't happen again for some years, we felt obliged to take steps to insure against any future occurrences. After consulting with several plumbing contractors, we discovered that the two existing drains emptied into dead-end gravel pits. Neither was connected with a subterranean exit or channel leading off the property.

The wooden and wrought-iron chandeliers throughout the Old Mission were the gift of Karl Karcher, the proprietor of Carl's Jr. Restaurants.

I had an acquaintance years ago who was the fundraiser for one of the mendicant orders. He was good at it because he had served personally in missionary areas and was able to portray his needs in terms that motivated others to assist in those projects. I recall that he said it was easy enough to raise funds, except for plumbing. "No one wants to pay for installing a sewer line." Admittedly that is among the most unattractive needs of any institution.

I became personally aware of what his challenges were. We were facing an enormous plumbing bill ($28,471) to replace the sewer lines that have been serving the Old Mission since the 1930s. The piping had disintegrated and the entire system had to be dug up, removed and reinstalled. Actually the fact that these antiquated lines lasted as long as they did is a minor miracle. We have upwards of 35,000 people a year using our facilities and it is astounding that the system hadn't broken down before.

Electric

Over time we have experienced some extensive power outages. We noticed that these occurred on especially hot days. Electricians discovered that some of our boxes were not sufficiently insulated from their surrounding walls. Hence, when the afternoon heat was at its highest, the system simply shut down. Actually that was a good thing because it alerted us of potential fire dangers.

Electricians spent several days moving and/or relocating the circuit boxes. Apparently it is important that air be able to circulate around the containers. Workers had to dig some new recesses in the walls and then fill in the old ones. They did a good job and no one is able to see where one box was removed and another installed. Why did it take all these years for this problem to surface? It's hard to say. But those boxes were old and their wires crumbling. All I knew is that we needed to make some adjustments.

In 2002, we converted the nineteen rooms of the *convento* from incandescent lights to high efficiency, low voltage halogens. With that change we began reducing our overall electrical voltage by almost half. The new lighting in our museums is state of the art. You'll notice that each one of our paintings and exhibits has its own illumination. In addition to using less power, the new system gives more light and that's an advantage anywhere.

Walkways

The walkways are constantly in need of repairs. The ground hereabouts has been settling again and we didn't dare run the risk of people

Ritz Weber.

stumbling. Hopefully that will be the last time that this will be necessary for a while, or so we were told by the concrete contractor.

San Fernando, Rey de España Mission, is a "work-in-progress", as one of our visitors observed. That remark was prompted by the yellow "caution" flags around the grounds in July of 2002. We were having the walkways fixed and that's a gigantic project since some of the existing broken concrete walkways had to be cut out and replaced.

Shelties

In November of 2005, Brewster, my sheltie sheepdog, died after a long illness. I have often been asked why so many shelties have shared my life. Well, here's the official story.

The Shetland Islands, which lie north of Scotland and east of Norway, are home to the Shetland Sheepdog. Due to the poor condition of the land, all the livestock there is small, for example, the Shetland Pony. In the middle of the nineteenth century, the islanders began to breed small agile dogs, called "Toonies," to keep livestock away from their precious crops.

Around 1890, British dog fanciers noted that Toonies were becoming rare and decided to preserve them. Today Shetland Sheepdogs range in size from 13 to 20 inches at the shoulder. Although the American

Peacocks have been associated with San Fernando Mission since 1874.

Kennel Club standards only allow 13 to 16 inch high dogs to be entered in shows, many pet quality dogs are larger than this. Shelties are found in many colors, including sable, black, blue merle and tricolor. Although they have thick coats, shelties do not do well if left out in the weather for extended periods.

They make affectionate and intelligent pets and are good with children. There are two challenges to living with a sheltie. The first is that the dogs need a lot of grooming, at least one brushing weekly and daily brushing during the shedding season. Second, they are notorious barkers.

Some shelties are very sensitive to heartworm medications, so owners must check carefully before using these. Shelties are popular dogs and, in 1992, they reached their peak, being the ninth most popular dog in America and third most popular in Japan. There were shelties at many of the California missions. Wire fencing was expensive and rare. Happily we decided to re-introduce those wonderful canines.

Peacocks

We are frequently asked about what happened to the peacocks that once roamed over the grounds and flew through the skies around San Fernando Mission. The easiest and quickest answer is: "They are hibernating."

Stories abound about the peafowl during their years in Mission Hills. One lady called to say that, "one of your storks has landed in my backyard, what should I do?" I resisted telling her to snatch the baby and

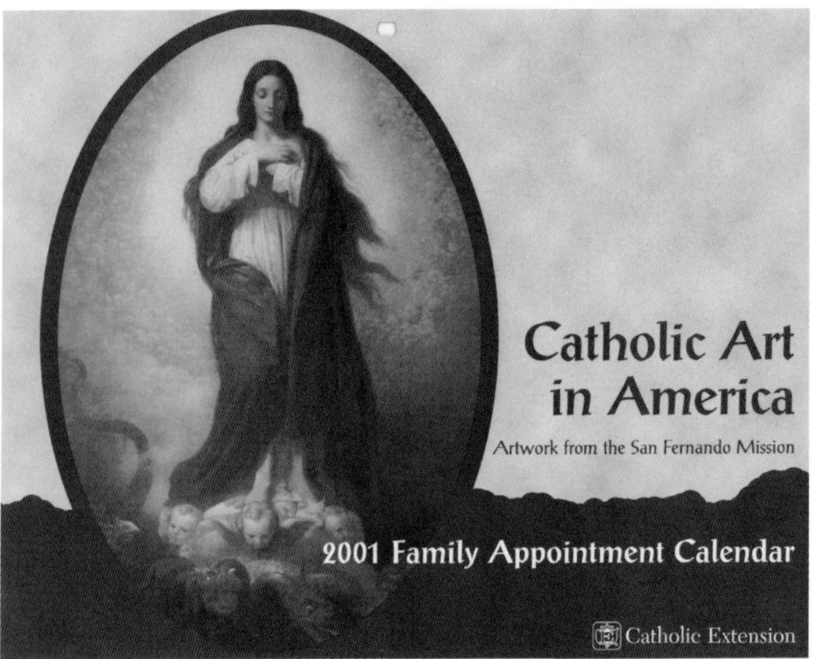

take it to the nearest foundling hospital. Another distraught neighbor reported that the birds had eaten her roses and geraniums.

We used to pass out questionnaires to the thousands of school kids who came here each year asking what they found most interesting at the Old Mission? The almost unanimous response was the peacocks. Few of the youngsters had ever seen such colorful birds.

There is a century old tradition about peafowl at the Mission. Claude Bain visited the area in 1874 and recorded seeing, "several beautiful peacocks allegedly brought to the West Coast from India."

We still miss the unique "chatter" of our bevy of birds and hope that one day they can return to San Fernando Mission. In the meantime our forty-two winged friends have been relocated to friendly homes where they spend a good deal of their time "hibernating."

Paintings

Few if any of the California Missions have as much art work as San Fernando, Rey de España.

In a pinkie for July 3, 2002 I noted that "Just a little over two years ago, one of my close friends, Anita Watson, died. I had known her since

Educational wall hangings for children at the Old Mission.

the years when I used to serve Mass in the old archiepiscopal residence in Fremont Place where she attended daily Mass.

In her will, she left me two paintings. When they arrived we had them hung in prominent places in the *convento* building. One is a Madonna and Child, oil on canvas, in a gilt-wood frame; the other is a portrait by G.G. Stevenson of the Madonna in a blue shawl and that, too, is framed.

> Anita was part of the Watson family. Her people were very prominent in the years after the mission era. The Dominguez and Watson families were inter-married. I was in her home in Fremont Place many times over the years and I must have commented about the paintings in question. If so, I had good taste because they are both quite exquisite.
>
> They are now deeded to the Old Mission and will hang here many years after the Old Country Priest has been carted off to the boneyard. I hope you and many others will enjoy these works of art in the years ahead.
>
> Paintings at the Old Mission have grown in quantity as well as quality.

Let me quote an essay that appeared in an issue of *The Tidings.*

> A substantial portion of what once constituted the private art collection of the late Bishop Joseph Sarsfield Glass (1874-1926) has been placed on permanent exhibit at San Fernando Mission.
>
> The Glass family were prominent Los Angeles pioneers. After his ordination as a priest for the Congregation of the Mission, Father Joseph Glass served many years at Saint Vincent's College and was that institution's president when it closed in 1911.

Cardinal Lapola, Governor General of Vatican City, and the OFM's visit the mission on November 8, 2008.

During his subsequent tenure as pastor of Saint Vincent's parish, Father Glass became a close friend of Edward Laurence and Carrie Estelle Doheny and it was through his ministrations that Mrs. Doheny entered the Catholic Church Oct. 25, 1918.

Glass was a longtime patron of the arts, an interest developed during his years of study in Rome from 1897 to 1899 and while on a trip through Spain in 1913 to survey ecclesial architecture.

In 1915, Father Glass was appointed Bishop of Salt Lake City. During his decade there, the Dohenys provided for many of his temporalities, including a Pierce Arrow automobile.

The Dohenys also financed a collection of statuary and some forty paintings which Glass purchased in Europe during 1924 and 1925. In addition to what became the "Collection of the Madeleine," which is presently housed in the Pastoral Center at Salt Lake City, the Dohenys encouraged Bishop Glass to acquire a smaller but no less exquisite number of paintings and art works for his own personal use.

This latter collection was eventually bequeathed to the bishop's sister, Mary Glass Pope, who lived in Saint Martin of Tours Parish in Brentwood, California. Soon after the completion of a new parochial church, Mrs. Pope arranged with Father Augustine Murray to have the paintings and certain other art items installed in the church, where they remained for the next quarter century.

In mid 1988, the Glass Collection was removed from the church and, in virtue of an agreement between Msgr. Lawrence O'Leary and

Mrs. Leona Pope, it was given to San Fernando Mission. The largest of the dozen paintings, affectionately referred to by Bishop Glass as "the Lady of the House," is an early 17th century portrayal of the Immaculate Conception attributed to Jusepe Ribera.

The oil painting of Christ Crucified, the work of the Hungarian artist, Neogrady, is dated 1712. It has been placed on exhibit in the Grand Sala of the mission's *convento* building. Two other 17th century oils depict the Death of Saint Joseph and Saint John the Evangelist. The latter is encased in a handsome Dutch frame.

Five of the smaller paintings are hung in Cantwell Hall. The subjects of those artistic masterpieces are the Pieta, God the Father, the Temptation of Saint Anthony, the Massacre of the Innocents and Saint John the Divine.

Other Paintings in the collection are a 17th century rendition of Nefrotiti, an 18th century Adoration of the Magi and a Florentine depiction with Saints Jerome and Catherine of Siena.

Finally, atop the doorway leading into the Archival Center is a small reproduction of Luca Delia Robbia's 15th century *Cantoria* or choir balcony in the Cathedral of Florence. This four panelled diorama, enclosed in a gold-leafed wooden frame, probably dates from the turn of the present century.

Seeing the treasures of the Joseph S. Glass Collection is just another of the many compelling reasons for scheduling a visit to San Fernando Mission.

Blessing of Statue of the Sacred Heart at San Fernando Mission Cemetery. Art by Isabel Piczek for the Sacred Heart Sisters.

In 2001 Utter McKinley San Fernando Mission Mortuary's calendar featured twelve of our very best paintings which were included in the Catholic Church Extension Society Calendar. Here's the content of a letter sent out to our people on July 25th.

> You will recall that we allowed the Catholic Extension Society to feature the artwork of San Fernando Mission on its calendars for this year of 2001. I have received a dozen or so of the calendars from parishes all over the country.
>
> Recently we discovered that Catholic Extension calendars were sent to 3,500 parishes, which is about 16% of the total number of parishes in the continental United States. Put another way, that means that upwards of 10 million people this year are being touched by the Old Mission.
>
> Sometimes we here at the homestead don't realize what a treasure we have in this historic place. Now, with this latest coverage, we even soar beyond the other establishments along California's *El Camino Real.*

The various paintings are described in several places. Here's an essay on the portrayal of Our Lady of Guadalupe in the Church, which appeared in one of our weekly bulletins.

> The oil on canvas painting of Our Lady of Guadalupe, colorfully and artistically restored at the South Coast Fine Arts Conservation Center in Santa Barbara, has been re-hung on the south wall of the Church. We are hoping that someone might be willing to pay for the restoration ($1,525). Here is the treatment process as described by the restorer:
>
> "The painting was removed from the wood panel and the wrinkles around the edge of the canvas flattened. The surface was cleaned with .05% ammonia stopped with naphtha and acetone. A honeycomb aluminum panel with a linen innerliner was adhered to the back of the painting with BEVA-371 adhesive. The damaged areas of the painting were filled with vinyl paste where required, sealed and inpainted with Mimari and Golden conservation paints. Finally, several coats of B-72 acrylic varnish were sprayed to the surface of the painting for protection.
>
> Because the original wood panel was simply nailed to the back of the frame, it was necessary to add a wood molding to the back of the frame to allow the painting with its new support to be attached to the frame. New wire was also attached."
>
> According to the signature on the painting, it was executed at San Luis Potosi, Mexico, in November of 1914, by Austin Jimenez. Here is a history of the painting's association with San Fernando Mission as told by Mary Ortega who heard this account from her mother when she was a small girl.
>
> "It seems that Dona Catalina Lopez—of the family of Don Pedro Lopez—who was a grand old lady at the time—allowed the owner of the painting to stay at her home. He was a refugee from Mexico during the revolution and apparently from a well educated family. No one knew

Mayor Richard Riordan at San Fernando Mission.

whether he had actually painted the picture, or had gotten it from someone else. When this man left the Lopez place he asked Dona Catalina if he could leave the painting with her for safe keeping, saying he would return for it later, as he had his living to make and the picture was difficult to carry with him.

"Years went by and the man did not return for his painting so that when the temporary chapel was furnished in the Convento at San Fernando Mission, around 1920, the Lopez family gave the painting which was still in their possession to San Fernando Mission. It remained in the little chapel while the chapel was in use and then when the Church of Santa Rosa was established in 1925, Father Charles Siemes, the Oblate father in charge of the Mission, loaned it to the pastor of the new church, where it remained until 1958. In 1958 a new painting of Our Lady of Guadalupe was obtained for the church and the pastor, Fr. Whelan, had promised to give the original painting of Our Lady to someone else. When Miss Ortega learned of this, she went to Fr. Whelan and informed him that the painting belonged to San Fernando Mission and should be returned there. For verification of her claim, she had the photograph taken of the little chapel which is published in Fr. Zephyrin Engelhardt's book, which shows the painting of Our Lady of Guadalupe on the Gospel side of the altar. Fr. Whelan agreed that if the painting belonged to the Mission it should be returned, and this was done. The painting now hangs on the south wall of the Old Mission Church where it seems to blend with the atmosphere of the Indian paintings and early Church furnishings."

The wooden panel on which the painting was mounted, is an old door. We would be happy to give the original mounting to the one who would pay for the restoration of Our Lady of Guadalupe. It is now mounted on a 40x60 inch aluminum panel.

A series of olive trees was planted to replace the aging trees that have grown old in their service to the Lord.

Most recently we were given a painting of the *convento* corridor of San Fernando Mission executed by Jean Krieg Irwing in 1969. And Rosa Villalvazo presented us with a *molcajete* that belonged to her mother, Amparo Zavalza. Those two acquisitions are prominently exhibited.

Building Painting

Years ago, we devised a schedule for painting our buildings which allows us to stretch this major expense over a half dozen years. Unhappily, the adobe surface of our buildings absorbs the paint more than ordinary structures. Since adobe is basically a form of "mud" it tends to melt when excessive rains descend upon Mission Hills.

Retablo *presented to San Fernando Mission by Clarence Liles. Originated in Mexico, about 1750.*

The building chosen for painting in 2005 was the archives. The existing exterior was painted and the wooden eaves hydrowashed to remove oxidation and surface dirt. Cracks in the plaster walls were patched using an acrylic textured plaster compound. The prepared surfaces also received two coats of industrial enamel.

The total cost of this project was $13,800, plus another $260 for the seven metal light sconces on the patio wall. Admittedly that's a lot of money. But there really weren't any alternatives. Leaving this project for even another year would have probably doubled the cost. Maintenance is, in the long run, our cheapest expense.

Trees

Trees are a blessing but they are high maintenance. Alternate Februarys here at the Old Mission are times when we have our trees trimmed.

It's a gigantic project and one that we dare not overlook. Unless trees are trimmed at regular intervals they will eventually topple over because of their own weight. Take a careful look and see what a fine job was done by Trees 'n' Things.

Kevin Feeney, our business manager, did a count of the trees. We now have thirty-three palm trees, fifteen olive trees and 116 shade/ fruit/ ornamental trees. In other words there are 164 trees that have to be looked after every other year. The cost is high—$6350 a hefty sum. But that's part of the overall cost in keeping this venerable institution open and attractive to our many visitors.

One problem keeps surfacing—that our olive trees are dying. Each year they move closer to extinction. In 2008, we devised a plan to replace six of the olive trees.

Ten Commandments

In mid-September, we sent out the following letter:

In mid-May, we were given a stone reproduction of the Ten Commandments which we have mounted on the north outside wall of the baptistry in the cemetery.

Happily do we acknowledge Farida Molina, Alex Ojascastro, Bobby Desiderio, and Linda Poblite who are associated with The Soldiers of Salvation, who cut the stone, engraved the lettering and delivered the tablets.

Holy Scripture tells us that the inscriptions on the original tablets were engraved by God himself. There is every reason to believe the tradition which connects the decalogue with Moses. (Exodus 24:1-18,12)

We know that the gift of the divine law was destined not only for Israel, but also for the "new Israel", the Christian Church.

If you haven't seen the mounted decalogue, please do so at your earliest convenience. I am sure you will agree that this is a wonderful addition to the Old Mission.

Chairs

We replaced the chairs in Cantwell Hall in 2000. Here's a copy of our appeal:

Probably you were among those who sponsored a "chair" for Cantwell Hall during June and July. We gathered enough funds to purchase eighty of those fine arm-chairs, along with two carriages for storage and moving. Surely our affairs in the Hall will be much more enjoyable in the future. Many thanks.

Through a grant that we received from the California Missions Foundation, we rehabilitated a room in the *convento* which has never been open to the public. Shelves and cases were fabricated to house many of the historical mementos we had in storage. By the mid-Fall of 2005 we had that project completed. The entrance to the driveway has been altered to allow a safer and easier access. The stone wall was extended, the asphalt repaired and new shrubbery has been installed.

Windows

In October of 2004, many of the wooden window casings in the south side of the wing, just to the east of the *convento,* needed replacement. For some reason, the windows on that side had deteriorated faster than the others. There were seven that were either full of dry rot, consumed by termites or just worn out by the constant rays of sunshine.

Finally we located a craftsman in Sun Valley who could rebuild the windows with their casing. It was really a tedious challenge and one that was very expensive. Removing the bars, the window casings, fabricating new ones and then putting the finished product in place was $900 each. Expensive as it was, the finished windows cannot be distinguished from the originals, yet they contain low heat glass and wood that has been treated to resist future termites and dry rot.

Cabinetry

Early in 2002, we had some cases made to house two of our oldest and most interesting historical artifacts—the tile maker and the host-oven encased to keep our overly enthusiastic tourists from touching or otherwise harming them. Of course, this was an expensive project but one which really needed doing.

The lady who looks after the exhibits at the Los Angeles Public Library fashioned the wooden cases. We hadn't been able to exhibit those items earlier because there was no way to make them "kiddie proof". Later we had two additional exhibit cases made for the other side of the Indian Craft Room. Lighted inside, they display some of the oldest materials we have here at the Old Mission. And they do it with class.

Madonna Room

Over the years, the most popular exhibit is the one in the Madonna Room where there are about three hundred depictions of Our Blessed Mother. That room is a special favorite of the kiddies during the school year. As many will recall, the room itself served the mission in earlier days as a *carcel* or prison. It probably wasn't used very often.

Convento Ceiling

The big news in 2006 was the painting of the ceilings in the *convento* building. Our late friend, Dr. Norman Neuerberg, always wanted the ceilings restored to their original color. Visitors will notice how much brighter the rooms are now. Would you believe that the workers used 130 gallons of paint! That must be a record.

Teatro

As mentioned in our earlier volume, El *Teatro de Fray Junípero Serra* in the *convento* building early on became one of our favorite attractions, with its state-of-the-art laser disc system offering three different historic film selections for visitors.

With the passage of time, two earthquakes and thousands of screenings, the laser disk system finally burned itself out. Only then did we realize how much people liked the three available films.

On May 8th, 2001 we installed a new, commercial-grade, DVD system in the theatre along with a microprocessor to bring the *teatro* into the 21st century. The rich colors of the presentations have been

Bob Hope and Paulette Goddard appeared in the Ghost Breakers *in 1940 from Universal Pictures.*

THE BOB HOPE
MEMORIAL GARDEN
San Fernando Mission
Mission Hills, California

DEDICATION
July 27, 2005

...in loving memory
by
Dolores and family

enhanced and we also made available to viewers part of Huell Howser's television series on the California missions.

High quality technology like this is costly, but we felt it was a wise investment for many reasons. According to questionnaires handed out to visitors the theater is one of our more popular attractions, even without popcorn. We consider it to be a very valuable educational tool for Fourth graders from the Los Angeles Unified School District, as well as for the private schools that gather here.

Over the ensuring years, the reaction has been universally positive for the three films, one narrated by Huell Howser, about life at San Fernando Mission, another a presentation about Fray Junípero Serra and a final one on "Together in Mission" which tells about the Church in Southern California as it has evolved from mission times.

By 2004, the projector, after fourteen years of service, expired and we were advised that it wasn't worth reviving because of all the new technology available. So we purchased a 50 inch Mitsubishi VS-50803, big screen machine that cost (with installation) $4,202.13, which was paid for by the Fritz Burns Foundation. Check it out, you'll find it is even clearer and more responsive than its predecessor.

Chandeliers

Friends of San Fernando Mission will recall that the chandeliers in the *convento* were given to the Old Mission by Carl Karcher, a Catholic entreprenuer and popular restaurant chain founder. Carl returned his noble soul to the Lord on January 11, 2008. May he rest in peace.

Bob Hope Memorial Garden

In the year after Hollywood's legendary Bob Hope's death (1903-2003), arrangements were made to entomb his remains in the cemetery at San Fernando Mission. The Memorial Garden was blessed by Roger Cardinal Mahony on July 27th, 2005, the second anniversary of the famed entertainer's demise.

About a third of the Memorial Garden is located on what was formerly the Old Mission's cemetery. The other part backs up to what was seminary property. The historical fountain in the cemetery was connected to an intricate series of pipes that now provide a cascading waterfall, with water re-circulated for environmental reasons. About thirty trees were planted to further enhance the area as were hundreds of colorful plants and walkways paved with shaved stones.

The only access to the Bob Hope Memorial Garden is through the Old Mission. So we anticipate an upsurge of visitors in the years ahead. Dolores Hope also generously provided that our public bathrooms be

Bob Hope's tomb at San Fernando Mission.

brought up to code with provisions for the handicapped. In addition, she made a substantial contribution of $300,000 to the mission's Endowment Fund.

I issued the following statement for the dedication:

> It all began for this magnificent 235 square mile valley in 1797 when the San Fernando Mission was founded by Spain as the seventeenth of the outposts along California's historic *Camino Real.* A century later came Great Britain's contribution to the valley with the arrival of Leslie Townes (Bob) Hope.
>
> For most of his hundred years on old planet earth and for all of his public life, Bob lived in the San Fernando Valley, just down the way, alongside Toluca Lake.
>
> On his many travels to the far corners of the world to entertain the nation's troops, his returning plane banked over the Old Mission as it made its way to Hollywood-Burbank and what is now the Bob Hope Memorial Airport. In 1940, he starred in the movie "Ghost Breakers", a Paramount production filmed at San Fernando Mission.
>
> Finally he has returned to the Old Mission which he knew so well, here to wait with the rest of us for the general resurrection.
>
> We welcome him home and rejoice that he will henceforth share his many memories with his friends and his fellow travelers.
>
> Happily, Mrs. Dolores Hope paid to have our public bathrooms brought up to code and that necessitated installation of handicapable facilities which we have long desired. The gardens in and around the bowl area in the cemetery were renovated and updated.

Dolores Hope visits the Hope Memorial Garden.

We were also mandated to install a larger area for handicap parking on our front lot. Now the area is van accessible, another long over due improvement.

Then, some months later, again through the generosity of Dolores Hope, we installed a ramp for wheelchairs on the approach to the

BOB HOPE
MEMORIAL GARDEN
San Fernando Mission
Mission Hills, California

BOB HOPE
ENTERTAINER, PATRIOT
and HUMANITARIAN
1903 - 2003

[PROFILE FOR STUDENTS]

Cub Scout "Estefano" at Holy Mass in San Fernando Mission, August 20, 2007.

church. Everyone who attends Mass at the Old Mission signed a birthday card for Dolores for making the ramp possible, which we delivered on her 97th birthday, May 25, 2006.

We have also converted one of the museum cases into an exhibit honoring Bob Hope, a unique talent on the Hollywood scene, who was successful in five major entertainment media—vaudeville, stage, radio, film and television.

Over the ensuring years, Dolores has retained her interest in the Old Mission and in 2008 she paid for having the pews in the church refinished.

On May 27th, 2009, Dolores observed her hundredth birthday. Cardinals Mahony and McCarrick (of Washington) were the principal celebrants for Mass in the Marian Chapel at St. Charles Borromeo Church in North Hollywood. Afterwards a number of friends were invited to the Hope residence in Toluca Lake for a reception. Dolores was in great form and sent a message of greeting to the good people of the Old Mission.

Inventory

In 2005, *Glen Langton* a candidate for Eagle Scout, inventoried much of the exhibits and holdings in the public areas of San Fernando Mission for the archives. Then in 2007, Brian Sears, another aspiring Eagle Scout, prepared two illustrated volumes, *Inventory of Items on Exhibit in the Convento of San Fernando Mission*, in which he enumerated 235 mission artifacts. Brian received the Archdiocesan Christian Service Award for his work in 2008.

Alia

There were many other additions and updates at the Old Mission over the past decade, including six new wrought-iron benches on the approach to the church, and a set of automated sprinklers in the east garden. Four large exhibit cases were built into the walls of El *Teatro de Fray Junípero Serra*, and another six in a hitherto unused room in the *Convento* in which we added new displays.

Filming

Almost from the beginning of the last century, San Fernando Mission has been a favorite of Hollywood film-makers. Well over a hundred movies and television programs have been shot on the grounds, along with a fair number of commercials. In the last decade, our interests have been looked after by Cast Locations, one of the industry's leading firms. Here's a list of the most recent productions.

2000	Breakers	Feature Film
2000	The Titans	Feature Film
2001	Bandits	Feature Film
2001	The Matador	Feature Film
2001	Coca Cola	Commercial
2001	The Banger Sisters	Feature Film
2001	Alias	Television Series
2002	*Te Amare en Silencio*	Spanish Language Soap Opera
2003	She Spies	Television Series
2003	Cruel Intentions 3	Feature Film
2004	Merge	Reality-based Television Series
2005	*El Muerto*	Feature Film
2007	Viva Laughlin	Television Series
2007	Heroes	Television Series
2008	Enel Energy	Commercial
2008	Make Your Own Hero	Webisode Series

Painting

In the early summer of 2009, San Fernando Mission inherited a sizeable monetary gift from the estate of Virginia DeNublia.

Restricted in its purpose, the grant was to be used only "for restoration". After much consultation, it was decided to paint the exteriors of all the buildings. In deference to a longtime suggestion of the late Norman Neuerburg, plans were also made to paint the ceiling of the church white in an effort to provide more light to the interior. Incredibly, over 45 gallons of paint were utilized in carrying out Norman's wishes.

* * * * * *

In conclusion, I would like to share a letter sent out on July 7, 2006:

> When the new archival facility for the archdiocese was completed in 1981, Cardinal Manning asked if I would come back to Mission Hills where I would also serve as director of San Fernando Mission.
>
> As an incentive for my giving up the pastorate of San Buenaventura Mission, the cardinal offered to elevate San Fernando Mission to the status of a canonical parish. After considerable thought and prayers, I concluded that this area didn't really need another parish. Nor did I think the neighboring pastors would welcome such a move.
>
> In any event, I never dreamt that my tenure at this, the seventeenth of the California missions, would stretch over another quarter century. Actually it's been a real delight ministering to the good people who come here for Sunday Mass.

The Dolores Hope Memorial "Ramp" outside the church at San Fernando Mission.

A lot has changed since 1981. We now have two (and sometimes three) Sunday Masses and, with your loyal assistance, we have made many improvements to the "mission" the latest of which is a wheelchair ramp into the church. Even the legendary Bob Hope has joined our little community.

With all due humility, I feel that San Fernando Mission has become the "showplace" of the *El Camino Real.* Our exhibits and grounds are without peer and all this despite the devastating Northridge earthquake of 1994.

Of course, I recognize that all this is due to the generosity and support of the wonderful People of God who worship here on Sundays. And I know you want to continue that tradition.

5

Archival Center-Chronicle

During the years when I was *President* of the Association of Catholic Diocesan Archivists, the position of Episcopal Moderator became vacant due to the demise of Joseph Cardinal Bernardin. In 1997 I recommended that Roger Cardinal Mahony be named to that position by the United States Conference of Catholic Bishops. The Archbishop of Los Angeles occupied that role until 2003, when his six-year term expired.

On March 24, 2003, we addressed a special intervention to the Leadership Team for the Archdiocese of Los Angeles which read as follows:

> Because the method of financing for the Archival Center is *unique* in the archdiocese, I would like to explain ever-so-briefly how that function has been funded over the years. May I also preface these remarks by pointing out that the archives are one of the few activities of the local Church *mandated by the Code of Canon Law*. The code entrusts the archives to the Chancellor who, in our case, hands over that duty to an accredited archivist.
>
> The archives for the Archdiocese of Los Angeles were formally established in 1962 by James Francis Cardinal McIntyre in a newly-erected annex attached to the northeast side of the old Chancery Office on Ninth Street. In early 1981, the archives were moved to Mission Hills and installed in a handsome edifice on the grounds of San Fernando Mission with a grant provided by the Dan Murphy Foundation. About five years ago, parts and later the whole of the basement area of the adjacent Alemany High School were entrusted to the Archival Center for additional storage. The present space needs should be adequate for the next quarter century.
>
> During the first two decades of its existence, the archival program was financed as part of the ongoing operation of the curial office. Postage, supplies and other capital expenditures were provided on a need basis. The archivist's salary was paid first by Queen of Angels Seminary (where he taught) and later by San Buenaventura Mission (where he was pastor). There was no budget.

In 1981, the archivist was appointed Director of San Fernando Mission and was told that thereafter those two institutions would operate as a single unit as an extraterritorial "agency" or outreach of the Chancery Office. Mission income (from two Sunday Masses, baptisms, marriages, funerals and Gift Shop revenue) would, thereafter, support the Archival Center. Since then, we have submitted monthly reports which are on file at 3424.

By the late 1980s, with the acceleration of the program for document retirement, we reached and surpassed the ability of San Fernando Mission

A Quarterly Publication of the Archival Center, Archdiocese of Los Angeles, California

February 2010 Issue 113

Dear Friends,

It was this writer's pleasure to provide the preface to *My Memories*, the autobiography of Sister Maria Victoria Hernandez, O.P. Copies are available from Queenships Publishing at Post Office Box 220, Goleta, California 93116.

Preface

Sister Maria Victoria is among my favorite nuns of all time and she gets more precious with the passage of time. Her memories are stunning, a must read for Catholics and others walking along California's *El Camino Real*.

We know that Christ did not make faith dependent on the personal holiness and the worldy learning of His shepherds. It is supreme test of Catholic faith to believe in spite of the imperfect channels through which faith is transmitted. Let us join together to eliminate the impurities that accompany the flow of the waters, but let us not shut off the current.

The *Newsletter for the Friends of the Archives of the Archdiocese of San Francisco* (Spring-Summer, 2009) congratulates Deacon Jeff Burns on the 25th anniversary of his appointment as archives are new located in the basement of Saint Patrick's Seminary in Menlo Park. That same Newsletter tells our own link to the Bay Area with the following note.

Congratulations to Monsignor Francis Weber – 50 Years a Priest!!

Congratulations to Friend Monsignor Francis J. Weber, who is celebrating his 50th as a priest. Monsignor is the Dean of California Catholic historians, and has published many, many, volumes of history. He has done an outstanding job at the Archives for the Archdiocese of Los Angeles. He has built and maintained the marvelous Archives Center at Mission San Fernando. Not the least of Monsignor's accomplishments, Monsignor secured the job of archivist for me for the Archdiocese of San Francisco some twenty-five years ago. Thank you Monsignor for all your great work.

to meet the expenses of the Archival Center. It was in 1988, Cardinal Mahony authorized an annual subsidy of $125,000 which allowed us to hire a professional archivist and embark on other improvements and services already in place for the other major ecclesial document collections in the American Church.

Though our workload has continued to grow in the ensuing years, the initial subsidy has never been increased and, in fact, it was reduced twice to the present amount of $95,000. The last reduction demanded our putting our Sister on half-time and that forced us to cut back on the response time for the many requests that come from the ACC.

There have been other cutbacks in our overall income in recent times:

a) The reduction of our funerals by 18%, due to the opening of a chapel at Mission Hills Catholic Mortuary: ($6,300.);
b) The imposition (in 1993) of "Together in Mission"—despite the fact that San Fernando Mission is not a parish and has no normal mailing list: ($6,758.61);
c) The gradual diminution of income caused by fewer tourists and the economy downturn which is reflected in a lowering of the Sunday collection from our congregation (mostly tourists).

A further reduction of the subsidy would cripple our operation. If the archivist were to retire, that would not diminish the overall cost to the archdiocese since he would be making almost the same retired as active.

I personally bring in to our overall financial picture about $45,000 each year, from a wide range of sources, including foundations, gifts and other funds. Without that income, the Archival Center-San Fernando Mission would be even more depleted.

For the above reasons, I am asking the Leadership Team not to reduce any further our annual subsidy.

Newsletter

Since the inauguration of The Friends of the Archival Center, we have issued a quarterly newsletter which allows supporters to know what we are doing, where we are going, what we have accomplished and what our goals are. Those wishing to read about our accessions are encouraged to join the friends which automatically entitles supporters to the newsletter. Since August of 2001 the newsletter has borne the moniker *El Camino Real.*

Department Heads

The following address was given to the Department heads at the Archdiocesan Catholic Center.

Alzheimer's Disease is one of the most distressing illnesses that can befall a person, especially if that individual has led an active and productive life.

Patients having that disease in its advanced form have no memory of or interest in the past and pay minimal attention to the present. Otherwise healthy people, they can live long lives but they do so in an almost subhuman state.

Institutions can also have Alzheimer's Disease and it is manifested when employers and employees know nothing or, worse, care nothing about the history of their institution, when it was founded, by whom, for what, etc.

I once knew a lady who worked for thirty years in the employ of Arm and Hammer Baking Soda. She told me that the founder of her company was Armand Hammer, the industrialist and art collector. And, when I attempted to set her straight, she nodded and said—"who cares, as long as I get my check."

The local Church, too, can suffer from a form of Alzheimer's when its members and/or its employees exhibit no curiosity or interest in its purpose, its goals, its works or its organization.

I mention this only because last week, after working in this complex for thirty-four years, an employee asked me if I was Cardinal Manning. I didn't bother to explain that he went home to God years ago, but I was tempted to tell Human Resources that we had a forty-year-old brain-dead person on the payroll.

Fortunately, for the Church and other institutions, there is a cure for Alzheimer's Disease and it really doesn't involve all that much effort—just a little, healthy motivation.

Increasingly, the past decade and a half, companies have been investing heavily in record management and archival programs. Invariably they are finding that it is a superb investment which pays rich dividends, far outdistancing the cost.

Happily, the Catholic Church has long recognized the usefulness of archives. Since the Middle Ages, Rome has been a treasure trove of the past. So valuable were the Vatican Archives, that Napoleon once stole them and moved them to Paris.

Thanks to the foresight of James Francis Cardinal McIntyre, the Archdiocese of Los Angeles has had a canonically constituted archives since 1962. In that context, this area of the Lord's vineyard was light years ahead of most other American ecclesiastical jurisdictions.

Since 1981, the Archives have been located in a building adjacent to the San Fernando Mission which you are all invited to visit—and, more importantly, to support by sending your retired and obsolete files.

Whenever you have something in that category, just call me or someone at Mission Hills and we will arrange to have it picked up—usually on a Wednesday. Don't sort it, that's our job. We pretty much know what should be retained and what can be discarded.

And all items entrusted to the Archival Center can be retrieved with a phone call. Generally we file things in the same internal order of the parent agency or department.

Those wishing to define or describe the Archives for the Archdiocese of Los Angeles could say, in computer terminology, that the Archives are the "memory bank" for the Catholic Church in Southern California.

People whose memory bank is impeded or burned out have very little to talk about. So would it be with the Church. And, after all, we have a lot to tell the world—twenty centuries worth of heroic activities for the Lord.

Francis Bacon shrewdly observed that "there can be no history without documents." The Church. which means God's people, has a glorious history and it needs to be told. Countless numbers of people have been first attracted to Catholicism by reading about its unique and glorious track record. And that's very good.

Commercials on television and radio, and in newspapers and magazines, advertise their products most effectively by appealing to their performance ratings or endurance. Consumers are impressed when they hear, for example, that 65% of all the Mercedes Benz automobiles ever built are still in operation, that Neutrogena hand lotion has been used since prehistoric times or that Ever Fresh water is melted from centuries' old glaciers.

Whatever our particular role or vocation in life, we all share the common obligation of telling the world about Christ—who He was, what He did and why we should subscribe to His blueprint for salvation.

The greatest story ever told could not have been related without the scriptures—which are nothing more or less than the footprints of Christ on planet Earth.

We are to this century what the apostles were to theirs. We record what we do in documents—and we must, therefore, be aware of their importance and the need to properly house and care for them.

Because—without a past, we have no future.

Friends of the Archives

The Friends of the Archival Center continue as a vibrant part of the overall retention policy for the Archdiocese of Los Angeles. Though membership is rather stagnant, at about 200 members, the Friends have amassed an endowment fund which provides the Archival Center with approximately $25,000 every year. That's a remarkable feat for a non-profit group which only had two events a year, dues, an end-of-the-year appeal and occasional auctions.

Between 1988 and 2006, the Friends sponsored eight Auctions/Book Fairs and during that time raised $81,644 for their Endowment Fund. Unfortunately, in 2006, the overall returns were the lowest ever, for a number of reasons. At the auction, for example, we had only five bidders, even though we sent out 120 invitations, most of which were returned marked, "no longer here". Small book shops have succumbed to the Internet. While the quality of the auction was high, the market had almost dried up. Nor did our members support the sale. So the decision was made to shut down the event. The whole operation was no longer cost-effective.

Since 2000, eight members of the Board have died:

Anita Weyer, IHM—April 28, 2000
Richard Farrell—February 1, 2003
Suzanne Meyer—June 2003
Nicholas Scrivetti—April 2004
Mary Gormaly—August 2004
Margaret Seltzer—October 18, 2004
Robert Campion—May 1, 2006
James Cremin—April 2, 2007

We plan to continue the newsletter *El Camino Real*, for several reasons, and there continues to be a lot of support for that quarterly publication.

Sr. Mary Rose Cunningham, C.S.C.

Sr. Cecilia Louise Moore, CSJ

Sister Cecelia Louise, or "CL" as we all knew her, will emerge as a giant when the final chapter of the Catholic Church in Southern California is written. She excelled in her own community, rising to the prestigious and influential position of President of Mount Saint Mary's College and then to the helm of our archdiocesan school system where for many years she occupied all of the leadership positions.

Finally, she became Chancellor of the Archdiocese, the first woman ever so honored. In that later position she was the canonical head of the archives and as you all know, no greater position exists in any archdiocese, except, perhaps, the Ordinary.

Sr. Mary Rose Cunningham, CSC

Between 1987 and 2005, Sister Mary Rose Cunningham, CSC served as Associate Archivist for the Archdiocese of Los Angeles.

Sister Mary Rose Cunningham was born on May 20, 1920, the youngest of four children brought into the world by Matthew and Ann (O'Gorman) Cunningham, at the family home, in Saint Agnes Parish, Los Angeles.

She attended Nativity Parochial School, Saint Agnes High School and Mount Saint Mary's College prior to entering the Congregation of the Holy Cross in 1942, and taking vows in 1944.

Professed in 1947, Sister Mary Rose held several teaching assignments in the Western region of her community including San Joaquin (Fresno), Holy Rosary Academy (Woodland), Saint Catherine's (San Buenaventura), Saint Agnes (Los Angeles), Holy Cross (Mountain View), Bishop Gorman (Las Vegas), Saint Mary of the Wasatch (Salt Lake City), Bishop Kelly (Boise), Mater Dei (Santa Ana), Saint Francis (Mountain View), and Judge Memorial (Salt Lake City). For nineteen years Sister Mary Rose served as either Dean of Women or dean of Studies at various secondary schools.

Sister Mary Rose, retired in June of 2005, and is presently living at the motherhouse of the Sisters of the Holy Cross, at Notre Dame, Indiana.

A Glance Backward

Possibly readers of this tome would be interested in a page from our 2007 Newsletter about an earlier "Father Weber" (1865-1935).

> On April 27th during a visit to my native city, I was given a tour of the archives for the Archdiocese of Indianapolis by the Vicar General, Msgr. Joseph F. Schaedel. I am happy to report that the files are well organized and carefully preserved.

The good monsignor then graciously took the time to give me a personal tour of the parish where my great uncle, Father Joseph F. Weber (1865-1935), served as pastor for most of his ministry.

The original church, located in West Indianapolis, is still standing and is now a Byzantine parish under the patronage of Saint Athanasius.

Demographics have changed considerably in subsequent years. There are presently forty-five families served by the Ruthenian Rite church, which is part of the Diocese of Parma. The original red brick schoolhouse, closed for several decades, has been acquired and hopefully, will re-open soon as a learning center.

Msgr. Schaedel then drove me to Holy Cross Cemetery on South Meridian Street for a visit to the priests' plot and Father Weber's grave. The genial Vicar General believes that his father was named after Father Weber. Msgr. Schaedel was born and raised in Assumption parish.

Some of you may recall the miniature book about Father Weber that appeared on the bookstalls in 1975. Here's a description of that tiny volume written by Robert O. Hanson.

Mayor of Indianapolis Father Joseph F. Weber.

A moving tribute to the author's great uncle, Father Joseph Weber, was proclaimed as "Mayor of West Indianapolis" for the duration of the city's

This colorful window enshrined in the archivist's office depicts the coat-of-arms of Archbishop John J. Cantwell. It was removed from the chapel at old Saint Vincent's Hospital in Los Angeles.

isolation caused by the worst flood in Indiana's history. For a period of forty-one years, the Pastor of Assumption Catholic Church provided spiritual guidance to his many parishioners as well as contributing mightily to the community at large.

Acquisitions

Attempts are made to list our major acquisitions in the quarterly newsletter. Several of the major, non-documentary items include a beautifully framed rendition of the Madonna of the Chair, which was given to Archbishop J. Francis A. McIntyre when he left New York in 1948; a large bust of Cardinal McIntyre which was housed at Saint John's College in Camarillo until that institution closed; a wrought-iron table from the former archiepiscopal residence at Fremont Place with a ceramic coat-of-arms of Archbishop John J. Cantwell and a stained glass depiction of Bishop Timothy Manning's coat of arms as titular bishop of Lesvi.

Stained Glass Installation

During the Christmas season of 1995, Edith and Isabel Piczek took an old glass rendition of the late Cardinal Timothy Manning's coat-of-arms and framed it into a colorful window in the archivist's office. Given to Father Lawrence Donnelly by Manning shortly after his episcopal consecration in 1947, the window had never before been seen. It was and continues to be an artistic jewel. Then, a few months later, the Piczeks offered to match the earlier window with a coat-of-arms of Archbishop John J. Cantwell that had been installed in the chapel of old Saint Vincent's Hospital in the 1920s. What a marvelous combination of color these two windows make. One visitor said the archivist's office "looks like a chapel—and is prettier than most I have seen." Our humble thanks to the Piczeks for this latest kindness. Do come and see!

One More for Serra

In my office are eight shelves of books, pamphlets and brochures, which I have long referred to as "a complete collection of writings by, on or about *Fray* Junípero Serra." Or so I thought.

And then Zamoranoan, Ken Karmiole, came along to tell me of a book about Serra that had never entered my radar zone.

After offering me a copy of Daniel Magee's "*An Original Leaf from Francisco Palou's Life of the Venerable Father Junípero Serra*", (1787), Ken casually mentioned that "there was another leaf book with a page from Palou that predated the Magee book by twenty-eight years!" And he had one for sale from another Zamorano member, the late John Class.

Entitled *The Miracle of the Anchor*, the seven page *opuscula* tells about the long-delayed ship, the *San Antonio*, in 1770, its eventual arrival in San Diego and how "the want of an anchor saved California for Spain."

The book is signed by Douglas S. Watson "as a Christmas greeting" from San Francisco in 1930. A penciled note states that "only 43 copies (were) printed." No printer is indicated, but the copy bears the book-plate of Robert Strong of the Grabhorn Press.

Measuring 10¾ x 7 inches, the book is bound in green wrappers, stitched with a white label printed and decorated in black on front.

Further research determined that *The Miracle of the Anchor* was indeed printed by the Grabhorn Press. It is described by Elinor R. Heller and David Magee in their *Bibliography of the Grabhorn Press* in 1940.

Never say "*complete*".

Photographic Collection

In 1993, the Archival Center was entrusted with a collection of 9,000 negatives of buildings, persons and events covering the years 1940 through 1975. It was an important period during which California hosted one of history's greatest migrations. In the wake of that

John Henry Nash.

migration, Los Angeles and California experienced a newness of people, languages, customs, culture and economics. That whole period lives on in these photos. However, the collection was useless in its condition and we desperately needed to have those negatives printed, indexed and made available to researchers.

As early as 1994, we began approaching local foundations, such as the Ahmanson, L.J. Skagg and Van Nuys, to no avail. Richard Farrell, our late board member, spent most of three years trying to interest the National Foundation for the Humanities, but that also proved fruitless because they kept adding conditions, which, clearly, pointed to the need of hiring a grant writer whom we could not afford.

In early 2000, we had the whole project re-bid. Based on the lowest of three bidders, the program broke down this way: For approximately 18,000 prints, the total cost would be $82,800.00. Much of the cost involved the labor needed to execute the project. We determined that by eliminating a second copy of each print, as well as its sleeve, numbering, etc., we could reduce the cost by some $28,000.00. With this reduction, the project was revised again, and the total cost to print and label 9,000 prints came in at $54,000.00. After ascertaining what the project would cost, in its revived format, we set out again canvassing foundations. It was a slow process because we didn't want to approach more than one foundation at a time.

On April 26th, a request was sent to the Carrie Estelle Doheny Foundation. There were several additional telephone inquiries. And then, on May 11, 2000, we were informed that the Foundation would give us half of what we wanted, provided that we match the grant.

In June, I answered, promising to provide from other sources the residue of the money needed ($27,000) by the end of the year. *Las Damas Archivistas* pledged $2,000, a member of the board $1,000 and the Friends approved a suggestion made by Pete Mauk at our meeting of August 17, 1996 (that the end of the year appeal be designated for this project), ($7,620). I checked with the President of the Friends who told me that the pledge still stood.

The board advanced us the remainder of the needed funds on the condition that the contributions from the end-of-the-year appeal and the proceeds from the upcoming Book Sale be designated for that purpose. We went ahead and signed the contract with Allied Micrographics.

John Henry Nash at Mission Hills

The Archival Center for the Archdiocese of Los Angeles has a formidable collection of books, broadsides and other ephemera printed in San Francisco by the late John Henry Nash (1871-1947). Renowned as a printer of fine books, Nash is especially remembered in typographical circles for his masterful formats, the technical perfection of his workmanship and the completeness of his detail.

The Nash imprint is recognized as synonymous with quality. He was a sound and able craftsman who patiently strove for perfection and one who came closer to that goal than many others of his generation.

It was perhaps in the creation of his broadsides, made frequently "for the joy of doing," that Nash allowed himself the greatest latitude and in those lovely specimens of his art, his personality found its fullest expression. Those "lesser pieces" are now quite scarce, even though they are little known to the general public because of their limited circulation.

The collection at the Archival Center encompasses those books and broadsides from the Estelle Doheny Collection with a California theme, together with several dozen acquired through the years from other sources. Nash's artistically-designed borders and decorative plates, often the work of Frederick Coyle, are the Nash trademark. He used them lavishly to enhance the works of poets, artists and authors.

Nash himself was an outstanding individual, once described as tolerant but stubborn, self-assertive but humble and ostentatious but simple. He was a man of outspoken likes and dislikes who personified the observation of Stanley Morison that "the fine printer begins where the careful printer leaves off."

Whether he was printing beautiful books, promotional broadsides, Christmas cards or elaborate announcements, Nash sought to distinguish his work by the careful use of superlatives.

Among the Nash treasures at the Archival Center is *A Tribute to Mr. Edward Laurence Doheny*, a eulogistic memorial written by Bishop Francis Clement Kelley of Oklahoma City-Tulsa in 1935. Housed in the same slipcase is *A Sermon of His Excellency, Most Reverend John J. Cantwell, D.D.* which was preached at the Requiem Mass offered for Mr. Doheny in Saint Vincent's Church, Los Angeles on September 11, 1935. Both of these beautifully printed and elaborately bound books were made exclusively for Carrie Estelle Doheny. Neither is listed in a *Catalogue of Books Printed by John Henry Nash* compiled by Neil O'Day in 1937. Possibly they are unique.

Though Nash was not a Catholic, one couldn't sense that from his work on behalf of churchmen and other religious figures in the Bay Area. In 1935, for example, he printed a lovely book on *The Great Archbishop* which contained "Evening Service upon the Twenty-Fifth Anniversary of the Consecration of Most Reverend Patrick W. Riordan, Archbishop of San Francisco." There were only one hundred copies, two of which are at the Archival Center. Fully a fourth of his other books and broadsides have a Catholic theme. Archbishop Edward J. Hanna publicly acknowledged that service to the Church when he personally presided at an open house at Nash's home in San Francisco.

Recognition of 40 Years

Each year the Archdiocesan Catholic Center stages a "Staff Recognition Day". The archivist was informed on January 31, 2003 that he would be honored...." for 40 years of continuous service."

Cardinal Mahony graciously wrote that he "doubted this record has ever been matched anywhere in the country, and it surely will not be matched here in this archdiocese in the future. Your leadership in the field of archival expertise is unparalleled, and you have helped so many other archdioceses and dioceses to see the great importance of good archives and sound archival policy and methodology. You have truly been a great gift to us!"

In the Winter, 2002 issue of *SMRC REVISTA* (Southwestern Mission Research Center) was the following note:

> FORTY YEARS OF ARCHIVES, 1962-2002, is the headline of a news release from the Archdiocese of Los Angeles. The history of "the most extensively-organized and carefully-preserved archdiocesan facility in the United States" had its origin in 1842 with the arrival of Fray Francisco

Seeing eye dog assists elderly priest outside Archival Center.

Garcia Diego y Moreno at Santa Barbara as the proto bishop of Both Californias.

One hundred and twenty years later, it was announced in the *December 28, 1962* issue of *The Tidings* that "Father Francis J. Weber, biographer and historian, has been named Archivist for the Archdiocese of Los Angeles."

Early the following year, work began on a two-story annex to the northwestern end of the curial offices at 1531 West Ninth Street in downtown Los Angeles to house the archival collection. In a simple but richly symbolic ceremony, James Francis Cardinal McIntyre blessed and formally inaugurated the Chancery Archives as an autonomous department on July 8, 1963.

During January of 1981, the archives were moved to their present quarters in a newly erected building on grounds adjacent to San Fernando Mission in Mission Hills and, in September 13, 1981, Timothy Cardinal Manning blessed the facility that was thereafter designated as the Archival Center.

Additional storage space was acquired in 1995 in the nearby basement level of Alemany High School, where the Cathedral Archives were also located in 2002.

About a month earlier, *The Tidings* reported that, "on December 28, Msgr. Francis J. Weber would mark his 40th year as archivist for the Archdiocese of Los Angeles. Appointed by Cardinal James Francis

McIntyre, Msgr. Weber oversaw the construction of a two-story annex at the former archdiocesan headquarters on Ninth Street in downtown Los Angeles that was completed and blessed by Cardinal McIntyre in 1963. In 1981, the archives were moved to their present quarters in a newly erected building on grounds adjacent to San Fernando Mission in Mission Hills. Additional storage space was acquired in 1995 in the nearby basement level of Alemany High School, where the Cathedral Archives were also located in 2002. The extensively organized and carefully preserved archival collections include materials gathered by proto bishop Fray Francisco Garcia Diego y Moreno in 1842.

Archdiocesan Catholic Center

Among the challenges of selling the archdiocesan building at 3424 Wilshire Boulevard, in early 2008, was that of condensing twelve floors of offices and files into five. Overnight the Archival Center inherited several thousand boxes of materials, including letters, ledgers, publications, etc. Happily, because of the installation of space savers, over the previous eight years, the Archival Center was able to absorb the mountain of materials, once again proving its value to the overall operation of the archdiocese.

With the reassignment of offices within the Archdiocesan Catholic Center in 2008, the cubicle occupied by the archivist was moved to the fifth floor, katiwampus of that used by the Chancellor.

Example of Usefulness

Archdiocesan and diocesan archival centers in the United States demonstrated their value to the Catholic Church in a special way during the pedophilia scandals in the early years of the 21st century. In many areas where diocese and archdiocese were insured against such breaches of clerical discipline, the primary evidence of such coverage was found in ecclesial archives. Happily the Archdiocese of Los Angeles, was able to produce names and documentation of insurance carriers along with original copies of policies.

Quinquennial Report

Every five years, all the archdioceses and dioceses throughout the world are required to submit detailed reports to Rome. Here is the excerpt pertaining to the Archival Center for the years 1998-2002.

Artistic and Historical Patrimony of the Church

A. **Statistics**

1. **The California Missions**

The most historically significant sacred buildings within the Archdiocese of Los Angeles are those associated with six of the missions along California's *El Camino Real*:

California Missions	Established	Operated today by
1. San Gabriel Mission	1771	Claretian Fathers
2. San Buenaventura Mission	1872	Archdiocese of Los Angeles
3. Santa Barbara Mission	1786	Order of Friars Minor
4. La Purisima Concepcion	1787	Owned and operated by the State of California.
5. San Fernando Mission	1797	Archdiocese of Los Angeles
6. Santa Ines Mission	1804	Capuchin Franciscans

Each of the aforementioned institutions has its own public museum. There are substantial historical libraries at missions Santa Barbara, San Buenaventura and San Fernando. The Assistencia de Nuestra Senora de los Angeles is a pueblo church founded in 1784.

2. **Historical Churches**

Among the churches in the archdiocese that are architecturally outstanding and historically significant, would be:

- St. Vincent, Los Angeles
- Saint Brendan, Los Angeles
- Blessed Sacrament, Hollywood
- Saint Monica, Santa Monica
- Saint Joseph, Pomona
- Saint Andrew, Pasadena.

There are published works available on the history and art work in those and many other churches filed in the Archival Center.

Also, on deposit in the Archival Center are several hundred institutional studies about churches and institutions in the three-county archdiocese. Specially prepared monographs are available on the cemeteries, high schools and hospitals in the archdiocese, as well as one on Catholic Action as it has evolved in California's southland since the days of Pope XI.

3. **The Archival Center**

The Archival Center, located in its own building adjacent to the San Fernando Mission, in Mission Hills, serves as a repository for documents, books and related materials pertaining to the history of the Archdiocese of Los Angeles, and its predecessor jurisdictions in California since 1840. Its purpose is to collect, preserve, interpret and provide access to these materials. The Archival Center also conducts a variety of "reach out" programs involving the editing and publication of materials for the benefit of the historical and ministerial community.

Over the past three years, a subterranean area at Alemany High School has been outfitted to serve as an Annex to the central building of the Archival Center. Now fully operational, the Annex has a series of Space Saver devices that greatly expand storage capabilities for the overall holdings. With special high-tech locks and a sophisticated alarm protection, the Annex should be adequate for the next two decades.

B. **Description**

Chancery Archives

The use of the Chancery Archives is accorded to qualified and/or certified scholars and researchers. In compliance with archival procedures followed in other ecclesial institutions, researchers are expected to abide by the guidelines drawn up by the Chancellor and Archivist and approved by the Archbishop of Los Angeles. Permission to use materials housed in the Archival Center must be secured from the Archivist, in writing. Scholars and researchers are required to sign a Permission Request form, indicating the nature of their work and the specific documents requested for viewing. All copying of materials is to be done on the premises with pencil or typewriter.

The archivist, adjunct archivist and associate archivist are all members of the Academy of Certified Archivists (ACA). The archivist is past President of the Association of Catholic Diocesan Archivists for the United States; the adjunct archivist serves also as Business Manager for the San Fernando Mission. The associate archivist functions as the cataloguer for books and documents.

In addition to the numerous finding devices prepared and available on in-house computers, a series of eleven calendars of documents and related historical materials housed in the Archival Center has been published and circulated to research centers in the United States and abroad in which 22,674 of the documents (1840-1970) are enumerated as to author, recipient, date, place of origin and digest.

Each of the 12,301 books in the library attached to the Archival Center has been professionally catalogued according to the system used at the Library of Congress, in Washington, D.C. That collection, covering American Catholica, Californiana and a host of related fields continues to expand as new titles are published and old ones surface in bookstores.

For forty years the archivist for the Archdiocese of Los Angeles has been collecting historical and artistical mementos associated with California's Catholic heritage. Today, those items are housed in sixteen handsome display cases. Several times each week, *Las Damas Archivistas*, a docent group founded in 1981, opens the Historical Museum to visitors. A book on *California's Catholic Treasury* is available to docents wherein the thousands of items featured are described as to their relationship in the overall pageantry of the states' ecclesial history. In summary, the Archival Center provides the following services:

- ❖ Serves as the official record repository for the Archdiocese of Los Angeles;
- ❖ Operates two distinct historical museums for the enlightenment and edification of tourists and other visitors;

- ❖ Responds to numerous written and verbal requests for historical information pertaining to the history of the Catholic Church in California;
- ❖ Accommodates upwards of 150 historical researchers each year;
- ❖ Functions as a resource center for questions dealing with the foundation and development of the Roman Catholic Church in Western America;
- ❖ Serves as the coordinator of the Archconfraternity of Blessed Junipero Serra;
- ❖ Houses and makes available to researchers the Estelle Doheny collection of Western Americana;
- ❖ Hosts the Saint Francis Historical Society.

The historical and archival ministry in the Archdiocese of Los Angeles is in total conformity with the Code of Canon Law and the directives and suggestions contained in the Circular Letter of February 2, 1997 from the Pontifical Commission for the Cultural Heritage of the Church.

Cathedral Archives

An adjunct of the Archival Center is the Cathedral Archives for the newly completed and dedicated Cathedral of Our Lady of the Angels. According to its mission statement:

> The Cathedral Archives, located at San Fernando Mission, serves as a repository for documents, books and all other media resources related to the history of the Cathedral of Our Lady of the Angels. Its purpose is to collect, preserve, interpret and provide access for qualified researchers to these materials. The Cathedral Archives also conducts a variety of "outreach" programs for the benefit of the historical and ministerial community.

At present, the Cathedral Archivist, Sister Mary Joanne Wittenburg, S.N.D., is in the process of gathering, accessioning and cataloguing various documents, photographs, artifacts, audio-visual materials, etc. in the areas of art and architecture, advisory boards/committees, construction, development, media relations, operations and publications, a process that should take a minimum of three years after which time the collection will be open to qualified researchers.

Sister Mary Joanne Wittenburg has a Masters degree in History from Loyola University, Los Angeles, and has been employed by the Archdiocese of Los Angeles since 1988, first as Research Associate for the Department of Catholic Schools, and later as Director of Student Data and

Research for the Catholic Education Foundation. Prior to that Sister taught American and European History as well as Latin at Notre Dame Academy, a high school for young women in west Los Angeles.

On May 26, 1998, Archbishop Francesco Marchisano, President of the Pontifical Commission for Cultural Affairs of the Holy Roman Church, responded, and here we repeat only that part which pertains to the Archival Center:

> ". . . I was particularly struck by the wonderful Archival center and the many activities sponsored there which include a variety of praiseworthy outreach programs, the set-up of historical museums open to the public—thanks to the exemplary dedication of Las *Damas Archivistas*—and the distribution of fine publications, as well as important initiatives in the field of preservation of archive material. A special word of thanks to the Archivist and members of the staff, whose professional talents represent a precious asset to the entire Archdiocesan community I'm sure, for conducting model efforts like the preparation of specific guidelines on this subject.

Immaculate Heart Archives

On January 6, 2009, I was authorized to move the archives of the Immaculate Heart Sisters to the Archival Center for safekeeping. Over the following months, I made an inventory of the holdings material but found, to my dismay, that nothing beyond the personal files of individual members was shared or entrusted with the Immaculate Heart Sisters at the time of the division. This was clearly contrary to Roman directives issued at the time.

Researchers

The number of clients using the Archival center for research continues. We have also hosted several groups, including the 22nd annual gathering of the California Mission Studies Association.

Academy of Certified Archivists

Since the inauguration of the Academy of Certified Archivists, the archdiocesan archivist at Mission Hills has been certified or re-certified three times, a recognition given for "achievements within the profession that have merited distinction".

"Where Is It?"

Often we are asked "how to find" items in the Archival Center. Here are two examples of the indexing and inventorying process which we provide to researchers:

The Academy of Certified Archivists

on recommendation of

Society of American Archivists

and its

Interim Board for Certification

hereby declares that

Msgr. Francis J. Weber

having met the requirements of

Certification by Petition

is designated

Certified Archivist

October 21, 1989

Date

President, Academy of Certified Archivists

President, Society of American Archivists

a) *Finding Aids to Materials located in storage containers in the Archival Center for the Archdiocese of Los Angeles, Mission Hills, California.*
b) *Archival Center Shelf List*—updated December 1, 2006 Pp. 470.

Space Savers

Early in 1996, when plans were finalized for the closure of Queen of Angels Seminary here in Mission Hills, the entire basement area of the west wing was consigned to the Archival Center.

In July of that year, we moved cabinets and storage boxes into about a third of the basement in what had become, by that time, Alemany High School. Unfortunately, fully half of that space fronted the Boiler Room, which required outside venting. The area was constantly covered with layers of dust that severely and negatively impacted the materials stored there. With the opening of the new high school auditorium in July of 2001, the northern part of the basement was vacated, thus making it possible for us to abandon and seal off the Boiler Room access.

On July 15th, we actually took possession of the north end of the basement where we found that the carpeting was damaged beyond repair, the walls required cleaning and painting, and the furnishings had to be completely replaced.

In order to achieve maximum use of the area, we contracted with the McMurray-Stern Company to install a fifty-unit SPACESAVER filing device at a cost exceeding $100,000. Happily we were able to acquire funding from the Dan Murphy Foundation and the Ernest and Helen Chacon Tust.

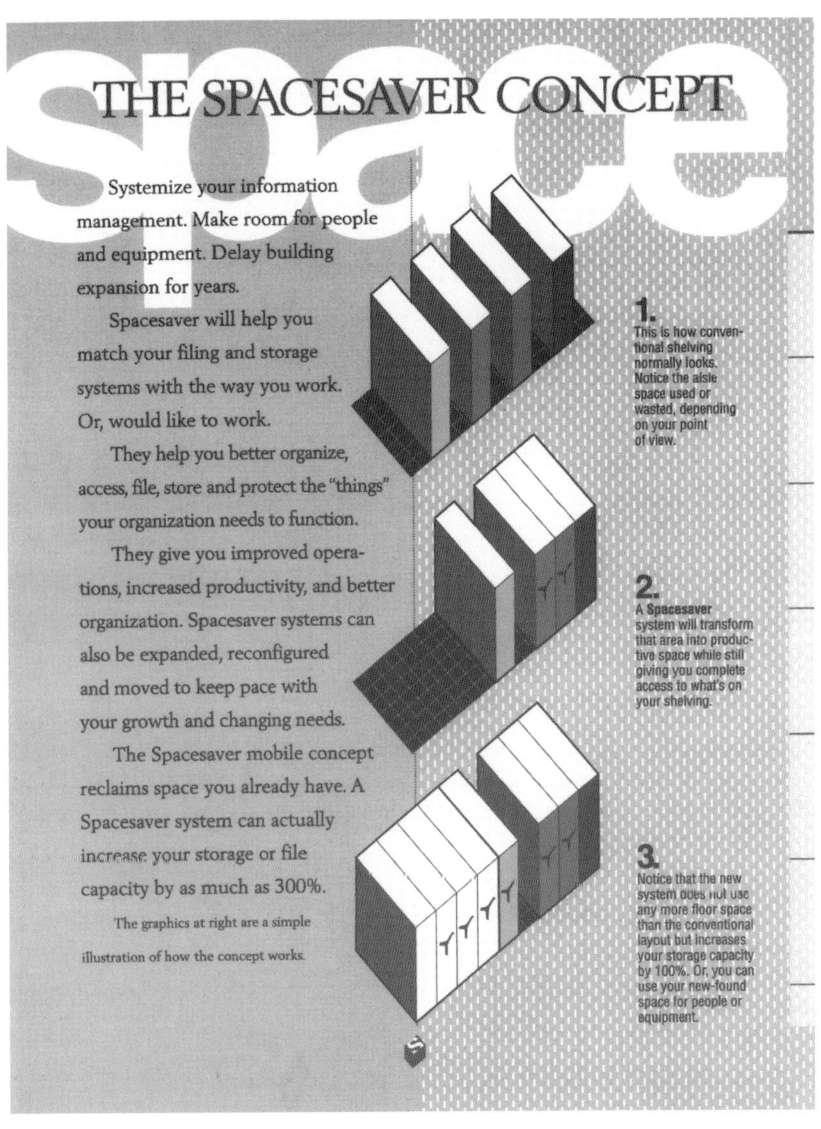

The installation and refurbishment project stretched over three months. On October 10th, we began transferring materials from closets, attics and garages both on and off site at the Old Mission to the new **Archival Center Annex.**

Neither historians nor archivists are generally known for their prognosticational abilities. Be that as it may, it became obvious, about a dozen years ago, that file cabinets had just about served their time.

With the proliferation of Xerox copies of documents a new age was dawning and it was time to re-think our storage facilities. The Space Savers already installed in a portion of the annex were the obvious response for future document storage, so we contracted the local representative McMurray-Stern to make a long-term plan for their product in the six rooms of the annex.

Several local foundations were asked to participate in purchasing and installing nine Space Saver units between 2001 and 2008. Following is a breakdown of the costs.

SPACE SAVER EXPENSES

2001	First Set (Racks #1-30)	$80,260.25
2001	Second Set (#31-50)	$57,211.60
2002	Locking Doors to first two sections	$9,754.00
2005	Blueprint Shelving Cathedral Archives	$6,760.76
2006	Second Set Extensions (#51-66)	$57,104.03
2006	Museum Cabinets Cathedral Archives	$22,127.74
2007	Third Set (#67-75)	$37,195.80
2008	Fourth set (#76-103)	$76,390.00
TOTAL:		**$352,504.18**

Memorial Plaque

Dr. Doyce B. Nunis, the President of the Friends of the Archival Center, suggested that we erect a plaque displaying the names of our major donors (minimum donation of $5,000 or a gift in kind). It has been hung near the entrance to the Archival Center Library and to date, expresses our gratitude to:

Patricia Adler Ingram

William H. Hannon

Robert Covey

Ernest & Helen Chacon Trust

Christie Bourdet

Dr. Emil Massa

Anita Watson
Doyce B. Nunis Jr.
Margaret Seltzer
Marie Walsh Harrington
Roger Larson
Edward D. Lyman
Peter T. Conmy
Patricia Duque Byrne
Virginia Mary DeNublia
Ynes Viole O'Neil
Dr. Richard Doyle
Sir Daniel Donohue
Edward Reed
Helen & William Close
The Leavey Foundation
Richard Curtiss
Irene Winterstein
Carrie Estelle Doheny Foundation
The Dan Murphy Foundation
Connie & Chuck Realivasquez
Stan & Virginia Hayden Foundation
Dolores Hope

A Noble Fragment

In 1987, when the Archdiocese of Los Angeles sold the Estelle Doheny Collection at auction, the Archival Center was allowed to retain for its research library the 887 volumes which comprised the Estelle Doheny Californiana collection, still a valuable research tool for visiting scholars.

Also remaining at the Archival Center were six individual pages of the Gutenberg Bible, each of which had been issued as a leaf book by Gabriel Wells of New York in 1921. Included in each volume was a bibliographical essay by A. Edward Newton.

In mid 2004, Roger Cardinal Mahony authorized the presentation of one of the 1921 books to the Henry Huntington Library in San Marino for inclusion in their extensive collection of Bibles.

Then, in preparation for the dedication of the new Bill Hannon Library at Loyola Marymount University in 2009, another "fragment" was placed on permanent exhibition at the new library on the Westchester Campus.

A few weeks later, a third fragment was entrusted to the care of Dr. Gary Kurutz at the Sacramento State Library in Sacramento.

History Module

In one of our requests for grants in 2001, we enclosed the following thumbnail sketch of The Archival Center, which may be worth repeating here.

> The dedication of the new Archival Center for the Archdiocese of Los Angeles is the latest phase of a program inaugurated almost two decades ago by the late James Francis Cardinal McIntyre.
>
> Though an archivist had been named for the old Diocese of Los Angeles-San Diego, as early as 1927, Msgr. Peter Hanrahan never functioned in any other but a titular role. He later described the collection of those early days as "a mass of unarranged materials in a walk-in vault with a combination lock at the old cathedral rectory."
>
> Charles C. Conroy served the ecclesial community of Southern California for many years as unofficial historiographer. A retired university professor, Dr. Conroy utilized the archives for his monumental treatise on *The Centennial 1840–1940*, but he never made any headway at organizing the holdings.
>
> In the final months of 1962, Cardinal McIntyre had a new wing added to the northeastern end of the Chancery Office, which was located at 1531 West Ninth Street in Los Angeles. An archivist was formally appointed and, on the following July 8th, the Chancery Archives were formally blessed and designated as an archdiocesan department.
>
> A reporter was present for that ceremony and he later ventured the opinion in the *Los Angeles Times* that the Chancery Archives would "eventually constitute the largest collection of ecclesiastical documents in the Western United States." Indeed there was a prophetic ring to those words.
>
> During the ensuing nineteen years, efforts were made to augment and catalogue the widely diversified assortment of documents, brochures, books and other historical mementoes associated with the development of the Catholic Church in California's southland.
>
> The initial holdings were quadrupled within the first decade and it became increasingly clear that the quarters on Ninth Street would not be able to adequately serve the ever-growing needs of the archdiocese.
>
> On a number of occasions, the necessity for larger quarters was discussed with Timothy Cardinal Manning and Msgr. Benjamin G. Hawkes. Several possible solutions were presented, all of which were carefully studied by His Eminence and the Vicar General. Early in 1980, Msgr. Hawkes, a member of the Board of Directors for the Daniel Murphy Foundation, presented a letter from the Cardinal requesting a grant with which to build a wholly separate structure for the archives on property adjacent to San Fernando Mission.

With the endorsement and encouragement of Sir Daniel Donohue, the foundation generously agreed to erect a building which would serve as the major participation by the Catholic Church in the bicentennial celebration for *El Pueblo de Nuestra Senora de los Angeles*. Ground was broken on the Feast of Saint Pius V, April 3rd. On the following February 5th, the first of twenty-three truckloads of historical materials arrived from the Chancery Office, thus launching the Archival Center on its tenure of service.

It is especially fitting that this first independent archival facility erected under diocesan auspices in the United States be located within the shadow of a California mission—for it was among these venerable foundations that it all began for Christ along *El Camino Real*.

The Other Doheny Collection

Most readers recall our participation in the disbursement of the Estelle Doheny Collection of Rare Books, Works of Art and Manuscripts. When the transaction was completed I wrote an extensive article outlining where, how and to whom the treasures were entrusted. Here's an article about the "other" Carrie Estelle Doheny collection.

Very few bibliophiles knew, until recently, that there was a second Carie Estelle Doheny Collection of Rare Books, Manuscripts and Works of Art, and a formidable one at that, located at Saint Mary of the Barrens Seminary in Perryville, Missouri.

The relationship of the Dohenys with the Congregation of the Mission (the Vincentians) was a long and pleasant one that dated back to the turn of the last century when Edward Laurence and Carrie Estelle first occupied their palatial home at #8 Chester Place in Los Angeles, California.

There they got to know a young Vincentian priest, Joseph Sarsfield Glass, who served as president of Saint Vincent's College and pastor of the attached parochial church. It was Glass who introduced the Dohenys to the Catholic faith. As Bishop of Salt Lake City, he baptized Carrie Estelle at Saint Patrick Cathedral in New York City, on October 25, 1918 and it was he who encouraged the Dohenys to become the chief benefactors of the new Saint Vincent Church at West Adams and Figueroa.

Glass was a longtime patron of the arts, an interest he developed during his years of study in Rome and Spain. After he became a bishop, the Dohenys provided for many of his temporalities, including a collection of statuary and some forty paintings that Glass purchased in Europe during the mid-1920s, some of which are now on permanent display at San Fernando Rey de España Mission.

There was a small chapel on the top floor of the Doheny mansion where the Vincentians came to celebrate Holy Mass. In the years after Carrie Estelle's eyesight failed, Father William Ward, by then the pastor, became a daily visitor who guided "the lady," as she was known, in her charitable activities and in the formation of the Carrie Estelle Doheny Foundation.

After her husband's demise, Mrs. Doheny began accelerating her collecting activities. In the early 1950s, she began channeling part of her bibliophilic and other treasures to the Vincentians at Perryville in memory of Bishop Glass and the other priests engaged in the parochial ministry of her parish.

The collection at Perryville eventually got its own quarters where many of the more prominent items were placed on public exhibit. Unhappily, as was the case at Camarillo, very few outsiders knew about or appreciated the collection. An exhibit of twenty-seven choice treasures from Perryville was mounted by Kathryn De Graff at De Paul University in Chicago, during May of 1999. That event attracted wide attention and drew many visitors including members of the Caxton Club.

Recently the seminary was closed for lack of clerical candidates and its buildings were leased to the University of Missouri. At that juncture, the Vincentians decided to sell their collection. Wisely, they chose Christie's of New York to handle the auctions.

Among the Doheny memorabilia at the Archival Center in Mission Hills is a typescript outlining the holdings of the Perryville collection. It was indeed a significant gathering of books, manuscripts and assorted works of art. Though the quantity of materials at Perryville was far less than the one at Camarillo, its quality was equally as high as its west coast counterpart.

Christie's issued two magnificent catalogues featuring the Estelle Doheny Collection at Perryville, one dedicated to fine books and manuscripts and the other to antique glass paperweights and decorative arts.

The first auction, held at Christie's New York City headquarters in Rockefeller Center on December 14th, 2001 featured 136 bound incunabula containing works from eighty-eight different presses in thirty-one cities in five countries. Included therein was the entire Gospel of Saint John from the Gabriel Well's copy of the Gutenberg Bible and a variety of works from other such well-known presses as those of Peter Schoeffer, Anton Koberger, Conrad Sweynheym and Arnold Pannartz. The post incunabula collection of well over a hundred biblical works in more than a score of languages included such volumes as first editions of the Douay and King James Bibles and the New Testament of Erasmus and Coverdale. Several hundred other volumes included works of world famous printers, artists and binders. There was also a library of approximately 800 first editions of American authors such as Samuel Clemens, Nathaniel Hawthorne and Walt Whitman, as well as about 700 volumes prized for their elaborate bindings.

The carefully annotated 451 lots, with numerous colorful illustrations, was prepared by Francis Wahlgreen and his talented staff of bibliophilic experts and presented in a handsomely bound red leather catalogue matching the earlier Camarillo volumes. The second, smaller paperbound volume presents 265 lots of paperweights (154), furniture, snuff bottles, carvings, figurines and assorted porcelain artifacts. The second auction took place on December 17th. Crown jewel of the paperweights, a Baccarat composed of a large cobalt-blue and white primrose with a red and white cane center, was similar to one in the Camarillo collection.

Mrs. Doheny was generous with other institutions also. The books and manuscripts that she gave to Immaculate Heart College in Hollywood were sold by the California Book Auction Galleries at San Francisco on May 10, 1980. Happily the treasures bearing her bookplate at the Henry E. Huntington Library in San Marino remain there as an enhancement to the other holdings of that wonderful institution.

There's room here only to mention some of the highlights of the collection. Surely the centerpiece was its Gutenberg fragment of fourteen consecutive leaves containing the complete Gospel of Saint John and the prologue to the Pauline epistles. This unique treasure is encased in a retrospective binding of half light-brown morocco, stamp decorated, beveled oak boards with braided straps, the work of K.J.D. Lamey. Earlier belonging to Frank Brewer, this fragment was acquired by Mrs. Doheny from A. S.W. Rosenbach in 1941.

A work of special interest to Californians was a mint copy of William Everson's *Novum Psalterium Pii XII* which was number twelve of forty-eight copies printed by Brother Antoninus on his hand press at Saint Albert College in Oakland. Bound in blue morocco at the Lakeside Press in Chicago, the pages of this unfinished folio edition were acquired by Carrie Estelle Doheny who had them gathered into book form with a forward by Robert O. Schad and title pages printed by Saul Marks at his Plantin Press.

Paramount among the presidential letters was one written at Philadelphia on May 4, 1794 wherein John Adams, the nation's second chief executive, challenges the legitimacy of the Anti-Federalists and deplores the dangers of party politics. Another choice letter was penned by Thomas Jefferson in 1801, calling for a reduction in the size of the Federal government and, finally, a missive by George Washington, written in 1782 in which the general addresses military matters and the establishment of winter quarters in New York. Many of the other presidential letters were arranged into lots for the sale.

Prices realized for the 451 lots of fine printed books and manuscripts auctioned December 14th and the 265 lots of antique glass paperweights and decorative arts on December 17th can be obtained from Christie's Website: christies.com.

The name of Edward Laurence Doheny appears in practically every textbook on American history written in this century. Few there are who cannot recall the accomplishments of California's famed oil developer. "Teapot Dome" has become a favorite term in crossword puzzles.

Interestingly enough, a half century after Doheny's death, his widow has emerged from the annals almost as well known or maybe even more so than her husband. And the reason is that while Edward L. Doheny was bringing in oil wells in Mexico and the United States, his wife was equally busy putting together what eventually became one of the world's most exquisite collections of rare books, manuscripts and works of art.

Like the accomplishments of many notable people, her reputation has grown considerably since her death in 1958. Especially has the name of Carrie Estelle Doheny become familiar since 1987, when the decision was made to return many of her treasures to the open forum. A new generation of people is now aware of the marvelous collection this remarkable lady put together in the years before women did such things.

Carrie Estelle Doheny was not only a talented business person, a generous benefactor, an exemplary Catholic and a gracious lady, but she was also a pioneer in a field that had been and still is largely dominated by men—that of book collecting. In her own lifetime, Carrie Estelle Doheny became the "first lady" of bibliophiles.

With only a modest education, she became the shrewdest and most knowledgeable female book collector of this century. And she did it all within the walls of her home at #8 Chester Place in Los Angeles.

Roots

Among the outreaches of our Archival Center is a page we distribute to all genealogists. A copy of which we include here:

Ever wonder about your ancestors—who they were, where they came from, what they were like or how they got here? In recent times, the study of genealogy has become almost a national past time.

Perhaps the following guidelines will be useful for those interested in pursuing their familial "roots."

It is wise, for practical purposes, to restrict the search to only one of the ancestral lines. Probably the one bearing the family name will be the most appealing.

First of all, search the attic, basement and other areas in the family homestead. Look for names, dates and places. Earlier generations often listed such information in Bibles or prayer books.

Interview elderly relatives. Find out where they originated and when they moved to this country, state, or city. Carefully write down marriage and birth dates. Do not presume that memory will serve you infallibly.

Check out cemeteries. In previous times, families tended to prefer "cluster" graves. Very likely a dozen or so relatives would be buried in the same section. Their tombstones usually disclose dates and even birthplaces. Inscriptions are also useful. The character of a deceased person may be reflected in the epitaph. The simplicity or grandeur of the headstone can provide an insight into the decedent's character.

School and college records may also provide useful information. Fraternities keep membership rosters which are often helpful. School magazines and newspapers are invaluable sources.

Churches are especially useful to genealogists because of their sacramental records. When writing, give name, approximate dates, along with your relationship. (These records are private and access is often restricted to relatives). Always include a stamped, self-addressed envelope.

Libraries often have information in their local history department. One of the finest genealogical departments in the nation is housed at the Los Angeles Public Library, at Fifth and Grand. Neighborhood and county newspapers and advertisers often have "morgues" which are exceedingly useful to genealogists.

Do not overlook the National Archives (General Services Administration, Washington, D.C., 20408). Records of every census since 1790 are filed there. They reveal the names of everyone in a given household, the year of their immigration, country of origin and occasionally religious background. The National Archives can also provide pension records and military information for those who served in the armed forces prior to 1917.

The names of immigrants who arrived in the United States after 1820 are often listed in the passenger arrival lists of ships (Form GSA-7111, available from the National Archives, is an official request for passenger lists).

The Immigration Office is another excellent source for naturalized citizens. Further information about an ancestor's country can be obtained from writing that nation's embassy in Washington, D.C. Often they will give addresses of foreign records offices. The world's largest collection of genealogical data is on file in the central library of the Mormon Church, in Salt Lake City. They have there the names and data on people who immigrated to America 1538-1885) from over forty countries.

For a minimal charge, the United States Government Printing Office (Supt. of Documents, Washington, D.C., 20402) will send booklets on how best to locate certificates of birth, marriage, divorce or death.

There are professional genealogists who research these materials for a modest fee, but for a satisfying, stimulating experience, try on your own. The rewards of a successful search are worth the effort.

Those wishing to know more about the Archival Center for the Archdiocese of Los Angeles are advised to subscribe to or get a hold of a copy of the quarterly newsletters mailed to members by The Friends of the Archival Center.

By the time my tenure expired, a world of changes had come to archival practices. The old "paper trail" was gone and a new era of complete technology had set in. It was obviously time for me to step aside. I have no regrets because I was in at the beginning of the necessity for records management.

Happily through a series of grants and careful management, the archives for the Archdiocese of Los Angeles embarked with the "space saver" age.

Now archives are an accepted part of ecclesial management. Having a small part in convincing Church authorities about the necessity of archival retrieval is reward enough itself. For the good of the Church let the new age prosper.

My farewell to the Association of Catholic Diocesan Archivists was sent in 2010.

> I would like to say "goodbye" to the past, present and future members of the Association of Catholic Diocesan Archivists for whom I have the greatest esteem and gratitude.
>
> Since our initial meeting at the Bergamo Center in 1979, I have attended all the meetings of this group. Earlier I had worked with Father Michael Gannon and a few others on drafting the statement that was adapted and released by the National Conference of Catholic Bishops in 1974.
>
> There was a trinity of founders: Dr. James O'Toole, then Archivist for the Archdiocese of Boston and now Professor of History at the University of Massachusetts, Fr. Leonard Blair, Archivist for the Archdiocese of Detroit, and now Bishop of Toledo and myself.

Happily the ACDA has become a permanent fixture of the Catholic Church in the United States and I commend all of its members for their work establishing and maintaining this great association.

After 48 years of archiving, I will soon be retiring in order to prepare for that great archives in the sky.

May I rest in pieces!

6
Outstanding Acquisitions

Lyman Collection

It was while reading the newsletter mailed out to the Friends of the Archival Center that Gladys Lorigan Lyman learned about the deficiencies in our library holdings. Before moving to Los Angeles, Gladys Lorigan taught history and later became the principal of the nationally-known Lowell High School in San Francisco, an exalted position for a woman to hold in those days!

On June 23, 1960, Gladys, a lifelong Catholic had married Edward Lyman at San Carlos Mission in Carmel. A distant cousin of Ed's first wife, Gladys remained active in her numerous charities, including the Ladies of Charity. She moved into the spacious Lyman mansion in Hancock Park where she continued her academic and charitable activities. In 1977, she became a member of the Equestrian Order of the Holy Sepulchre.

Doyce B. Nunis, Jr.

It was only a few days before her demise, on October 16, 1985, that Gladys instructed her lawyer, Carl J. Schuck, to add a codicil to her Will stipulating that "such books, pamphlets and other documents in my library . . . having to do with the religious background and history of early California" were to be left to the library of the Archival Center.

On May 13, 1986, Dr. Doyce Nunis and I visited the Lyman home at 355 South Windsor Boulevard to select those books falling under the provisions of Mrs. Lyman's Will. (After one look at the stately home, I recalled having delivered newspapers there forty years earlier).

The books were pretty much arranged on the shelves as they were in her late husband's time. They had been collected by Edward Dean Lyman (1881-1962), a prominent attorney, who co-founded the law firm of Oberton, Lyman, Prince and Vermille in 1915. A native of Virginia City, Nevada, Mr. Lyman had a long-time interest in books. He was an early member (from 1928 onward) of the prestigious Zamorano Club and a frequent speaker at the club's monthly meetings.

A graduate of Stanford University and the law school of the University of Southern California, Mr. Lyman was admitted to the California State Bar in 1910 and the United States Supreme Court in 1922. According to the San Francisco *Examiner* for October 20, 1985, the several dozen boards he sat on included the Farmers and Merchants National Bank, the Pacific Electric Railway Company, Stanford Research Center, Friends of the Huntington Library, the Pierpont Morgan Library and the Honnold Library Society. He served for many years as a trustee for Claremont's Men's College. In 1929, he was named President of the Automobile Club of Southern California. He later served as President of the Los Angeles Bar Association.

In an issue of *Hoja Volante*, a publication of the Zamorano Club, is a reference which says that "only a very successful man would have chosen the unusual field for book collecting that Ed Lyman has pursued for many years. That is to assemble the 1,000 rarest items of Californiana. The halfway mark has been passed but the list yet to be acquired becomes rarer and more expensive day by day. As if this were not enough for a collector, there has been an active interest in the extensive field of modern fine printing."

Though it appeared that a substantial quantity of the volumes had been dispersed some years earlier, there still remained a copy of Palou's *Relacion Historica* which was and remains the cornerstone of any Californiana collection.

Mr. Lyman was an Episcopalian, but his bookish interests were truly "catholic" in every way. The Archival Center was greatly enriched through the benefaction of his widow. The bulk of the other bibliophilic holdings were consigned by Mrs. Lyman's Will to the Honnold Library of the Associated Colleges of Claremont.

Peter T. Conmy

The acquisition of the books from the Lyman estate was easily the most important single gift received up to 1985. When the books had been cleaned, repaired, restored (where needed), catalogued and placed in the library of the Archival Center, our holdings were greatly strengthened and our resources vastly enhanced. All of this was due to the kindness and generosity of Gladys Lorigan Lyman, who will long be remembered as one of the Archival Center's most munificent friends.

Peter T. Conmy Collection

Over the last decade, many items have been acquired by the Archival Center for the Archdiocese of Los Angeles, none of which exceeds the books, and memorabilia of Dr. Peter T. Conmy. Here's a short explanation that appeared in *The Tidings*:

> Not only does the Archdiocese of Los Angeles have the largest number of Catholics in the nation, it also has an archival facility which has been described by the State Librarian for California as the finest "of its sort in the United Slates."
>
> The holdings at Mission Hills were dramatically expanded a few weeks ago by the acquisition of the massive Peter T. Conmy Collection of materials relating to the history of the Catholic Church in Northern California.
>
> Born at San Francisco July 8, 1901, to Thomas Cherry Conmy and Mary Henrietta (Richter), Peter made his initial studies in the local public schools. During the subsequent yeas, he established a distinguished educational pedigree, with degrees from the University of California, Stanford University and the University of San Francisco in Library Science, education, history and law.
>
> From 1926 to 1943, Dr. Conmy was a certified teacher in the San Francisco Public School system, as well as debate coach, counselor and evening school administrator. On November 1, 1943, he was appointed librarian for the City of Oakland, a position he held for over a quarter century. Upon his retirement in 1969, Conmy was named historian for the City of Oakland.
>
> On July 11, 1928, Peter married Emiliette Constance Storti at Saint Francis of Assisi Church in San Francisco. His two children were raised at the family home on North Ardmore in Piedmont.
>
> A lifelong member of the Knights of Columbus, Peter served as Grand Knight for two terms. He was named a Knight of Saint Gregory by Pope Paul VI in 1964 and a Knight of Malta in 1976. Conmy occupied many fraternal roles, including historiographer for the Order of Alhambra, official historian for the Native Sons of the Golden West, the Young Men's Institute, the Serra Club, the BPOE and the Rotary Club.
>
> A prolific author, Peter wrote on practically every aspect of California Catholic life. In a series of brochures issued by the Native Sons of the Golden West, he composed essays on such luminaries as Stephen Mallory White, Fray Junípero Serra, Philip Augustine Roach and Romauldo Pacheco.

A Parochial and
Institutional History
of the
DIOCESE OF OAKLAND
1962-1972
and two centuries of background

by
Peter Thomas Conmy

Edited and prepared for publication by
Doyce B. Nunis, Jr.
With a Preface and Bibliography by
Msgr. Francis J. Weber

SAINT FRANCIS HISTORICAL SOCIETY
Mission Hills, California
2000

His encyclopedic 433-page tome, *"Seventy Years of Service, 1902-1972,"* a history of the Knights of Columbus in California, is without peer and, a quarter century after its appearance, is still hailed for its distinctive style and informative content. At the request of Bishop Floyd L. Bergin, Peter spent several years preparing a history for the Diocese of Oakland, the manuscript for which is a superb example of historiography.

> In mid-1995, plans were drawn up whereby Dr. Conmy, still active at 94 years of age, entrusted his vast collection of historical notes, writings, books and ephemera to the care of the Archival Center for the Archdiocese of Los Angeles. The actual transfer took place on July 6, when two large truckloads of books and files arrived in Mission Hills.
>
> In addition to 120 boxes of books on practically every aspect of California history and the Catholic Church in the northland, the archival materials consist of eight large file cabinets. Twenty-five of the drawers contain clippings, brochures, handwritten notes, manuscripts, newspapers and related items arranged in a coded sequence. There are also two drawers of parochial materials, three drawers of items relating to the Knights of Columbus, one each for the Native Sons of the Golden West and the *Grizzly Bear*, and four devoted to miscellaneous ledgers and scrapbooks.
>
> Dr. Conmy's materials, filed in an elaborately numbered code system, can be easily located by referring to eight drawers of alphabetically arranged filing cards.
>
> The acquisition of the Peter T. Conmy Collection by the Archival Center greatly expands the database of the Archival Center, and makes the archdiocesan facility a truly statewide resource for the story of the Catholic Church in the Golden State.

Associated with the acquisition of the Conmy Collection was a manuscript on the history of the Diocese of Oakland, which the Archival Center and the Saint Francis Historical Society agreed to publish. Here is a portion of the Preface to that book which I wrote in 2000:

> The genesis of this book can be traced back to the days of Floyd L. Begin's tenure as the proto bishop for the Diocese of Oakland (1962-1977). In an effort to give his 1,467 square mile diocese an identification apart from that of its parent jurisdiction, San Francisco, Bishop Begin approached Dr. Peter T. Conmy (1901-1996) with the proposal and later commission that the then Librarian for the City of Oakland prepare a history of the newly-created ecclesial enclave.
>
> I had known Dr. Conmy since the early 1960s and during those years he was always enthusiastic and generous in his support and assistance to my work as historian and archivist for the Archdiocese of Los Angeles. During one of my visits with Dr. Conmy, at the Mercy Retirement and Care Center in Oakland, he alluded to his manuscript about the diocesan history, noting disappointment that it had never materialized in print. Busy man that he was, Peter had finished the manuscript after the demise of his patron. When he presented the completed manuscript to Bishop Begin's successor, he found little or no enthusiasm. And when Bishop John S. Cummins failed to honor the earlier promise of financial subvention, Peter put the project aside and moved on to other things.
>
> In December of 1995, I wrote to Dr. Conmy offering to publish his manuscript under the mantle of the Saint Francis Historical Society. Peter responded by telephone, expressing great pleasure about the possibility. In

Reverend Monsignor
Francis Matthew Osborne

the meantime, I assembled an essay about Conmy, which appeared as Volume IV in the "California Catholic Miscellany" series. Entitled *Prominent Catholic Chronicler. A Bio-bibliographical Study of Peter Thomas Conmy (1901-1996),* the monograph, envisioned as a tribute to a distinguished California historiographer, also contained a commendation from Pope John Paul II.

Dr. Conmy returned his noble soul to the Lord on July 27, 1996. About a year later, Thomas Conmy wrote to say that his father's heirs (Thomas Conmy, Mary Miles, Theresa Larkin, Emily Moberly and Thomas E. Prothero) had agreed to fund publication of the manuscript on the Diocese of Oakland. The manuscript needed considerable editing, a task that was entrusted to the prominent Western Americana historian, Dr. Doyce B. Nunis, Jr., editor of the *Southern California Quarterly* and Distinguished Professor Emeritus of History, University of Southern California.

Several caveats about this book are in order. First of all, the manuscript concluded in 1972 and it was considered inopportune to extend the coverage beyond that date. Secondly, the editor, Dr. Doyce B. Nunis, was not asked nor expected to alter the manuscript, except grammatically. Finally, like all books, this one reflects the views and conclusions of its author, not the editor or the publisher.

Historical publications are rarely, if ever, definitive. Others will surely build on, expand and even correct aspects of this presentation. Yet, whatever its deficiencies might be, this book is a seminal work of unparalleled importance, a monument to its author and a tribute to its patrons.

Francis Osborne Collection

A second extremely useful and extensive collection was given to the Archival Center near the end of the century. It consists of newspaper and magazine clippings related to local, national and international Catholics and Catholic-related incidents that occurred during the sixty-plus sacerdotal years of its assembler, Msgr. Francis Osborne. (1912-2004)

Here is the explanation of the collection taken from our newsletter:

> The massive collection of newspaper and periodical references assembled by Msgr. Francis Osborne, a priest of the Archdiocese of Los Angeles, is now open to researchers at the Archival Center in Mission Hills.
>
> Gathered over the span of six decades, the collection is especially strong in social issues, papal announcements, controversial topics and catechetical materials.
>
> A longtime moderator of the Holy Name Society, Osborne concentrated on putting together a notable assortment of pamphlets, articles and related items. He monitored such topical issues as abortion legislation and carefully recorded developments as they appeared in religious and secular journals.
>
> Msgr. Osborne remained active in retirement as pastor emeritus of Our Lady of Grace parish in Encino. He continued to be a keen observer on issues impacting ecclesial life, especially in Southern California.
>
> Comprising 1716 lineal inches and arranged in sixty-six file drawers, the collection was originally presented to the Archival Center just prior to the Northridge earthquake. It was arranged and made accessible to researchers in 2000.

Msgr. Osborne was a towering figure among the clerics of the archdiocese. Following are the remarks I made at his diamond sacerdotal jubilee in 1998.

> The ingredients for these reflections began falling in place a dozen years into this century when Francis Matthew Osborne was baptized in Saint Andrew's Church in Pasadena. It was a smaller world in those days of Pius X, Woodrow Wilson, Hiram Johnson and the Tournament of Roses.
>
> Then, sixty years ago on this very day, Archbishop John J. Cantwell ordained Francis Osborne for the Archdiocese of Los Angeles in Saint

Vibiana's Cathedral. His earliest priestly years were spent administering the Sacraments at Holy Spirit, Saint Anselm and Saint Brendan parishes.

During World War II, Father Osborne joined the Navy as a chaplain where he served at bases in the Caribbean, Cherry Point, North Carolina and Guam in the Pacific. By the end of the war, he was a Lieutenant Commander with a chest full of decorations for bravery.

Back in the archdiocese, he ministered at Saint Ignatius, Saint Finbar, Good Shepherd and Saint Cornelius. When he was posted to Encino in 1959, Ventura Boulevard was still a two-lane road. In those pre-freeway days, this parish site was nestled in an orange grove. For a quarter century and more, Father and later Monsignor Osborne guided this parish to its present status as the spiritual flagship of the San Fernando Valley.

Should you want to know where his monument is—look around you. This beautiful church is monument enough for a half dozen priests. Its adornments are extensions of the man who designed and erected it.

Yet statistics and accomplishments do not fully describe any man especially today's jubilarian. Father Osborne has been considerably more than a busy administrator or a successful leader. He has been primarily and most importantly a shepherd of souls who assiduously looked after his flock in good days and in bad. Of all his many accomplishments, none meant more to him or others than the simple title of priest. That word says it all.

Like every priest should be, Father Osborne is a voracious reader. A few years ago, he gave the archdiocesan archives his monumental clipping file which he had amassed over the previous half century.

Hidden away in one of those packed drawers of historical goodies is a copy of a letter written by Father Thomas A. Judge, founder of the Missionary Servants of the Most Holy Trinity, to a young priest. That letter could have been (and maybe was) addressed to Francis Osborne. In any event, the sentiments expressed therein bear repeating for they greatly influenced today's jubilarian. Here is what it says:

Let not your wisdom be of this world.

Let your wisdom be of Christ.

Be a priest, ardent . . . for the things of God . . . zealous for

God's Holy Church.

Freely you have received, freely give.

You are to preach the Gospel, you are to be a light to those in darkness, and you are to proffer the Bread of Life.

May the sick know you, especially the poor sick . . .

May you have a tender heart for those who are stricken and who are very dear to the stricken Christ.

May your name be familiar in the homes of the poor and the lowly.

Christ is the Good Shepherd and wants His priest to be good shepherds.

He was poor and lowly, and He opened that wonderful school of the Sacred Heart where He wishes His priests to qualify in meekness and humility . . .

He raised you to a dazzling height, but the law of advancement is this: that those who wish to go higher should seek out the lowly and the most humble.

He wishes His priests to . . . have a heart for sinners . . .

The first law of the priest is the salvation of souls.

We are here today to celebrate priesthood and to rejoice that God, in His infinite mercy, has allowed Francis Osborne the joy and consolation of having shared that precious gift for sixty years.

Probably no aspect of our holy faith has been more discussed and written about in this post-conciliar era than priesthood, something that surely is exceedingly interesting and meaningful. Who would have thought that in these last days of the 20th century, there would be so much interest in this sacrament, which is given to so few and esteemed by so many.

These brief reflections won't add anything to the notion of priesthood. If one were to put all the papal letters, synodal exhortations, theological tracts, canonical and episcopal directives about priesthood into some sort of a giant blender, the end result would not alter, to any appreciable extent, the notions that have been associated with the role of the ministerial priesthood since apostolic times. Perhaps we would best be served by a moratorium on the subject.

I am more concerned today about the perspective of priesthood held by the people in the pews. In the final analysis, form follows function and especially is that true of priesthood. I have a feeling that priesthood is far better understood by the faithful than most writers and experts would suspect. Call it supernatural instinct or vision, the faithful see Christ in the priest and no one will convince them otherwise, especially when it comes to the sacraments.

People tend to look beyond the individual priest, with all his human faults and foibles, and they see themselves beholden to the priest for their very life of grace with God. They reverence him in whom the image of Christ is visible and through whom God's merciful powers are exercised.

Today's educated lay-people understand the real reasons that set the priest apart from them: the mystery of Christ incarnate again in the priest, through whose unworthy and stained hands flow the graces and blessings of redemption.

Priest and lay-people alike are humbled as they recognize the love and wisdom of God who deigns to use the very human person of a priest, not an angel, to transmit the supernatural gifts of His love to those who may be superior in every other way.

The laity might admire priest educators, writers, philosophers, theologians, social workers, psychologists and even archivists, but what they

really want and rightly demand is the priest who (1) gives them guidance to God, (2) knowledge of His ways and (3) a reassurance of His love and mercy.

In my opinion, Francis Osborne is just such a man. I am here to testify that he has fulfilled admirably the role of mediator, prophet, leader and offerer of sacrifice. For two generations and more he has been (1) bringing people to God, (2) teaching them about the Lord and (3) interceding for them before the divine tribunal.

In today's breviary reading, Saint Paul provided the Hebrews with the best description of the jubilarian we honor today when he observed: "No name of father or mother, no pedigree, no date of birth or of death: but there he stands, eternally, a priest, the true figure of the Son of God."

The Tidings Morgue

In 2007, the Archdiocesan Catholic Center on Wilshire Boulevard, along with fifty-five other pieces of real estate, was sold by the Archdiocese of Los Angeles in order to finance the settlement of its pedophilia cases.

Though the Chancery remained at 3424 Wilshire Boulevard, its space was reduced from twelve floors to five. Affected by that move was *The Tidings* Morgue, which had been maintained for more than seventy-five years.

Twelve filing cases of the morgue were trucked in May of 2008 to the annex of the archdiocesan archives in Mission Hills, along with sixty-one volumes of the Catholic newspaper.

The Tidings Morgue, divided between historical materials and selected illustrations, remains mostly intact, with most of it filed alphabetically by subject or person names. Watching carefully over the transfer was Hermine Lees, editor of the *Archdiocesan Catholic Directory*, who had cared for the morgue for about two decades.

7

Cathedral of Our Lady of the Angels

Among the observations made by Cardinal Mahony after reading my *Memories Of An Old Country Priest* was his wonderment about the lack of any reference to the new Cathedral of Our Lady of the Angels. "I mention this," he said, "only because of your very important role from the earliest days in the Cathedral project." He hoped that my "humility would still allow some reference and credit for your extraordinary commitment to the new cathedral and your very active role in its realization." Inasmuch as humility has never been one of my dominant virtues, I gave his idea some thought and decided to at least outline my involvement with this once-in-a-lifetime endeavor.

Despite the cardinal's kind words, my role was really quite minimal and confined mostly to that of resource advisor. Like most of the archdiocesan clergy, I had given little if any thought to the notion of a new cathedral for Los Angeles. Having been ordained at Saint Vibiana, my natural bent was to keep fixing up that noble historical edifice which embodied so much of our local heritage. The Northridge earthquake changed my mindset and, when Sir Daniel Donohue offered to help finance the erection of a new mother church for Los Angeles, "the old order began to change, giving rise to the new." It was time to move on and provide the Church in Southern California with a new cathedral for the 21st century.

It was while enroute home from Ottawa in 1994 that my associate, Kevin Feeney, contacted me by phone aboard an Air Canada flight saying that the cardinal wanted more information about a reference in one of my books to Saint Vibiana Cathedral. There it was recounted that Pope Pius X had granted permission "to remove the present cathedral in order to erect a larger church in a more suitable area of the town."

Upon arriving home, I checked the minutes of the Diocesan Consulters for January 27, 1904, wherein it was stated that Bishop Thomas J. Conaty had indeed petitioned Roman authorities for authorization to build a new cathedral which would be "sufficiently large and entirely adequate" for the Diocese of Monterey-Los Angeles. Happily, the rescript and its cover letter granting permission were still in place in the archdiocesan archives under the date of July 20, 1904.

The story of what eventually happened to Conaty's grandiose proposal has been related elsewhere and needn't be repeated here. Though no action was taken at the time, there wasn't any time limit attached to the rescript, which therefore remained open-ended. *The Code of Canon Law* was and is very strict about dismantling consecrated churches but, in this case, the earlier appeal to Rome and its favorable response was still intact. The fact that it took ninety years to implement the rescript wouldn't bother Rome where time is dealt with in centuries, not in decades. Hence, looking backward, it was easy enough to surmount the first obstacle in what became an eight-year project.

Nomenclature

I've always had great empathy for the biblical Zachariah. Struck deaf because of his hesitancy about the angelic salutation regarding the birth of a son in his and Elizabeth's old age, he next appears on the pages of holy writ when relatives proposed several names for the newly-born son. He solved the question definitively when he wrote on a pad (or traced in the sand), "his name will be John." Zachariah became my hero for the next hurdle which dealt with the very name of the new cathedral.

Back in the middle ages (1968), I thought that the nomenclature of Our Lady of the Angels would be resolved with the appearance of my book on *El Pueblo de Nuestra Senora de los Angeles*, a study offering convincing evidence that *la reina* (queen) was a spurious interpolation attributable to a few early chroniclers, none of whom belonged either to the Church which canonized the term or the country which popularized it. So effective was my argument for exclusion of *la reina* that the *Pueblo de los Angeles* State Historic Park Commission, on February 11, 1970, endorsed *El Pueblo de Nuestra Senora de los Angeles* as the only valid title for the city. But skeptics die hard and even today there are those who insist on using the "queenly" title, which is historically, and in every other way, wrong in this context. Years earlier, I had proposed to Cardinal Manning that the patronage of Saint Vibiana be changed to that of Our Lady of the Angels. For some years, certain historians and archeologists had doubted whether Vibiana was truly a martyr. Manning settled for moving Vibiana to a less prominent place in the old cathedral, replacing her shrine above the main altar with a gigantic ceramic statue of our Lady of the Angels.

Early on, I sent a copy of my treatise to Cardinal Mahony with the suggestion that he leave the queenly title for the old Plaza Church. Noting that it was inappropriate there too, I reasoned that it would allow a necessary distinction between the earlier church and the new cathedral. My case was further strengthened by coming up with the designs from Philip Milbert Froman for Archbishop John J. Cantwell's never-built cathedral, on Wilshire Boulevard, also dedicated to "Our Lady of the Angels." I also pointed out that Arcadio Cardinal Lercaro, Prefect of the Congregation of Rites, suggested in 1962 that he felt "it would be very opportune to change the title of the cathedral by adopting that of the Blessed Virgin Mary."

Later, there came up the question of when to celebrate the Feast of Our Lady of the Angels. I pointed out that the feast day was celebrated on August 2nd in the Seraphic Missal. In 1981, Cardinal Manning asked Roman authorities to transfer the feast to September 4th to coincide with the anniversary of the city's founding in 1781. From the beginning of the planning, it was hoped that the dedication of Mahony's cathedral could take place on September 4th, but the Labor Day weekend proved more logical because of traffic congestion.

Committee

On March 1, 1996, Ira E. Yellin invited me to attend the interviews being conducted by the Architectural Selection Committee. During the previous December, the committee had sent out a fifteen page "Request for Qualifications" to sixty-seven architectural firms, some as far away as Japan, Germany, Spain and England.

Listening to their presentations was a fascinating experience as each of the candidates produced a model of a chapel for the board, a process superbly explained by Kevin Starr. From my vantage point, it looked like a contest between Frank Gehry and Jose Rafael Moneo from the beginning. I would have voted for Gehry chiefly because of his residency in and identification with Southern California. What probably worked against his candidacy was the then raging controversy about the overrun expenses at the Walt Disney Concert Hall.

I don't function well on committees, probably because of my impatience. My first pastor was forever saying: "Patience and forbearance will make a bishop of Your Reverence. And that's why you'll never be a bishop." Anyway, when the cardinal initially asked if I would serve on the Cathedral Advisory Committee in 1995, my response was that "I would prefer not to serve on the board . . . but I would remain available at any time to assist in the planning" of the cathedral. When asked a second time, I regarded it as an occasion for doing penance for my many sins. And, actually, it proved to be a rewarding and enjoyable interlude to my otherwise uneventful lifestyle.

Interventions

Generally speaking, I kept my mouth stifled during the meetings. However, on November 25, 1996, I wrote to the cardinal complaining about several items. He said it was "essential that you raise your voice and express your views openly for the whole group to hear." So I prepared an intervention that was given at the next board meeting on January 28, 1997:

> First of all, I am very pleased with the interior design and I applaud the architect and those who have worked so hard with him in identifying the needs of the interior. Especially am I pleased that the interior design will allow future generations to make the adaptations that will surely come in liturgical practice.
>
> The first of my concerns deals with the entrance to the cathedral. I know of only two major churches in the world where the principal access is not through the front or main door; a) the underground Basilica of Saint Pius X at Lourdes where the contour of the land demands it; and b) the massive, barn-like church at Taize which has no overall design, but just grew haphazardly.
>
> If memory serves me correctly, the notion of entering the proposed Los Angeles cathedral from the side originated more from liturgical considerations than from architectural expression.
>
> The rationale behind this notion was that of placing an immersion pool for baptism at the main entrance, something to which there is no precedent in any existing Catholic cathedral. Most, if not all, cathedrals have either a separate baptistry chapel or a tower area off the central vestibule.
>
> In recent years, the Church, in recognition of an ancient practice, has once again allowed baptism by immersion. It is important to note, however, that the practice of immersion is allowed, not mandated and, given the negatives, it will likely never become the norm.
>
> Before advocating a widespread return to immersion, it might be well to recall why that manner of baptism was discontinued in the early Church. The reason is not philosophical nor liturgical, but practical. Too many babies and not a few adults died from pneumonia and other infections acquired in the sanctified but often polluted waters.
>
> Apart from the spectacle of seeing someone like myself adorned with a liturgically appropriate bathing garment, there are some practical considerations that should influence our decision about an immersion pool.
>
> One deals with a defrocked Catholic priest who is now the self-proclaimed "archbishop" of a large religious community in the nation's capital. Recently, while baptizing an infant in an immersion pool, he slipped and dropped the baby which eventually died. He is now involved in a multi-million dollar lawsuit.
>
> The other deals with a newly erected church here in Southern California with an immersion pool at the front entrance. Just a day after

the church opened, a lady stumbled into the pool and broke her ankle. Now the pool is fenced in with a most unattractive wrought-iron barrier.

Finally, will OCIA demand that we keep a lifeguard on duty whenever the church is open and will the waters need to be chlorinated to keep the "holy" water from attracting mosquitoes?

Proponents of this practice remind us that Christ was baptized by immersion in the Jordan River. But, if we want to be so slavishly symbolic, then maybe we should have acquired beachfront property along the Los Angeles River for our cathedral.

To obstruct the main entry of our cathedral out of deference to a long abandoned manner of baptism does not make a lot of sense to this observer. I contend that immersion is unsanitary, unsafe and impractical. And, I rather like entering a church through its front door.

My other concern is that of aesthetics. It has been my privilege to see many of the great cathedrals in the world. And when I think about them, distinctive phantasms pop into my mind—whether it be Chartres, Cologne, Palma, Canterbury, Notre Dame, Coventry and even San Francisco. People remember great churches and probably other notable buildings from their initial impression.

When I went home after seeing the proposed design of our cathedral, I kept trying to remember what it looked like. All I could remember were massive walls of concrete. Then I saw the model in the paper—I listened as others talked about it and I came to the conclusion, ***salva reverentia***, that the design is boxy, ugly, pedestrian and non-distinctive. There is nothing about the exterior design that excites imagination nor elicits artistic admiration.

To the extent that the straight and parallel lines bring about maximum usage of natural light in the cathedral, might I point out that we are living in the age of electronics, in an area of the world where electronics have produced the magic of the motion picture industry.

Not only can we produce any kind of light artificially, but we can do it better and with less damaging effects to the environment. Any dermatologist will testify that natural light has a devastating effect on skin, something not usually true with artificial light. Should we not be using the developments of this age in our cathedral, rather than harkening back to the times when there were no electronics?

Not being an architect, I don't know what precisely is wrong and/or missing; but at this moment, the design is very pedestrian, more reminiscent of a massive Sav-On drugstore than a majestic cathedral. In my opinion, a cathedral should reach up into the heavens, it should fit into and even dominate the skyline of the city over which it presides.

I have seen and been impressed by Moneo's train station in Madrid and his museum at Palma de Mallorca. But we are not building a train station or a museum, we are building a world-class cathedral and I would hope that eventually it will do for us what the world famous cathedrals of yesteryears did for their cities.

My intervention got about as much attention as it deserved. When I sat down, the cardinal looked out at the group and said: "Next please."

My self-imposed passivity on the committee was overcome another time with the proposal by John Bear and his bronze sculpture described as the "Spirit of the Earth." It was, in his own words, a "contemporary interpretation of American Native peoples." When the design came before the committee, I couldn't resist speaking out that it was pure paganism, with no redemptive qualities. What bothered me more was that it would be forever located on our property, at the north end of the complex, near the bell tower, and would cost $50,000 which was, in itself, exorbitant. Only two other members of the committee supported my view so, once again, and for the final time, I reverted to my role as "observer." It is still my opinion that most native-Americans, especially those who have embraced Christianity, will find the sculpture offensive and utterly out-of-place in a Catholic Cathedral.

Father Richard Vosco was a prominent and influential voice in all the Committee's deliberations. He had the primary role of identifying the liturgical art, adornment and furnishings needed for the cathedral. He is a very pleasant man whom I personally liked very much. But he did have some ideas that seemed impractical in many areas. As the designated liturgical consultant, he often presented his personal views as official and definitive. Interestingly enough, Roman directives rarely speak in absolutes and they should always be interpreted to fit local circumstances. I personally resented being told what was best for the Church in Southern California by a resident of New Jersey.

Anyway, I wrote to the cardinal in August of 1999, pointing out that, "not all of Father Vosco's clients are happy troopers." I have always been fascinated as to why bishops pay so much attention to liturgists and seemingly so little to theologians and scripture scholars. Many of the liturgical practices now in vogue are derived from an obscure document, *Environment and Art*, published by the NCCB's Liturgy committee in the late 1970s. I must have gone a little too far when I wondered why "the Father Voscos of the world who are paid handsomely for their ideas, get more attention than their counterparts in other disciplines." I enclosed with my letter an article from *AD 2000* by Paul Likoudis on "How a Canadian Church was saved from destruction." The cardinal said he was "deeply saddened both by the tone and the contents of my letter." He presumed that I knew who Paul Likoudis was and characterized him as "one of the most strident, arrogant and self righteous people I ever met in my life." The cardinal was "surprised and saddened that you would give him any credit."

Carillon at the Cathedral were formerly in the tower at San Fernando Mission.

In my response, I expressed regret for having bothered him and assured him that I didn't even know Likoudis. Later, he softened his tone and said:

> Your interventions surely have not bothered me; rather, they give me the opportunity to think through various issues and situations, as well as to respond to you in writing. Since you are our resident archivist and historian, I want to make sure I leave behind no unanswered letters from Frank Weber!

From that time onward, I pretty much avoided expressing my personal viewpoints on the cathedral. And I must say that, in the final analysis, the edifice came out quite well, in spite of me!

The Carillon

For many years, San Fernando Mission housed the only true carillon in a Catholic church west of the Rockies. The saga of that magnificent instrument, with its thirty-five electronically-operated bells has been told in great detail in several places.

Originally installed at Saint Monica's parochial church in 1931, the carillon never reached its maximum service because the church's enclosed tower inhibited maximum transmission of the sound waves. During the devastating earthquake of February 9, 1971, the tower

Escaray Rererdos *at the Cathedral.*

suffered severe structural damage and was judged unsafe to support the massive weight of the bells.

Later, when San Fernando Mission was restored after suffering damage in the same earthquake, Msgr. Benjamin Hawkes decided to move the carillon twenty-four miles to the north where it was installed in the refurbished bell-tower.

After extensive rewiring, the carillon was ready for use on December 4, 1974. Some years later, a digital control system was added whereby the Westminster sequence of hours, the *Angelus* and other motifs could be activated electronically.

When plans were being made for the new cathedral, I suggested, on September 30, 1996, that the carillon originally donated by Johanna Shanahan be moved a third and last time to the new archdiocesan mother church where its melodious tone could be shared by the whole city.

Cardinal Mahony was "really excited" to learn about the carillon and expressed the view that "if properly computerized and if the more modern ringers and electrical wiring were employed, the carillon would be a great addition to the new cathedral of Our Lady of the Angels." He forwarded the offer to Jose Rafael Moneo and the architect, too, was elated, promising to "stop out at the mission to view the carillon" personally. He did and the Shanahan carillon is now one of the major features at the new cathedral.

Pattarino statue of Our Lady of the Angels given to the Archival Center by Msgr. Benjamin Hawkes in 1981.

Reredos

With the closure of the minor seminary in 1995, there was no longer any reason why the historic and artistic reredos or retablo installed there in the mid-1950s should not fulfill the original purpose for which it was acquired, namely the adornment of a proposed Cathedral for Los Angeles. Granted, it was a different cathedral than the one envisioned by Archbishop Cantwell, but surely the appropriateness remained.

I had spoken to the cardinal about the possibility and, on June 2, 1995, he asked for "fuller advice about utilizing the reredos from Queen of

Angels Seminary in the new cathedral." I sent him a brochure that I had written some years earlier when a portion of the altar piece was installed in the sanctuary of San Fernando, Rey de Espana mission.

Specialists from the Getty had volunteered to refurbish the reredos and, after removing it from Mission Hills, experts spent several months examining and restoring the historic work-of-art. While I had hoped that the reredos would be used in one of the chapels, the decision was made to install it along the inside entranceway to the church where it looks very majestic, if somewhat out-of-place architecturally.

Pattarino

Early in 2002, I acquired one of the now rare ceramic renditions of *Mater Ecclesiae* which Professor Pattarino produced just after the opening of Vatican Council II. It had come into the possession of Bishop Harry A. Clinch in Rome while he was attending the council in 1962. Later it became the property of Richard Menn of Carmel who gave it to me on April 11th. I offered it to Cardinal Mahony if he would find a place for it in the new cathedral. On May 20, he informed me that he was "greatly struck by its beauty" and would see that it found a place in the

Relics for the cathedral High Altar are encased in a silver reliquary at the feet of the altar.

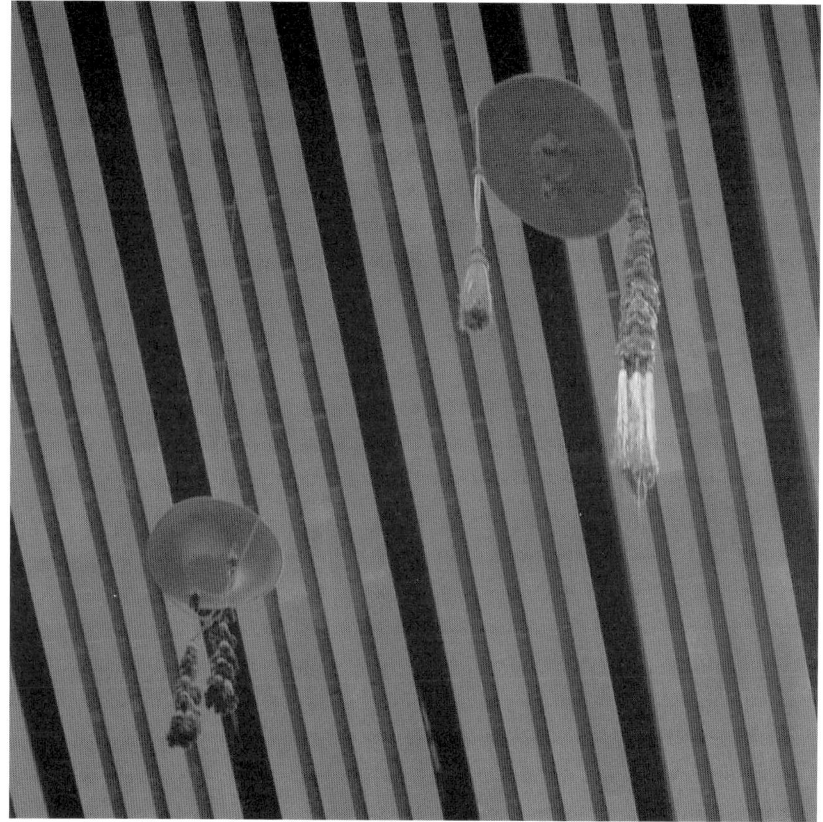

Galleros *hanging from the Cathedral ceiling from Los Angeles' cardinals.*

main sacristy of the cathedral. Eventually it was erected in the Cardinal's rectory. The Pattarino stations that once hung in Saint Basil's rectory are now erected in the crypt church.

Saint Peter

Others of my suggestions didn't fare so well. An example would be one about the real-size bronze reproduction of the statue of the Prince of the Apostles that is such a popular source of attention in Saint Peter's Basilica in Rome. The then Bishop John J. Cantwell had purchased it in 1926 for the foyer of Los Angeles College, where it remained until the seminary was demolished. It was then taken to Saint Peter Church on San Vicente Avenue. When that parish was entrusted to the Maronites, the statue was stored for some years in the mausoleum at Holy Cross. Then, in the mid-1960s, it was transported to Queen of Angels Seminary in Mission Hills and placed in the garden area south of the chapel.

The windows in the crypt of the Cathedral were formerly in Saint Vibiana's Cathedral. They were fashioned in Europe.

I thought it would be eminently reasonable to have that statue "placed in the new cathedral to symbolize our devotion to the See of Peter."

Several other times I followed up on the issue until, on July 19, 2002, the cardinal informed me that the statue was "permanently installed at All Souls Cemetery in Long Beach" and he felt that, "given its size and the fact that it has a permanent home," it was best to leave it as it is.

Happily there is still much adornment to be done at the new Cathedral of Our Lady of the Angels. Maybe one of the cardinal's successors will find my suggestion in the archives and think better of the whole idea.

Relics

One of my pleasant activities in connection with the new cathedral was that of arranging the relics for the main altar. Those chosen for this distinction were Saints Emydius, Patrick, Francis of Assisi, Candidus, Vibiana and Blessed Junipero Serra. The relics were encased in a small wooden box and placed in a crevice at the base of the altar, rather than in a crypt of the altar table itself as was the practice until recent years. Other relics were also acquired which will be used at other places in the cathedral, probably in connection with the saints portrayed in the tapestries.

Galeros

In August of 1992, well before plans for the new cathedral began to unfold, I approached Cardinal Mahony about the centuries-old but discontinued practice of distributing *galeros* (or red hats) to cardinals. The one bestowed upon James Francis Cardinal McIntyre in 1953 was hung at Saint Basil Church where he lived the final years of his life.

The design of the unique hat, reproduced in each cardinal's personal coat-of-arms, is as simple as it is singular. Its crown is small and shallow; the brim flat, rigid and very broad. Attached to the crown are two crimson-colored cords, each of which terminates with fifteen tassels arranged triangle-wise. (The hats were fabricated by the Roman firm of Tanfani & Bertarelli, on Via S. Chiara.)

Anyway, I had contacted Maximiliano Gamarelli in Rome and he could produce galeros for Cardinals Manning and Mahony. Thus the Church of Los Angeles would be honoring a tradition that dates back to the Middle Ages.

The cardinal agreed and several generous benefactors came forward to pay for the galeros. Initially we planned to hang them in Saint Vibiana Cathedral. However, before they could be set in place, work had begun on a new cathedral. Cardinal Mahony decided to "suspend the galeros through the wood ceiling" where future generations could get a glimpse of the splendid role of cardinals in the universal Church. Today they are visible high above the Cathedral sanctuary.

Endowment—Crypts

It was in September of 1999 that I suggested to the cardinal that some thought should be given to an endowment for the cathedral. I recalled my time in Anaheim when some of us were given a tour of the Crystal Cathedral in Garden Grove.

> Dr. Schuller personally greeted us and was exceedingly gracious in every way. During the question period, I asked him if he had any regrets. In addition to being upset about the acoustical problems, he responded that it was a major mistake not to include, in the original fund drive, any provisions for endowment. (I think he later partially-remedied that oversight by opening a mausoleum.)

March 1, 2010

Dom Brendan Freeman, O.C.S.O.
Abbot
New Melleray Abbey
6632 Melleray Circle
Peosta, IL 52068

Dear Abbot Brendan Freeman:

You may recall a few years ago I purchased a fine casket from New Melleray Abbey for my own personal use. It is located in my crypt in the Mausoleum of the Cathedral of Our Lady of the Angels here in Los Angeles, awaiting the day when the Lord calls me home to eternal life.

I am writing to offer my personal testimony about the hand-crafted quality of Trappist Caskets, and to encourage others to consider obtaining one now (pre-need) or at-need. Given the beautiful wood forests at your Abbey, it is surely appropriate that you and your monks are engaged in such an important work for the good of all peoples.

When someone purchases a Trappist Casket, they are not only obtaining a unique piece of craftsmanship, but they are helping sustain the spiritual power of the Abbey and the sanctity of your members.

I would encourage everyone to consider purchasing one of your hand-crafted caskets.

Sincerely yours in Christ,

+ Roger Cardinal Mahony

His Eminence
Cardinal Roger M. Mahony
Archbishop of Los Angeles

555 West Temple Street, Los Angeles, California 90012-2707 TEL (213)680-5200 FAX (213)620-1982

To the point. We appear to be doing very well in raising funds for Our Lady of Angels Cathedral. Possibly we are even ahead of schedule. Might you consider advancing the overall cost by another 30 million dollars, all of which would be set aside irrevocably to maintain the cathedral?

I understand that it takes about $50,000 a day just to operate Saint Patrick's Cathedral in New York City with guards, clerical and lay staff, utilities and maintenance, etc. Our costs will probably approach that figure.

CATHEDRAL OF OUR LADY OF THE ANGELS

CATHEDRAL CHAPTERS

Cathedral Name Honors Our Lady and Our City

"Our Lady of the Angels" is the patroness of the City of Los Angeles. Therefore, it seemed appropriate from the outset that the new Cathedral, the mother church for the Archdiocese of Los Angeles, would be named in her honor.

The name has both a spiritual and historical significance. The Franciscan friar Juan Crespi was a member of the expedition headed by Gaspar de Portola that came through the area in 1769. An expedition diarist, Crespi noted that the explorers' arrival was on the vigil of the feast of Our Lady of the Angels.

The group named the river (which would later be known as the Los Angeles River) "El Rio de Nuestra Señora de los Angeles de Porciuncula,"meaning the river of Our Lady of the

El Pueblo de Nuestra Señora de Los Angeles—was on September 4, 1781, which would later become the feast day of Our Lady of the Angels. On September 4th in the year 2000, Los Angeles will again celebrate the feast of Our Lady of the Angels with the dedication of a new Cathedral in her name.

We have chosen Our Lady of the Angels of Porciuncula as the image on our logo for this project. The photograph is taken from a statue of Our Lady which was designed and fired by Professor E. Pattarino, a famous ceramicist from Florence, Italy who died about ten years ago.

Cardinal J. Francis McIntyre commissioned three originals of the statue in the mid-1950s.

According to the archivist for the Archdiocese of Los Angeles, one of the statues is at St. Anastasia's, Cardinal McIntyre's titular church in Roma. A second one was originally placed

CATHEDRAL CHAPTERS
THE ARCHDIOCESE OF LOS ANGELES
3424 Wilshire Boulevard
Los Angeles, CA 90010-2241

The cardinal responded that "the matter of an adequate endowment for the Cathedral of Our Lady of the Angeles in not only under study, but is in its active development." He mentioned a special account called "Our Lady of the Angels Fund" whose secondary purpose was "to begin an endowment fund for the cathedral." He then revealed that a mausoleum was under study and that "proceeds from the mausoleum will all go directly go into the Cathedral Endowment Fund." That was good news to hear.

If I recall correctly, the notion of a mausoleum in the crypt area of the new cathedral was not part of the original plans. Surely it was a providential development, however it originated. Many people have said that the crypt area is the most attractive part in the entire cathedral and I tend to agree. Others are quire surprised and pleased to find there the relics of Saint Vibiana, the windows (beautifully back-lighted) and the main altar from the old cathedral.

In December of 1998, the cardinal mentioned "I plan to move all of the bishops from the mausoleum at Calvary to a new section beneath the Cathedral, and of course, Cardinal Manning would remain exactly where he is. Bishop Carl Fisher would be moved from the ground to the new mausoleum since he requested that he be buried near my own burial plot. My current burial plot is at Calvary in the priests section and, consequently, there would be no difficulty in having him moved."

The plan for transferring the bishops to the cathedral ran into a small snag when I received a call from Aileen Cantwell who, along with her two cousins, objected to moving Archbishop John J. Cantwell. She reasoned that since he had built the Episcopal Vault at Calvary, he obviously would prefer to remain there. I passed the information on to the cardinal and she followed that with a letter wherein she mentioned that other members of the Cantwell family were buried nearby in the mausoleum. But she did say that if his remains had to be disinterred, it would be acceptable "to move him outside into 'priests' plot" where the many priests with whom he served are presently at rest." I later discovered that Cantwell was moved into the grave vacated when Auxiliary Bishop Carl J. Fisher's remains were transferred to the cathedral. Aileen later relented and, on September 25, 2003, Miss Cantwell agreed to have her uncle placed in the cathedral.

I was present on June 12th at Calvary Mausoleum when the tombs of Cardinal McIntyre, Archbishop Cantwell and Bishops Thaddeus Amat, Francis Mora, Thomas J. Conaty and Carl Fisher were opened. They were moved to the new cathedral in the early morning hours of the 22nd and, again, it was my privilege to be there for that historic event. The remains of Cardinal McIntyre had to be placed in a new coffin, as the earlier one had seemingly been damaged years earlier when put into place in the Episcopal Vault.

It was my suggestion that The Triumph of David, given to the archdiocese by Bernardine and Daniel Donohue in 1974, be moved from St. John's College Seminary to the cathedral. It now hangs on the backdrop of the stairwell in the cathedral conference room.

Cathedral Chapters

In the spring of 1996, I suggested to His Eminence that, "we must soon begin a catechesis for our people about the new cathedral." I went on to say, "They must be made to understand that we are not planning to replicate one of the great cathedrals of former centuries. Ours will be unlike any ever built because it will reflect the Church as it exists in the third millennium. Whether my proposal was the impetus is unknown, but the first issue of *Cathedral Update* appeared the following September and that was followed the next year by *Cathedral Chapters* which was published quarterly until September of 2002. A typical edition consisted of a letter from the cardinal, updates on the fund drives, listing of donors and essays about other aspects of the proposed edifice.

CATHEDRAL
OF OUR LADY OF THE ANGELS
MSGR. FRANCIS J. WEBER
Saint Francis Historical Society
Anno Domini 2004

Time Capsule

Back in April of 1999, I was asked to provide a list of items that might be appropriate in a time capsule for the Cathedral. Here is the list that I submitted:

Significant issues of *The Tidings*
Medallion of the papal visit
Brochure on Archdiocesan history
Calling cards of Los Angeles bishops
Booklet on your cardinalatial investiture
Booklet issued for papal visit
Set of 2000 US coins,
(Superior Gallery will have these early in the new year.)
Cathedral brochures of various kinds
Pastoral Letter announcing cathedral
Select group of photos of cathedral
2000 Catholic Directory for Los Angeles

Though mine was a minor role in the overall project of erecting the magnificent Cathedral of Our Lady of the Angels, I will always consider it a singular grace to have been associated with what has already become one of the most historically significant and culturally relevant houses-of-worship in the United States.

In no other place in the world has a church of this magnitude been erected and paid for in so short a time. Blessed be Sir Daniel Donohue who conceived the idea, Jose Rafael Moneo who designed it, Roger Cardinal Mahony who guided it to completion and that army of benefactors, workers and supporters who brought this dream to fulfillment.

Where else but in Los Angeles!

Book On Cathedral History

The genesis of the book on the Cathedral of Our Lady of the Angels can be traced to December 21, 1995 when I asked the cardinal if he "would be interested in my doing a book on the history of Saint Vibiana's Cathedral down to and including the new edifice scheduled to be opened in the year 2000." Realizing that it was "early to think about this," I pointed out that he had "no idea how much time such a project entails." At that time, plans called for erecting the new cathedral on the site of the older one. The narrative would include a new and updated history of Saint Vibiana, telling "how the new complex came to be." Included in my letter was a suggestion that he "set aside a few thousand dollars along the way to pay for the book."

This history of the

Cathedral of Our Lady of the Angels

is presented

with the gratitude and blessings of

the Roman Catholic Church in the

Archdiocese of Los Angeles

+ Roger Cardinal Mahony

Archbishop of Los Angeles

Anno Domini, 2004

By return mail, the cardinal replied that he was "absolutely thrilled" with the "offer to do a book on the history of the cathedral." Wanting the project to begin at once, he did not anticipate any problem with funding, noting that, "many would want to be benefactors for this book." He asked Sister Lois Ann Linenberger, C.S.J., to send me copies of "all the minutes since we began the project—starting with the historic meeting in October 1994, at which the College of Consulters, the Council of Priests and others met to discuss the proposal and vote on it." The cardinal felt that preserving "the history of the former cathedral, as well as everything necessary to construct the new one on the same city block was important to preserving our historical destiny."

Over the following months and years, in addition to updating the story of the earlier cathedral, I began gathering a detailed collection of

Archival Center

Archdiocese of Los Angeles

On Tuesday, the 11th of May 2004
the lead-filled and remarkably preserved casket bearing the
earthly remains of the
MOST REVEREND JOHN J. CANTWELL
(1874 - 1947)
Bishop of Monterey - Los Angeles
(1917 - 1922)
Bishop of Los Angeles - San Diego
(1922 - 1936)
and
Archbishop of Los Angeles
(1936 - 1947)
was removed from a temporary vault
in the Doheny Chapel
at Calvary Mausoleum
to the
Cathedral of Our Lady of the Angels
where it was entombed with other
members of Southern California's hierarchy.

Fred Balak
Mr. Fred Balak

Br. Hilarion O'Connor
Br. Hilarion O'Connor, O.S.F.

Msgr. Francis J. Weber
Archivist

newspaper, periodical and other published accounts of the overall cathedral program, including the controversies about renovation, demolition, and acquisition of a new site.

Ever so gradually over the following months I began to sense a lessening of enthusiasm for my role as author of the book. For example, I got a letter from Amanda Mansour, Director of the Cathedral Campaign, in which she said:

> I gathered from the last Cathedral Advisory Board that there was some doubt as to whether or not you would be producing a book about the construction of the Cathedral Complex. While I think that everyone agreed that such a book should be done, there was additional question as to what kind of book it should be. I, for one, think that the idea of a coffee-table book, with beautiful pictures and drawings, would be particularly valuable. I know that such a book was published when the Getty Center opened, that included the plans and information about the architect. It was sold with great success at major bookstores.

Amanda went on to observe that, "regardless of what kind of book is produced, I am writing to inform you of the value such a book will have for our donors." She had grandiose plans for giving major contributors a signed copy at a Benefactor Dinner scheduled for November 22, 1998. In other words, she expected the book to be finished even before the cathedral building was concluded.

I responded to Amanda, noting that there has "been some misunderstanding about the cathedral book. Originally I was thinking of a work that would trace the cathedral notion since the 1870s," but obviously "the cardinal has something else in mind." I did suggest an alternative plan, the issuance of a miniature book in a press run of 400 copies that could be given to donors for a relatively small outlay of funds. And I mentioned that the "coffee table book was also a possibility," but that we would have "to look elsewhere for that kind of production."

The cardinal had asked that I speak to him about the overall project after the next Advisory Board meeting. I strongly felt that the book could not be finished prior to the dedication of the cathedral because of the impossibility of anticipating history.

When I talked with the cardinal, he had already begun discussions with Dr. Michael Downey, his theologian, for a coffee-table type book that would indeed be finished about the time of the cathedral's dedication, and he subsequently remarked that he felt that "we are looking for two different types of books"

> "Certainly we want a coffee-table type of book that would have many photographs, drawings and some text. There are many examples of such a pictorial book available, and we need to be planning ahead for this type

Msgr. Jeremiah Murphy helps to honor Sir Daniel Donohue at the latter's ninetieth birthday at Cathedral rectory 2008.

of production. It would be a very popular item for us, a gift to donors and eventually for sale in the cathedral gift shop."

But the cardinal also reiterated that:

> "We also need a comprehensive book that details the history of the Cathedral Project, leading up to the planning, design, construction and dedication of the new cathedral. This more historical piece would have all of the information and processes involved in the planning over the many years beginning with the early attempt to remodel and expand the old Saint Vibiana's Cathedral."

When later I met with Dr. Downey, we agreed between ourselves that the "formal history would come later after all the construction work is done." However, at that time I told the cardinal that the actual writing of such a book "couldn't even be started until all the papers are in place" and that process would probably take several years to complete. Meanwhile, I assured him that "I would continue attending all the meetings, collecting documentation and gathering whatever else is needed for the eventual history."

Pilgrims from Los Angeles standing atop floor inscription in Saint Peter's Basilica for the Cathedral of Our Lady of the Angels, 2003.

After getting some further discordant signals, I do recall, after one of the Advisory Board meetings, suggesting the possibility that Kevin Starr, the Librarian for the State of California, might be interested in doing the formal history. He was extremely qualified as a writer and as a trained historian and his books on the state's history were best sellers. By that time, the cardinal had met Starr and was impressed by him.

Nonetheless, I was surprised to hear after an Advisory Board meeting in December of 1998, that the cardinal had indeed arranged with Starr "to write the history of the cathedral." I believed then and still do believe that he would have done a commendable job. Surely I did not have any proprietary claim for the assignment.

> Thanks so much for your letter of December 14, 1998 with respect to the historical work that would chronicle the history of the building of the Cathedral of Our Lady of the Angels. My desire all along has been that you yourself be the author of this work, but on one occasion you seemed to emphasize quite strongly that you did not see this as a work that you yourself would wish to undertake. That is the reason that I have been encouraging others to at least make the offer to do the longer historical piece. My first choice for the book is you yourself since you have been so much a part of the history of the old Saint Vibiana's and the new Cathedral of Our Lady of the Angels. No one would be better able to do such a work.

But, in the last sentence of his missive, the cardinal said that "it would seem to me that much of the work could be done on the book prior to the dedication of the cathedral since we have all the records, minutes and actions taken beginning in 1988 forward. He wanted me to "reconsider the possibility."

So we were back to square one. In the best of circumstances, it would take a year for all the pieces to come together. I had never been asked to write about something before it happened. It just could not be done, at least by me.

The next thing I knew about the project was when a copy of Kevin Starr's contract was sent to the archives. By that time I was neither surprised nor disappointed. My enthusiasm level had descended to a minus three. Not long afterwards I had dinner with Kevin who wanted to borrow my extensive collection of clippings. I agreed to place them on deposit in an office provided for Starr at the Archdiocesan Catholic Center where they remained for the following months. That decision was formally approved by the first pastor of the cathedral, Monsignor Kevin Kostelnik, in a letter to Starr in which he said that "one of the starting points for your understanding the chronology of how the cathedral site was chosen might be to review all of the press articles and clippings that were part of this scenario."

On July 24, 2001, Starr wrote to the cardinal and submitted "a brief and informal quarterly report relating to the project." Having reviewed all the materials from me, he said he was "midway through this process" and could determine the final sequence of the book. He divided the proposed text into thirteen chapters, which he said would allow "for a fast paced book possessed of a forward narrative momentum." By the following August and September, Kevin planned on "completing the breakdown of the material and conducting interviews." He would begin the composition in the fall, planning to have "the first draft completed by February 1, 2002."

With that missive the Starr involvement fell silent. No more letters came from Starr. Subsequently he contacted Bill Close and asked to be released from his contract, giving no reason for the request. In a subsequent letter to Close, Starr promised to send whatever materials he had collected, "together with secondary sources." He admitted that "these may not be of much use" to another writer, "since his approach will most likely be based upon a selection of primary documents oriented to a more official presentation."

In a subsequent letter, the cardinal said that "his own worst fears were confirmed". He had wondered and worried that Kevin "had really not done anything on the cathedral book over the past year and a half." Mahony admitted that this left us "with a very daunting task indeed."

It was at this juncture that Mahony hoped that I would be open to the possibility, given the other commitments with which I was already dealing, to take up the unfinished project: "You have been involved intimately with the project from the earliest days, and your ability to capture the history would be superior to anyone else." He wondered if "it would be possible for you to consider doing the book for us. I realize that it would consume a great deal of your time, but you would certainly be the best choice to do the work."

On March 17th, I answered the cardinal's request, telling him that "since God so often writes straight with crooked lines," I had concluded that the whole Starr scenario "must be the Lord's way of telling me to get busy with the cathedral history." And with the cardinal's formal commissioning, I asked him "to be patient and maybe say a prayer that I can live long enough to finish this project."

On March 2nd, Starr notified me that he was "shipping by UPS four boxes of materials" he had accumulated regarding the Cathedral of Our Lady of the Angels. Enclosing the "chapter outline" that he was following, he looked forward "to verbally annotating it over the telephone sometime this week," something that never materialized.

In a letter to Bill Close, I recounted the arrival of the four boxes and early on determined "that their content is about as close to useless as it could ever be." I told how internally many of the "bundles are not organized" and that it would take several weeks just to make any sense out of it. I concluded, "that it would be better for me to start over." Still wondering if there might be some text, I asked Bill to contact Starr to see if indeed there was something.

I wrote to Kevin Starr early in July apprising him of how the cathedral history was progressing. I hoped to have the work done by early 2004, "unless some catastrophe falls into place." I reminded him that this was a project "that I really never wanted to do. However, as the days have rolled on, I have overcome that obstacle and now am most enthusiastic."

Every historian has his or her own work ethic. In my case getting all the available facts together was about 85% of the effort. Writing is actually the easiest part for me. Once I had gathered, organized, sifted and refined all the ingredients, it came time for composing. Writing took about ten weeks in all, except for the endless "tweaking" that went on to the every end.

The Dan Murphy Foundation subvented publication of the book with a generous check for $50,000, which allowed the Cardinal to present copies to all of the American Hierarchy.

Reviewers were generous in their accolades for the book. Matthew Gallegos, writing in the *Catholic Historical Review* stated that the volume was" packed with the circumstances and decisions that brought about the Cathedral of Our Lady of the Angels". He noted that the author "was uniquely positioned to write this book as an *ex-officio* member of the most senior of Cardinal Mahony's advisory committees". Another reviewer said the volume "is a must for Catholics who yearn for inspiration from episcopal leadership that can both bless and demonstrate business acumen".

The Cardinal himself was pleased and in a letter to me about another matter, he referred to the treatise as a "masterful work". Once again he congratulated me "on a magnificent contribution to the historical recording of all the steps that went into the planning, design, construction and utilization of the cathedral and its complex".

Miniature Book

During the time when it appeared that I wouldn't be writing the history of the cathedral, mostly to keep my oar in the water, I composed a twelve page miniature book on *Our Lady of the Angels Cathedral* which was published by the Mar Michael Press in 2000. Printed by Regis Graden and bound by Marianna Blau, only 150 copies were produced, and I gave them to people who played key roles in the erection of the cathedral. Only the cardinal and Jose Rafael Moneo took the trouble of sending an acknowledgement. The Spaniards are well-mannered people.

Perhaps this already scarce treatise should be here reproduced for those who didn't get a copy.

> The selection of Our Lady of the Angels as the patroness for the southland's magnificent new cathedral has a historically long and richly significant precedent, which dates back to 1769 and the beginnings of Christianity in Alta California.
>
> The provenance of the title itself can be traced to Fray Juan Crespi (1721-1782), the Mallorcan-born friar who accompanied the Gaspár de Portolá expedition of 1769-1770 as diarist. All subsequent writers accepted his generic terminology, though not a few were guilty of textual corruption.
>
> Crespi recorded that late in the afternoon of July 31, 1769, the explorers crossed an *arroyo* of muddy water and stopped a little further on in a wide clearing. He had stated that the next day was one of rest "for the purpose of exploring, and especially to celebrate the jubilee of Our Lady of Los Angeles de Porciúncula," a liturgical commemoration observed only in the Franciscan calendar.
>
> The following morning, on the vigil of the feast, the expeditionary force continued its journey and came through a pass between two hills into a broad valley abounding in poplar and alden trees.
>
> A beautiful brook crossed the valley and later turned around a hill to the south. After traveling three more leagues, the Spaniards camped along a river which they appropriately named "in honor of *Nuestra Señora*

Sr. Mary Joanne Wittenburg, SND

de los Angeles de Porciúncula," a title derived from the day's sanctorial cycle.

Authorities are in general agreement that the name of the town established adjacent to the *Río Porciúncula* in the fall of 1781, was taken from the title of the nearby river. Fray Francisco Palóu (1723-1789), a contemporary observer, related that, "work was begun with a few families in founding the projected town of *Nuestra Señora de los Angeles* on the banks of the river named *Porciúncula*."

When Felipe de Neve decided to set up the town, he incorporated the religious title of the river and the popular appellation of Assisi's chapel in the name and the result was *El Pueblo de Nuestra Señora de los Angeles de Porciúncula.*

The initial church in the *pueblo* was erected as an *asistencia* of Mission San Gabriel. Its name was taken from that of the town in much the same way as the *pueblo* received its title after that of the river, a fact confirmed by the first entry in the baptismal register of the church, written in the hand of Fray Gerónimo Boscana (1775-1831), which read: "*Dia 4 Marzo de 1826, en la Iglesia de este Pueblo de Ntra. Sra. de los Angeles. . . .*"

By the time that Bishop Thaddeus Amat moved the seat for the Diocese of Monterey-Los Angeles to the southland in 1859, the official patroness of the jurisdiction was Saint Vibiana and it was under her patronage that Amat's cathedral was erected in 1876.

In 1943 Archbishop John J. Cantwell revealed his intention of building a new cathedral for the Archdiocese of Los Angeles which would be placed under the patronage of Our Lady of the Angels. On July 11, 1945, Cantwell issued a pastoral letter about the proposed new cathedral which he planned to locate atop a block long site on Wilshire Boulevard at Hudson Avenue.

With Cantwell's demise and the installation of a new archbishop in 1948, priorities changed and plans for a new Mother Church were put aside in favor of educational facilities.

Several times during the ensuing years the existing cathedral was renovated and otherwise restructured until the venerable edifice suffered irreparable damage during the Northridge earthquake of 1994.

As early as 1962, Roman officials hinted at the desirability of changing the patronage of Saint Vibiana Cathedral to that of Our Lady of Angels. Subsequently, the remains of Vibiana were removed from their place of prominence and replaced by a life-size porcelain statue of Our Lady of the Angels by the renowned artist, Pattarino.

Meanwhile in 1981, Timothy Cardinal Manning thought it would be appropriate to seek Roman authorization for changing the traditional feast day of Our Lady of the Angels from August 2nd to September 4th, the day on which the City of Los Angeles was founded in 1781. For the last twenty years, Los Angeles has been among the five American jurisdictions identifying title and patron.

It was shortly after the Northridge earthquake that Sir Daniel Donohue proposed the building of a wholly new cathedral for which he volunteered to be the major contributor.

About the time that the initial plans to erect the cathedral on the site of the earlier edifice were put aside in favor of a new location alongside the Hollywood Freeway, Roger Cardinal Mahony decided to invoke the earlier Cantwell patronage of Our Lady of the Angels.

Fittingly, the first cathedral in all the world erected in the third millennium of the Christian era, will be named for Mary, the mother of the Savior.

Cathedral Archives

Finally, there was the question of archiving the enormous collection of letters, blueprints and other related documents pertaining to the erection of the Cathedral of Our Lady of the Angels.

During the final months of 2001, Vicki Steele, Director of the Research Library at the Los Angeles campus of the University of California, approached officials at the soon-to-be-finished Cathedral of Our Lady of the Angels about the disposition of the vast array of documents and related materials generated during the five or so years since the overall project began in 1995. Steele offered the services and facilities at UCLA to both catalogue and store the materials.

Bill Close, Co-Chair for the Cathedral Campaign, expressed his view and that of others that the materials in question should become part of

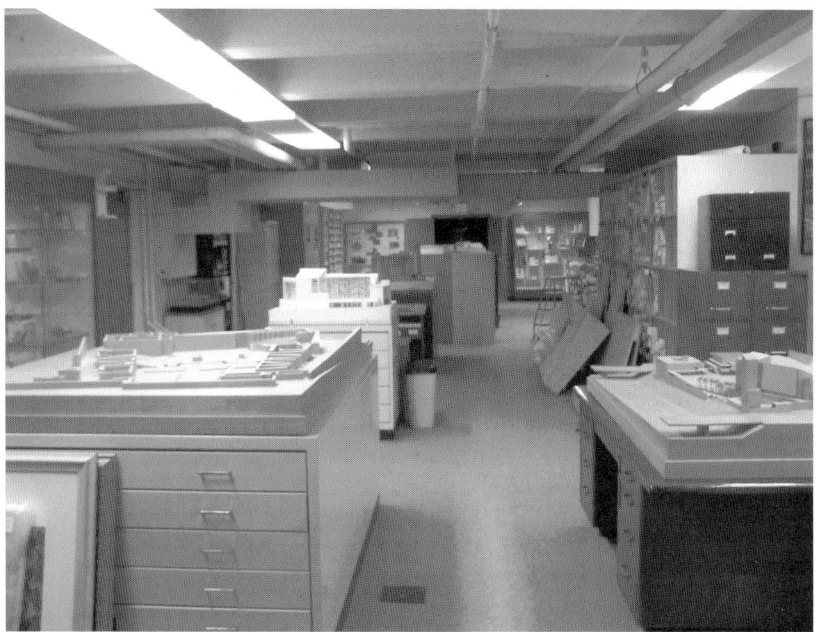

Cathedral Archives

the repository at Mission Hills known as the Archival Center for the Archdiocese of Los Angeles.

With the approval of Roger Cardinal Mahony, a meeting was called of concerned people, including Msgr. Francis J. Weber, Kevin Feeney, Brother Hilarion O'Connor and Dr. Kevin Starr. At that conclave, it was decided to establish an archival committee consisting of Drs. Kevin Starr (Chair), Doyce B. Nunis, Gloria Ricci Lothrop, Brother Hilarion, Msgr. Francis J. Weber, Admiral Ray Smith, Steven Lanzarotta, William Close, and Kevin Feeney.

At the initial meeting of that committee, the decision was made to house the Cathedral Archives in an unused section in the basement at Alemany High School, adjoining the facilities of the Archival Center.

During the following weeks, a SPACESAVER was installed and a series of modifications were made in the designated area, bringing it more into conformity with archival practices.

Inasmuch as the magnitude of the documents, correspondence, work orders, photographs, models and other materials demanded a full-time professional organizer and manager, Sister Joanne Wittenburg, SND, was hired for a three-year term as the initial Cathedral Archivist, beginning February 2, 2002. In her position, she would be a member of the staff at the Cathedral of Our Lady of the Angels, working under the direction of the Archivist for the Archdiocese of Los Angeles.

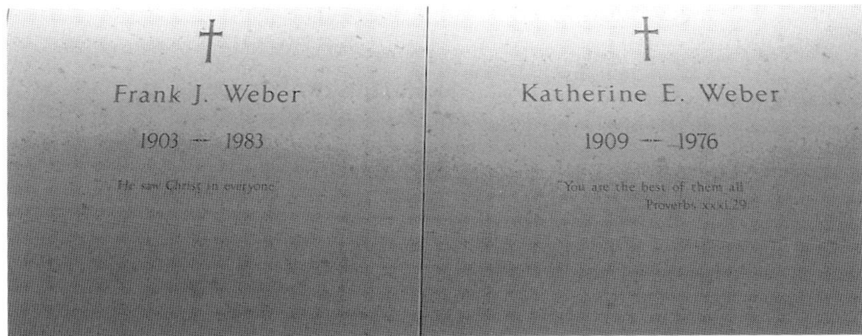

With the completion of the preliminary planning, it was announced that the Cathedral Archives would formally be inaugurated on April 1st, 2002. The mission statement for this newest archdiocesan agency reads as follows:

> The Cathedral Archives, located at the San Fernando Mission, serves as a repository for documents, books and all other media resources related to the history of the Cathedral of Our Lady of the Angels. It's purpose is to collect, preserve, interpret and provide access to these materials. The Cathedral Archives also conducts a variety of "outreach" programs involving the editing and publication of materials for the benefit of the historical and ministerial community.

The Cathedral Archives serves as a repository for documents, books and all other media resources related to the history of the Cathedral of Our Lady of the Angels. Although the collection is youthful in age, the Archives has received several interesting items.

- ❖ Files released by the Office of Worship indicate that as early as 1990 conversations were taking place concerning the renovation of St. Vibiana's. An architectural firm had been hired when the 1994 earthquake affectively ended the discussions. The correspondence, however, show that the process used to identify the architect was a relatively simple one in comparison to the national and international search that ended with Professor Jose Rafael Moneo's selection as Design Architect for the Cathedral of Our Lady of the Angels.
- ❖ *The Cathedral of St. Vibiana: A History and Appraisal* was put together by Thomas R. Vreeland & Associates in February 1996 in order to clarify the future of the former cathedral. Part IV contains a detailed description of its construction together with a number of photographs illustrating the previous efforts to reinforce the building.
- ❖ Artifacts from the Dedication of the Cathedral include the *Book of Workers* from Morley Construction Company containing the names of the

individuals who contributed to the Cathedral project; a set of signed drawings from Leo A. Daly, Executive Architect/Engineer as well as the silver bowl and trowel used to cement the relics into the altar floor.

It is anticipated that the process of gathering and cataloguing items such as these would take a minimum of three years at which time the collection will be open to qualified researchers interested in the history, construction and decoration of the Cathedral of Our Lady of the Angels. Eventually the Cathedral Archives also hopes to conduct a variety of "outreach" programs involving the editing and publication of materials for the benefit of the historical and ministerial community.

Entombment of Parents

When my father died, Mary Alice and I temporarily rented and then sold the familial home at 454 South Mansfield Avenue. With my share of the assets I purchased a small condo in San Buenaventura, across the street from the county museum. Initially I planned to live there in retirement but, with the passage of time, I felt that it would be better to remain in Los Angeles. The condo was offered for sale.

In 2002 I sold the condo for approximately $200,000 (which was double what I had paid) and set my sights on Saint John of God Retirement Home at Western Avenue and Adams Boulevard.

Having no need for the cash, I decided to give it to the Cathedral of Our Lady of the Angels. Bill Close, a good friend of many years and the "overseer" of the cathedral's erection, asked me if I wanted to "name" anything in exchange for the gift.

Ultimately, he suggested I might like a vault in the cathedral's mausoleum. The funds were enough for me to move my parents from Holy Cross Cemetery. I could only imagine what my father would say on judgment day, when he comes forth onto Grand Avenue in downtown Los Angeles.

Arrangements were made with officials at Holy Cross to disinter my parents in exchange for a gift of the graves for some future worthy decedents. In any event, I was there on April 30, 2003 when my parents arrived at their new home.

Cardinal Mahony wrote to say that he was pleased that I had arranged for my parents "to be buried in the cathedral mausoleum." He very graciously added that "you have had such a vital part in the entire cathedral project, it seems fitting that the Weber family be a part of the cathedral for hundreds of years to come.

Working Together

To Prevent Child Sexual Abuse

Keeping Ministerial Relationships Healthy & Holy

April, 2010

Archdiocese of Los Angeles

When I called my sister and told her that our parents had a new address, she was not overly amused. Later, she and her husband John visited the site and were very pleased.

Now this is all to explain how the Webers from Valley Mills, Indiana came to be interred in the nation's largest cathedral!

Obiter Dicti

In October of 2002, I expressed a concern that the oil painting of Saint Vibiana's Cathedral by Ben Abril needed a more prominent home. The Cardinal responded and after a few years in the rectory of Saint Brendan's church, the painting was moved to the Vibiana Chapel of the new cathedral.

8
Pedophilia Scandal

The clergy sexual abuse charges and its subsequent fall-out that surfaced in 2002 will surely be remembered as the greatest scandal in the history of the Catholic Church in the United States.

For those who might be interested, a superb and objective chronological account of this unpleasant chapter in our annals is that by Nicholas P. Cafardi, in his book *Before Dallas*, published by the Paulist Press in 2008.

In the Archdiocese of Los Angeles, there were 647 creditable charges leveled against 211 local priests, extern clergymen, religious clerics and brothers, a deacon, a seminarian, and even one bogus priest alleging events that occurred between 1932 and 1999.

Years hence some enterprising scholar will write about this matter, probably at considerable length. Here I am only going to relate my own reaction and how I attempted to handle it in Mission Hills.

In the weekly bulletin at San Fernando Mission, for April 14, 2002, there was a brief reflection addressed to some of the queries at the local level:

A Pause To Reflect

Occasionally we must divert our attention from the usual Gospel message to matters that touch us as a family. And like so many family problems, this particular one is unpleasant to the utmost degree. I speak, of course, of the pedophilia infection that has surfaced among certain clergymen in recent months.

In most cases, these incidents in question occurred ten or twenty years ago. We like to think that our screening process at the seminary has been working effectively in recent times.

While a single case of this malady is reprehensible, I would point out that the problem is not as rampant as newspaper and television reports would indicate. Statistics are few, but one survey of 2400 priests in the

Archdiocese of Chicago over a forty-year period puts the percentage rate for all kinds of sexual misbehavior at 1.8, which is considerably beneath the incidence in the general population. Priests are human beings and, as such, they reflect all the traits, good and bad, that enhance or taint human nature.

The bishops have been accused of "covering up" the whole matter and, to some extent, that may be true. In their defense, up until fairly recent times, most psychologists have believed that pedophilia was treatable. Now we are told there is no cure.

In earlier times, acting on what was the best available advice, a number of pedophiliacs were sent to treatment and then some few were put back into active service. Now, belatedly, the bishops are better informed and have wisely adopted a zero tolerance for these cases. But we can be assured, however, that critics will keep regurgitating the well-intentioned mistakes of the past.

No group in society is more upset at this whole problem than the 99% of priests who are just as put off by pedophilia as anyone else. We deplore it, we encourage identifying and treating victims, and we are embarrassed by the horrendous publicity that our errant brothers have unleashed on the Church and all its ministers.

It didn't take Catholic bashers long to seize on this malady as an occasion to vocalize their criticism of every aspect of the Church. They are unwilling to let us solve this problem internally, which is the best way to solve any family problem. Whatever the Pope says is "too little", whatever the bishops do is "too late" and whatever other Church leaders do is a "cover-up".

Last week, someone asked me what I thought of a columnist for a major local newspaper who makes his living by trashing the Church and its ministers on every possible occasion. My answer would be an exhortation to upgrade the veracity of his informants and to reflect on the Pauline injunction that "certain things are better left unsaid."

Those who like to think that bigotry is dead or on the back burner need only to observe the reaction in the press when something unpleasant happens in or to the Catholic Church or one of its members. The feeding frenzy that occurs then is proof enough that charity and forgiveness do not occupy center stage in modern society.

Unfortunately, down through the ages, there have been scandals, indiscretions and outright crimes perpetrated by the clergy in almost every century. Today's scandals, bad as they are, are simply the latest manifestation of the power of evil in the world.

The French king once took Cardinal Richelieu to task for not complying with one of his directives. He yelled at Richelieu "Your Eminence, I will destroy the Church if it doesn't comply with my wishes." The cardinal smiled and said: "Your Majesty, our priests have been trying to do that since apostolic times and have been unsuccessful."

Listening carefully to God's word during our recent Lenten journey, we have been reminded that from arid deserts will come streams of running water and out of the deepest darkness will come the light of God's peace and good news. Darkness gives place to sunlight in the early hours of every day.

This horrible scandal will pass, but it will probably take a long time for its wounds to heal because communications today are immediate and universal. I would exhort everyone to remember that the Lord has promised to be with His poor, mud-splattered Church until the end of time. Forgive your priests, pray for them and encourage vocations. For some inexplicable reason of Divine Providence, priests are designated ministers of the sacraments, which are the normal means for communicating God's graces to His people.

Don't allow this latest scandal to compromise or minimize your faith. God has chosen to publicize the sins of His chosen people from the time of David, the King. Even among Christ's innermost apostolic family, one of the twelve denied Him, another doubted Him and a third betrayed Him. But the early Church was strengthened by the scar tissue of those unpleasantries.

Then on February 22, 2004, I passed out the following comments.

DURING the coming week, you will be reading or hearing about the results from a survey of Catholic dioceses in the United States about sexual abuses by members of the clergy. It will not be a pleasant read or listen. The numbers reported for Los Angeles will be larger than others because of the area's size and the diversity of its population.

PURSUANT to that, we are inserting in this week's bulletin a series of guidelines that have been formulated and promulgated by the Archdiocese of Los Angeles. I would like to speak briefly on this matter because many Catholics will understandably be shocked, angered, despondent, disgusted and demoralized over the quantity of allegations of sexual misconduct among priests, as well as the manner in which many of their cases were mismanaged by Church leaders.

THOUGH it is not a new phenomenon, perpetrators are not limited to priests, Available data indicates that approximately 2% of Catholic priests have had some involvement with minors, mostly teenage boys.

RESEARCH from Saint Luke's Institute in Maryland suggests that although the number of offenders is large, the figure also applies to male clergy from other religious denominations. And it is likely lower than the number of sexually offending men in the general population.

RESEARCH with other occupational groups such as teachers, coaches, scout leaders indicates that sexual abuse of children occurs in those and other groups at a frequency comparable to that among Catholic priests.

OF COURSE that doesn't minimize or diminish culpability. Obviously any sexual abuse of minors is horrific, immoral, unethical and illegal. To assume, however, that priests are any more likely to be sex offenders than men in other groups or from the general population is simply not supported by current research.

NEWSPAPERS and others will likely exaggerate to a significant degree the number of priest sex offenders. But it is important to keep in mind that while a small percentage of Catholic clergy have sexually engaged with minors, they have not done so in greater proportion than other men.

In these troubled times we need to keep this whole tragic chapter in perspective.

THE local press, radio stations and television commentators have been and will probably continue to be hostile to all aspects of religion. Especially will they dwell upon the human failures of the clergy.

OUR chief consolation is that the bishops have now taken steps that will insure that these horrendous things will not happen again. The Catholic Church was strengthened after the Reformation. Hopefully this unfortunate experience will have the same long-term effect.

In the *History of the Archdiocese of Los Angeles*, published in 2006, I wrote the following essay on the "Safeguarding the Children" program.

As a response to what future historians will surely classify as the "worst scandal ever in the American Catholic Church," the Archdiocese of Los Angeles adopted a "Safeguarding the Children Program" in 2002 whereby victims harmed by sexual abuse at the hands of priests, religious, deacons or other ministers of the Church could obtain therapy and spiritual direction.

Though the scandal touched most areas of the Catholic Church in the United States, it affected the Archdiocese of Los Angeles more severely than many other places because of the sheer numbers of people comprising the largest ecclesial jurisdiction in the country.

In the files for the Archdiocese, is a mountain of materials tracing the evolvement of the scandal from its outset as it unfolded in the newspapers, magazines, journals, radio reports and television commentaries. With the passage of time, a future sociologist-historian will be able to prepare a study of what transpired and how it played out in the nation as a whole and the archdiocese in particular. Even at this early stage, norms adopted and implemented by the National Conference of Catholic Bishops have taken hold whereby the Church can deal aggressively with this problem.

While a single case of this malady is reprehensible, it needs to be said that the problem is not as rampant as newspaper and television reports would indicate. Statistics are few, but one survey of 2,400 priests in the Archdiocese of Chicago over a forty-year period puts the percentage rate for all kinds of sexual misbehavior at 1.8%, which is considerably beneath the incidence in the general population. Priests are human beings and, as such, they reflect all the traits, good and bad, that enhance or taint human nature.

Gary Schoener, a nationally recognized expert on sexual abuse, expressed a widely accepted opinion that "true pedophilia is very rare among all clergy, and now there is no evidence that it is more common among clergy than laypersons."

And it should be observed that sexual abuse of young people is not just a Catholic problem. *The Christian Science Monitor* reported on April 5, 2002, that most American Churches being hit with the child sexual abuse allegations are Protestant, and most of the alleged abusers are not members of the clergy or staff, but church volunteers.

Though comparative data is not readily available, there are indications that this is not a problem just in the Church. For example, the Gallup Organization reported that 1.3 million children were assaulted in 1995. Most instances of abuse take place in families, where it remains a hidden but very real problem. According to Dr. Garth A. Rattray, "about 85 percent of the offenders [of child sexual abuse] are family members, babysitters, neighbors, family friends or relatives."

A second and troublesome aspect of this scandal has been attempts made over the years by bishops and others of "covering up" the whole matter. To some extent, that is true. In their defense, up until fairly recent times, most psychologists have believed that pedophilia was treatable. Now we are told there is no cure.

In earlier times, acting on what was the best available medical and psychological advice, a number of pedophiliacs were sent to treatment and then some few were put back into active service. Belatedly, the bishops are better informed and have adopted a zero tolerance for these cases. We can be assured, however, that critics will keep regurgitating the well-intentioned mistakes of the past.

Roger Cardinal Mahony and other members of the hierarchy have openly acknowledged "the failure of bishops and other Church leaders to deal wisely with this misconduct." The president of the Catholic League has noted that "there is much blame to go around. Among the culprits are the Archdiocese of Los Angeles, some priests, many therapists, some lawyers, some alleged victims and some in the media."

Christians are reminded that from arid deserts will come streams of running water and out of the deepest darkness will come the light of God's peace and good news. Darkness gives place to sunlight in the early hours of every day.

Tomorrow will be a better day!

Finally, let me quote from a letter Roger Cardinal Mahony sent out to the faithful of the archdiocese on July 18, 2007.

As you have heard, this past week our Archdiocese settled 508 civil cases involving clergy and lay persons accused of sexual abuse. The emotional pain of the victims of this abuse remains intense, and I invite each of you to join with me in praying for them on their difficult journey toward healing.

I again apologize personally, and on behalf of those who led the church in past decades, to all those who were abused, regardless of how long ago the abuse took place.

As much as we might wish that the past could be reversed and the harm undone, it cannot be. But we can work to ensure that our parish ministries are as safe as we can humanly make them for all of our parishioners, especially our children and young people.

Throughout our Archdiocese, in our parishes and schools, our priests and lay people have worked hard over the past several years to create safe environments for our children. At this important moment in our Local Church's history, as we remember our past failings, it is also appropriate to reflect on what has been accomplished so far:

- There is no priest or lay person currently in ministry in the Archdiocese who has been found to have abused a young person.
- Complaints of abuse are promptly reported to civil authorities.
- A Clergy Misconduct Oversight Board receives complaints of inappropriate conduct and makes recommendations about the disposition of individual cases.
- More than 40,000 priests, teachers, lay employees, coaches and volunteers have been trained in abuse prevention techniques under the Archdiocese's Safeguard the Children program.
- Before being allowed to work alone with children, church employees and volunteers are being fingerprinted and will clear a criminal background check.
- More than 350,000 of our children and youth already have been trained in age-appropriate programs that teach them to distinguish between appropriate and inappropriate behavior and how to report inappropriate behavior to a parent or guardian.

Who's To Blame?

It is easy and somewhat of a cop-out to blame only contemporary bishops for the pedophilia scandal that has rocked the Catholic Church in recent times. Viewing human events apart from the historical context is always simplistic and rarely accurate.

There is an old dictum: *Corruptio pessima optima*, or "corruption at the highest level is the worst." The leadership in the Church in the United States has been compromised to the extent that since the 1960s the bishops have been grossly negligent in exercising their spiritual authority.

The background for this episcopal complacency to secular events that developed in the United States was manifold, but I personally believe that much of it developed from the caliber of bishops selected during the years when Jean Jadot served as Apostolic Delegate (1973–1980). I have an observant friend who once said it would take several generations to "get over the so-called Jadot bishops". Interestingly, Jadot, still living, was never made a cardinal as were all his predecessors.

The first indications of this downward trend can be traced back to the issuance of *Humanae Vitae* by Pope Paul VI in 1968. The Holy Father unequivocally and definitively declared that artificial birth control was a grave sin and totally unacceptable. The so-called "pill" was not allowed by Roman Catholics.

Unhappily the bishops "winked" at this encyclical and most failed to implement it or did so rarely and reluctantly. I remember hearing confessions in West Hollywood where penitents who bothered to admit practicing birth control confided that the Jesuits in nearby Blessed Sacrament told them to "follow their consciences" which was nothing less than a green light.

In 1968 when a group of fifty-two priests issued a public "statement of conscience" objecting to certain provisions of *Humanae Vitae*, James Francis Cardinal McIntyre asked that the United States Conference of Catholic Bishops issue a public endorsement of the papal encyclical. Though the bishops approved of McIntyre's intervention, the President of the NCCB, Archbishop John Dearden of Detroit, never forwarded the original statement to Rome. When McIntyre subsequently confronted Dearden directly, he was told that the actions of the bishops had been shelved for parliamentary reasons!

Then came *Roe vs Wade*, which legalized abortion in the United States. Once again the Church's leadership paid only lip service to its opposition. Those few bishops who publicly counseled non-observant Catholics in public offices to refrain from receiving Holy Communion were ostracized by the USCB and none of those who did so received any further positions of leadership or advancement at the national level.

Finally and most recently, when the California Supreme Court struck down the prohibition against same-sex marriages, there was only minimal response from the state's Catholic Bishops.

Today's corruption derives from the failure of bishops to take action in areas that desperately needed attention. Interestingly, the Pro Life movement originated with the laity, not the hierarchy.

It would be historically short-sighted to view the pedophile scandal apart from the gradual drift that the Church's leadership began in the 1960s. While no bishops then or now publicly condoned birth control, abortion, same sex marriage or pedophilia, few took any more than negligible steps to oppose those affronts to Catholic morality.

The present generation of bishops has allowed the complacency of their predecessors to become the norm. Even those who paid attention to warnings about pedophilia in the 1980s did nothing to implement it, little imagining that such a position would return to haunt them.

Chances are that the pedophilia scandal, admittedly the worst ever to rock the Bark of Peter, will eventually fade into the woodwork, but the damage is catastrophic and will be felt for decades. Catholics must demand that their episcopal leaders return to the level of responsible administration evident in the pre-conciliar Church. Loving the Church means denouncing corruption wherever and however it is manifested. All aspects of the *New Catechism* must be implemented. The era of smorgasbord Catholicism was a disaster.

The bishops must never again be complacent in their relationship with secular society. Whenever ecclesial agencies begin to take account of earthly purposes, they become corrupt and truly cancerous.

Our goal is to be squeaky clean, not subservient to worldly standards.

While surely the sex abuse scandal is indeed "painful," John Allen points out in his book *All The Pope's Men* that the American press invested incalculable resources broadcasting the failures of the Catholic Church, but made no similar effort to publicize anything the Church did right. To provide just a bit of context, in the same year that the sex abuse scandals finished on the front page of the New York Times for forty-one days in a row, 2.7 million children were educated in Catholic schools in the United States, nearly 10 million persons were given assistance by Catholic Charities USA, and Catholic hospitals spent 2.8 billion in providing uncompensated health care to millions of poor and low-income Americans.

9
Publications

In 2001, I inaugurated a series of publications dealing with otherwise mostly unknown and/or unpublicized ministries in the Archdiocese of Los Angeles. At least one of these volumes went into a third printing.

156

Books, Books, Books, A Selection of Book Reviews
(Mission Hills, Saint Francis Historical Society, 2001), Pp. XIV, 347

In his *Apologia pro Vita Sua*, John Henry Newman extended the concept of "apology" beyond its traditional meaning to include the notion of "explanation." In that vein, the preface of this book endeavors to tell how and why this book came to be.

To those who feel that reproducing book reviews of yesterdays is redundant, might I point out that the considerable time and effort involved in writing reviews is practically always restricted to the readers of the journals or newspapers in which they appear. Hence relatively few people have the opportunity of reading and profiting from whatever insights they might offer.

Secondly, the books in question are still around and book reviews reveal a lot about the authors, their prejudices, shortcomings and background. In addition to pointing out factual errors and inaccurate interpretations, critical reviews often expand the topic or person under consideration or update old ones. Finally, the threat of book reviews helps to keep overly enthusiastic authors on track.

As will be evident, the range books reviewed from 1962 to 2000 is quite extensive (193). Every book, even those out-of-field, was carefully read and described in measured language. Though I never kept a log of books reviewed, a reasonable guestimate would put their number at about 400. Only half of them have been located and, in some cases, I was

unable to identify the journal in which they appeared. Several were (apparently) never published and only one was rejected by the editor who requested it. The length of the reviews has no relationship to the importance of the volume under scrutiny. Generally, the editor of the journal stipulated the number of words.

This collection of reviews has been arranged topically and, within the various categories, they appear alphabetically by author. Little, if any, editorial changes have been made from the original format.

An interesting final feature in this book is an appendix "on reviewing books" which repeats some of the canons or criteria that should govern reviewers.

157

A Remarkable Legacy
The Story of Secondary Schools in the Archdiocese of Los Angeles
(Mission Hills, Saint Francis Historical Society 2001), Pp.xx.154.

The remarkable and unparalleled accomplishments in the field of Catholic education in the area now comprising the Archdiocese of Los Angeles are unique in the annals of American Catholicism.

This volume is an historical, compendium of the secondary schools from 1890 to the present. Schools are divided into categories of private (22), parochial (6) and archdiocesan (23) including prep seminaries and special service institutions. The twenty-three schools which have been closed are included, each with an historical background sketch.

Preparing this book was indeed a challenging project for many reasons. Even where there was a traceable paper trail, accreditations reports and other pertinent data were scarce and, in some cases, non-existent. One school never opened (Catharine McAuley,) 1970); several changed their patronage (Saint John Vianney to Daniel Murphy, Regina Caeli to Queen of Angels Academy and Saint Joseph to Pomona Catholic); three schools operated under the same name (Marymount-Los Angeles,) Santa Barbara and Palos Verdes; a couple merged (Conaty-Our Lady of Loretto and Cantwell-Sacred Heart); others were sold (Marymount in Santa Barbara and Corvallis in Studio City); one moved to another's campus (Saint Matthias to Pius X); and six became part of the Diocese of Orange (Cornelia Connelly, Marywood, Mater Dei, Rosary, Saint Michael and Servite.)

158

A Tradition of Outreach
Examples of Catholic Action in the Archdiocese of Los Angeles
(Mission Hills Saint Francis Historical Society, 2003). Pp xii, 106

Early in 1934, the Bishop of Los Angeles-San Diego began preparations for a "Catholic Action Week" which was to be held between April 29th and May 3rd. For that occasion, Bishop John J. Cantwell issued a thirty-six page *Catechism on Catholic Action. Its Theory and Practice* whose purpose was that of giving "our Catholic people a clearer understanding of the meaning of Catholic Action." In retrospect, it is clear that the Church in Southern California was considerably out in front of its sister ecclesial jurisdictions in the field.

This book contains forty randomly chosen examples of Catholic Action inaugurated along the Western Shore of the United States since 1865. It is not intended as providing an in-depth coverage of the groups enumerated. A reviewer in the *Catholic Historical Review* said that the "book's interesting and information-laden summaries can, along with a brief background on the concept of Catholic Action, serve as a ready reference for scholars and general readers."

159

A Legacy of Healing
The Story of Catholic Health Care in the Archdiocese of Los Angeles
(Mission Hills: Saint Francis Historical Society, 2003) Pp.viii; 84

This modest book attempts to sketch the story of Catholic healthcare in what is now the Archdiocese of Los Angeles. The concentration here is on the historical establishment and subsequent evolvement throughout the ensuing years. Little attention has been paid to the recent challenges brought on by the ever-growing burden of financial costs.

Preparing this book was something of a challenge for a host of reasons. Even where there was a traceable paper trail, there were almost

Santa Margarita de Cortona *Asistencia*

A FORGOTTEN MISSIONARY FOUNDATION ALONG CALIFORNIA'S *EL CAMINO REAL*

MSGR. FRANCIS J. WEBER

with graphics and layout by

TERRY RUSCIN

Saint Francis Historical Society
Anno Domini 2003

insurmountable factual challenges. One of the hospitals never opened, the names of several others were changed and ownership of others remains unclear.

The five chapters of this book touch on Catholic Health Care, Heroines of Catholic Healing Center, Individual Hospital and Medical Centers, Individual Skilled Nursing Facilities and Closed and/or Sold Hospitals.

160

Santa Margarita de Cortona Asistencia
(Mission Hills; Saint Francis Historical Society, 2003) Pp. 42.

This is the story of a forgotten missionary foundation along California's *El Camino Real*, complete with graphics and layout by Terry Ruscin. This is the first and only book about the elusive *asistancia*.

The reasons why the *asistencia* has eluded historians for so long are manifold. There are virtually no documents available; the earliest visitors to the Pacific Slope rather consistently omitted all but passing references to Santa Margarita; the area in question never became a thriving metropolis; and, finally, the actual ruins have been privately owned since their confiscation in the 1830s.

While the continued lack of evidence does not allow for any startling revelations in these pages, there is some satisfaction in bringing Santa Margarita de Cortona out of the dim shadows of the distant past and into the real world of the third millennium.

Much happened at the *asistencia*, perhaps much more than its founders ever envisioned. As contemporary and future people gaze at its ruins, they would be well-advised to recall the old scriptural adage: what one person plants, another reaps. The whole story will be revealed when the archives of heaven are opened on resurrection day, for nothing escapes the notice of the recording angel. Perhaps this book will serve as an interim account.

161

Requiescant in Pace
The Story of Catholic Cemeteries in the Archdiocese of Los Angeles
(Mission Hills; Saint Francis Historical Society, 2003) Pp. vii, 92.

According to one reviewer, *Requiescant in Pace* "features photos, anecdotal material, a fascinating chapter detailing the first local Christian burial (1782) and closed or abandoned burial grounds." Another reviewer who did his homework well, remarked that "the author . . . is no stranger to the funeral industry, having spent part of his youth in the employ of a Los Angeles mortuary.

Divided into four chapters, including historical background, Mission cemeteries, closed, abandoned or alienated cemeteries, twelve functioning cemeteries and a series of appendices, the book describes how California's southland's Catholic Cemeteries are among the oldest publicly recognized ministries in Christendom.

Probably one of the most interesting essays in this book tells the story of J.A. Doric - who he was, what he did and how he came to be buried in the priests plot at Calvary Cemetery in Los Angeles.

162

Unity in Diversity
The Story of Ethnic Ministries and Eastern Rites in the Archdiocese of Los Angeles.
(Mission Hills, Saint Francis Historical Society, 2004) Pp.vii, 87

Historical commentators are quick to observe that almost everything in Southern California has been imported-plants, flowers, shrubs, trees, water and even religion! More than three decades ago, the late Carey McWilliams pointed to the unprecedented influx of peoples as a factor that today accounts for the multi-ethnic nature of the onetime *Pueblo de Nuestra Señora de Los Angeles.*

The final book in this series traces the history of ethnic ministries and Eastern Rites as found in this "most diverse Catholic population of any jurisdiction in North America."

There are forty-four historical and current photos in the thirty-six different ethnic and religious sections. Besides the thirty ethnic groups, all of the churches of the Eastern Rite are included with interesting statistics as to origin, forms of worship and pioneering founders.

163

Cathedral of Our Lady of the Angels
Los Angeles Saint Francis Historical Society, 2004) pp.x1, 364

This book had several false starts, as indicated in an earlier chapter. Reviewers unanimously praised the book. One writer in the *Catholic Historical Review* said that the author "was uniquely positioned to write this book as an *ex-officio* member of the most senior of Cardinal Mahony's advisory committee." He went on to note that "to future scholars of Church architectural history this book will be a primary interpretation source."

The overall cost of printing and binding the book was subvented by a generous grant form Daniel Donohue and the Dan Murphy Foundation.

164

The California Missions.
(Strasbourg, France: *Editions du Signe*, 2005). Pp. 253

This book tells the story of the California missions in a manner directed to inquisitive students, casual readers and even serious scholars. The

treatise makes no serious effort at being definitive inasmuch as all of its subject headings could, in themselves, be further elaborated into book-length volumes. For over forty-five years, queries have come daily to the Archival Center for the Archdiocese of Los Angeles about various aspects of the mission story. The format and contents of this book are an attempt to answer many of those questions in a simple but straightforward manner.

By all rights and logic, this book should have been written by a seraphic historian. For most of the 20th century, such Franciscan giants as Zephyrin Engelhardt, Maynard Geiger and Francis Guest provided the Western American bibliophilic landscape with dozens of erudite books and learned articles on practically every aspect of the California missions. One hopes and prays that soon the Order of Friars Minor will once again encourage and educate its friars to work, speak and write in a field now depleted of a Franciscan presence.

In an era when critics and soothsayers are gaining a totally undeserved prominence for their undocumented portrayals and inaccurate interpretations of the accomplishments of Alta California's 142 friars, this writer decided that it was time to take up the torch, even if by default. As a member of the Third Order of Saint Francis for over half a century, maybe there is some justification for my daring to tread in the footsteps of Engelhardt, Geiger and Guest.

The book received numerous accolades and reviews none of which was esteemed more than the one from Dr. Gary Kurutz from the California State Library: "You have done another spectacular book. You are outdoing Engelhardt and Bancroft. Your book makes me want to go on a trip visiting the missions. Congratulations. I will be ordering additional copies for the Library."

On Saturday, May 20th, Dawson's Book Shop held one of their "Los Angeles Salons" at which a goodly number of books were signed for bibliophiles. The book became an entry of the Gem Guide Book Company in Baldwin Park.

165

A History of the Archdiocese of Los Angeles and Its Precursor Jurisdictions in Southern California 1840-2007
(Strasbourg: Editions du Signe, 2006) Pp.431

This history of the Catholic Church in California's southland, issued to commemorate the seventieth anniversary of the Archdiocese of Los Angeles, is really the capstone of almost a half century's work as archivist and historian.

Most of my other books, periodicals articles and newspapers essays prefigured or anticipated, in one way or another, this monumental treatise which was described by Roger Cardinal Mahony as the "most extensive, comprehensive and elegant of any of its kind yet published in our nations annals."

Appended to this volume were appendices of parochial foundations by Hermine Lees and histories of grammar schools by Sister Mary Joanne Wittenburg, S.N.D.

The French publisher, Editions du Signe, sent representatives to all of the parishes of the archdiocese in an effort to circulate the 433 page book as widely as possible. No fewer than 35,000 copies were printed in the initial press run.

In a letter accompanying a dozen or so complimentary copies, Cardinal Mahony said:

> It is with great pleasure that I send you a copy of the history of the Archdiocese of Los Angeles, 1840-2007.
>
> As many are aware, the Archdiocese of Los Angeles has been the largest Archdiocese in the United States for quite a long while, and that reality is reflected in the vast coverage of this book.
>
> For the first time, a cross section of Catholic activities in the counties of Los Angeles, Ventura and Santa Barbara is presented, complete with charts, graphics and pictorial glimpses.

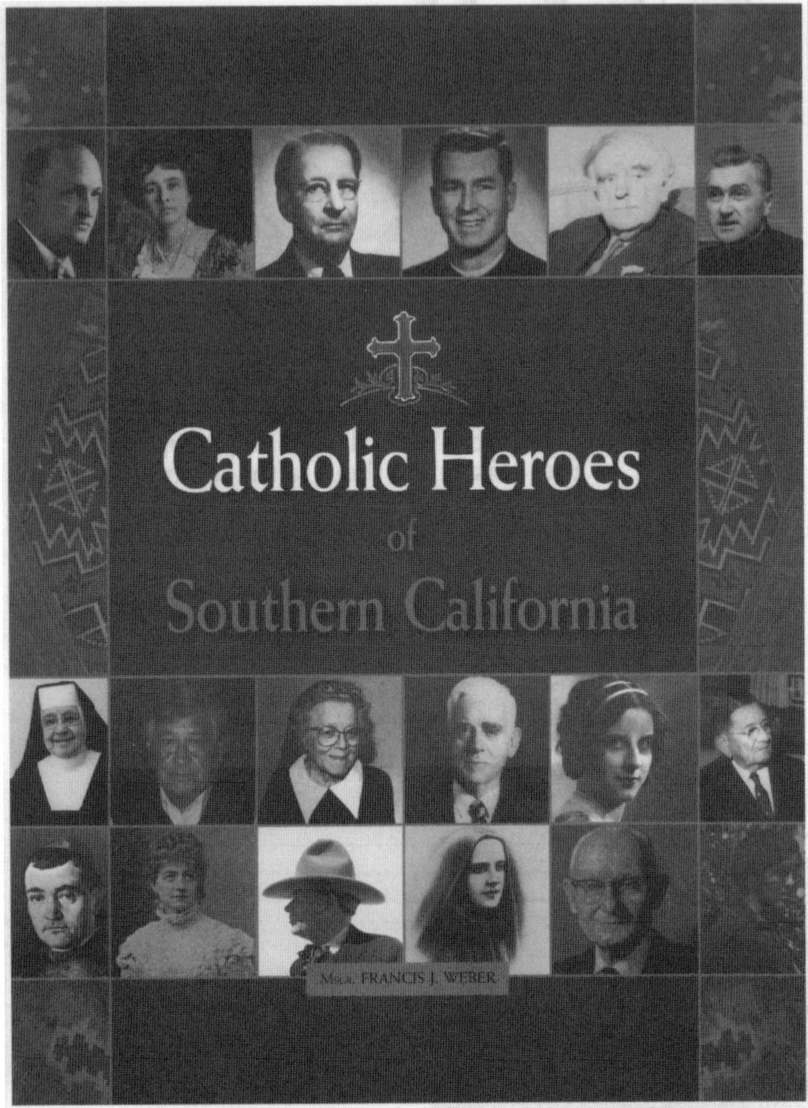

166

Una Historia de la Arquidiocesis de Los Angeles
y sus jurisdicciones precursoras en el sur de California, 1840-2007
(Strasbourg: Editions du Signe 2006); Pp. 431.

This translation, the work of Elizabeth Espinoza Roa, was a literal rendition of the English text.

167

Catholic Heroes of Southern California
(Strasbourg: Editions du Signe, 2007) Pp. 191

Here the author declares that a society which rejects its heroes is spiritually doomed. To ensure that the local Church will not forget those who have blazed and enhanced its trail the author has provided eighty samples of Catholic's from all walks of life whose endurance is the pursuit of their faith commitment are worthy of emulation by those who follow in their footsteps. The copiously—illustrated book concludes with a tribute from a Protestant minister who stated, in 1903, that the "Catholic Church is the grandest organization in the world."

168

San Fernando, Rey de España Mission
(Strasbourg: Editions du Signe, 2008) Pp. 64

This colorful edition incorporates several new aspects of Fray Fermin de Lasuens's mission, published for the first time, including the burial place of Bob Hope, the papal visit to the States' seventeenth mission, the celebrated Madonna Room and the visit of Spain's Crown Prince.

169

Blessed Fray Junípero Serra
An Outstanding California Hero
(Strasbourg: Edition's du Signe, 2007). Pp. 152

It is significant and highly appropriate that this last of the Weber books deals with a personal hero, Fray Junípero Serra. Though already the most written about personage in California annals, the influence of the gray friar continues to motivate, enrich, encourage and dominate the state's literary landscape.

170

Las Misiones de Californias
(Strasbourg, France: *Editions du Signe*, 2005). Pp. 255.
(actually published in 2008)

This is a translation into Spanish of *The California Missions* book by Elizabeth Espinosa R.

Seguramente el distintivo mas notorio de Alta California es su cadena 21 Misiones, establecida a lo largo de "El Camino Real" desde

San Diego a San Francisco Solano", explica Monseñor Weber en su libro titulado simplemente "Las misiones de California".

Estas misiones son las mas visitadas por los californianos y los viajeros; las mas mencionadas en libros corrientes y series, revistas y periódicos; las más honradas por premios, citas y placas; las mas estudiadas por los investigadores e historiadores; las más copiadas por arquitectos y constructores; las mas conmemoradas en estampillas de correo (cinco naciones), sobre las cuales ban escrito mas los historiadores, novelistas y guionistas; las más fotografiadas entre cualquier edificio de los Estados Unidos; las mas visitadas por jovenes de las escuelas publicas y privadas y las mas adaptables y versatiles de todos los sistemas de transformacion del Nuevo Mundo.

Las misiones en California pueden entenderse y apreciarse dentro del contexto de los tiempos y las areas en las cuales existieron, en los valores de los que las dirigieron y sostuvieron, y en la aceptacion y respuesta de los que se beneficiaron de su existencia. Como todos los esfuerzos nobles, las misiones no existirian sin sus difamadores".

Hagamos un repaso entonces a estos 21 majestuosos monumentos religiosos que forman parte de la historia de nuestra California.

(for the rest of this lengthy review, cf—*La Vida Nueva* for July 6, 2009)

171

History of the Newman Club of Los Angeles
(Strasbourg, France: *Editions Du Signe*, 2009) Pp. 144.

Msgr. Francis J. Weber has once more published his "penultimate" volume—this one on the auspicious Newman Club once described by the

THE HUNTINGTON LIBRARY

The Huntington Library in Pasadena (actually officially San Marino, California) has a large collection of miniature books, mostly from gifts of Msg. Francis Weber, a longstanding Miniature Book Society leader as well as a collector and publisher of miniature books. Alan Jutzi is the curator of rare books at the library. Here is his report:

"In 1991, Msgr. Francis J. Weber donated his 6, 000 volume miniature book collection to the library, and since then he has made two additional gifts including a fine collection of reference books and journals on the history of miniature books. The Huntington's own collection of about 1,000 volumes which include many early English and Continental works, along with gifts such as Grace Broecker's donation of a nearly complete set of doll-house size books by Barbara Raheb. The total number of miniatures is currently estimated at 10,000 volumes. (Lenora Shull in 1996 wrote an article in *Miniature Book Society Newsletter* summarizing the Huntington's holdings.)

All of these miniatures are not catalogued but many of them are available through an interleaved copy of Doris Welsh's *A Bibliography of Miniature Books* where the books and sets are numbered and listed. This includes many 20th century sets, which are arranged by genre or subject. A separate listing of "Limited Edition Press" books provides access to contemporary late-20th century imprints.

Plans are underway to integrate recent additions by Msgr. Weber and to catalog his fine library of reference works. A small semi-permanent exhibition of the Weber Collection is also planned. The Huntington regularly shows selections of rare material to visiting groups and those attending conferences and lectures. The latest presentation of miniature books was to a group of writers of children's books.

The person to contact at the Huntington about miniatures is Alan Jutzi, Curator of Rare Books, ajutzi@huntington.org."

Los Angeles Times as an "organization of a strong Catholic Literary Association" bearing the name of the late John Henry Cardinal Newman. (That editorial comment appeared a day after the inaugural meeting of the Newman Club, May 25. 1899.) On the anniversary of that auspicious beginning, this handsomely illustrated volume is appropriate. The chronicle encompasses the club's beginning, inspired by Bishop George Montgomery, to the Current roster of members—with sufficient data in between to satisfy any history aficionado.

Although Bishop Montgomery "felt something special was needed" to offset all the bigotry besieging Catholics, it was John Fillmore Francis, a convert, who initially headed the group. He was staunchly supported by the intrepid lawyer Joseph Scott, who served as secretary, and many other distinguished local leaders dedicated "to consider and discuss subjects germane to Catholic thought and history."

Prominent men comprised the group, but women were invited as guests and at the second dinner meeting the famous actress Madame Helena Modjeska delivered a paper on the influence of Christianity on the stage. The variety of monthly presentations followed the dictum of the bishop "that membership in the club be limited exclusively to laity prominent in their profession . . . on some topic germane to Catholic thought." The record for the most talks, however, belongs to "the humble scribe" who gave 11 presentations."

Hermine Lees

Miniature Books

My interest in miniature books has continued in the years since the turn of the century. I have attended most of the conclaves and on one occasion sponsored a "Rump Conclave" here at San Fernando Mission.

During July of 1999, when it became apparent that only four Californians were planning to attend Grand Conclave XVII in Koblentz, I decided to host a mini-gathering for the stay-at-homes at San Fernando Mission in Mission Hills. Although invitations were sent out only to Californians and, as a courtesy, to the President of the Miniature Book Society as well as the editor of the MBS newsletter, we received several out-of-state responses, mostly because of a series of negative letters, which appeared on the Internet.

Those invited were asked to bring along some bookish items for the auction along with a check for $25 to cover the tasty dinner provided by one of Hollywood's outstanding caterers. Accommodations were available for those wishing to stay overnight at the local Best Western Motel on nearby Sepulveda Boulevard. Tables were offered for those wishing to buy, sell, exchange, appraise or otherwise discuss miniature books.

Attendees were feted with two freshly-released miniature book keepsakes, one from the Junípero Serra Press and the other from the Mar-Michel Press of Missy Crahan. The former was a personal memoir

YOU ARE INVITED TO PARTICIPATE IN

"Rump" Grand Conclave XVII
of the
Miniature Book Society

Sunday, September 5, 1999
from 12 noon to 6:00 p.m.

at

San Fernando Mission
15151 San Fernando Mission Blvd.
Mission Hills, California

Event Schedule

Reception: 12 noon to 1:30 p.m.
Book Fair: 2:00 to 3:30 p.m.
Auction of Bibliophilic Treasures: 4:00 to 5:00 p.m.
Barbecue Dinner: 5:00 p.m.

Please bring an "auctionable" item. Profits will go to the Miniature Book Society!

If you want to "stay over," please contact:
Best Western Hotel
10621 Sepulveda Blvd.
Mission Hills, CA 91345
(800) 528-1234 / (818) 891-1771

Keep this top half for your information!

If you are interested, please complete, cut & mail this bottom half in the envelope provided.

NAME: ______________________
ADDRESS: ______________________
CITY: ______________ STATE:____ ZIP:______
PHONE # (_____)______________

I (We) will attend Grand Conclave☐ Number of people in my group☐
Enclosed please find my check for $25. per person.
(If interested in an exhibit table, please add $5. for each table.)
Please make check(s) payable to San Fernando Mission.
Rare keepsakes will be given!!!

about Earl Warren, three-term Governor of California. Measuring 2-¼ x 7-⅞ inches, the fourteen-page mini carries a 29 cent commemorative stamp of the one-time United States Chief Justice. The other is an essay about the Shroud of Turin, with a stamp issued in 1997 by the Italian government. Both books were handsomely printed at the Nut Quad Press by Regis Graden and bound by Mariana Blau. The latter was a gift of Michel "Missy" Crahan.

The day's festivities began when a number of those signed up for the conclave gathered in the Old Mission church for the 10:30 Mass celebrated by Father Joseph Curran, the parish priest of Waltham, Massachusetts.

The conclave itself began at high noon with exhibitors arriving to set up their miniature wares. Eighteen tables of bibliophilic "goodies" were adorned with all sorts of tiny books and related materials. Among those exhibiting were Mariana Blau, Robert Bradbury, Margaret Class, Eileen Cummings, Joseph Curran (Kurbel Books), Agnes and Muir Dawson (Dawson Book Shop), Glen and Mary Helen Dawson, James and Joan Lorson, Barbara Raheb, Georgianne Matthews, Lloyd Neilson and Marvin Hiemstra (Juníper von Phitzer Press), Peter Thomas, Kathy Miller (Iron Bear Press) and Corey Nethery.

Everyone emerged from the conclave with his or her own treasures. My "discovery of the day" was a rare copy of *Two Letters written by Margery Brews to John Paston at Saint Valentine's Tide* in 1937 and printed by Crispin Elsted at the Barbarian Press in 1983. There were only twenty-six copies of this book issued as a tenth wedding anniversary presentation.

At 12:30, members were treated to a deluxe tour of San Fernando Mission by senior guide, John Pancratz. Since there were two weddings also scheduled for the afternoon, members were able to witness the busy ecclesial life still in vogue at the seventeenth of the California missions.

Around 2 o'clock guests began flooding the areas set aside for the conclave. Almost a hundred visitors responded to advertisements in local newspapers. Even the mayor of nearby San Fernando was there, mixing among others who were seeing miniature books for the first time. As collectors snatched up the available little books, onlookers were astonished by the beauty and precision inherent in the tiny volumes.

At the auction, scheduled for 4 o'clock in the Archival Center library, there were thirty-six items available. A hastily-prepared catalogue had been made of the items, all of which were donated by members. Among the more noteworthy entries was a *History of the Bible* (New London: Starr & Co., 1859) which was presented by Glen Dawson. Only two copies are recorded of this rare Thumb Bible by Ruth Adomeit.

The highest price realized was for *Genesis Prima*, a gorgeous copy of the "chained" Book of Genesis produced at the Juníper von Phitzer Press by Marvin Hiemstra and Lloyd Neilson. The $1,125 raised at the auction was earmarked to offset the myriad of expenses associated with the one-day affair. Throughout the day members were treated to fruit and salad plates, finger sandwiches and cold drinks. Our auctioneer, Joseph Curran, was assisted by eighty-seven year old Glen Dawson, a fixture of the Grand Conclaves since they began in Tipp City seventeen years ago. At the conclusion of the auction, Missy Crahan presented a lovely butterfly piece of jewelry to Muir and Agnes

Dawson in memory of her mother who died several years ago during an earlier conclave.

After the auction concluded, everyone assembled in Cantwell Hall for a tasty barbeque dinner prepared in the Hollywood Kitchen of Chris-n-Pitts, one of the west coast's premier caterers. By 6:30 everyone was homeward bound after a full day of fun and recreation at the last of the century's Grand conclaves. Fittingly or otherwise, this writer was presented with the first "Rump Cup" hosting the first Conclave of its kind for the Miniature Book Society.

Whether regional gatherings will become a reality of life for the MBS in the years ahead depends on a number of things. When traveling to the Grand Conclaves becomes too costly, too burdensome or too out-of context for those who speak only English, other options will likely emerge. Deviating from the traditional Labor Day weekend is probably not a good idea. Seventeen years of association with that date has worked well in the past.

The "Rump" conclave held at Mission Hills was a most pleasant and upbeat experience enjoyed by all who attended, all of which proves that there is life beyond the narrow confines in which people often confine themselves.

Early in 2008, the curator of the William Andrews Clark Memorial Library at the University of California exhibited the collection I gave them some years ago of all the publications of Achille J. St. Onge.

My book on *The Bayeux Tapestry* brought to a close the twenty-seven year publishing history of the Junípero Serra Press in 2003. Begun at San Buenaventura in 1976, with the issuance of its proto book, *Interfaith in Action*, the press published sixty-eight miniature books under its imprint.

With most of its books printed by the late Francis Braun and Roger Pennels, the Junípero Serra Press has also utilized the talents of Regis Graden (Nut Quad Press), George Kinney (Castle Press), John Lathourakis (Tabula Rasa Press) Susan Acker (Feathered Serpent Press), Patrick Reagh and Paul Bohne (Bookhaven Press).

Complete collections of imprints from the Junípero Serra Press, as well as the other miniature books written and/or edited by the undersigned are known to exist at the Huntington Library (San Marino), Azusa Pacific University (Azuza), the Lilly Library (Bloomington, Indiana), the J. Pierpont Morgan Library (New York City) as well as the private collections of such bibliophilic luminaries as Joseph Curran and Caroline McGehee.

The book on *The Bayeux Tapestry* was inspired by a visit to that largest tapestry in the world some years ago. It is illustrated by a commemorative stamp featuring one of the many scenes depicted on the great eleventh-century masterpiece.

My association with the Junípero Serra Press has been a most pleasant interlude in my life, and one which I will always cherish. But now it's time to move on for, as some wag once noted, "it's better to jump than to be pushed," a dictum I feel should be embraced by anyone in his 70s. It's been real fun.

The issuance of my miniature book on *The Veil of Veronica* in 2004 marked the proto publication of El Camino Real Press.

My own miniature books here kept apace and, since 2000, I have written no fewer than ten books as here indicated.

112. Weber, Francis J., *Our Lady of the Angels.* Los Angeles: Mar Michel Press, 2000. 2 ¼ x 2 1⁄16. 12 pp. letterpress by Regis Graden, Nut Quad Press, white cloth spine, white paper over boards, gilt title by Mariana Blau. Frontispiece.

113. Weber, Francis J., *The First Mass in California.* Monterey, CA: Old Monterey Book Company, MM. 2 7⁄16 x 2 ⅛. 18 pp. letterpress by Roger Hilleary and David Salinas, printed cloth spine, paper over boards. Postage stamp frontis. 80 copies.

114. Weber, Francis J. *The Bayeux Tapestry.* Mission Hills, CA: Junipero Serra Press, 2003. 3 ¼ x 2 5⁄16. 17 pp. letterpress and bound by Regis

Graden, Nut Quad Press, printed wrappers. Color frontispiece. 275 copies.

115. Weber, Francis J., *The Veil of Veronica*, a personal memoir. Mission Hills, CA: El Camino Real Press, 2004. 3 ⅙ x 2 ⅛. 27 pp. letterpress by Regis Graden, Nud Quad Press, brown cloth, title stamped in orange. Illustrated. 150 copies.

116. Weber, Francis J., *Blessed Teresa of Calcutta*. Mission Hills, CA: El Camino Real Press, 2004. 2 15⁄16 x 2 ¼. 18 pp. letterpress by Regis Graden, Nut Quad Press, blue cloth, title stamped in silver. Postage stamp frontispiece. 150 copies. This book was chosen by the judges for the Western Book Exhibition.

117. Weber, Francis J., *The Ronald Reagan Presidential Library*. Mission Hills, CA: El Camino Real Press, 2005. 2 ⅞ x 2 ⅛. 13 pp. letterpress by Patrick Reagh, silver-stamped green cloth by Mariana Blau. Postage stamp & color photograph. 150 copies.

118. Weber, Francis J., *John Paul the Great, a eulogy*. Mission Hills, CA: El Camino Real Press, 2005. 2 13⁄16 x 2 3⁄16. 12 pp. letterpress by Patrick Reagh, gilt red leatherette by Mariana Blau. Postage stamp frontis. 150 copies.

119. Weber, Francis J., *Bob Hope Memorial Garden*. Mission Hills, CA: El Camino Real Press, 2006. 2 ⅞ x 2. 14 pp. letterpress by Patrick Reagh, gilt green letterhead by Mariana Blau. Postage stamps and wrappers. 175 copies.

120. Weber, Francis J. *Hershey*. Mission Hills, CA: El Camino Real Press, 2007. 2 ¾ x 2. 16 pp. letterpress by Patrick Reagh, brown leatherette by Mariana Blau two postage stamps plus wrapper of Hershey's Krackel.

121. Weber, Francis J. *Toward Equality in Our Schools. Mendez vs. Westminster* Mission Hills, CA, El Camino Real Press, 2007. Pp.14, 2 ¾ x 2. Postage stamp and one tipped-in photograph. 150 copies.

122. Weber, Francis J. *The Space Needle* Mission Hills, CA, El Camino Real Press, 2008. Pp.14, 2 ¾ x 2 ⅛. Postage stamp Seattle World's fair. 150 copies.

123. Weber, Francis J. *A Memoir 1959—2009,* Mission Hills, CA, El Camino Real Press, 2009. Pp.13, 2 ¾ x 2. Postage stamp 50th Anniversary, Devil's Tower. 300 copies.

124. Weber, Francis J. *Air Force One,* Mission Hills, CA, El Camino Real Press, 2009. Pp.13, 2 ⅞ x 2. Postage stamp. 50 copies.

125. Weber, Francis J. *Cezar Chavez,* Mission Hills, CA, El Camino Real Press, 2009. Pp.13, 2 ⅞ x 2 ⅛. Postage stamp frontice. 100 copies.

126. Weber, Francis J. *Benjamin Franklin,* Mission Hills, CA, El Camino Real Press, 2009. Pp 15. 2 ⅞ x 2 ⅛. Postage stamp frontice. 160 copies.

Since the initial transfer of my miniature books to the Huntington Library additional gifts have been sent to San Marino, one in 2005, another in late 2007, and a final gift in 2009.

My attendance at the Conclave in Seattle, meant to be my swan song as a member of the Miniature Book Society, resulted in the publication of a miniature book on the Space Needle. Happily however, I was able to attend the conclave in 2008 at San Diego.

10
Articles and Essays

The flow of articles and essays has diminished in quantity over the last decade. Hopefully the quality has kept apace with the pre-2000 offerings. The reason for the overall lessening is not alone age, but a realization that most of my historical goals have been accomplished.

With our acquisition of the Peter Conmy Collection, I felt that there was enough new material for another thirty years of Weber newspaper essays. Hopefully some youthful historian will take advantage of that treasure trove.

Following is a collection of essays and articles written over recent years.

Maynard Geiger

Father Maynard Geiger has always been one of my heroes. Commencing in 1934, the late and highly-esteemed Father Maynard J. Geiger (1901-1977) began keeping a meticulous daily diary in which he enumerated and described his correspondence, scholarly pursuits, Franciscan happenings, world travels, historic events and just about everything else that touched upon his busy academic and religious life.

Several times I asked him about his "hidden years," the ones between 1901 and 1934 before he inaugurated his diary, which eventually stretched into thirty-one volumes. Then one day, I think it was in 1972, there arrived in the mail a thirty-six page typescript copy of his "early life" which he asked me to file in the archives for the Archdiocese of Los Angeles. It appears to have been written in 1967.

Because of Maynard Geiger's unique place in the historiographical montage of California, I took the time to edit that manuscript for publication. It really is a charming account which tells the simple yet

Rev. Maynard Geiger, O.F.M.

fascinating story of a remarkable man who aspired for nothing else in life than being a seraphic follower of Francis of Assisi.

Poised to write, I hesitated momentarily and peered through the window of my monastic cell that opens upon the mission garden. Years of effort had been expended to make the garden a thing of beauty and a source of perennial joy. It is a noiseless spot as tranquil as the depth of a forest except when school children on a tour pass through the lower corridor chattering like liberated magpies. The colors are all pleasing: green, red, blue, gray and canary yellow, a soothing view for eyes that daily pour over ancient manuscripts. Palms and poinsettias, cactus and roses thrive in their daily, silent growth. The gray, sandstone walls of the mission church stand sturdy with age like an old fortress of faith that seems destined not to die. In the distance, across a green lawn and flowers, the old Indian workshops of earlier times have been replaced by a two story wing where, over thirty years ago, I studied theology. Red tiles redolent of the Mediterranean cover the canary yellow walls and above all is the serene, azure sky.

FRAY ESTEVAN TAPIS, O.F.M.
(1754-1825)

by Maynard J. Geiger, O.F.M.
Edited by Msgr. Francis J. Weber

REPRINT FROM
SOUTHERN CALIFORNIA QUARTERLY · VOLUME LXXX · NUMBER 4

There is a fountain in the center of the garden placed there as recently as 1872. Should not a fountain form the axis of every garden? There is music too, melodies more ancient than man, from the throats of a variety of birds that pass by here every spring ushering in the day as I awake to my daily tasks. At night when the moon is at its full, eerie shafts of light and darkness redecorate the walls and foliage after blotting out the colors of the day.

This garden has been here now for many years but it was not always precisely a garden. As a patio, it was originally without grass on its floor and lacking flowers or trees to enhance it. In mission days it was a gathering place for the natives where they were assigned their daily tasks. The lives these Indians led, as well as the history of the friars who guided and instructed them, has been the object of my interest now for many years. All are dead now and the tribe is extinct. I was privileged to bury the last full-blooded Canaliño, Tomás Ignacio Aquino, in 1952. The mission friars sleep in a crypt of the church, their passing reminiscent of the words of Sirach: "All the works of man are fugitive, and must perish the same as the rest. Yet shall their choicest works find favor, and in his work the workman shall live."

Yes, though those of earlier times are gone, but the work of their hands remain. Not only the buildings they erected but much of what they thought, said and did is preserved in the archive of which I have been custodian since 1937. By this time I feel that I know all of them personally for one cannot spend several decades on a past era without identifying with it. And communing with the dead, I discovered that they imparted wit, knowledge and wisdom to life. A document is like a tomb in its silence. But roll away the stone and there stands Lazarus come alive.

I rode with horsemen up and down *El Camino Real*. I sat with *padres* by candlelight composing their letters to governors and *presidio* commanders. I accompanied each creaking *carreta* laden with melons, pears and apples from northern missions to the governor, not forgetting the sweet oranges from Santa Barbara or an occasional cask of wine or brandy. There were moments of exaltation as well as of grief. Who could refrain from shouting *Viva* with Serra as he saw the sails of the *San Antonio* arrive at San Diego saving the day for California, or who would not join in the *Requiem* when Indians, 600 strong, came to burn that mission, clubbing Fray Luis Jayme to death as he exhorted to them: "Love God, my children!"

There were jubilant scenes as I reviewed the events of Santa Barbara in 1820, when the great *fiesta* was held upon completion of the final church edifice. There were tragic scenes too such as the crumbling of the great stone church of San Juan Capistrano in 1812 burying many who knelt in worship as the earthquake struck. With ship captains and cabin boys, *vaqueros* and *majordomos*, soldiers and muleteers as well as brave women who came here to tame the wilderness and found homes—I have traveled. Yesterday's flags and languages were different from mine, the laws and psychology were of a foreign stamp. But they were basically the same essential human beings we are today, with tears and laughter, goodness and malice and zest for life. I have touched some of their bones. Like Yorick, I knew them well.

I well recall a Wednesday afternoon in the spring of 1929. Father Patrick Roddy, O.F.M. and I were returning from our weekly walk. We had turned the corner of Los Olivos and Laguna Streets making our way to the worn front steps of the Old Mission. Our conversation had turned upon our possible future assignments, a matter of supreme interest to students about to complete their studies. I remember exactly Father Patrick's final words: "Well, as far as I'm concerned I would be content to remain in Santa Barbara for the rest of my life." My words re-echoed his and as it turned out, our wishes were realized.

The many pleasant years I've been privileged to spend in Santa Barbara, most of them within the hallowed walls of the mission, impel me to write these memories. "Count Your Blessings" is well-known song with a pointed moral. My life at the mission has been one long series of blessings that are now enshrined in my memory. These blessings have come to me as a result of being a seraphic friar and priest assigned to a particular work. All this I owe to the Franciscan Province of St. Barbara that accepted me, educated me and gave me the opportunities I have enjoyed, as well as position and status I have today.

As often as not I have been a person *from* Santa Barbara rather than a dweller *in* the city. Though assigned to the mission, I have often been away by reason of research and historical travel. But wherever I went the image of the Old Mission was with me. And no matter how long I was gone or how enticing and fruitful the travels and labors in distant parts, I counted the weeks and days when I would be back again with friendly brethren, to enjoy the common life of a Franciscan and align myself once more with the felicitous association of Santa Barbara. It is the story of my roaming abroad as well as of my periods at home that I hope to recall in these pages.

Now to identify myself for history I cannot leave my early years to assumptions, even though there is nothing in them too exciting or extraordinary. Born at Lancaster, Pennsylvania, on August 24, 1901, at 5 o'clock in the afternoon, in a home on North Reservoir Street, I was the first surviving child of Joseph and Catherine (Kray) Geiger. Lancaster is an old colonial city founded in 1734 before California became a part of the civilized world.

My parents had been married at St. Anthony's Church, Lancaster, June 12, 1895, by Father Anthony Kaul, who had founded the parish and ruled over its spiritual destinies for over fifty years. My father was a cobbler, a trade he had learned in his native Germany. He came to Lancaster as a youth of seventeen where he lived with relatives until his marriage. Upon his arrival he enrolled in night school to learn English and he learned it well, never speaking with a German accent. He had been born at Altobernodorff, near Rottweil, Wurtemburg, on June 26, 1872, the son of Joseph and Matilda (Meier) Geiger. His parents were poor and his early life was challenging, something he had in common with other Europeans. He had a fine constitution and enjoyed good health during practically his whole life. He was of medium height and stockily built. In his native land he went through a three year apprenticeship, learning his trade in the old Medieval fashion and living with his employer for whom he worked long hours. Wishing to avoid compulsory military service like many another of his countrymen, he decided to emigrate to America where he soon became a naturalized citizen.

My mother, a native of Lancaster, was born on May 4, 1873, of parents who were natives of Germany, Andrew and Margaret (Kaber) Kray. My mother was the youngest of four children. She survived her brothers and sister, dying in Los Angeles, February 16, 1960, in her eighty-seventh year. She was planning her sixty-fifth wedding anniversary, four months away. My father died at the age of ninety-three, in Los Angeles, November 22, 1963.

I was baptized on September 8, 1901, by Father Kaul, at St. Anthony's Church, Lancaster. My aunt Mary and uncle Andrew were the sponsors. My sisters, Mary, Catherine, Margaret and Loreta, were all born in Lancaster, whereas by brother Anthony was a native of Los Angeles.

My parents journeyed to Europe in 1900 visiting Belgium, Germany and Switzerland, where they spent six months. It was an extended wedding trip, but its final goal was that of a pilgrimage. The crowning point of their visit was the beautiful town of Einsielden, Switzerland, where is located the famous Benedictine Abbey of Our Lady of the Hermits. Having lost several babies in birth, my mother had recourse to prayer for children that would survive. On the anniversary of their return from Europe, I was born.

In Lancaster, my parents occupied a brick house at Duke and Locust Streets where they generated a store. Later they moved to a better neighborhood at 429 South Shippen Street. They owned both homes. I remember the first for only a few incidents. My uncle Andrew resided with us and lived on a modest income from his properties. He was an avid reader and I well remember the morning he recounted to me the disaster of the San Francisco earthquake and fire, April 18, 1906. I was then four and a half years old. Another recollection recalls the day I placed my left index finger into a cigar cutter and chipped off some flesh, a slight scar of which remained throughout my life.

It was from the Shippen Street house, however, that I retain most of my memories. From there I entered St. Anthony's Parochial School, taught by the Holy Cross Sisters of Notre Dame, Indiana. At St. Anthony's I was confirmed by Bishop Shanahan of Harrisburg on March 26 and made my First Holy Communion on April 23, 1910. That was the first year that the new legislation on early Communion, inaugurated by Pope St. Pius X, was put into effect. I happened to be the first of the class to become a Mass server in the parish church.

I do not recall my initial day in school, but we always had plenty of homework. I was somewhat slow at arithmetic but geography was a walk-away. Maps fascinated me from my earliest days. In later classes, I received high percentages in grammar, and early showed an interest in languages. I have nothing but the highest regard for the good nuns who taught reading, writing and arithmetic, the fundamentals upon which all subsequent education was built.

MOST REVEREND

JOSEPH THOMAS McGUCKEN, S.T.D.

Fifth Archbishop of San Francisco

March 13, 1902 - October 26, 1983

Eternal Rest Grant unto Him, O Lord

Though she had only six years of schooling herself, my mother was generous in helping us with homework. I found difficulty in learning certain big words in the catechism, one in particular, Extreme Unction, today called the Anointing of the Sick. Mother told me to think of three smaller words: "ax," "tree" and "monk." Later I learned the practice of association . . ..

Those who might want to continue this interesting saga can find the full text in *La Gazeta* (Winter 2000 — Spring 2007) which is published by the Friends of the Santa Barbara Mission Archives.

Archbishop Joseph T. McGucken

In 2003, Deacon Jeff Burns, the archivist for the Archdiocese of San Francisco announced a series of essays for the 150th anniversary of the archdiocese. I was asked to do the article on Archbishop Joseph T. McGucken which then appeared in the March 14, 2003 issue of *Catholic California.* It was later incorporated into a booklet entitled *Catholic San Francisco: Sesquicentennial Essays* from which this lengthy essay is excerpted.

Of the seven archbishops of San Francisco, only the first, Joseph Sadoc Alemany and the fifth, Joseph Thomas McGucken served in all the ecclesial districts or jurisdictions of what now comprises the State of California. McGucken served as auxiliary bishop of his home archdiocese of Los Angeles, administrator of the diocese of Monterey-Fresno, Bishop of Sacramento and finally, from 1962—1977, as Archbishop of San Francisco.

Joseph Thomas McGucken, the only son of Joseph A. McGucken and Mary Agnes Flynn, was born in a small residence near his grandfather's store at Seventh and Mateo Streets in Los Angeles. Shortly after his birth, on March 13, 1902, the youngster was baptized in St. Vibiana's Cathedral. Ireland figured prominently in the boy's background. His maternal grandfather came from Castleistand, County Kerry, ancestral home of the Flynns. Not long after Joseph's father died, his grandfather, moved the family from their home near the Fourth Street viaduct to more commodious surroundings at Wadsworth and 32nd Streets.

The youngster's early life was profoundly influenced by his grandfather who transported the boy about town on his grocery wagon. Joseph grew up in St. Patrick's Parish in Los Angeles under the watchful eye of Father Patrick O'Donoghue, who saw the young boy enrolled in the parochial school operated by the Sisters of St. Joseph of Carondelet. After completion of his primary education, Joseph entered Los Angeles Polytechnic High School, which at that time was the only institution in the Southland offering courses in electrical engineering.

Intellectual opportunities widened four years later when he transferred to the Vermont Avenue campus of the southern branch of the

University of California. In 1922, the, collegian expressed a desire to study for the priesthood. Father Francis Ott gave him and Alden J. Bell, later his successor as Bishop of Sacramento, private lessons in Latin, and made arrangements for their entry into St. Patrick's Seminary at Menlo Park.

At the recommendation of the Very Rev. Henry A. Ayrinhac, seminary rector, Bishop John J. Cantwell offered the seminarian the opportunity of completing his studies in Rome. It was a time when Pope Pius XI, then in the early years of an eventful pontificate, was taking the first steps towards restoring papal freedom during the Mussolini regime. While in Rome, Joseph lived at the old North American College. Although the North American College was known for the high percentage of its graduates who subsequently became members of the hierarchy, only two of Joseph McGucken's class of fifty—eight achieved that distinction: McGucken and Floyd L. Begin, who became Bishop of Oakland. The Los Angeles seminarian attended classes at the Urban College of Propaganda Fide, studying under such luminaries as Ernesto Ruffini and Gregory Agagianian, later to gain acclaim as distinguished members of the College of Cardinals. Joseph McGucken was ordained in the seminary chapel adjacent to St. John Lateran Basilica on January 15, 1928, by the Viceregent of Rome, the Most Rev Giuseppe Patica, Titular Archbishop of Philippi. The following July, Father McGucken was one of eighteen priests in his class to qualify for and obtain the doctorate in Sacred Theology.

Upon his return to Los Angeles, the newly ordained priest was named temporary administrator of Holy Trinity Parish in Atwater Park. In October of 1928, he assumed the duties of curate at St. Vibiana's Cathedral where he stayed until being transferred to Cathedral Chapel Parish on La Brea Avenue. In November of 1929, Bishop Cantwell named Fr. McGucken his private secretary, and for the next fifteen years he lived with the Southern California prelate in the episcopal residence. It was a mutually beneficial association, for the young priest's innate sense of humor proved an ideal tonic for the heavily burdened bishop of a widely scattered flock. On the other hand, the mark of Cantwell's influence on his secretary during those formative years was plainly obvious.

On Oct. 31,1938, a year after his appointment as papal chamberlain, Msgr. McGucken was named chancellor for the Archdiocese of Los Angeles and in June of the following year, he was advanced to the domestic prelacy. Though each step involved greater duties, the monsignor maintained a keen interest in the historical setting and development of Catholic life in the west, and in 1940 he wrote an informative article, "The Golden Fields of California," which appeared in *Extension Magazine.* Some years later, he showed his sustained concern for the subject by becoming a charter member of the Academy of California Church History.

An important part of this history took place when the growing Los Angeles jurisdiction, since 1936 a metropolitan seat, necessitated the appointment of an auxiliary bishop. It came as no surprise when Msgr. McGucken was named to the Titular See of Sanavo by Pope Pius XII, on February 4, 1941. The eighth native Californian named to the hierarchy received Episcopal ordination from Archbishop John J. Cantwell on the Feast of Saint

Joseph in 1941. By an interesting design of Divine Providence, the three prelates whom the new bishop would eventually succeed in Monterey-Fresno, Sacramento and San Francisco, were present in the sanctuary of St. Vibiana's Cathedral on that Wednesday morning for the ceremony.

The added cares of the episcopate multiplied Bishop McGucken's activities considerably. Archbishop Cantwell was advanced in years and anxious to turn over the more demanding tasks to his auxiliary. On February 19, 1944, Bishop McGucken was made pastor of St. Andrew's Church in Pasadena where, in addition to his other commitments, he took an active part in the various parochial functions of the Crown City's mother church. He divided the parish in sections, one for each of three assistants, supervised a census of the widespread area and instructed the curates to spend several hours a day making house-to-house visitations. Under his direction, enrollment in Confraternity of Christian Doctrine classes was tripled and special attention was given to the mission station of Our Lady of Guadalupe located within the parochial boundaries. The beautiful church begun by his predecessor was completed, and a new high school, grammar school and convent were built. Besides taking a personal interest in all these activities, Bishop McGucken participated in local civic affairs, even serving for a time as a member of the Board of Directors for the nearby Southwest Museum.

His multiple parish duties did not diminish the prelate's concern for other activities. As chancellor, and later as vicar general, the Los Angeles auxiliary was personally in charge of much of the planning for the two seminaries erected in the archdiocese: one at Camarillo in 1939, the other adjacent to San Fernando Mission in 1954.

Because of the serious illness affecting Bishop Philip Scher of Monterey-Fresno, Pope Pius XII, on September 24, 1946, named Bishop McGucken apostolic administrator of the Central California diocese, a position he held for four months until plans were formalized for appointment of a coadjutor.

At Cantwell's passing on October 30, 1947, the archdiocesan consultors selected Bishop McGucken as administrator for the Los Angeles jurisdiction. When the new metropolitan, the Most Rev. J. Francis A. McIntyre, was installed on March 19, 1948, Bishop McGucken was made vicar general.

While attending the investiture of Archbishop J. Francis A. McIntyre as cardinal, during January of 1953, the auxiliary bishop of Los Angeles quietly observed the silver jubilee of his ordination to the priesthood at the tomb of St. Peter where he had celebrated his first Mass. Two years later, Bishop McGucken accompanied Francis Cardinal Spellman and 329 pilgrims to the 36th International Eucharistic Congress in Rio de Janeiro. At the conclusion of the liturgical ceremonies, Bishop McGucken, representing the administrative board of the National Catholic Welfare Conference, attended the General Assembly of the Latin America episcopate called by Pius XII on July 25, 1955.

In the political sphere, the Southland auxiliary bishop was active in the campaign to remove the tax burden from California's parochial schools.

In addition to coordinating activities at the district level, he appeared a number of times before the Los Angeles Board of Supervisors on behalf of the educational program of the archdiocese.

On October 26, 1955 Bishop McGucken was sent to Sacramento as coadjutor, with right of succession, to the ailing Robert Armstrong. Upon the death of Armstrong, McGucken became the fifth bishop of Sacramento. He sounded a clarion call for vocations to the priesthood and the religious life; he focused attention on the need for a new diocesan seminary to replace the temporary structure at Rio Dell; he pressed for the expansion of the Catholic school system and for the intensification of the Confraternity of Christian Doctrine programs and he anticipated Vatican Council II with plans for spiritual renewal and the promotion of the lay apostolate.

How well Bishop McGucken succeeded in realizing his ideals becomes evident upon perusal of his achievements during the seventy-six months of his Sacramento episcopate. During that time, a veritable host of diocesan structures made their appearance along the Gold Dust trails, including churches (nine of them for new parishes), schools, rectories, convents and parochial halls, all of them sturdy and attractive buildings. His crowning achievement was the St. Pius X Seminary in Galt in which he was deeply interested.

These accomplishments were made possible by a corps of dedicated priests, religious and laity, all of whom were inspired by the leadership of their beloved bishop whose life's work and example forged a bond of diocesan solidarity.

On February 1,1962, Pope John XXIII appointed Joseph McGucken to succeed Archbishop John J. Mitty of San Francisco. He was installed on April 3, 1962, as the fifth Archbishop of San Francisco. He was the first native Californian appointed to that position, which he was destined to hold for fifteen turbulent years of ecclesial history.

One of the new archbishop's earliest tasks was the planning and financing of the new St. Mary's Cathedral to replace the old Van Ness Avenue Church which was destroyed by fire five months after his arrival. Despite the difficulties encountered and the archbishop's involvement in the sessions of Vatican Council II, the new cathedral at Gough and Geary Boulevard opened in 1970, a veritable monument to its great builder. In the meantime on March 19, 1966, McGucken was honored by the Holy Father by being appointed an Assistant at the Pontifical Throne.

Living up to his reputation as a diligent, hardworking shepherd, McGucken established fifteen new parishes, two missions, two high schools and seventeen grammar schools. He encouraged the building of three Catholic hospitals, all of this amid the climate of challenge and confrontation that marked the post conciliar period. Undaunted, he pressed on though, in due course, he began to show signs of his advancing years as well as the ill effects of an attack one evening by an assailant as he took his customary neighborhood walk.

On February 22, 1977, having nearly reached the recommended age of retirement for bishops, Joseph McGucken relinquished the heavy burdens

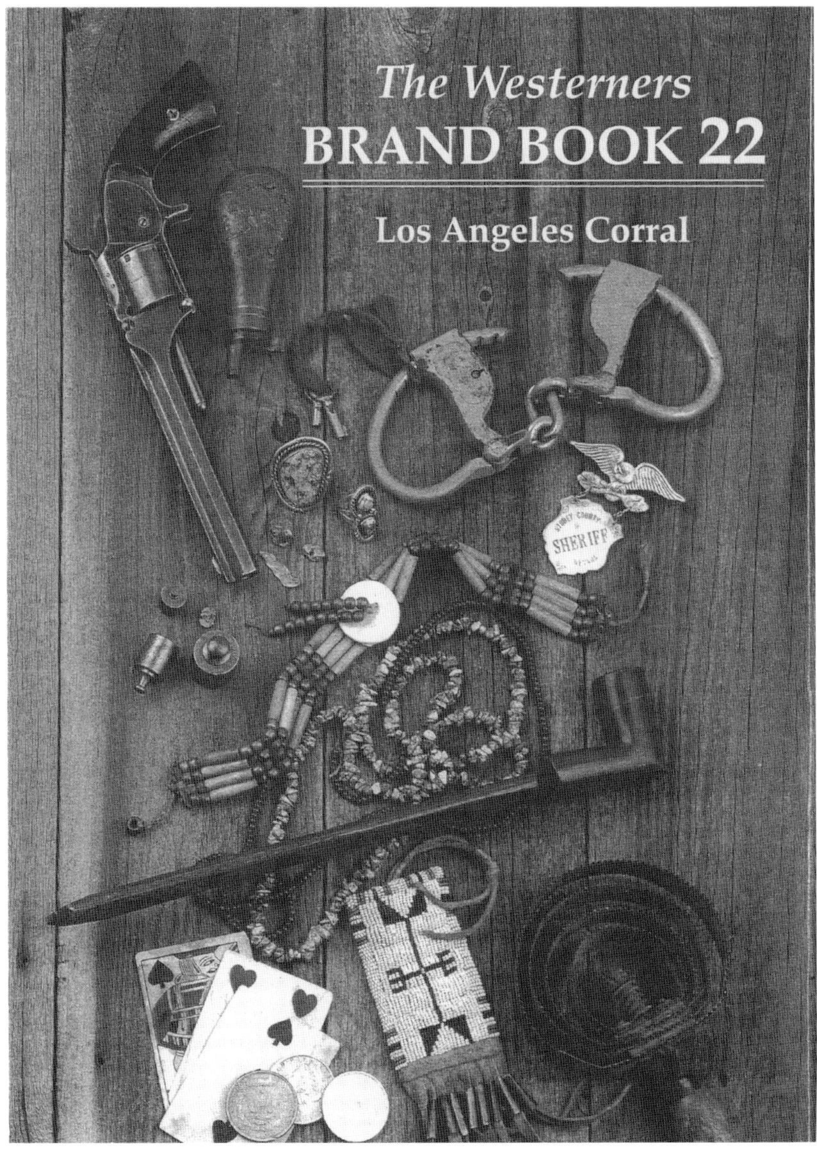

of his office and took up residence at St. Brendan's Church with his friend and one-time chancellor, Monsignor Donnell Walsh. There he maintained an interest in archdiocesan affairs and made himself available for parish priestly ministry.

Finally, suffering from a lung ailment, he entered St. Mary's Hospital where he passed peacefully to his eternal reward on October 26, 1983. His funeral services were held at St. Mary's Cathedral after which his mortal remains were taken to Holy Cross Cemetery in Colma where they await the resurrection.

There were those who decried McGucken's indecisiveness and some who disagreed with certain of his policies, but no one ever disliked the man because he epitomized what shepherdhood was all about. He was a churchman who lived totally and only for his flock and he always sought their best interest. He was intelligent, kindly, understanding, jovial and honest, a combination of virtues rare at any level of the priestly ministry.

Brand Book 22

In 2004, I wrote a lengthy essay on the California Missions for *Brand Book 22*, the annual publication of the Los Angeles Corral of Westerners. It is here reproduced in its entirety because most readers have no access to the *Brand Books*.

Surely the most distinctive feature of Alta California is its chain of twenty-one Missions established along *El Camino Real* from San Diego to San Francisco Solano. Those who keep records report that the missions still are the most visited by Californians and travelers; the most featured in casual and serious books, magazines and newspapers; the most honored by awards, citations and plaques; the most studied about by researchers and historians; the most copied by architects and builders; the most celebrated on postage stamps (five nations), the most written about by historians, novelists and playwrights; the most photographed of any buildings in the United States; the most toured by private and public school youngsters and the most adaptive and versatile of all the New World's reduction systems.

The missions in the Golden State in the world can best be understood and appreciated within the context of the times and areas in which they existed, in the values of those who staffed and supported them, and in the reception and response of those who profited by their existence. Like all noble efforts, the missions are not without their detractors. This writer has addressed some of those questions in the pages of the *Branding Iron*, published by the Los Angeles Corral of Westerners. This presentation restricts itself to a basic historical sketch of the twenty-one foundations arranged in the chronological sequence of their establishment between 1769 and 1823.

TITLE	FOUNDED	PATENTED
1. San Diego de Alcala	1769 (moved 1774))	May 23, 1862
2. San Carlos Borromeo	1770 (moved 1771)	October 19, 1859
3. San Antonio de Padua	1771 (moved 1773)	May 31, 1862
4. San Gabriel Arcangel	1771 (moved 1775)	November 19, 1859

5. San Luis Obispo	1772	September 2, 1859
6. San Francisco de Asis	1776	March 3, 1858
7. San Juan Capistrano	1775 (refound. 1776)	March 18, 1865
8. Santa Clara de Asis	1777 (moved 1779)	March 3, 1858
9. San Buenaventura	1782	May 23, 1862
10. Santa Barbara	1786	March 18, 1865
11. La Purisima Conception	1787 (moved 1813)	January 24, 1874
12. Santa Cruz	1791	September 2, 1859
13. Nuestra Senora de la Soledad	1791 (moved 1791)	November 19, 1859
14. San Jose	1797	March 3, 1858
15. San Juan Bautista	1797	November 19, 1859
16. San Miguel Arcangel	1797	September 2, 1859
17. San Fernando Rey de Espana	1797	May 13,1862
18. San Luis Rey de Francia	1798	March 18, 1865
19. Santa Ines	1804	May 23, 1862
20. San Rafael Arcangel	1817	October 19, 1859
21. San Francisco Solano	1823	May 31, 1862

1. San Diego de Alcala 1769

On July 1,1769, Fray Junípero Serra and Gaspar de Portola arrived in San Diego after a journey of forty-six days from the last of the peninsular missions, San Fernando de Velicata. While Portola moved on to search for the elusive Monterey harbor, Serra established the first mission in Alta California, placing it under the patronage of San Diego de Alcala. By the time of his return, Portola found the tiny settlement dangerously low on provisions. He decided that San Diego would have to be abandoned if supplies did not arrive by the Feast of Saint Joseph. The prayers of Serra and others were answered and the proto mission was assured of permanence.

Due mostly to the shortage of water and the proximity of the military camp, the mission was moved from Presidio Hill to its present site in 1774. On November 4th of the following year, a group of dissidents attacked the mission, killing Fray Luis Jayme and destroying many of the structures. The intervention of Fray Junípero Serra on behalf of the culprits did much to establish lasting peace at San Diego and within a few months, the outpost was once again a functioning and prospering establishment along *El Camino Real*.

At the peak of its prosperity, before the blight of premature secularization, there were 20,000 sheep and 10,000 head of cattle on the vast acreage of San Diego Mission. Its wines had become famous and its olive trees formed the mother orchard for the area's olive industry. Water for the vineyards and orchard—was conveyed by aqueduct from the San Diego River.

On June 14, 1846, Fray Vicente Pasqual Oliva closed the second volume of the *Libro de Bautismos* with its 7,126th entry, that of Jose Antonio de la Luz. That same year, Governor Pio Pico sold the mission to Santiago Arguello, but it was not until 1862 that twenty-two acres were restored to the Church.

On September 13, 1931, ceremonies were held at San Diego to mark the rededication of Alta California's proto mission. In his address for that occasion, Bishop John J. Mitty noted that "this is a holy spot; it has been sanctified by the prayers and labors of heroic people of God."

2. San Carlos Borromeo 1770

The initial site of the missionary outpost dedicated to San Carlos Borromeo overlooked the beautiful Bay of Monterey. On Pentecost Sunday, June 3, 1770, while bells rang, cannons fired and muskets saluted, the founding ceremony concluded with the traditional chanting of the *Te Deum Laudamus.*

A military *presidio* was also established, but it provided so many challenges to effective evangelization work that the mission was moved some miles inland to its present site on the Carmel River in 1771.

Because of its location, San Carlos is widely known as the Carmel Mission. Fray Junípero Serra made it his headquarters and from an adjacent hut the great missionary directed the affairs of the growing missionary chain. After secularization, San Carlos fell into disrepair until it was almost completely in ruins.

Although the earthly remains of the saintly friar reposed in the church's sanctuary, the title to the property eventually passed into profane hands. It was restored to the Catholic Church by President James Buchanan in 1859. After extensive repairs had been made, the old church was rededicated on August 28, 1884, one hundred years after Serra's death.

It was not until 1924 that a further series of restorations was undertaken, and eventually the mission became a thriving parish church. Harry W. Downie, an authority on mission architecture and reconstruction, was mainly responsible for transforming San Carlos into an outstanding California landmark.

Today, the numerous visitors to Mission San Carlos are captivated by the spirit of Serra and the early mission days, which pervades the premises. A wide assortment of historical treasures and artistic reproductions provide an authentic setting of the original mission. The use of stone in the construction of the church, built under the direction of Fray Fermin Francisco de Lasuen, was an unusual departure from the adobe used in most of the other contemporary missions.

3. San Antonio de Padua 1771

Encircled by the picturesque mountains of the Santa Lucia range, the Valley of the Oaks rests in singular splendor. Near a small stream, Fray Junípero Serra celebrated Mass July 14, 1771, in the presence of several companions and a lone Indian. On the same day, he established his third mission which he named San Antonio de Padua. "Here I will build the fist shrine of Saint Anthony," he exclaimed as he called upon the gentiles to come and hear the word of God.

The Jolon Indians responded well and within three years some 178 neophytes had been gathered together. By the time Juan de Anza stopped in 1774, a church and many dwellings and workshops had been erected. The present church was completed in 1813, but neglect and vandalism after secularization eventually reduced it to ruins. Happily, its continuance as a spiritual force was never fully thwarted.

The prosperity of the mission was indicated by the use of irrigation, construction of a water mill for grinding flour and the raising of golden colored horses known as *palominos*. Vast orchards and vineyards produced abundant fruit and wine, and livestock numbering upwards of 20,000. After secularization, all this rapidly disintegrated until only the church and a few arches remained. In 1862, President Abraham Lincoln restored the property to the Church, and, in 1929, the Franciscans returned to the mission. Bishop Aloysius Willinger, with the help of the William R. Hearst Foundation, initiated a rebuilding program in 1948.

Today, the mission stands rebuilt along the lines of its ancient beauty as it looked in its heyday. The bell that rings across the Valley of the Oaks is said to be more than 250 years old and the statue of Saint Anthony, before which Indians prayed, hovers above the church's sanctuary. The mission is located about twenty miles south of King City, near the Hunter Liggett Military Reservation.

4. San Gabriel Arcangel 1771

The founding of San Gabriel Archangel Mission dates from the determination of Fray Junípero Serra to locate an outpost midway between San Diego and San Carlos Borromeo. Thus the fourth mission had its beginning on September 8, 1771, some four and a half miles southeast of its present location. The selection of a new site was most fortunate, for it enabled San Gabriel to become one of the most prosperous of all the frontier outposts in Alta California, perched at the early crossroads from Mexico and the United States.

The first land link with Sonora was completed when Juan Bautista de Anza arrived on March 22, 1774, with an exploring party, and on January 2, 1776, returned with a group of colonists bound for San Francisco.

In the latter year, the mission was moved to its present site. Fifty years later, the first of the famous mountain men, Jedediah Smith, with a party of trappers, blazed a trail across the desert. Given a generous reception at San Gabriel, Smith called "Old Father Sanchus" (Fray Jose Sanchez) his "greatest friend." After that, numerous overland parties visited the well-known mission. Within a few years after the arrival of the mountain men" San Gabriel and its entire inventory was turned over to a civil administrator and, within less than ten years, little of value remained.

The relationship of San Gabriel with the City of Los Angeles dates from the arrival of forty-four *pobladores* accompanied by a company of soldiers, who crossed the *Rio Portiuncula* and founded the *Pueblo de Nuestra Señnora de Los Angeles de Porciuncula*. This historic event took place on September 4, 1781, just a decade after the establishment of the mission.

For years, San Gabriel was the spiritual center of the community. The last Franciscans withdrew in 1852 and five years later, President James Buchanan returned the property to the church. The Claretian Fathers have administered the mission as a parish since 1908. It remains a scenic spot for visitors who find there interesting Indian art, paintings, statuary and a hammered copper baptismal font donated by King Carlos of Spain.

5. San Luis Obispo 1772

Almost midway between Los Angeles and San Francisco stands the mission dedicated to San Luis Obispo de Tolosa. It was founded by Fray Junípero Serra September 1, 1772, his fifth missionary outpost in Alta California. The picturesque location had favorably impressed him during his first trip from San Diego.

The early diarist, Fray Juan Crespi, described the location as a broad vista known as the *Canada de los Osos* or Valley of the Bears. It was in this region that Governor Pedro Fages staged the famous bear hunt that saved the missions from starvation in 1772.

Fray Jose Cavaller was placed in charge. With only five soldiers and two Indian neophytes, he began the construction of a chapel and other buildings made of poles and roofed with tule grass. The mission was set afire several times by hostile Indians and, on one occasion, everything but the chapel and granary was burned to the ground. Then the friars got the notion of baking clay in the sun and making tile roofs, which became the practice of the other missions. After seventeen years of service, Cavaller died December 9, 1789, and was buried near the sanctuary railing of the church.

Although the mission prospered, it never enjoyed a large population. The last entry in the baptismal register in 1841 was No. 2909. As early as 1830, five years before secularization took place, the neophyte village was almost in ruins and the front of the church, which was completed in 1793, was in such disrepair it had to be taken down.

In 1844, the neophytes lost their affiliation and the mission was declared a *pueblo*. Governor Pio Pico sold the entire property for a paltry $510 in 1845. Fourteen years later, the United States Government returned it to the Bishop of Monterey and restoration of the church was commenced. While misguided remodelers altered its historic beauty, later modifications resulted in a somewhat faithful restoration of the original edifice.

6. San Francisco de Asis 1776

Immediately after Juan Bautista de Anza arrived at Monterey with 240 colonists from Sonora early in 1776, he proceeded up the peninsula and selected sites for the future *presidio* and mission of San Francisco. Seven years earlier the first white man beheld "the great arm of the sea" and only the year before, Captain Juan Bautista de Ayala brought the first vessel through the Golden Gate.

San Francisco de Asis, or Mission Dolores, founded by Junípero Serra on October 9, 1776, was his sixth mission. When plans for the missions in Alta California were originally made, the *Presidente* asked: "And for our founder, there is none?" Jose de Galvez reportedly stated that, "If Saint Francis desires a mission, let him show us his harbor, and he will have one." Although the mission's official name is San Francisco de Asis, it is more popularly known in the chronicles as Mission Dolores, located as it was on a long, dried-up lake.

When Lieutenant Jose Moraga led the colonists up a creek called *Arroyo de los Dolores*, Fray Francisco Palou celebrated the first Mass in a little arbor, just prior to the first Fourth of July. Shortly thereafter, timbers were cut for the initial church, about one-half mile northwest of the present structure. The cornerstone of that church was laid April 25th, 1782. The mission became an important center in the Bay area and was visited by George Vancouver and many other explorers. By the time the American flag was raised at San Francisco in 1846, the mission was partially in ruins.

When secularization began, chroniclers placed the valuation of Mission Dolores at a fraction of its real worth. A fraudulent title to the property by Governor Pio Pico was voided and the mission was later restored to the Archbishopric of San Francisco, but the records do not show what final disposition was made of the surrounding mission lands.

7. San Juan Capistrano 1775

The bells of historic San Juan Capistrano Mission rang out for the first time on All Saints Day in 1776, four months after the signing of the Declaration of Independence by the thirteen American colonies. Today, those same bells still beckon parishioners and visitors to weekday and Sunday Masses.

It was the seventh mission to be founded by the Franciscans under Fray Junípero Serra, in the devoted crusade for civilizing and Christianizing the native peoples of California. The friars built well. Their aqueducts, storm drains and cisterns are still usable. Laboratory experiments made on the tile walls of the smelter kilns indicate that temperatures of 2200°F were obtained in the smelting of metals, a great engineering feat even in modern times.

The brightest facet of San Juan Capistrano, the jewel of the missions, was its church. Begun in 1797, it was thought to be the most magnificent in all California. Its arched roof of seven domes had sheltered Indian neophytes for less than a decade when a tragic earthquake leveled the beautiful structure in 1812, leaving only part of one dome and the sanctuary wall standing. Today, a modern replica church serves the area.

The mission itself has been restored for many years to its early dimensions, a wonderland of quaint and lovely scenes. San Juan Capistrano is located in a thriving town bearing the same name, in Orange County, fifty-six miles south of Los Angeles along the old Santa Fe Railway. It serves as the parish church for Catholic families residing in the vicinity.

8. Santa Clara de Asis 1777

The penultimate mission founded during Fray Junípero Serra's lifetime and the last church to be dedicated by him, was that of Santa Clara de Asis. Located immediately south of San Francisco Bay, it was placed under the patronage of the foundress of the Poor Clares on January 12, 1777. During that summer, Lieutenant Jose Moraga arrived from San Gabriel with a group of colonists to establish a *pueblo* in the vicinity, the present city of San Jose.

Like many of the California missions, Santa Clara suffered many changes. Heavy rains necessitated removal from the original site in 1779. The old church, dedicated by Fray Junípero Serra, May 16,1784, was badly damaged by earthquakes in 1812 and some years later it was replaced by another edifice. The mission was withering away under secularization when it was assigned to the care of the Society of Jesus who opened Santa Clara University in 1851. After a series of restorations, the present church resembles numerous features of the original structure.

Remains of other buildings of the historic establishment exist in the form of adobe walls, which give a picturesque grandeur to the university grounds. Rich in relics and archival materials from the period of spoliation, historic memorabilia include paintings, furniture, vestments and a crucifix that belonged to the saintly Franciscan, Fray Magin Catala. The Serra Cross in front of the church, made of old rafters, contains encased an authenticated relic of the original mission cross behind a small glass pane. Mounted on a cement pedestal, it bears the inscription: "November 19, 1781. Second site of Mission Santa Clara."

9. San Buenaventura 1782

Delayed for numerous years, the establishment of San Buenaventura Mission came at last on Easter Sunday, 1782. It was an aging and infirm Fray Junípero Serra who traveled north from San Gabriel to officiate at the founding of the ninth in California's chain of twenty-one missions. Little more than two years later he died, after thirty-four years of missionary labors in the New Spain, fourteen of these having been spent in California.

San Buenaventura became one of the most enduring of the missionary establishments. Except for the month of December 1818, when the friars moved the natives to nearby hills because of Argentinean pirates then ravaging the area, the mission afforded its people uninterrupted religious services.

Despite rebuilding and restoration, the church that serves modern-day San Buenaventura is the same as that dedicated September 9, 1809. Fifteen years in the building, the church's walls are six and one-half feet thick. The earthquake in 1812 rendered the buildings unsafe for almost half a year.

San Buenaventura has a treasure of antique statuary and ecclesial furnishings. In a central niche on the main altar stands a statue of Saint Buenaventura brought there in 1801. From its belfry comes the toll of bells cast between 1781 and 1815. Still in use is the mission's original baptismal font.

To the right of San Buenaventura's main altar is an historic painting of Our Lady of Guadalupe. San Buenaventura was the only mission to have wooden bells, one of which can still be seen in the museum. The scenic beauty of what is now Ventura County, a verdant valley bordered by mountains and ocean, motivated Fray Junípero Serra to establish a mission where today there are a host of parishes and schools.

10. Santa Barbara 1786

The frontier outpost of Santa Barbara, the "Queen of the Missions," is one of the most notable shrines of Christianity in the West. Its historic twin towers, ancient stone fountain in front, museum rooms and cemetery garden are redolent of all that was historic, beautiful and artistic in early California.

The tenth mission established in the Golden State, it was the first founded by Fray Fermin Francisco de Lasuen in his role as *Presidente*. Founded on the Feast of Santa Barbara, 1786, this mission is the only one served uninterruptedly by the Friars Minor to the present time.

In 1842, the first Bishop of Both Californias, Fray Francisco Garcia Diego, took up residence at the mission. Upon his death, he was entombed in a vault beneath the sanctuary of the church, which houses many of the early day friars, as well as Governor Jose Figueroa.

Santa Barbara Mission possesses a vast store of historical material relating to the life and work of Fray Junípero Serra and it is the headquarters of those who direct the cause of his canonization. Second to the nation's Capitol, the Old Mission is among the most photographed buildings in the United States. The cornerstone plaque at Santa Barbara Mission commemorates the founding in 1786, its devastation by earthquakes in 1812 and 1925 and its restoration in 1927 and 1953.

11. La Purisima Concepcion 1787

Although it was part of Fray Junípero Serra's original plan to erect a mission midway between San Luis Obispo and Santa Barbara, it remained for his successor to establish it. This took place on December 8, 1787, shortly after the United States Constitutional Convention and one year after Santa Barbara Mission was founded.

Named La Purisima Concepcion in honor of Mary's Immaculate Conception, the mission became a center for teaching the industrial arts. In 1803, Fray Mariano Payeras was placed in charge and, during the remaining twenty years of his life, he developed a flourishing mission.

Disaster in the form of a severe earthquake in 1812 leveled the buildings, including the church, which had been completed in 1802. The friars then moved the foundation northeast across the Santa Ines River and erected a long, narrow adobe structure and two other buildings.

Although Fray Mariano Payeras was later named *Presidente* of the California missions, he remained at La Purisima. Following his death in 1823, a serious revolt took place, from which the mission never fully recovered. Ten years later, fewer than 350 neophytes remained and the number of livestock had diminished substantially. After secularization, maladministration resulted in the sale of all the mission property for a paltry financial payment. Restored to the church by the United States Land Commission, the buildings subsequently passed into private hands and ultimately became heaps of rubble.

In 1935, after the Federal Government acquired the lands and the ruins, the work of reconstruction began. Painstaking research and skillful craftsmanship resulted in a faithful reproduction which incorporated the new building into what was left of the crumbling walls. Exact reproductions of carved mission furniture may now be seen in the State Historical Park near Lompoc.

12. Santa Cruz 1791

Santa Cruz Mission was founded August 28, 1791, on the seventh anniversary of Fray Junípero Serra's death. Fray Fermin Lasuen raised the cross and offered the first Mass for the twelfth California mission, which was located twenty-five miles directly north of San Carlos Borromeo across the Bay of Monterey. Formal ceremonies took place September 25.

In 1797, Governor Diego Borica established the town of Branciforte opposite the mission on the San Lorenzo River. The *Presidente* complained bitterly, that the mission could not prosper near a *pueblo* settlement.

The site for Santa Cruz was well chosen. Its soil and climate were excellent and the Indians were exceedingly receptive. Yet, five years after its founding, the mission had reached its zenith. Of the 500 neophytes in 1796, less than half remained by the end of the century. The town and even its name disappeared, but it lasted long enough to compromise the success of the mission.

The initial church of 1794 was damaged by a violent storm and flood and, five years later, had to be rebuilt. That restored church, the model for the contemporary replica, was completely destroyed by an earthquake on January 9, 1857. Bishop Thaddeus Amat acquired 16.9 acres of the original property two years later. The present brick church was completed on the original site in 1891. Some 250 feet away stands the smaller replica built by Gladys Sullivan Doyle.

When the property was secularized in 1835, it was valued at $50,000. Four years later, Inspector William E. P. Hartnell found only seventy Indians and a small portion of the livestock. Of the original buildings, little remains today beyond the original baptismal font, some statues and paintings.

13. Nuestra Señora de la Soledad 1791

The mission bearing the patronage of Nuestra Señora de la Soledad served as an important link and contributed greatly to the development of the Salinas Valley during the Franciscan era. Fray Fermin de Lasuen decided that a mission was needed midway between San Antonio and Carmel. A site was chosen in the treeless valley and the establishment was launched on October 9, 1791, only a few weeks after the foundation of Santa Cruz Mission.

The precedent for the patronage of Our Lady of Solitude stems from the historic expedition of Gaspar de Portola in 1769. During an encampment at this spot, Fray Juan Crespi opined that it would be a good place for a mission; An Indian who visited the camp uttered a word sounding like "*soledad*," the Spanish term for loneliness.

Soledad was never an imposing structure as were some of the other missions. The brushwood shelter, dedicated in 1791, was not replaced by adobe until several years later. There was little need for a large church because the number of Indian neophytes never exceeded 700. Even with little rain, scarcity of food and much sickness, the lonely mission survived until secularization in 1835. In May of that year, Fray Vicente de Sarria's emaciated body was found at the door of the church. He was transported over the hills for burial at San Antonio Mission, leaving behind a deserted Soledad, which came to be known as the outpost where a friar starved to death. Gradually, the remaining structures melted into ruins and desolation.

In 1846, the lands were alienated. By the time the United States Government returned ownership to the Church most of the habitations had disappeared. The Native Daughters of the Golden West sponsored rebuilding of the chapel which was dedicated October 9, 1955.

14. San Jose 1797

Overlooking the southern end of San Francisco Bay, a site fifteen miles north of the *pueblo* San Jose was selected by Fray Fermin Francisco de Lasuen for the fourteenth of the California missions in June, 1797. Dedicated to San Jose, the mission at first consisted of small wooden structures roofed with tule and grasses stitched together by Indians. While it was never comparable in size or magnificence with the other missions, it occupies a significant place in California history. During the gold rush it was converted into a trading post for miners and was described in glowing terms by visitors.

After a slow start,. the mission had nearly 2,000 Indian neophytes and tens of thousands of livestock by 1831. Six years later, the properties were evaluated at $155,000. Within two years after secularization its assets had been completely dissipated. The United States Government nullified sale of the land by Pio Pico and twenty-eight acres were subsequently returned to the Church.

The name of Fray Narciso Duran will forever be associated with San Jose Mission. Arriving in 1806, he remained for twenty-seven years during which time an adobe church and workshops were built. An accomplished musician, Duran trained an Indian orchestra with homemade instruments which they played on festive occasions. There was never a dull moment at the mission, located among occasionally hostile tribes. By the time Duran became *Presidente* in 1830, an office he held until his death in 1846, the mission system was already doomed.

Today, only a few rooms of the adobe monastery, a grove of olive trees and a replica church remain as the living memory of the historic premises.

15. San Juan Bautista 1797

Less than two weeks after founding San Jose Mission, Fray Fermin de Lasuen moved into a little valley midway between San Carlos and Santa Clara. Here, on June 24, 1797, the feast of Saint John the Baptist, he planted the cross for Mission San Juan Bautista. Within six months there were several adobe buildings which included a church and monastery. In 1800 more than 500 Indians resided at the mission. The increasing numbers of neophytes caused Fray Felipe Arroyo de la Cuesta to erect the largest church in the province and the only one of its kind constructed by the Franciscans in California. Nine bells rang their joyful chimes throughout the peaceful valley. When the church was completed in 1812, the Indian population had greatly dwindled from the peak of 1,100. The two sides of the building were walled off, which reduced the interior to a size comparable to the other mission churches.

The Franciscans at San Juan Bautista devoted a great deal of attention to musical activities. Fray Estevan Tapis and later Fray Narciso Duran taught music and organized Indian boys choirs. Notes were printed in black, yellow, green and red to indicate the various voices. These are still to be seen at the mission, along with an interesting barrel organ, which was reportedly the gift of the English explorer George Vancouver. As the handle was turned, the instrument produced strange music that pleased the Indians. Many gay fiestas were held at this historic site. But all was not music and signing, for marauding Tulares Indians occasionally threatened destruction of the mission. Once it was saved by playing the barrel organ.

San Juan Bautista shared the sad fate of the other missions when word came that the orchards and fields and even the fine church had been illegally sold. Although U.S. military authorities ordered priests to remain in charge of the church, the Indian neophytes had already been scattered. During gold rush days, stagecoaches changed horses in the little village by the mission. In 1859, President Buchanan restored the buildings to the

Catholic Church. Today, the Castro and Zanetta houses nearby as well as the mission itself have become historic monuments for tourists.

16. San Miguel Arcangel 1797

While the mission named for San Miguel Archangel is one of the lesser known foundations along *El Camino Real*, more people have passed within a stone's throw of the place than of any other mission. It is located adjacent to busy Highway 101 and the Southern Pacific Railroad, midway between Camp Roberts and Paso Robles.

This was the third mission founded by Fray Fermin Lasuen in the year 1797. On July 25, soon after having established San Juan Bautista, he personally erected the cross near the juncture of Salinas River and Estrella Creek. It was a promising fertile valley, with plenty of water from the springs of Santa Isabel.

The mission prospered and, within a few years, over a thousand Indians had been baptized. Vast herds of livestock roamed the area, exceeded only by those at San Juan Capistrano. In addition to a church, numerous structures were erected where the natives engaged in various simple trades. A fire in 1806 destroyed most of them, but new adobes with tile roofs soon took their place. A larger church was started in 1816 and its final decorations were added in 1821. The artistic embellishments are the most interesting features since this mission is the only one where paintings and decorative effects have not been retouched in subsequent years.

San Miguel Mission declined rapidly after secularization in 1834. The population dwindled from 1,200 to thirty within the following seven years. The last missionary, Fray Ramon Abella, left in 1842 and two years later, Fray Narciso Duran reported that there were no lands or cattle. Although Governor Pio Pico sold the property, the United States Government declared the sale illegal and, in 1878, Bishop Francis Mora appointed a resident priest. The Franciscans returned in 1928 and began restoring the mission structures.

17. San Fernando Rey de Espana 1797

Fray Fermin de Lasuen founded San Fernando Mission, Rey de España, September 8, 1797, the seventeenth in the chain of twenty-one missions. Francisco Reyes, an early settler in the San Fernando Valley, furnished temporary shelter. The permanent church, dedicated in December 1806 was severely damaged by an earthquake in 1812.

The church was repaired and made operational by 1818. The appeal of Christianity and the opportunity for civilization and a settled culture drew the scattered Indians of the valley. The mission flourished and soon its ranches extended to many adjoining areas.

San Fernando Mission was secularized in 1834. Governor Manuel Micheltorena restored the mission to the Franciscans in 1843 but, after his overthrow, it again became the victim of despoilers and was sold by

Governor Pio Pico in 1846. General John C. Fremont and Pico signed the treaty whereby California was ceded to the United States.

In 1862, the new nation confirmed ownership of the mission to the Church. Title was issued to Bishop Joseph S. Alemany of Monterey. The quadrangle of the mission was in ruin, and the chapel and *convento* were without roofs in 1896, when Charles F. Lummis and friends began the long task of restoring San Fernando Mission. The church was rededicated on September 7, 1941.

Today, San Fernando Mission is enjoying new life and fresh interest. Adjacent to its ancient walls are the buildings of Bishop Alemany High School where 1,600 youngsters are being trained in the classics. Also adjoining the property is the new San Fernando Mission Cemetery, which serves the northern San Fernando Valley.

Before the arched cloister of San Fernando Mission stands a bronze monument of Fray Junípero Serra. He appears to be resting, looking out over the valley, his walking stick in his right hand, his left arm resting on the shoulder of an Indian boy.

18. San Luis Rey de Francia 1797

San Luis Rey de Francia Mission, stands five miles inland from Oceanside in a beautiful sheltered valley in San Diego County. Established June 13, 1798, on a site selected by Fray Fermin de Lasuen, it was the last mission founded by him, the eighteenth in the chain. The permanent church was completed in 1815.

Fray Antonio Peyri was assigned to the mission as its resident priest and served San Luis Rey for thirty-four years. It became one of the most influential of all the missions. Although prosperous, San Luis Rey shared the fate of the other missions in the period of secularization. The Indians withdrew to the hills and secluded valleys, and the mission was reduced to almost complete ruin.

Within the peaceful walls of San Luis, Rey de Francia Mission, as many as 3,000 Indians would assemble for instructions in Catholic teachings. The mission was their home, school and civic center. Soon the Indian settlement began to thrive. Livestock was introduced and crops were sown. Some thirty years after the coming of the friars large sections of the countryside were under cultivation. The mission owned, in the name of the Indians, some 27,000 cattle and 26,000 sheep.

In the same chapel where soldiers of Spain worshipped in the eighteenth century, United States Marines from nearby Camp Pendleton now occasionally gather and recite the Stations of the Cross. Points of interest at San Luis Rey are numerous. One feature is the Mortuary Chapel, a small octagonal-shaped room off the main church. In the courtyard is reportedly the first pepper tree planted in the West.

One of the largest collections of provincial vestments in the United States is housed inside the mission. Also exhibited are early chalices, furnishings and vellum-bound books once used by the friars. In the museum is a facsimile of the original deed signed by President Abraham Lincoln restoring the mission property to the Church, following the period of secularization.

19. Santa Ines 1804

When founded on September 17, 1804, Santa Ines Mission showed more promise than any of the frontier outposts that preceded it. Densely populated with Chumash Indians, the area was well adapted for agriculture and grazing. And it afforded an excellent buffer to the Tulare tribes to the north and east.

After its establishment by *Presidente* Estevan Tapis, an extensive building program was launched. This included an adobe church, an adjacent *convento* building and the characteristic quadrangle of workshops, storerooms, guardhouse and living quarters. Disasters and misfortunes that dotted its brief but colorful history did not permit it to live up to early expectations.

Peaceful mission life was interrupted by the Hidalgo revolt in Mexico in 1810, followed two years later by a devastating earthquake. The church and other buildings were either completely destroyed or seriously damaged. Rebuilding under the direction of Frays Estevan Tapis and Francisco Uria restored most of the mission, and on July 4, 1817, the present church was dedicated.

Then came the independence of Mexico in 1821 and, shortly after, a destructive attack of rebel Indians upon the mission itself. The "secularization laws" in 1834 provided the concluding chapter in the turbulent history of Santa Ines.

Today, in the town of Solvang, about forty miles northwest of Santa Barbara, Santa Ines still stands as a prominent monument of the Spanish period. Outstanding among those who helped to preserve the church and the adjoining *convento* from lapsing into complete ruins was Father Alexander Buckler, who for more than twenty years supervised a program of restoration. The museum contains a wide assortment of provincial treasures, including vestments, artifacts and Indian art.

20. San Rafael Arcangel 1817

The mission dedicated to San Rafael Archangel began as a sanitarium for Indians who were wasting away from disease at Mission Dolores. Governor Pablo Sola suggested that the sickly neophytes be removed to a milder climate.

The sunny oak-studded slopes north of the Bay, about twenty miles from Mission Dolores, were selected. Here *Presidente* Vicente Sarria raised the cross and celebrated the first Mass December 14, 1817. Fray Luis Gil, who had considerable medical knowledge, volunteered to take charge of San Rafael.

The new establishment was intended to be only an *asistencia* of Mission Dolores, where all its records were kept. However, the prospects for new conversions as well as material prosperity were so promising that in 1822, it became a mission in its own right. At the end of the first year, 382 neophytes resided there and that number soon doubled.

San Rafael was less imposing than other missions. A composite adobe structure with a tule-covered corridor along the side served as monastery, hospital and chapel, which had no tower or campanile. Bells were suspended from crossbeams in front of the L-shaped buildings.

Although coming late in the missionary period, San Rafael made remarkable progress, principally because of Fray Juan Amoros who labored there for thirteen years. It was the first of the chain to be secularized. Tiles and bells, orchards and buildings vanished, until nothing remained but a lone pear tree. In 1909, a singular mission bell marked the site. Today, a replica church reminds visitors of California's twentieth mission.

21. San Francisco Solano 1823

San Francisco de Solano has the distinction of being last of the mission chain founded along California's *El Camino Real,* the farthest north, and the only one established during the Mexican period. It existed only a brief while as a mission, because secularization was decreed just a decade after Fray Jose Altimira raised a cross on the site, July 4, 1823.

There appears to have been no special reason why this historic date in American history was chosen, but it augured events soon to follow. By terms of the Treaty of Guadalupe Hidalgo, San Francisco de Solano was now situated on United States soil. More than that, it became the scene of the American revolt against Mexican authority in 1846, when the California Bear Flag was raised at Sonoma, within the shadow of the mission. The Mexican general, Mariano Vallejo, was staying at Sonoma, where the Americans captured him. By this time, mission activities had been discontinued and the entire chain reduced to desolation. Heartbroken, Altimira had long since returned to his native Spain.

As a young friar, he was among the last of the Franciscans to come to California. At Mission Dolores, his missionary zeal impelled him to plan a new establishment in the hinterland beyond San Rafael. Without the customary material assistance from other missions, he plunged ahead and by the following year had erected a wooden church. Unfortunately, he was forced to leave within two years. After the mission was founded, until 1881 when it passed into private ownership, the building served as a parish church. In 1903 it was purchased by the California Historic Landmark League and the mission site served as a museum. Since 1961, the carefully preserved historic buildings have been a national monument.

El Caminito Real

Closely akin and related to the missions were the *asistencias,* presidios and *estancias* scattered along the Pacific Rim. The *asistencias* were set up as branches or extensions of fully established and flourishing missionary foundations. By definition, an *asistencia* was a mission on a small scale

SOCIETY OF
SOUTHERN
CALIFORNIA

TOILETRY AT THE CALIFORNIA MISSIONS

by Msgr. Francis J. Weber

REPRINT FROM
SOUTHERN CALIFORNIA QUARTERLY · VOLUME LXXXI · NUMBER 3

with all the requisites for a mission, and with religious services held regularly, except that it lacked a resident priest. Of the five *asistencias* functioning in Provincial California, only one, that of San Rafael, ever achieved full mission status. There were also chapels at the military presidios and in many of the ranch outstations or *estancias*.

The missions stand on their own merit. They need little apologies by onlookers. Yet, one does recall the remarks of Thomas Jefferson Farnham who came to California in 1840. In his Travels in the Californias, the Maine-born author said: "I could not forbear a degree of veneration for those ancient closets of devotion; those resting-places of the wayfarer from the desert; those temples of hospitality and prayer, erected by that band of excellent and daring men who founded the California missions, and engraved on the heart of that remote wilderness, the features of civilization and the name of God."

Senior Connection

I also compiled a series of articles on the California Missions, which appeared in *Senior Connection*, published by Churchill Publications in 2004-2007. The following are the issues which came into my possession.

San Diego de Alcala	September 2004
San Gabriel	February 2005
San Luis Obispo	March 2005
San Francisco de Asis	May 2005
San Juan Capistrano	June 2005
San Fernando Rey de España	July 2005
San Buenaventura	September 2005
San Juan Bautista	December 2005
San Luis Rey de Francis	January 2006
Santa Cruz	July 2006
San Jose	September 2006
San Francisco Solano	November 2006
San Rafael	January 2007

More Unpublished Geiger 2005

Another jewel crowded away in my files at the Archival Center was Father Geiger's description of the rise and fall of San Diego de Alcala Mission. It is here excerpted from *The Branding Iron* for Spring 2005.

The placid waters of the South Sea, as the Pacific was known to the Spaniards, were first gazed upon by European eyes, when Vasco Nuñez de Balboa, in 1513, from the mountains of Panama, stumbled upon the world's largest ocean. No longer was the Atlantic to be the only theatre of maritime traffic and colonial adventure. Spanish vessels crept along the coast to the south until Peru and Chile were added to the Spanish domain.

They reconnoitered the coast to the north, at first falteringly, then with greater boldness, until another navigator, in the service of

Hernando Cortés, discovered Baja California in 1533. Six years later Francisco de Ulloa reached the headwaters of the Gulf of California, proving that the land to the west was a peninsula and not an island. If the mysterious land to the north was to be reached by water, future voyages would have to be made along the western shores of Baja California.

The return to Mexico of Cabeza de Vaca after eight years of unbelievable heroism and hardship in the wilderness of Texas and Mexico, revived interest in the northern country. Francisco Coronado was sent north by land while Francisco Alarcón sailed along the coast from Acapulco to the Colorado River. The ambition and desire of the Spaniards was to find a strait connecting the Atlantic and Pacific. The impasse of the isthmus of Panama spurred renewed efforts to find that strait in the north.

In 1542, Juan Rodriguez de Cabrillo, a Portuguese in the Spanish service, was sent north from Navidad, Mexico, to continue the search for a strait. On this memorable voyage, he discovered a magnificent harbor, later to be known as San Diego. He entered it on Thursday evening, September 28, 1542. Cabrillo named the harbor San Miguel in honor of the Saint whose feast fell on the following day. Cabrillo departed on October 3. On the return voyage, Bartolome Ferrelo, Cabrillo's pilot, reached the port again. From then until 1602, no white man disturbed the unruffled waters.

In that year Sebastian Vizcaino explored the coast of California and, on Sunday, November 10, 1602, dropped his anchor in San Diego Bay. He described the bay as "the best to be found in the whole South Sea." A tent was pitched on what is today known as Ballast Point and here Mass was said by the Carmelite friar, Fray Antonio de la Asención. On this occasion, the name of the port was changed to San Diego in honor of St. Didacus, the Spanish Franciscan. On November 20, Vizcaino left the harbor and sailed north.

Despite the fact that San Diego harbor was "the best to be found in the whole South Sea," its waters lay untroubled by Europeans for another 167 years. In 1769, California's occupation by Spain became necessary to ward off the encroachments of the Russians in the north. California, a buffer area, would protect the wealth and civilization of the New Spain of Mexico. Entering Indian territory, Spain employed her benevolent policy of nearly three hundred years, namely to subdue the natives with as little force and bloodshed as possible, by enlisting the service of the missionaries who would offer the blessings of Christianity and European culture to the aborigines. Franciscan friars were entrusted with the evangelization of Alta California, and the region that had only a place on the map was to find a place in the sun. San Diego became the cradle of Christianity and culture, of a glorious and prosperous state.

On April 11,1769, the *San Antonio* under Capitan Juan Pérez, bearing two Franciscans, Juan Vizcaino and Francisco Gómez, entered San Diego Harbor and anchored near Ballast Point. On April 29, of the same year, a ship under Captain Vicente Vila, and bearing the Franciscan, Fernando Parrón, likewise entered the bay. On May 14, the first land expedition led by Captain Fernando de Rivera and accompanied by Fray Juan Crespi reached "this excellent port of San Diego." On June 29, Caspar de Portola, with the second land expedition, reached the port. Fray Junípero Serra, the famous founder of the future California missions, came to the port with the main body on July 1st. On the following day, a solemn high Mass of thanksgiving was sung. On July 3, Serra wrote to Mexico, describing his arrival "at this truly beautiful and justly famed port of San Diego."

From 1542 to 1769 is a long span in human history and during these two centuries the stage was being prepared for the enactment of a drama which even today lives in everlasting memory. Spaniards occupied San Diego. From here was to begin the spiritual conquest of Alta California. San Diego, the first mile-stone of the new *El Camino Real,* became the site of the area's first mission, the initial jewel in a crown of twenty-one.

Sunday, July 16, 1769, was selected as the day for the formal establishment of San Diego Mission. Serra, aided by his companions Fray Juan Vizcaino and Fray Fernando Parrón, raised a cross on the site of a future chapel. This according, to the original record, "was within sight of the harbor." A crude building, but better than others, was selected as a place for divine worship, until a better could be built. Thus commenced the Christian era at north San Diego or Old Town in the memorable month of July, 1769. The first year was so poor in spiritual results and so devoid of material comforts that Governor Portolá decided to abandon San Diego. But under Divine Providence, it was owing to the determined boldness of a Fray Junípero Serra, that San Diego was not abandoned. He decided to wait until March 19, 1770 on which day his patience and prayers were rewarded by the appearance of the relief ship, *San Antonio.* San Diego and California were saved! Popularly expressed, that was the day when San Diego got its second wind.

In April 1773, Fray Luis Jayme wrote to Serra, then in Mexico, stating that: "We were thinking whether this mission could not be moved, while the *presidio* remains here. . . In case the *presidio* stays here, however, it is not expedient that it be near the mission, on account of the annoyances of which Your Reverence is aware." Then Jayme continued: "We tell you this that as long as the mission is in present location, it will never have a firm basis. Nor should there be a mission here, on account of the scarcity of water; for we see that this year there are little hopes for wheat." It is evident that San Diego's first mission site at Presidio Hill was a makeshift institution during the incipient days of missionization. Anxious eyes cast about for a site whose permanency would be assured by the presence of water and the fruitful produce of the fields.

The viceroy of Mexico authorized the transfer of the site and in 1774 Fray Junípero Serra was able to write: "It was determined to move the mission within the same *Cañada* (mountain valley) of the port toward the northeast from the *presidio,* at a distance of a little less than two leagues, about four miles. This place is much more suitable for a population, on account of the facility of obtaining the necessary water and because of good land for cultivation. This place is called Nipaguay."

The change from Old Town to Mission Valley was actually effected in August, 1774. By December of the same year, a church of poles, roofed with tules, was constructed, measuring 53 by 17 feet. This, however, was not as yet the beautiful building of a later day.

Disaster soon fell on the new establishment Some rebellious native Americans attacked the mission buildings and savagely murdered Fray Luis Jayme. This occurred on the night of November 4, 1775. On July 11 of the following year Serra arrived at San Diego from Monterey to get a first hand view of the situation. He determined on the restoration of the ruined mission. Meanwhile the old site near the presidio, once again was the center of Christianity. On August 22, 1776, work commenced on a new structure in Mission Valley. By October 17, of the same year, a new church and a friary were ready for use. Soon this mission became inadequate and a more spacious building began to take shape. The exact date of its dedication is not known, but it was sometime prior to December 8, 1781. The building measured 84 by 15 feet. Built of adobe, its walls were three feet thick, with beams of pine and rafters of poplar. The interior was neatly and elegantly done. The final church building, which was erected and was to become the Mission San Diego, was begun on September 29, 1808. Despite the earthquake of 1812, which destroyed the missions of San Juan Capistrano and Santa Barbara, the unfinished building at San Diego was not affected. Finally it saw completion and its dedication is recorded in the following words: "On November 12, 1813, the day of the glorious St. Didacus, this holy church was blessed with all the appropriate formalities and solemnities." Thus the San Diego Mission of picture and story, with which a whole nation is familiar, became a reality.

From 1813-1834, San Diego Mission prospered. The final Franciscan attached to San Diego was Fray Vicente Oliva who entered the last baptism in his register, June 14, 1846. What sad desolation had come to this center of Christianity in 1849 is best described by Lieutenant E.O.L. Ord.: "I followed this bed of sand through its valley (Mission Valley) amongst low cactus covered clay hills, seven miles, to the mission. There I found the old walls tumbling in and everything going to ruins." With California's entry into the American Union, the mission lands were claimed by Bishop Joseph Sadoc Alemany. On December 18, 1855, the United States Land Commission restored the property to the Catholic Church in virtue of the Spanish laws on the matter. The bishop received exactly 22.21 acres of land surrounding Mission San Diego.

The buildings, however, continued to decline, so that Henry Chapman Ford penned his sad picture of San Diego in 1883:

> *But little is left of the former buildings, except portions of the church and the adjacent dormitories. The chapel is used as a stable; several colonies of wild bees have taken possession of the cavities over the lintels of the*

doors; and a family of owls startle the visitor with their screams as he intrudes upon their solitude.

San Diego Mission stood a desolate ruin for many years, and the mother mission of the Pacific Coast appeared to be a neglected shrine. In the 1930s the mission was restored to its pristine splendor by patriotic citizens, and once again the hollowed shrine became a sign and a symbol to inspire future generations.

Reverence for the past is a noble virtue because it refrains from ascribing all good things to the present. Respecting the drudgery of the pioneers who blazed the paths of civilization, it seeks to tell the heroic story of the past to a modern generation who may listen, wonder and admire, and in turn carry the golden truth down across the span of centuries.

San Diego burgeons forth with history. Every bend of its beautiful harbor and its every hill tells its own story. The interest of its citizens in its history is to be highly commended. Visitors come to San Diego as to a national shrine where they walk in the footprints of mighty heroes. So great a regard for truth should be observed that the visitor should carry away impressions as exact and as exalting, as if they had obtained them first-hand among the musty tomes of a silent but revealing archive.

In conclusion San Diego had five mission churches. The first, was a temporary shelter on Presidio Hill, founded in 1769; the second, in Mission Valley, was destroyed in 1775; the third was a warehouse on Presidio Hill, temporarily used as a place of worship; the fourth, in Mission Valley was an adobe structure finished in 1781 and the fifth and last, which became "the" mission, in Mission Valley, was dedicated in 1813. This structure continues in part down to our own day, the old walls being incorporated with the new. Thus for so many years Mission San Diego de Alcala in Mission Valley has stood as a sentinel over the Mission Valley of San Diego, once a hearth of religion and culture, now a shrine forever dedicated to zealous and hardy pioneers and an inspiration for generations to come.

Occasional Newsletter

I served as transitional editor for the *Occasional Newsletter for the Order of St. Gregory* in 2006. Among other articles prepared by the Old Country Priest was one on Sir Kenneth Olsen, along with an overview sketch of Villa San Guiseppe:

Sir Kenneth O. Olsen

(This first in a series of essays about members of the Los Angeles branch of the Knights of Saint Gregory features Ken Olsen, created a knight by Pope Paul VI. He was interviewed at the Wilshire Country Club on August 31st in a room

overlooking the golf course onto which Howard Hughes crashed-landed an experimental airplane in the late 1930s.)

Born of Norwegian ancestry eighty-seven years ago, Ken was one of two children hailing from Brooklyn, New York. After attending John Adams High School, he went to work for Standard Oil Company who sponsored his night attendance at New York University where he majored in annuities and benefits.

He enlisted in the United States Army just prior to World War II and was sent to the "flatlands" of Los Angeles in charge of a regiment charged with setting up an anti-aircraft unit adjacent to what became Loyola Marymount University.

It was while camped out at Loyola that Ken met Father Carl von der Ahe who subsequently invited him to a dinner at his family home. (For those of you who read between the lines, you are right in concluding that it was during that dinner that Ken met Father V's younger sister, "Dickie", who became Mrs. Ken Olsen in 1942.) While working with his regiment, Major Ken Olsen helped to set up a scanning device, which allowed for tracking incoming hostile aircraft. Happily the program never had to be activated.

After leaving the service, Ken returned to Los Angeles and went to work for the elder von der Ahe who had been in the grocery business since 1906. His first years were spent as a meat cutter in a store at 9th and Alvarado. Ken worked his way up in the hierarchy of Von's until 1946 when the chain was sold. He remained on as President and CEO until 1983. Even after his departure, he stayed on as a consultant until 1991.

An evangelical Lutheran since birth, Ken was "prayed into the Church" by his wife and their seven children, becoming a Catholic in 1948.

As a Catholic, Ken was anything but a passive observer. He was active with the Holy Family Adoption Service, Saint Anne's Hospital, the Little Sisters of the Poor, Jesuit Charities, Saint John of God Hospital, Catholic Big Brothers and *Nuestros Pequenos Hermanos* and practically every other of the Church's many outreach programs. He was also affiliated with the City of Hope and the Braille Institute and received the Humanitarian Award by the National Conference of Christians and Jews.

His happiest moments were those in which he was able to know Christ more intimately. He received the Cardinal's award in 1994. To his fellow knights, Ken epitomizes what being a Catholic is all about.

Villa San Guiseppe

When ground was broken for the new Cardinal Manning House of Prayer, the memory of Earle C. Anthony cast a long and memorable shadow over the proceedings.

The property on which the new facility is located, more recently known as the Villa San Giuseppe, was developed by one of California's most innovative and fascinating characters. Earle C. Anthony was a radio executive (KFI), a composer ("What Hawaii Means to Me"), a bridge-builder (San Francisco Bay Bridge) and a television pioneer—all in one lifetime!

But above all those accomplishments, Earle C. Anthony is credited, as early as 1927, with making Los Angeles "a completely motorized civilization." Anthony sold Packard automobiles to Los Angeles as a total way-of-life.

Kevin Starr tells how he did it: When a person purchased a Packard from Anthony, he bought into a club as well as a franchised service system. Anthony established a chain of gasoline stations, which he lighted with neon lights (a concept he imported from Europe), so that his clients might gas up or have their Packards serviced in uniformly identifiable surroundings.

"Like Helena Rubenstein or Ralph Lauren in the years to come, Anthony understood that in conditions of emergent taste, a brand, a label, a neighborhood, a specific make of car anchored identity. Nowhere was this anchoring more necessary than in Los Angeles of the 1920s and nothing could do it more dramatically than an automobile, especially a shiny new black Packard."

Anyway, in 1923, Anthony acquired eight and a half acres in the Los Feliz area overlooking Los Angeles, Hollywood, Burbank and Glendale. There he decided to build his dream home. Earle dreamed big. He and his wife traveled throughout Europe gathering thousands of photographs of castles and other historic buildings. He entrusted the plan for the building to renowned architect, Bernard Maybeck, who had earlier designed such landmarks as San Francisco's Court of Honor.

Maybeck, a proponent of mixing styles, eventually settled on a medieval, Gothic-styled mansion unlike any other ever erected in the west. Stone was imported from France, tile from Spain and wood from Italy. The completed specifications called for a classical Mediterranean estate, patterned after the early Renaissance. Beginning in 1927, the building of the mansion stretched over three years. When completed, it covered over 23,000 square feet and became the largest house under one roof on the west coast, with twenty-eight rooms and sixteen bathrooms.

The Earle C. Anthony estate was purchased in the 1950s by Sir Daniel and Countess Bernardine Donohue. It was then christened Villa San Guiseppe in honor of Saint Joseph. The Donohues landscaped the gardens and added European art treasures throughout the mansion. The property was deeded to the Sisters of the Immaculate Heart of Mary in 1971 and has since become the community's motherhouse. Donohue Manor, now used as a convent, was added in 1983.

Earle C. Anthony's wife died within the embrace of the Catholic Church. Surely she and her husband would rejoice at seeing how their estate at 3431 Waverly Drive is being used seventy-five years after its birth in the Los Feliz Hills.

Zamorano Anniversary

As part of the keepsakes issued for the eightieth anniversary of the Zamorano Club in 2000, Victoria Daily reproduced a portfolio of works by "many eminent members of the Zamorano Club" that contributed "a great deal to California literacy and bibliophilic history". I was honored to have my 1978 book on Benjamin Cummings Truman included.

1978

DAWSON'S BOOK SHOP: LOS ANGELES

Msgr. Francis J. Weber's contributions to California history are legion: his research into the Missions and Catholic history; his compilation of various bibliographies; his interest in miniature books; and his work as Archivist for the Archdiocese of Los Angeles have made him a well known and respected scholar. This work on Los Angeles pioneer Ben Truman, (1835-1916) is illustrated with rare photographs by early Los Angeles photographer A. C. Vroman (1856-1916). It was published by Dawson's Book Shop in the Los *Angeles Miscellany* series and was printed by Grant Dahlstrom, giving it a complete Zamorano pedigree.

A series of articles on The Archdiocesan Synod appeared in the *Tidings.*

September 25, 2001
October 5, 2001
October 12, 2001
October 19, 2001
October 26, 2001

These essays already appeared in *Past Is Prologue II.*

Recently I looked through my files and determined that several of my articles and essays had never been published. Examples would be one sent to *Vincentian Heritage* entitled "From Vincentian Giants" which sketches the lives of members of the Congregation of the Mission, which has a long and distinguished pedigree of service to the church in California beginning with Bishop Thaddeus Amat, C.M., who came to the area in 1855. No reason was given for the refusal of the editor. Perhaps it was an oversight.

Another was an article commissioned by Rachel Serlen editor of the *Yale Dictionary of American Law* in 2004. The 505 word essay treated John Thomas Doyle, a prominent Catholic lawyer in California during the years of Archbishop Joseph Sadoc Alemany and Patrick W. Reardon.

> American law is in many ways the story of the United States itself, allowing for its unmatched individual freedom and economic strength. To understand law, one must understand its leading figures. This book gathers together for the first time in a sing1e volume, concise yet comprehensive biographical entries on the men and women who have devised, replenished, expounded, and explained American law. These figures are the most significant in the history of American law and have had lasting impact and influence as judged by contemporaries or by history.
>
> **Doyle, John Thomas** (1819-1906). Lawyer. Doyle was born in New York City and reared there and in Ireland. He graduated from Georgetown in 1838 and, after studying law at Columbia College, was admitted to the New York bar in 1842. On vacation in Nicaragua in 1851, he met the industrialist Cornelius Vanderbilt, who induced him to manage an investment company in Nicaragua that Vanderbilt was establishing to finance a canal across the isthmus. That project failed the next year, and Doyle moved to San Francisco. In Nicaragua he had become interested in the former Spanish colonial administration and its relation to the Roman Catholic Church, and he now represented the church in California in recovering possession of old Spanish missions. He established the illegality of the sales by the Mexican government when it controlled California and reclaimed the buildings and immediately surrounding lands for the church.

Doyle is remembered mostly for his four-decade association with the Pious Fund. In the early 1700's wealthy Spanish Creoles in Mexico founded a trust for the support of the California missions. Mexico seized the assets of the trust fund in 1842 but soon defaulted on payments. On behalf of the San Francisco archdiocese Doyle investigated the origins of the claim for the lost income, and in 1870 a Mixed Claims Commission appointed by the United States and Mexico awarded a judgment of $904,000 to the church. This was the first case of international arbitration before the court of arbitration in The Hague.

Civic-minded, Doyle was a member of the initial board of regents for the University of California in 1868 and of the state board of commissioners for transportation in 1877-78. His call for rail rates based on the classification of goods and distances to be carried, helped lead to the development of the modern tariff. Doyle was a founder of the San Francisco Law Library and, in 1870, was the first person to urge the establishment of the California Historical Society. He moved to Menlo Park in 1866 and, after his retirement from law practice in 1888, ran a vineyard in Cupertino. He became known for his interest in viticulture and his experiments to develop a disease-resistant type of grapevine; and he served several terms as the viticulture commissioner of California. Impatient but "good natured at heart", Doyle materially aided younger lawyers. He shunned "public notice and, worldly acclaim, preferring . . . the pleasure of his home, his books, his vines and fruit trees."

Doyle promoted interests vital to the Roman Catholic Church, publishing an edition of Francisco Palou's *Noticias* in Spanish—he also read French, Italian, and German,—and writing several long articles on the early history of the California missions and a history of the Pious Fund. His library was a repository of varied lore, especially Shakespeare, Horace, and Cervantes. Doyle lived a simple life in the seclusion of his vineyards. His emotional and sentimental writings contrasted with the aggressiveness and occasional irascibility he displayed in his legal practice.

Then there was the essay on Saint Brendan's Parish in Los Angeles, which can here be reproduced because it touches on my own years living in that Hancock Park enclave.

Saint Brendan Parish

While young people fantasize about the future, their elders often take comfort in recalling the past. One of my favorite memories reverberates around the vibrant spiritual life of the Los Angeles parish of Saint Brendan and its indefatigable pastor, Father Thomas F. Fogarty (1902-1966), in the 1940s. The Catholic density of that mid-Wilshire district exceeded by far that of other parts of the city, mostly because Fogarty kept abreast of available houses to buy and apartments to rent. A remarkable percentage of the parishioners had come to this second smallest parish in the archdiocese of Los Angeles at his personal behest. Realtors and pastor worked hand-in-hand and, if there were a commission or finder's fee, Fogarty would enter it as the initial offering on the census cards he meticulously kept in three neatly organized wooden boxes in his tiny rectory office.

Fogarty, himself, could have walked out of a Charles Dickens' novel. Irish-born, he always claimed Chicago as his birthplace because he felt that people wanted a native-born clergy. He was a perpetual-motion machine whose turtleback Buick moved up and down the streets of Hancock Park with the regularity of the Wilshire bus. He knew every one of his people (and all the kids in the school) by their first names. A workaholic, his masterfully prepared sermons anticipated many aspects of the post Vatican II Church. Punctuality was one of his hallmarks and people could set their watches by the beginning of his services. He parceled out jobs to practically everyone on the parochial list and Saint Brendan parish had the politest ushers, the most enthusiastic greeters and the best-trained altar servers in the west.

In those days, there were six crowded Masses on Sundays at 7, 8, 9, 10, 11 and 12 o'clock. People expected and received well-conducted liturgies, theologically sound homilies and professionally trained choral accompaniment. On Saturday afternoons and evenings there were long lines at all three confessionals. Evening services were scheduled on Sundays (Rosary), Mondays (Miraculous Medal novena), Wednesdays (Holy Hour) and Fridays (Sorrowful Mother novena) at 7:45 p.m. There were annual missions, solemn novenas and Stations of the Cross twice on the Fridays of Lent. Each of the services was concluded by Benediction of the Blessed Sacrament. Truly the parish offered a wide variety of experiences for every level of the spiritual spectrum.

Most all the parishioners belonged to one or another of such parochial organizations as the Altar and Rosary Society, the Third Order of Saint Francis and the Holy Name Society. Each of those groups had a monthly Mass and breakfast at which their respective banners were unfurled in their colorful splendor.

Father Fogarty was bigger than life in every way. An example would be the radio Mass broadcast on Sunday mornings at 10:00 o'clock to all parts of Southern California. The broadcast, the first of its kind in the west, was financed wholly by the parish and featured the talented commentaries of Pedro de Cordoba and the spirited musical renditions of Bob Mitchell and his internationally known Boy Choir. The unsolicited letters that flowed into the rectory from hundreds of shut-ins was motivation enough to keep the program on the air, even in times of financial distress.

The two full-time, able-bodied assistants (now called associate priests) attached to Saint Brendan parish spent the majority of their time teaching catechetics in the school, bringing Holy Communion to the ill and infirm, conducting Pre-Cana and convert classes and taking door-to-door census. The single car for both priests was used primarily for making hospital calls to parishioners in neighboring hospitals. Dinner was a time for

BOOKS
BOOKS
MSGR. FRANCIS J. WEBER
BOOKS

exchanging daily experiences, keeping one another updated on the spiritual and physical well being of the parishioners and strategizing on expansionary plans for the future. The younger of the priests looked after training the altar servers who abounded in numbers and excelled in service. Annual investiture in the Knights of the Altar was a public event anxiously anticipated by the boys.

Living conditions in the two-story rectory at 311 South Wilton Place were cramped. There was no air conditioning, precious little heat and a plumbing service that barely worked. Three priests, an occasional clerical visitor, housekeeper, cook and secretary all lived in the ramshackled duplex, which dated from the early years of the century. The sextant lived in a tiny apartment behind the garage.

The school was the apple of the pastor's eye. His "kids" ran away with a host of sports trophies and literary awards. Conducted by eight Sisters of Charity of the Blessed Virgin Mary from Dubuque, the school's convent was small and inadequate, with two ends of the upstairs hallway cordoned off for bedrooms. The schoolhouse was antiquated, but neat and clean. A live-in custodial couple kept the classrooms and campus in good order. There was no food service for the 375 youngsters jammed into an area that had earlier served as both church and school for the parish. The nuns were outfitted in full-length habits and no one had ever seen one out-of-uniform. Often, their afternoons were occupied visiting the homes of sick children. Though funds were scarce, the nuns always managed to leave behind a piece of candy or a cute little toy. They walked two-by-two in those days before they were allowed to drive.

There was even a parochial choir school located on an adjacent parcel of land on Manhattan Place. A priest director came each day for classes in music and, for many years, the Saint Brendan Boy Choir provided chant for several of the Sunday Masses.

Saint Brendan parish was affectionately known as a "priest factory" and for good reason. Each September, the pastor and school principal began measuring up candidates for priesthood and sisterhood. Rarely did a graduation pass that didn't find Fogarty announcing that one or another youngster was entering the seminary or convent. Between 1938 and 1960, there were nine ordinations to the archdiocesan priesthood and six to the Jesuits.

When Fogarty was handed his appointment as pastor, the archbishop also entrusted him with an indebtedness of 1.2 million dollars, a phenomenal amount of money in those depression years. Yet, by the time of his demise, the debt was paid, the shell of the church had been completed and consecrated, the convent was renovated and later completely rebuilt, the schoolhouse was first modernized and then replaced and the rectory was relocated and built anew.

There are few today who remember the priest once referred to by the Los Angeles Times as a "three ring clerical circus." There's only one priest in the parish and a single nun in a school with 313 enrollees from a Catholic populace slightly exceeding that of fifty years earlier. There are five weekend Masses, one of them in Korean.

As to whether the post conciliar parish of Saint Brendan can or will rebound after sixty years is a question beyond the competence of this observer. Today the mix is eschewed, the rules have changed and the goals are different. But as long as the young can dream, maybe history will repeat itself. After all, anything is possible with God's grace.

11
Representative Book Reviews

In 2001, I published a collection of my book reviews (1962-2000) wherein I pointed out that relatively few people have the opportunity of reading or profiting from whatever insights such reviews might offer.

Here I am producing a handful of book reviews written over the last decade and arranged in chronological order.

An Account Of The Voyage Of Juan Rodriguez Cabrillo

Edited by James D. Nauman.
(San Diego: Cabrillo National Monument, 1999. 97 pp. $9.64 paper.)
Copies available at Cabrillo National Monument Foundation,
1800 Cabrillo Memorial Drive, San Diego, California, 92106.

Juan Rodriguez Cabrillo was one of the richest landholders and most intrepid adventurers in the New Word. Author, slaveholder, shipbuilder and professional navigator, he was also a family man, perhaps even a religious one. The account of his voyage to Alta California constitutes the oldest written record of human activity along the west coast of the present United States.

This slim, factually-laden and attractively-presented book is a fully illustrated account of Cabrillo's voyage in 1542 and 1543. It is filled with maps, photos, illustrations and commentary which, when combined with Thomas E. Case's new translations of the trek as reported by surviving crew members, presents a vivid and accurate portrayal of the epoch-making, six month trek.

Among the most compelling aspects of this book are its graphics whereby a host of ancillary topics are presented in short but pungent essays and imaginative charts. Among these informative portrayals is one by Debbie Stetz featuring Fray Julian de Lescanso, the Augustinian monk "whose duty it was to maintain the Catholic faith among the crew members." It was also his responsibility as the ship's chaplain to administer the sacraments and act as spiritual advisor.

Two pop-up charts portray an inside and outside view of the San Salvador, the small (100 feet long and twenty-five feet wide) galleon which served as the flagship for Cabrillo's expedition. Constructed in Guatemala, the 200-ton ship carried staples enough for the one hundred or so crewmen to subsist for two years. One of the informative charts identifies Cabrillo's route by enumerating the places, names and locations comprising to the voyage, which lasted from July 3, 1542 to January 29, 1543.

While readers who want the full story of the voyage can find it masterfully told in Harry Kelsey's monumental and scholarly treatise *Juan Rodriguez Cabrillo* (San Marino, 1986), those who are looking for a handy, graphically attractive and factual synopsis of this proto chapter in Alta California's history need look no further than this publication sponsored by the Cabrillo National Monument Foundation.

Frontier and Region: Essays in Honor of Martin Ridge

Edited by Robert C. Ritchie and Paul Andrew Hutton.
Albuquerque: University of New Mexico Press, 1997.
263 pp. Index. Cloth, $29.95.
Order from University of New Mexico Press,
1720 Lomas Blvd., NE, Albuquerque, NM, 87131-1591, (800) 249-7737.

This is a collection of essays honoring Martin Ridge on the occasion of his retirement as senior research associate at the Henry E. Huntington Library in San Marino. These papers reflect the vitality of the field in which the honoree dedicated his long and fruitful career.

Divided into four sections, one each for "Locating the West," the "Political West," the "Popular West" and the "Historiographical West," the 261 page book addresses a wide spectrum of interest, including "just where the West is," the influence of political parties "as the proper vehicle for change," the "key figures as they emerged in the frontier legends" and the place of "historical romanticism about the West." While the authors express differing viewpoints on the nature of the overall field, they are united by their commitment to the importance of the West.

Each reader will find a favorite among the essays. Mine was Walter Nugent's essay on development as exemplified by such places as Pasadena, California, an "Indiana colony," which demonstrates the motives, means and ingenuity of the old-time propagandists. A runner-up: Hurtado's superb account of the so-called "Drake Plate of Brass" which captivated even such prominent scholars as Herbert Eugene Bolton.

There's something for everyone in this anthology, from Annie Oakley to Buffalo Bill to the senate debate on plans for constructing an artificial lake in the Hetch Hetchy Valley of Yosemite National Park. Happily, my own hero, Ray Allen Billington, receives much attention and credit for extending, by another nineteen years, the work of Frederick Jackson Turner at the Huntington Library.

Typically, Festschrifts are boring, lack cohesion and add little to the overall reputation of the honoree. This book is a happy exception, probably because the genius of the "master" rubbed-off on his twelve apostles.

Dark Side Of Fortune
Triumph and Scandal in the Life of Oil Tycoon Edward L Doheny

By Margaret Leslie Davis.
(Berkeley and Los Angeles: University of California Press, 1998. 339 pp. $35.00.)

It was once said of Edward L Doheny, "In a future day when the complete story of the winning of the West is set down by some historian, his name will stand out in bold letters as a rugged personality whose outstanding achievements were marked by the unostentatious manner in which he lived and the scores of real friendships he found time to form during a busy and eventful career that is well worthy of emulation." That day has come. In this magnificent book, Margaret Leslie Davis has produced a "revisionist" view of Edward L Doheny, which will necessitate the re-writing the history of oil development in the United States.

Edward was born at Fond du Lac, Wisconsin, on August 10, 1856, the son of Patrick and Eleanor Doheny. Upon graduating from the local high school in 1872, he went to work for the federal government as a public surveyor in Kansas, the Indian territories and New Mexico. He worked as a hard-rock miner throughout the West and Southwest from 1880 to 1891 and then prospected for gold before arriving at San Bernardino, where he and Charles A. Canfield formed the Pacific Gold & Silver Extracting company.

The story is told how Doheny was sitting one day in 1892 in front of his Los Angeles hotel when he spotted a wagon coming down the street loaded with a dark, tar-like earthen material. A closer inspection revealed it to be "brea", a substance used for fuel in the local ice plant. Doheny contacted Canfield and the two set out to exploit this newly discovered "black gold." Though unable to lease El Rancho de la Brea, the prospectors sunk a shaft at the corner of Second and Glendale Boulevard. Their primitive methods brought in the initial well on November 4, 1892, the first of Doheny's eighty-one wells in Los Angeles. It was for him the beginning of one of the most picturesque and profitable careers ever recorded.

In 1897 Doheny began acquiring lands adjacent to the Santa Fe Railway in present-day Fullerton, near the south slope of Puente Hills. Soon thereafter, he branched out to the San Joaquin Valley area west of Bakersfield. He purchased a block of land in the Coalinga fields in 1909 and organized for its development the American Petroleum Company. The holdings were later expanded by formation of the American Oil Fields company and the Midway Petroleum Company. After some years in Mexico, where he brought in the greatest gusher in history, Doheny came back to California in 1916 to form the Pan American Petroleum Company composed of land in Maricopa and the Casmalia districts.

With all his success, Doheny's life was not without its tragedies. His only son died in 1929, and five years earlier the "Dean of Western Oil Producers" was indicted for supposedly offering a bribe to Albert B. Fall, the Secretary of the Interior. Although declared innocent by two successive juries, the cloud of "Teapot Dome" remained the rest of Doheny's life.

The oil magnate's benefactions to Southern California were manifold. With the encouragement of his wife, Carrie Estelle, whom he married in 1900, Edward Doheny built Saint Vincent's Church and the library at the University of Southern California. Death came on September 8, 1935, to Edward Laurence Doheny, empire builder, philanthropist, and member of that host of trailblazers which followed the Argonauts into the western frontiers and took up the work where those rugged pathfinders left off.

The late Lucille V. Miller, longtime personal secretary to Carrie Estelle Doheny, recalled that on the very day of Mr. Doheny's funeral, his widow and her sister, Daisy Anderson, personally burned all Doheny's papers in the basement furnaces at 8 Chester Place. According to Miss Miller, who was an eyewitness to the conflagration, Mrs. Doheny felt that "destroying all the evidence, favorable and otherwise, would forever bring down the curtain on the alleged and never proven misdoings of her husband in the Teapot Dome affair." Indeed it was a chapter in her life she wanted to forget. In retrospect, burning the papers proved to be her single most disastrous decision.

Yet, from the ashes of that disastrous fire has come new life. The author, with the determination of a detective, utilized three principal unexplored sources of materials to provide the grist for this book. First she discovered a collection of letters between Doheny and Albert Fall which had long languished unrecognized in the Zimmerman Library at Albuquerque; next she and her friend, Nicholas Curry, traced down the papers of Frank J. Hogan, Doheny's lawyer, which were found intact, with several dozen scrapbooks and all the court transcripts of the famous trials and, finally, she gained access to the files of the Los Nietos Trust which heretofore had been unavailable to researchers. She was even able to get a transcript of the murder investigation of Doheny's son from the Beverly Hills Police Department.

A couple of very minor blemishes confirm that perfection alludes most if not all historical productions: Oklahoma was not an archdiocese in the days of Francis Clement Kelley; R. C. Kearns was really Richard Kerens of Saint Louis; Cantwell was Bishop (not archbishop) of Monterey-Los Angeles in 1935, his vestments at Edward Doheny's funeral were black not white, and Father O'Mallett was Martin J. O'Malley, C. M., legendary pastor of Saint Vincent's parish. Also, this reviewer hopes that a future researcher will flush out Doheny's relationship with Santa Anita Racetrack, Lake Arrowhead and *Casiana* (Doheny's yacht) and the *Estelle* (Doheny's private railroad car).

It has taken sixty-five years for historians to catch up with Edward L. Doheny. No longer can his achievements be dismissed or his motives questioned. From hereon he takes his rightful place beside America's great oil tycoons, John D. Rockefeller and Andrew Mellon. Thank you Margaret Leslie Davis!.

Fritz B. Burns and the Development of Los Angeles

By James Thomas Keane
(Los Angeles: Historical Society of Southern California, 2001).
Pp. 287. $25.

During the numerous biographical interviews with James Francis Cardinal McIntyre during the 1970s, His Eminence was asked about his relationship with civic leaders, business people and outstanding Catholics in Southern California. One name that surfaced frequently was that of Fritz B. Burns whom McIntyre characterized as "one who gave unstintedly, never wanting or accepting any recognition in return." He recalled how plans were quietly made to name a high school for Burns in Westchester where he had provided the property. Burns adamantly refused the honor and only after much coaxing did he agree to allow the name of his grandfather to be placed on the institution.

Born at Minneapolis, Fritz B. Burns (1899-1979) studied at La Salle Institute and the University of Minnesota. A good student, he devoted what extra time he had to such entrepreneurial efforts as delivering newspapers, watering and cutting lawns and clerking for a local real estate firm. He served briefly in World War I and was mustered out as a "Sixty-Day Lieutenant."

Coming to Los Angeles in 1921, he proved to be an extraordinary salesman in an area where real estate was the mother lode. He began buying, subdividing and selling large chunks of land in and around Los Angeles.

The Serviceman's Readjustment Act of 1944 totally changed the marketing of real estate in the United States. The G. I. Bill guaranteed returning World War II veterans a free college education and interest-free home mortgages. In and out of partnership with Henry J. Kaiser, he developed a wholly new concept of affordable housing. Estimates placed the total number of houses constructed by Burns and his associates between 1935 and 1975 in excess of twelve thousand. More than a hundred thousand residents in Southern California have lived in those neighborhoods in Panorama City, Westchester, North Hollywood, Playa Del Rey, Monterey Park, Ontario, Compton, Echo Park, Sylmar, Burbank, Torrance and Windsor Hills. The man once honored as "Mr. Housing, U.S.A." was at heart a builder of communities, a visionary with the rare ability to carve hundreds of homes out of a bean field and a neighborhood out of a cow pasture. The Burns imprint extended beyond the west coast of America to Hawaii where he helped to make that area into one of the world's most attractive and profitable resort centers.

Burns served the commonwealth too. He was president of the Home Builders Association, an early investor in the Los Angeles Buccaneers (the first National Football franchise in Southern California) and a "near-candidate" for Mayor of Los Angeles in 1953. Named "Builder of the Year" in the mid-1950s, he was described as a man "whose vision, civic awareness and building integrity helped to create" whole neighborhoods. He won a national reputation as a speaker for his outspoken advocacy of private land ownership as a remedy for social ills.

Burns' association with Loyola College, Loyola University and, finally, Loyola-Marymount University began in 1927. He was present for the groundbreaking of the new campus in the Del Rey Hills and served as a regent from 1950 until his demise. His gifts totaled several million dollars and, in 1998, the university's Westchester location was named the Fritz B. Burns campus. Among the other institutions favored by Mr. Burns were Saint Anne's Maternity Home and Loyola Law School.

Unlike so many of his contemporaries, Fritz Burns looked beyond the grave by establishing a foundation that would continue his philanthropic endeavors. Assisting institutions across the religious, social and political spectrum, the Fritz Burns Foundation, under the careful stewardship of Burns' family members, friends and business associates, has distributed over a hundred million dollars since 1983 for education, medical and social services.

A personal postscript. I first heard the name "Fritz Burns" when I was a teenager living in the Hancock Park area of Los Angeles. Each Christmas, Mr. Burns would bring a flock of deer, remarkably similar to those used for the flying, sleigh-pulling reindeer of myth, to his "Home of Tomorrow" at Wilshire Boulevard and Highland. There, thousands of youngsters from the asphalt jungle flocked to see the descendants of animals imported from the fabled Hearst Ranch at San Simeon. That Burns thought and cared so highly for youngsters is a gauge of his civic awareness. Few people in public life had a greater claim to a full-length biography and this volume is a creditable tribute to a truly remarkable Catholic pioneer.

Metropolis In The Making: Los Angeles in the 1920's

Edited by Tom Sitton and William Deverell.
Berkeley: University of California Press, 2001.
371 pp. Illustrations, Notes, Index.
Cloth, $55; Paper, $22.50.
Order from University of California Press,
2120 Berkeley Way, Berkeley, CA 94720 (510) 642-4710.

This anthology, comprising fourteen original essays, explores topics of scholarly interest and dynamism in early twentieth century Los Angeles. Much of what we now recognize as Los Angeles, its vast sprawl, its reliance on the automobile, its predominance as a business and financial center and the lure of Hollywood took shape in the 1920s. During that hectic era, Los Angeles annexed forty-five adjacent communities spreading into the San Fernando Valley and southward to the harbor at San Pedro. The Pacific Electric's Big Red cars became the nation's largest streetcar system.

Oil discoveries just south of the city made the Los Angeles basin into one of the world's great petroleum producing areas. The City of Our Lady of the Angels emerged as first in movie production, ninth among the country's industrial centers, and the aviation capital of the United States.

That literary curmudgeon, Carey McWilliams, attributed the area's eccentricities not to its "fabled climate," but to its incessant growth. An avalanche of emigrants made Los Angeles a haven for evangelistic sects, cults and "freak religions."

The essays in this volume are a successful attempt to create a richer, more detailed analytical tableau of the city's past, stressing the extraordinary variety in the Los Angeles experience. The contributors to this 370 page book tested earlier chronicles and historical accounts, accepting what remains viable and discarding what is no longer relevant. They validate Carey McWilliams' caricature of this "land of bright colors, flowers and perpetual sunshine" as the most fantastic city in the world.

Adapting In Eden: Oregon's Catholic Minority, 1838—1986.

By Patricia Brandt and Lillian A. Pereyra.
(Pullman: Washington State University Press, 2002. 216 pp.) $21.95

The planting of the first definably Catholic community in the Northwest came about through the Hudson Bay Company which, in 1821, extended its operations to the Columbia River. In 1838 John McLoughlin convinced Hudson officialdom that Catholic priests could help retain loyalty of the French Canadians then being proselytized almost exclusively by Protestant American missionaries. When word of this opening to the Church came to the Bishop of Quebec, he selected Father Francis Norbert Blanchet to be his Vicar General in the Territory on the Columbia. Shortly after his arrival, Blanchet befriended and then brought into the Catholic fold McLoughlin who even then was recognized as the virtual "Emperor of the Oregon country".

Francis Norbert Blanchet (1795-1883), a mature, earnest, devout and widely-experienced priest with visionary plans, moved easily among the leadership of an area which proved to be unlike any other in the United States. One needn't venture too far into the study of American ecclesial history to affirm the sentiments given years later by Archbishop Charles Seghers over his beloved predecessor: "Francis Norbert Blanchet was to Oregon what Saint Boniface was to Germany, what Saint Augustine was to England, what Saint Patrick was to Ireland".

As a pioneer who almost single-handedly created the second metropolitan province in the United States, Blanchet laid the foundation for an archdiocese that only now is bringing his dream to reality.

Blanchet's successor, the unrequited missionary Charles John Seghers, led the Oregon church out of the pioneer era, consolidated its boundaries and introduced administrative order. Oregon's first American-born archbishop, William Hickley Gross, brought the Oregon church into the mainstream of the American Catholicism, welcomed many new religious communities and encouraged the start of many institutions and religious observances.

Alexander Christie oversaw an explosive growth of parishes and institutions, while the long administration of Edward Daniel Howard brought new and expanded institutions, increased social awareness, greater lay activity, and culminated in the changes of Vatican Council II. In an administration marked by transitional turmoil but continued progress, Robert J. Dwyer struggled to maintain traditional Church structure and doctrine while facing school closures and a major decline in numbers of priests and religious. Finally Cornelius M. Power quieted turmoil with his gentle demeanor and openness, while restructuring the Church's exploding bureaucracy and delegating authority with competency. His leadership ushered Oregon Catholics into an era of even greater changes than those recorded in the earlier century and a half.

This eminently appealing account of the Catholic community in Oregon from 1838 to 1986, with its astounding twenty-eight pages of documentary notes, outstanding array of bibliographical sources and comprehensive index ranks this study among the most readable and entertaining ecclesial histories yet written in the United States. Into the 172 pages of text is crammed a remarkable quantity of details which the authors have deftly woven into an attractive narrative.

It isn't often that talented writers come upon and then portray the feats of such outstanding personalities and characters—even in Eden! This book affirms that such pleasantries can still happen.

Witness to Integrity by Anita Caspary

(Collegeville: The Liturgical Press, 2003), Pp. xx, 287

Historians will welcome this treatise because it makes available, for the first time, the files and archives of the Immaculate Heart Community as well as the innermost thoughts of the woman who choreographed what surely constitutes an epochal chapter in American ecclesial history. It is a special act of providence that has allowed Anita Caspary to complete this book which only she could have compiled.

The election of Anita Caspary to the superiorship of the California Institute of the Sisters of the Most Holy and Immaculate Heart of the Blessed Virgin Mary in 1963 opened what might be called the penultimate chapter in the life of a religious community founded at Olot, Spain in 1848. For almost a century, the Immaculate Heart Sisters were among the most precious adornments of the Catholic Church in California. Founded in Catalonia's small town of Olot by Canon Joaquin Masmitja, the congregation was brought to the Diocese of Monterey-Los Angeles in 1871 by Bishop Thaddeus Amat. From their humble beginnings, the Sisters prospered and expanded until they found themselves scattered over the entire Pacific Coast. Given canonical autonomy in 1924, the community ultimately became the largest single component in the educational system operated by the Archdiocese of Los Angeles. No fewer than 197 nuns taught and/or staffed twenty-eight elementary and eight secondary schools throughout the four county jurisdiction.

Caspary's book might better be classified an historical novel than a serious historical narrative. And, as is the case with every novel, there has to be a villain. Though Anita Caspary denies passing "judgment on the life and work of Cardinal McIntyre," she pretty much trashes his reputation with a series of selective and nuanced observations many of which are couched in such vague remarks as "the cardinal was reported to have said . . ." One doesn't get far into the text without realizing that the author is frozen in a time warp of the heady 1960s. And, unhappily, none of her convictions has mellowed or matured with the passage of four decades.

Caspary was generous enough to spread some of the blame beyond Cardinal McIntyre. It was not he alone, "who forced us to abandon canonical status in the Catholic Church," but "a vast ecclesiastical system that for centuries has used every ploy to keep women beholden to its curiously antiquated rules and regulations. Bishops, cardinals, priests have inherited the legacy of domination over women, especially over women religious, who by built-in dependencies of their lifestyles were made subservient to male clerics."

In many respects, this treatise is more memorable for its omissions than its contents. The author, for example, appears to be totally unfamiliar with *Magnificat. The Life and Times of Timothy Cardinal Manning* which takes up the story of the IHM controversy in the years after McIntyre's retirement. Admittedly with McIntyre off the scene, the Sisters lost their villain and were reduced to arguing their case on its own merits and that proved a hard sell to the rank and file Catholics of Southern California, to say nothing of the Sacred Congregation of Religious in Rome. Also, despite all the affection Anita expresses for Mother Eucharia Harney, she fails to state (did she know?) that her predecessor's vows were renewed on her deathbed by Cardinal Manning. William Coulson gets only a paragraph despite his subsequent and quite accurate role in what he called the "destruction of the Immaculate Heart Community."

Sadly, but understandably, Anita Caspery remembers and emphasizes only what strengthens her case. Quotations are taken out of context and, not infrequently, her memory misfires or recalls inaccurately. This book will change few minds or recruit many followers. She is indeed an important player in one of the most controversial moments in all U.S. Catholic history. But there were no winners in the long and complicated struggle nor could there have been. However one interprets her activities and those of her cohorts, it cannot be denied that their action marked the beginning chapter in the demise of the greatest instrument of evangelization the Universal Church has ever witnessed, the American parochial school system.

Witness to Integrity

The Crisis of the Immaculate Heart Community of California

Anita M. Caspary, I.H.M.

THE LITURGICAL PRESS
Collegeville, Minnesota
www.litpress.org

Converting California
Indians and Franciscans in the Missions.

By James A Sandos.
(New Haven: Yale University Press, 2004. 251 pp. $35.00.)

James A. Sandos, from the University of Redlands, once a bastion of Baptist theology, has written a treatment of the process of Catholic conversion practiced by the Franciscan order in eighteenth-century California that is not only unsympathetic but appears to be based on a questionable comprehension of the whole concept of missionary outreach and its place among Christians of all denominations.

The methodology of conversion, of course, has evolved over the centuries and will do so in the future. By taking the eighteenth century out of context, Sandos finds much to criticize in the manner by which the California missionaries attempted to "convert" the peoples of Alta California. While some of his observations are, in retrospect, partially true, there is much more that is questionable.

Using the standards of the Enlightenment, for example, to pass judgment on the conduct and policies of friars whose culture still clung tenaciously to the Baroque tradition creates an untenable premise. Nor should one evaluate the ways of Hispanic California with norms characteristic of the early twenty-first century. Leopold Van Ranke observed that "each generation is equidistant from eternity." Hence each generation has to be looked at by contemporary standards, not by those of a later time.

This book can best be classified as a reincarnation of the work by the late Sherburne F. Cook, Professor of Physiology at the University of California, who, in the 1940s, attempted to explain the demographics of conversion. Sandos enhances his narrative with fanciful accounts and legends, echoing Edward D. Castillo, Robert Jackson, David J. Weber, and a small cadre of other revisionist historians.

In 1979, the late Francis Guest published a detailed critique of S. F. Cook's works. Sandos alludes to that work in his bibliography, but there is no evidence that he assimilated its information on such basic questions as "forced" conversion, "spanking" of the Indians, and influences of the Enlightenment.

Like the man in whose shadow this book was written, Sandos frequently mistranslates, misreads, and misunderstands historical sources. He omits significant matter from certain passages, takes words and thoughts out of context, and assumes conclusions based on faulty translations and, as Guest notes about Cook, "selects evidence which seem to support his views while omitting facts which contradict them." Even with a bibliography stretching over twenty pages, the author uses no previously unpublished sources nor cites any un-translated materials.

Sandos has no acquaintance with or even references to such major documentary depositories as the Archives of Propaganda Fide (Rome), the Archives of the Indies (Seville), or the Archivo Nacional (Mexico City). Rather, he relies heavily on the writings of a small group of polemicists who have dominated the field over the last two decades.

To correct, explain, or otherwise cleanse the Sandos text of its errors of fact and interpretation would take more time and space than the book is worth. One area might serve as an example, and it deals with the so-called "beating" of the Indians.

Whipping Indians for their misdeeds, though rare in Alta California, certainly did nothing to improve their appreciation of Christianity. But observers need to know that whipping was an integral part of the culture from which the Spaniards had come, and they seem to have taken it for granted that this form of punishment was beneficial for those who received it. At home in Spain it was customary to spank children in school. So why should not the Indians, whom the missionaries frequently described as being like children, be given a similar kind of punishment? Captain Frederick Beechey, an English seaman who visited California in 1826, saw nothing wrong with it.

In Spain the friars preached sermons on the evils of beating their servants. But this only shows how common the practice was in aristocratic Spain. In Hispanic California it was not unknown for irate commissioned officers to cane enlisted men. And if soldiers could be treated in this manner why not Indians? In the Mexican period rancheros were known to have whipped Indian employees engaged in house service. And, of course, the flogging of criminals at this time in history was almost universal.

Though the Law of the Indies allowed "spanking" of the natives for specified violations, the extant evidence indicates that the vast majority of the friars, Serra included, avoided that form of punishment whenever possible. The missionaries did not look upon themselves as disciplinarians and, with rare exceptions, left the "policing" of the neophytes to the military. While the friars in Alta California may have countenanced "spanking," most of them (a) doubted its effectiveness, (b) preferred other methods, and (c) avoided, whenever possible, any part in its execution. Though Sandos gives no indication of being familiar or knowledgeable with the Spanish language, he complains that Guest and others translate such Spanish words as the noun azotes and the verb azotear into absurd meanings. In fact these words generally refer to "spanking" and not "beating." Ironically he calls Guest's translation a "torturous misreading" (p. 188).

The mission system was not without its flaws, and there are those who honestly disagree with the whole rationale of missionization. But critics need to attack the system for what it was, not what they make it out to be. Distorting the facts, misinterpreting the evidence, and validating

JAMES A. SANDOS

Converting California

INDIANS AND FRANCISCANS IN THE MISSIONS

Yale University Press
New Haven &
London

fourthhand traditions of poor scholarship is not a scholarly, honest, or fair way of proceeding.

Finally, I suspect that Sherburne F. Cook himself would be displeased with this book inasmuch as his biographers noted at the time of his death, in 1974, that he was "applying new techniques of analysis to California mission records, the preliminary results of which would indicate a more favorable verdict on California missions in terms of demographic impact than his previous studies."

Despite its prestigious publisher, favorable dust cover endorsements, and readable style, this book is a roadmap for driving down blind alleys.

Padre. The Spiritual Journey of Father Virgil Cordano.

Edited by Mario T. Garcia
(Santa Barbara Capra Press. 2005. Pp. xxx, 233. $17.95 paperback.)

As aptly described in Garcia's preface to this autobiography, Father Virgil Cordano "is a shining example of everything that is good about the Catholic Church." More than that, he is the acknowledged spiritual godfather of California's Channel City.

Born of Italian parentage eighty-seven years ago, "George" Cordano attended Catholic parochial school in his native Sacramento, where he recognized his priestly calling at the tender age of twelve. He entered Saint Anthony's Seminary in Santa Barbara and graduated in 1939 as class valedictorian. In the Franciscan novitiate he took the name of "Virgil." He completed his clerical studies at the Mission Theological Seminary at Santa Barbara, where he was ordained in June of 1945 by then Bishop Joseph T. McGucken.

After a brief stint as chaplain at Saint Mary's Hospital in San Francisco, he taught biblical studies, homiletics, and liturgy at Santa Barbara. Then it was off to The Catholic University of America for a degree in Sacred Theology. While in Washington, D.C., he was asked to preach for the 200th anniversary of Fray Junípero Serra's departure for New Spain at a ceremony honoring that legendary friar at Statuary Hall in the nation's capitol. His remarks for that occasion were printed in the *Congressional Record*.

Returning to Santa Barbara in 1950, he subsequently served as professor, master of clerics, seminary rector, parochial pastor, member of the definitorium, and three terms as guardian. Cordano's widely recognized prudence and insight explained how he came to be appointed three times as apostolic visitor to the Franciscans in Australia and New Zealand, those along the eastern seaboard of the United States, and the friars in Latin America.

Zamoranoans Michael Mathes, Glen Dawson, Doyce Nunis and Thomas Andrews in 2007.

For the past fifty-five years, Father Virgil has been a part of the Franciscan family at Santa Barbara, where he has witnessed the sometimes painful but always challenging renewal of religious life. While believing that change in the Catholic Church was long overdue, he was, like others, often perplexed about certain "misreadings" of Vatican Council II.

Nitpickers might quarrel with some of Father Virgil's viewpoints such as his unqualified statement that "women have always been marginalized in the Church." But those who suffered through most of the same post-Vatican II years will testify that Father Virgil has captured reasonably well the tensions, confusion, disappointments, and even surprises that beset a clergy educated in one era and compelled to live in quite another. It has been a bumpy ride, maybe more so than any other in the Christian era, but Father Virgil has verbalized quite accurately the ever resilient Church as it reaches out to the needs of peoples in every age of the human panorama. This is one of those rare books that is hard to put down. Readers will devour every word because its message explains how the Lord speaks to each century as it unfolds in time.

Santa Barbara, California, is known the world over for its historic mission, scenic seashore, native architecture, mild climate, and most of all, for Virgil Cordano, the friendly brown-robed friar who, for over half a century, has personified the Catholic presence to peoples of all religious persuasions.

12
Organizations

Zamorano Club

In my earlier book, I recalled that among my most pleasant and rewarding experiences, none surpassed that of being a member of the Zamorano Club. That selection of my memories was printed as an essay in the club's newsletter, *Hoja Volante*, in May of 2005.

Meanwhile, several of my offerings were used in *Hoja Volante*, including the issue of February 2000 which provided an overview of the most valuable books in the Library of the Archival Center at Mission Hills. Though, given enough time and resources, the tomes mentioned could eventually be replaced, it wouldn't materialize without substantial effort.

1. The *Jesuit Relations and Allied Documents* were released annually in French by the Cramoisys at Paris. The series at Mission Hills is the English translation, issued by the Imperial Press at Cleveland under the editorship of Reuben G. Thwaites in seventy-three volumes. Those books, representing a monumental editorial achievement, contain reports and observations by members of the Society of Jesus about their activities in North America from 1601 to 1791.

2. The first attempt at a history of California, published at Madrid in 1757, was based on a manuscript by Miguel Venegas written in 1739 and printed under the title *Noticia de la California, y de su Conquista Temporal y Espiritual....* Released in three volumes by the widow of Manuel Fernandez, the copies at the Archival Center are the exceedingly rare first edition.

3. In 1799, appeared the first English translation of Jean Francois Galaup de la Perouse's account of A *Voyage Round the World ...* in two volumes, together with an atlas. This best edition in English of the French voyage was considered by Warren Howell as "one of the finest narratives of maritime exploration ever written."

4. The three volumes of Otto von Kotzebue's *A Voyage of Discovery . . .* were published at Paris in 1821. This proto English translation, based on the original German edition of the same year, includes a table of comparative vocabulary for the languages of some islanders. One reviewer felt that Kotzebue's observations about the missions were mostly "based on hearsay from Mexican officials."

5. The *Voyage Autour du Monde, Principalement a la Californie . . .* by August Bernard Duhaut-Cilly was published at Paris in two

Zamorano at 80

MEMBERS HONORED AT THE ZAMORANO CLUB
80th ANNIVERSARY DINNER
FOR LOYAL MEMBERSHIP OF
TWENTY-FIVE OR MORE YEARS

FEBRUARY 6, 2008
at the University Club,
Pasadena

David Alexander (1972-73)
Saul Cohen (1967-68)
Glen Dawson (1971-72)
Tyrus G. Harmsen (1953-54)
K. Garth Huston Jr., M.D. (1983-84)
Alan H. Jutzi (1982-83)
George Kinney (1981-82)
Lawrence D. Longo, M.D. (1979-80)
Frank L. Mallory (1959-60)
Larry L. Meyer (1967-68)
Earl F. Nation, M.D. (1957-58) *
Doyce B. Nunis Jr. (1963-64)
Gerald Papertian, MD. (1983-84)
Edward Petko, M.D. (1970-71)
Loren Rothschild (1979-80)
G.W. Stuart Jr. (1973-74)
James Thorpe (1967-68)
Edwin Todd, M.D. (1982-83)
Hugh C. Tolford (1969-70)
Msgr. Francis J. Weber (1969-70)

*Deceased, January 1, 2008

volumes, bound in one, in 1834-1835. There are only a dozen known copies of this exceedingly rare first edition of a primary source on Mexican California. The French navigator's observations constitute the most extensive contemporary account of the California missions.

6. *Vischer's Pictorial of California Landscape, Trees and Forest Scenes* was printed by Edward Vischer by Joseph Winterburn & Company at San Francisco in 1870. Reproducing drawings made by the talented artist between 1858 and 1867, this two-volume, paperbound work is enclosed in a handsome leather case bearing the bookplate of Carrie Estelle Doheny. The Archival Center also has Vischer's *Missions of Upper California,* along with his *Notes on the California Missions,* which was intended as a supplement to the earlier pictorial edition.

7. *Noticias de la Nueva California,* telling the story of the California missions with Fray Junipero Serra moving in and out of the narrative, is regarded by most authorities as meriting a premier place

Zamorano Club Outing, September 21, 2003
Rancho Camulos Keepsake
Presented by Msgr. Francis J. Weber

among all the works on California. This work by Fray Francisco Palou, translated and prepared for publication at San Francisco in 1874 by John Thomas Doyle under the auspices of the first California Historical Society, was released by the firm of Edward Bosqui and Co. in a four-volume edition of 100 copies.

8. The massive, thirty-nine volume *Works* of Hubert Howe Bancroft, written and edited by Bancroft and his staff of research associates between 1882 and 1891, is represented by a complete run belonging to Carrie Estelle Doheny, together with a separate set of seven volumes comprising the *History of California* and a full complement of the *Chronicles of the Builders.*

9. Certainly the most beautiful title in this category is William Leon Dawson's four-volume set of *The Birds of California,* published at San Diego by the South Moulton Company in 1923. This complete, scientific, and popular account of 580 species and subspecies of birds in the state is illustrated by thirty photogravures, 120 full-page plates, and more than 1,100 half-tone cuts.

10. Finally, there is Carl Irving Wheat's monumental, six-volume work on *Mapping the Transmississippi West, 1540-1861.* Published by the Institute of Historical Cartography and printed at San Francisco by the Grabhom Press, Taylor and Taylor, and the James Printing Company, these volumes are among the most outstanding of the holdings in the library of the Archival Center.

Then in the issue of February 2001, was an article "So You Want To Write An Article:"

> That contemporary writers have more natural enemies than the endangered condors is evident in many circles. Page Smith, himself an accomplished author, recently wrote an essay for the Los *Angeles Times* in which he said it was entirely beyond his comprehension "why anyone should be valued or admired simply for having written a book." Such a person should "probably, and more appropriately, be stoned or treated like a common criminal." He went on to observe that "the notion that someone who has written a book is more intelligent or more worthy of being listened to respectfully than someone else who has not is balderdash. If the time spent writing many books had been spent watching sunsets, helping old ladies cross the street, rehabilitating alcoholics, listening to Mozart, or simply thinking, it would have been much more usefully spent." Others have shared his views for a long time. An inscription on an Assyrian stone slab dating from 2800 B.C. proclaimed, "Our earth is degenerate in these latter days. . . . Every man wants to write a book. . . . The end of the world is evidently approaching."
>
> Maybe there's something to such a viewpoint. Anyone browsing through Waldenbooks, Crown, Barnes & Noble, or Amazon.com must be staggered, for example, by the number of titles of "How-To" books. Why would someone write a book on how to take a bath, raise a puppy, relate to aliens, overcome boredom, get married (or divorced), win a million dollars, eat soulfood, practice Hinduism, or pass an exam? Maybe it's time for a moratorium. On the surface it looks like our decline as a civilization is being calibrated by the ever-increasing tide of books and pseudo-books, many of which would have been better left unwritten.
>
> Although there are too many books being published these days, I suspect that most of them are honestly motivated. Perhaps one way of diminishing their quantity would be adoption of a set of guidelines that potential writers would have to satisfy. These would apply to anyone aspiring to write a book. He should want to:
>
> 1. Share knowledge about a subject not widely known by others;
> 2. Correct, negate, or expand information already in the public arena;
> 3. Demonstrate an unusual facility with words and how they interrelate;
> 4. Facilitate easy reference for inquisitive readers;
> 5. Narrate visual material;
> 6. Provide a memoir of personal or observed accomplishments;
> 7. Record events that otherwise would not be remembered;
> 8. Assist in the learning process;

9. Explain or simplify complicated formulas or issues;
10. Entertain, edify, or delight the reader.

As mentioned in my earlier *Memories,* I served as editor of *Hoja Volante* for forty-three issues over ten years, 1984-1995.

In February of 2002, I was asked to temporarily re-assume the editorship, a challenge which stretched over four more issues, #216 through #219. The first issue included my appraisal of the newspapers then being published in the United States.

1. *The Wall Street Journal* is read by the people who run the country.
2. *The New York Times* is read by people who think they run the country.
3. *The Washington Post* is read by people who think they ought to run the country.
4. *USA Today* is read by people who think they ought to run the country but don't understand the Washington Post.
5. *The Los Angeles Times* is read by people who wouldn't mind running the country, if they could spare the time.
6. *The Boston Globe* is read by people whose parents used to run the country.
7. *The New York Daily News* is read by people who aren't too sure who is running the country.
8. *The New York Pos*t is read by people who don't care who is running the country, as long as they can report something scandalous.
9. *The San Francisco Chronicle* is read by people who aren't sure there is a country, or that anyone is running it.
10. *The Miami Herald* is read by people who are running another country.

Another article by the "scrivener" (a.k.a. the old country priest) addressed the "other" collection of rare books, manuscripts and works of art amassed by Carrie Estelle Doheny at Saint Mary of the Barrens Seminary in Perryville, Missouri. There was also my version of the Bible in fifty words:

God Made.
Adam bit.
Noah arked.
Abraham split.
Joseph ruled.

Jacob fooled.
Bush talked.
Moses balked.
Pharaoh plagued.
People walked.
Sea divided.
Tablets guided.
Promise landed.
Saul freaked.
David peeked.
Prophets warned.
Jesus born.
God walked.
Love talked.
Anger crucified.
Hope died.
Love rose.
Spirit flamed.
Word spread.
God remained.

In the next issue were several articles by outstanding bibliophiles about Glen Dawson, along with a check list of miniatures books bearing the Dawson imprint by Stuart Robinson. The August issue continued the upbeat quality of the *Hoja,* along with a "bibliophilic Hit List" containing the selection of my favorite ten books of all time.

Here I will attempt to explain how each of those titles came to be on that list. I am excluding of course the *Bible* which is the capstone of any sacerdotal library.

1

Henry Van Dyke (1852-1933) is enshrined as one of the all-time great storytellers. A clergyman/educator and writer, he served for some years as United States Ambassador to the Netherlands and Luxembourg. My nomination for the most memorable of his works is *The Story of the Other Wise Man* which was first published by Harper and Brothers in 1895. The author claimed that "the story of the fourth wise man came to me suddenly and without labor—while reading medieval accounts in the *Golden Legend* of Jacobus de Voragine. I have used an abbreviated version of this story as a framework for many Christmas homilies. Van Dyke was masterful at fashioning parables, which are little more than literary devices for teaching lessons. *The Story of the Other Wise Man* tells how a fourth "man from the east" also saw the star at its rising over Bethlehem and set out to follow it, but he didn't arrive with his brethren at the Manger. His frustrated desire and how it was denied, his many wanderings, his seeking and the strange way of his ultimate arrival at Mount Calvary, create the fabric of this devout and inspirational tale.

2

Since high school days. in the mid-1940's, Carleton J. H. Hayes (1892-1899) has been among my literary heroes. A former President of the American Historical Association, Hayes wrote a popular world history text-book that became a fixture in most of the nations secondary schools. The most unknown of his many works is, in my humble opinion, the best. Entitled *Wartime Mission In Madrid,* the volume was published by the Macmillan Company of New York in 1945. Like most historians then and now, Hayes was a liberal Democrat who exhibited a mindset against Franco's Spain. When the long-time Professor of History at Columbia University was asked by President Franklin Delano Roosevelt to serve as American Ambassador to the Caudillo, Hayes resisted with all his persuasive personality, but FDR was not easily turned away. In May of 1942, Hayes began a three-year stint in Madrid, during which he kept "an historian's candid and factual account of what he saw at first hand." The Hayes book, the first full authentic account of America's evolving policy toward Spain, is a most significant document. All of Hayes' books were well written but this one is especially dramatic and, to quote a recent literary hack, "a good read."

3

While never being accused of or recognized as a very knowledgeable theologian, I do have more than a passing interest in the basics of dogmatic, moral and ascetical theology. Included therein would be Mariology, the study of how the Blessed Virgin Mary fits into the overall montage of the Catholic faith. My favorite book on the subject was published by Reginald Garrigou Lagrange, a Dominican theologian who began teaching at the Angelicum in Rome in 1909. Entitled *The Mother of the Savior,* the book covers every aspect about Mary and explains why its author was so popular with Popes Plus XI Pius XII and John XXIII.

4

One of the great blessings of my life was that of knowing Will and Ariel Durant. They had a season box at the Hollywood Bowl and many times I was their guest for Pops concerts on Saturday evenings. After concluding their monumental ten-volume series on "The Story of Civilization", the Durants published a book on *The Lessons of History* in 1968. That book should be required reading for any aspiring historian. The Durants pointed out that the chronicle of history, far from being a chamber of horrors, is in reality a celestial city, a spacious country of the mind, wherein a thousand saints, statesmen, inventors, scientists, poets, artists, musicians, lovers and philosophers still live and speak, teach and carve, compose and sing.

5

In 1956, Carolyn Reading Hammer printed a chapter from Willa Cather's *Death Comes For the Archbishop* at the Anvil Press in Lexington, Kentucky. Set in American Uncial type, 200 copies of the book were released under the title, *Father Junípero's Holy Family*. In addition to the charming storyline, the non-paginated little gem, bound in white boards, certainly qualities as a Fine Press book.

6

H W. van der Vaart Smit took the first giant step in stamping out the carnival air of neon lights, pagan music and frenzied shopping that often smothers the true meaning of Christmas. His book, *Born In Bethlehem,* published by Helicon at Baltimore in 1963, is based on the solid principle that "science and faith are one, indeed must be one, since there is only one truth, which it is the duty and task of both faith and science to seek." By portraying Christmas as it really is, the author presents little known facts about Jesus' birth, which gives the observance exceedingly more meaning than pious legends. By van der Vaart Smits calculations, Christ was born near the end of August in the year 747, AUC. (7 B.C.) during the major conjunction of Jupiter and Saturn. The author explains that the present day observance, dating from 354, represents nothing more than a baptizing of the Teutonic Festival of the Fires, which has occurred on December 21st since the adoption of the Gregorian calendar.

7

While all great writers are gifted with an ability to use (and even misuse) words, few there are whose writing style is both attractive and magnetic. Rafael Cardinal Merry del Val was among that small cadre of authors. An influential churchman in the Roman curia for over three decades, Merry del Val's candidacy for the papacy itself was evident in two papal conclaves. In 1939, his *Memories of Pope Pius X* was posthumously published. That little book became an instant success and went through several editions. It is one of the few volumes that I reread every year and always it is an uplifting experience.

8

Unquestionably one of the greatest biographies of all time is Samuel Eliot Morison's 1942 treatise on the *Admiral of the Ocean Sea*. Though the distinguished historian wrote many fine books, his life work centered about the person and the voyages of Christopher Columbus. Himself a commissioned admiral in the United States Navy, Morison traced by sea and ship every nautical mile traversed by Columbus over eight years of frantic research. Unlike many similar volumes, this one is as readable as it is accurate.

9

Jim Bishop was a popular syndicated newspaper columnist whose daily essays were read by millions of people throughout the United States. His book. *The Day Christ Died*, reads like a fifth Gospel insofar as he fills in many of the little details overlooked in the standard narratives of Matthew, Mark, Luke and John. A meticulous journalist with a panoramic vision, Jim Bishop searched where others had failed to look thus supplying readers with much colorful data from everyday life in first century Palestine. Though surely not "inspired" in the normally accepted sense, Bishop's account is eminently more devotional than those of the "big four."

10

Bishop Fulton J. Sheen wrote even more books than the old country priest and certainly the quality of his writings far surpassed those of his distant admirer. Of all the thousands of commentaries written on the subject, Sheen's *Life of Christ* has no peers. He places Jesus in the very center of history and tells the story of the Redeemer's brief but glorious life with reverence and a profound knowledge of His mission on earth. Even the non-believer will find this treatise a truly magnificent reading experience.

So, there you have my ten favorite books of all time, enumerated in random order. Everyone knows that shrouds have no pockets, but maybe someday there will be coffins with built-in bookracks.

In November, a complete issue was dedicated to the legendary Henry Raup Wagner, to which I appended the following:

A Memoir of Thirty-Five Years

Dr. Gloria Ricci Lothrop asked me early in 2005 to record my association with the Zamorano Club in the preceding thirty-five years.

In my memory bank are many pleasant and rewarding experiences, none of which surpasses that of being a member of the Zamorano Club, a group of bibliophiles established in 1928 under the patronage of Agustin V. Zamorano who operated California's first printing press at Monterey between 1834 and 1836. I knew about the club from Lucille V. Miller, who had hosted members to a tour of the Estelle Doheny Collection at Camarillo on May 6, 1950. She gave me one of the keepsakes containing the addresses delivered on that occasion.

Born in PhiladelpHia on September 27th

Graduated from YalE Law School in 1886

Became involved iN mining profession

Worked in Latin AmeRica, years 1915-1917

Married in the Year 1917 to Henriette

1862  **1957**

1920 became a Western bibliographer

Published the *Plains And the Rockies*, in 1920

1922 - Henry E. HuntinGton bought Overland collection

Joined the ZamoraNo Club in *Anno Domini*, 1931

President, Historical SociEty of Southern California, in 1933

Died and BuRied at Forest Lawn

I was invited to a meeting of the club on October 4, 1967 at which time my friend, Doyce B. Nunis, gave a memorable lecture on "Books and Reading on the Far Frontier." Then, on November 6th of the following year, the program chairman arranged for me to address the club on "The Birth, Death, Burial and Resurrection of a California Mission Library," a talk outlining the history of the *Biblioteca Montereyenis-Angelorum Dioceseos.*

Late in 1969, I was delighted to receive a letter from Zamorano Club President George Whitney confirming that I had been invited to membership, sponsored by my historical colleague, Doyce Nunis. Many years later, during my own tenure as president, I discovered that my nomination had been initially opposed by Dr. Marcus Crahan, a prominent physician and noted book collector, who contended that "having a priest at the meeting would dampen the spontaneity of conversation." In those times a negative vote by a single governor would result in blocking a nomination. Member Ray Billington told Crahan that "if you want to block this candidate because he is unqualified or lacking in clubability, I might concur, but, if you keep him out just because he is a priest, this non-Catholic will resign." Billington's intervention carried the day, Marcus voted "yes" and my name was approved. Marcus and I subsequently became close friends. Others elected to membership in that year were Alvin Brizzard, Anthony Lehman, Norman Strouse and Hugh Tolford.

My first meeting as a member took place on December 3rd when I joined the other Zamoranoans for sherry at the club's book-lined room in the Biltmore Hotel in downtown Los Angeles. After dinner in one of the hotel's private rooms, we returned to our club's room on the third floor to hear a lecture from Roby Wentz on "The Other Winston Churchill."

In those days when my finances were less secure, I would generally have dinner with my parents and then arrive at the Biltmore for the meeting and lecture, thus by-passing what was, for me, the costly dinner provided by the hotel. Another member who regularly joined me in that unorthodox practice was Edwin H. Carpenter, bibliographer at The Huntington Library. We engaged in many spirited conversations while waiting for the others to gather for the monthly presentation.

Even though my calendar in those years was crowded with all sorts of commitments, academic and otherwise, I considered the first Wednesday evenings of every month a "half holyday" on which Zamorano received primary priority, even though it often involved driving all the way from Anaheim or San Buenaventura. I was able to share the privilege of being in the Zamorano Club with others over the years by helping to sponsor for membership Edward Petko, Bela Blau, Norton Stern, Anthony Kroll, Carey Stanton, Katherine Haley, Marla Daily, Regis Graden and Kenneth Karmiole.

The tenth joint meeting of the Zamorano-Roxburghe Clubs, scheduled for the weekend of September 26, 1970, took place at San Fernando Mission where I served as guide for a tour of the seventeenth of California's missions. The day was memorable because, after leaving Mission Hills, the buses were turned back at Castaic Junction by fires raging along both sides of the highway. The club's annual outing for 1979 was held at San Buenaventura Mission on June 28th. Zamoranoans were welcomed by the ringing of the historic mission bells. After a guided tour and a bountiful luncheon provided by the ladies of the Altar and Rosary Society, members were bused north to *Rancho Mi Solar* where Katherine Haley had arranged an exhibit of her Ed Borein collection. Then in 1981, as part of the observance for the bicentennial of Los Angeles, members once again assembled at San Fernando Mission, this time for a tour of the newly-opened Archival Center for the Archdiocese of Los Angeles. A formal dinner was served in the *gran sala* of the *convento* building featuring foods common in provincial times.

Each member of the Zamorano Club is expected to deliver an address occasionally and over the years I have spoken a number of times. As part of the celebration for the American bicentennial, I read my pledge of allegiance, entitled "Happy Birthday Uncle Sam," to the club on December 1, 1976. At the end of the meeting, each member received a miniature book released earlier that year with the text of the talk. The address to members on May 2, 1979 was entitled "California, The Golden State" which describes why the state is indisputably *"numero uno."*

In my address to members on November 4, 1981, I recalled my love for Hollywood, which dated back to childhood days when I was glued to Radio Station WLW in Indianapolis listening assiduously to "Breakfast at Sardi's." One of my ambitions in life was one day to dine in that restaurant, then located on Hollywood Boulevard.

The address given to the Zamorano Club on April 4, 1990 outlined my role as liaison for the Archbishop of Los Angeles with Christie's in the sale of the Estelle Doheny Collection. In it I told how each of the nearly 10,000 items was identified and inventoried and then sent to New York and/or London. The ramifications of the seven auctions were described in a process that made the name of Carrie Estelle Doheny a household word in bibliophilic circles throughout the world. Twice as many serious book people and art connoisseurs read about, saw and even caressed the book treasures as had done in the previous half-century. Fittingly, the title of that address was "The Estelle Doheny Collection—A Personal Memoir."

"Reflections of a Newspaper Editor," the topic for a presentation to members on November 6, 1991, recalled the issues of *The Tidings*, the weekly newspaper for the Archdiocese of Los Angeles, which I edited for seventeen weeks in mid-1990. On Ash Wednesday of 1994, I recalled some "Memoirs of the Stars," people encountered during the early years of my priestly ministry at Saint Victor's parish in West Hollywood. For that presentation, Ward Ritchie brought along his lifelong friend, actress Gloria Stuart, who was yet to star in her greatest role in the film *Titanic*, a wonderful capstone to sixty plus years in the motion picture industry.

"Trials and Tribulations of a Biographer," the subject for a talk on November 5, 1997, told about the book on James Francis Cardinal McIntyre. It concluded with the observation that "writing a biography can be dangerous to one's health, and overall well-being." It was a consuming project that almost became an obsession. After a while, a biographer begins to identify with the person he is writing about and therein lies the potential pitfall of losing objectivity.

In 1985 I was elected to a seven-year term as governor for the Zamorano Club. I was privileged to serve as the club's thirty-first president, 1991-1992. Several noteworthy accomplishments were recorded during my years on the board and as president, none more important than the happy resolution of the long-debated question of inviting women to membership. It was also during my tenure that we were able to publish a fifty-year Index for *Hoja Volante*, the club's official newsletter. Covering the years 1934 to 1984, it was compiled by Anna Marie and Everett Gordon Hager.

Of the many wonderful people in the Zamorano Club, none surpassed the gentle W. W. Robinson, long-time book reviewer for *Westways* and outstanding local historian. He was especially gracious to me personally and whenever one of my books appeared, he would mention and often elaborate on it in his monthly column for *Westways*. The one underlying virtue of all the members was and remains their graciousness. They were all practitioners of the natural virtue of kindness. Rarely if ever did I hear a harsh word or an uncharitable remark about a fellow member.

In 1981 James Greene asked me to take over the editorship of *Hoja Volante*, the club's quarterly newsletter. Nothing further happened, however, until the end of 1983 when Hugh Tolford, by then president, formally entrusted the position to me. The *Hoja Volante* had been published intermittently between 1934 and 1938 and quarterly since 1947. I slightly adjusted the focus to concentrate on modestly-sized essays about "bookish" events and topics. Prior to becoming editor, I had written several articles for the *Hoja Volante*, the most ambitious of which appeared in May 1972 under the title "The Editions of Palou's *Relation Historica*, 1787-1958," a chronological outline of the various editions of that monumental historical opus.

Because of the demise of Grant Dahlstrom the previous printer, my initial issue, February 1984, was designed and printed letterpress by Richard Hoffman who continued in that role until his own death in 1989. Richard and I were a good team and often I visited his press in Van Nuys to read proof, tip in illustrations or otherwise participate in the overall process. Later George Kinney and Patrick Reagh did the printing until that task was assumed by Regis Graden at the Nut Quad Press in San Fernando (and now in Chico).

Happily I was given the freedom of introducing a number of innovations into the *Hoja Volante*. In the issue of May 1984, for example, was the first tip-in, a colorful piece of marbled paper illustrating an article by Stephen Tabor on contemporary paper marbling. In later issues, there were other tip-ins, including Tony Kroll's etching of the Zamorano logo, Carrie Estelle Doheny's leather bookplate, a print of Carl Oscar Borg's depiction of Dawson's Book Shop and a commemorative United States postage stamp featuring Robert Frost.

In addition to several dozen of my own articles on different aspects of the "book," other members of the club were encouraged to submit essays. Earl Nation, Lawrence Longo, Norton Stern, Larry Myers, Carey Bliss, Henry Clifford and Stuart Robinson became regular contributors, along with old-timers Doyce Nunis, Tony Lehman, Ward Ritchie and Glen Daw-

THE LOS ANGELES CORRAL
of the
WESTERNERS

Acknowledges the substantial contribution
to the perpetuation of the spirit and culture of the Old West
and the creation and preservation of Western Americana
and with appreciation bestows

Honorary Membership

on

Msgr. Francis J. Weber

December 2000

Sheriff | Registrar of Marks & Brands

son. The greater mix of articles did much to stimulate fresh interest in *Hoja Volante*. Were I asked to nominate the article that contributed the most and the one which probably would never have been published anywhere else during the decade of my editorship, it would be the two-part essay about Emilio Valton (1879-1963), the ex-priest who came to Los Angeles in 1929 and befriended Glen Dawson. Over many years, Valton had his finger in almost every level of the book trade. And he was a mystery man to the very end as the essay amply testifies.

After a hiatus of some years, I returned to act as interim editor of *Hoja Volante* for four issues in 2002. During that time, the most important article was probably Robert C. Bradbury's enumeration of the ninety-two miniature books bearing the Dawson imprint.

Over the years I edited four books for the club: Carey Stanton's *Island Memoir* (1984), *The Zamorano Club Programs*, 1928-1991 (1992), *Zamorano Choice II* (1996) and *Zamorano Club Biographies and Memorial Tributes 1956-1997* (1998).

For those who keep track of statistics, only five of our eighty confreres outrank the old country priest in club seniority. Even after thirty-five years, my esteem for the Zamorano Club and my gratitude for being a member remains at fever pitch. It's been great fun and may the Lord bless those who have walked along side these many years!

The Westerners

My association with the Los Angeles Corral of Westerners has also been spelled out in some detail. Early in the new century, I was made an honorary member which meant that I no longer had to pay dues. Only nine members enjoy that esteemed status.

The Trail Bosses entrusted the editing of Brand Book 21 to this humble servant who wrote an essay about the publication in *Hoja Volante* for November, 2000.

> Among the best kept secrets of the historical world is *The Branding Iron,* which has been published by the Los Angeles Corral of The Westerners since March, 1948. The initial issue featured articles and comments from or about such local historical luminaries as Glen Dawson, Rodman Paul, Charles Yale, Carl Dentzel, and J. Gregg Layne.
>
> An open letter from editor, Dan Gann, in the issue of April, 1948, informed members of the Corral that *The Branding Iron* was "intended to draw you closer to our work and our activities here in Los Angeles." The primary purpose of the publication, according to Louis Percival, was "not to entertain but to act as a link between members."
>
> Originally planning a monthly publication, the Corral pledged itself with the issuance of #9 to a quarterly schedule of March, June, September, and December. Since March of 1949, it has appeared in Spring, Summer, Fall, and Winter. The basic format of *The Branding Iron* has remained fairly consistent over the years, with at least one feature article in each issue. Also included was a log of speakers and their topics, internal happenings of the Corral, and activities of members, many of whom were outstanding professional or amateur historians.
>
> The dimensions of *The Branding Iron* were determined to be 10 × 6 ½ inches with a pagination that has ranged from eight pages to as high as thirty-four. Paul Galleher commissioned John B. Goodman to design the official masthead, which portrays a buffalo skull arranged above lettering reminiscent of a cowboy's rope. Two branding irons at either side spell out LAW (Los Angeles Westerners).
>
> In March, 1961, editor Robert L. Dohrmann revised and expanded the quarterly's purpose as that of "a publishing medium for the historical articles which, because of brevity, do not lend themselves for inclusion in the *Brand Books.*" During those years *The Branding Iron* published articles, mostly by Corral members, on a wide range of topics, such as mining, western dress, cattle and ranching, guns, saddlrey, Indians, artists, outlaws, and kindred subjects.
>
> Response and participation have varied over the past five decades. In the issue for June, 1974, the "Foreman" threatened readers that *The Branding Iron* would be "going from 16 to 8 pages" because "we have nothing else to publish at this time." Complaining that the "well was dry," he placed the blame on "a lazy bunch of Westerners" who were not providing essays. The appeal had its desired effect and *The Branding Iron* was able to maintain both the quantity and quality of its feature articles.

In 1966, the Corral published an *Index Guide: A Score of Years and Fourscore Issues*, which enumerated and identified publications of the Los Angeles Corral of The Westerners, including *The Branding Iron*. Then in 1985, Anna Marie and Everett Gordon Hager completed their comprehensive *Index to the Brand Book and The Branding Iron*, which covered issues released between 1947 and 1983, as part of the Corral's fortieth anniversary. At that time, Sheriff Jerome R Selmer praised *The Branding Iron* for preserving research, tales, ideas, and visual images on a variety of pertinent subjects, as well as maintaining a record of Corral activities.

Early in 1996, the Trail Bosses of the Los Angeles Corral commissioned this writer to compile an anthology of the more outstanding feature articles that have appeared in *The Branding Iron* during the first half-century of its existence. It was to contain a small but representative portion of the more significant essays that had graced the pages of *The Branding Iron* since 1948. In an effort to achieve equality, no author is represented by more than a single entry. For the most part the articles appear as they were initially printed, with only a few stylistic alterations. Robert Blew participated in the selection process and Gladys Posakony read and corrected the galleys.

Brand Book 21, an anthology of seventy-five articles, is 334 pages long and is illustrated with the same photos and drawings that appeared in the original copies of *The Branding Iron*. Andy Dagosta, award-winning artist, designed and executed the jacket. Printed and bound by BookMasters, Inc. of Ashland, Ohio, in a limited edition of 350 copies, the book is printed on acid-free Finch Vellum Vanilla paper.

Newman Club

Since my earliest years as a priest, I have had a pleasant association with the Newman Club of Los Angeles. My first talk entitled "Shadows over American Catholicism; was delivered on November 21, 1963. Later I spoke about the origin of the club's history:

> The Newman Club was established, on May 25, 1899 by John Filmore Francis and several other Catholic laymen of California's southland with the avowed purpose of promoting religious to1eration in accordance with the Constitution of the United States, and considering and discussing subjects germane to Catholic thought and history and giving expression, on proper occasions, to the sentiments of members about matters of Catholic concern.
>
> According to John Alton, "the idea of such a club had its inception in the mind of that American Churchman whose memory we all revere and cherish, the late Most Reverend George Montgomery," during his years as Bishop of Monterey-Los Angeles. An early journalist noted that "the formation of the Newman Club came at a most opportune time, and its object was mainly to have a body of laymen whose tact and firmness would be a great assistance to the Catholic people in general." Such an observation is understandable when one considers that the Newman Club was launched in an era when many citizens believed that a Catholic American was not a fit person to be a citizen.
>
> Though it was essentially a literary organization, one of the Club's principal purposes was the defense of those few Catholics in public positions whose religious convictions subjected them to injustice or oppression. That the Newman Club achieved its purpose is obvious from remarks recorded just a few years after its establishment: "Whilst maintaining the strictest Catholicity, the club has done a noble work .... in giving to the Church in this community a standing among the non-Catholic body that it never had

before." It has done "a generous service in breaking down unhappy prejudices that have too long made enemies of those who should be friends."

These outstanding effects on the educational life of Los Angeles were recognized by Bishop Montgomery, who reckoned that the Newman Club was "one of the promising features of Catholic life in the city and for the diocese."

Men of prominence in the professional and business life of the community have always considered membership in the Newman Club a distinct privilege. Even in 1903, it was noted that the organization "is made up of some of our best men in almost every walk and profession of life. They are men who enjoy the respect and confidence of their fellow citizens, irrespective of party or denomination."

At the same time, social status has never been a criterion for membership. The Newman Club is open to Catholics in all walks of life, provided only that they have "a liberal education and sufficiently cultivated literary taste . . . to appreciate and discuss the activities, which under the purview of the constitution, may be brought up in the papers which each in turn will be required to present."

The passage of time has not altered the Club's original format. Since May of 1899, when Madame Modjeska read her paper before the group on "Christianity and the Stage," members have met monthly to hear and discuss the major problems encountered by the Church in an ever-growing community. Over sixty years ago, the Newman Club was referred to as "probably the only society of its kind in the United States," a distinction that would very likely go unchallenged even today.

It would be hard indeed to improve on the observations of the poet, publicist and author, James R. Randall, who wrote, in 1905, that "The Newman Club of Los Angeles is a splendid representative body of Catholic men. It is an admirable combination of religious and literary motives and purposes."

On May 15, 2008, I addressed the Newman Club for the twelfth time on Justice Paul J. McCormack who I discovered, served as President of the Club in 1918-1920.

Here is the text of the talk:

In 1945, a group of Hispanic parents in Orange County filed suit to end segregation in their schools. The case revolved around Sylvia Mendez, an eight-year old youngster, who was denied entrance into the 17th Street School in Westminster.

Two years later a pivotal legal precedent was established when San Francisco's 9th Circuit Court of Appeals, ruled that school districts in the area could no longer segregate children on the basis of national origin.

The resulting legal battle ended segregation eight years before "Brown vs. Board of Education" did the same for the nation as a whole. What the leadership of Earl Warren accomplished on the national level was pioneered by another Californian, Judge Paul J. McCormick (1879-1960).

Born in New York City on April 23, 1879, the enterprising jurist was raised in San Diego. He attended All Hallows College in Salt Lake City and Saint Ignatius College, later the University of San Francisco. He subsequently received his law degree from Loyola University.

Moving to Los Angeles in 1893, Paul "read" law as assistant to Thomas W. Robinson, the Los Angeles City Librarian. After being admitted to the Bar, he practiced law with Max Loewenthal. He taught legal procedure at USC from 1912 to 1924.

A Catholic lay leader in California's southland for over a half-century, Paul was made a Knight Commander of Saint Gregory by Pope Pius XII in 1953. He was also active in the Holy Name Society and the Saint Vincent de Paul Society. A charter member and first financial secretary of the Knights of Columbus, Council 621, he was Grand Knight and State Deputy in 1914-1915.

Paul married Josephine Redmond on June 25, 1908 in Saint Agnes church at Vermont and Adams Boulevard. The Right Reverend Thomas J. Conaty, Bishop of Monterey-Los Angeles, witnessed the exchange of their marital vows.

The youthful attorney served as assistant district attorney in Los Angeles County from 1905 to 1910. In the latter year he was named to the Superior Court of Los Angeles where he served until 1924. He was then appointed a judge of the United States District Court, Southern California, by President Calvin Collidge. Judge McCormick was chief judge of the District Court from 1940 to his retirement in 1951. For several years thereafter he served as substitute on special cases.

Among the thorny cases adjudicated by McCormick was the Elk Hill litigation along with the Teapot Dome case, which dominated the nation's newspapers in the 1920s. Edward L. Doheny and Albert B. Fall, Secretary of the Interior, were the central figures in that case which stretched over several years and ultimately resulted in the conviction of Fall and the exoneration of Doheny. Subsequent research has shown that the government withheld crucial evidence because of the threat to national security had the Japanese been informed about the country's oil reserves.

President Herbert Hoover later appointed McCormick to the Wickersham Crime Commission on Law Observance and Enforcement because of his national prominence.

After his retirement from the bench, Judge McCormick continued his active participation in various religious and charitable activities. He served for a while as Vice President of the Archbishop's Fund for Charity at the behest of James Francis Cardinal McIntyre. On December 6, 1960, the cardinal presided and gave the final absolution for McCormick at the judge's funeral at Saint Vibiana Cathedral.

McCormick always felt that his most important case was that in which he enjoined Orange County from forcing Hispanic young people to attend a particular grammar school, thus ending what was then *de facto* segregation in Orange County.

The importance of Judge Paul J. McCormick and the "Mendez vs. Westminster" case will be underscored by the United States Postal Service in the Fall of 2007 with the issuance of a 41 cent commemorative stamp entitled "Toward Equality in Our Schools."

Knights of Columbus

Years ago when I was pastor of San Buenaventura Mission, the Knights of Columbus, Council 2498, asked me to serve as their chaplain. It was an easy chore because the headquarters was across the street in an old, abandoned theatre.

Happily they have kept me on their rolls in ensuing years. The Knights of Columbus do wonderful things and are a great blessing to the church. Supreme Knight Carl Anderson visited San Fernando Mission on September 16, 2009.

ACDA

I was a charter member of the Association of Catholic Diocesan Archivists when the group was established in 1979.

Among the several talks given to the ACDA at the biannual gatherings at Mundelein, Illinois was one on "Before Disaster Strikes."

> If it is true that the best way to ensure longevity is to choose the right parents, then surely it must be equally true that the best way to avoid natural disasters is to live in areas where they don't occur.
>
> Unfortunately, people don't always enjoy the luxury of deciding where they live and work. Like potted flowers, we are expected to bloom where we are planted. And that means that we must learn, how best to adjust to circumstances as we find them.
>
> During recent years, California has been anything but a safe place. First there were riots, then looting and burning; that was followed by a series of forest fires, flooding and extensive mudslides and, finally, earthquakes. As one local newspaper writer put it, "something went wrong in paradise."
>
> Today, I would like to tell you something about the natural disaster sustained by the Archival Center for the Archdiocese of Los Angeles on January 17th of this year, what measures we have taken to repair the damage and, more importantly, what we are doing to ensure that any future incident of that nature will result in minimal damage.
>
> As you may have heard, our facility is located only three miles from the epicenter of the so-called Northridge Earthquake which measured a staggering 6.8 on the Richter scale. In what the *Los Angeles Times* called "the nation's largest and costliest natural disaster ever," Mission Hills moved seven inches east and eight inches up, while the greater Los Angeles Basin shrank by a half inch.
>
> My day starts early—at 3 a.m. following some prayers in the Serra Chapel, I had arrived at my office in the Archival Center about 4:10. After feeding the pooch and winding the clocks (a regular Monday ritual), I had

turned on my ancient IBM electric typewriter as a prelude for grinding out the first draft of an essay that I was writing for the local Catholic newspaper.

At precisely 4:31, there was a penetrating noise and the entire room began swaying. Something crashed down and gashed my head as I slid under my desk, the same desk that saved my life in the 1971 earthquake.

After what appeared like an eternity (it was more like 30 seconds), there was utter silence. It was pitch black as I began to crawl out of the building. It took about twenty minutes to get around, over and between the several thousand books that had rained down from the shelves.

We can avoid, in this presentation, further dramatics about the event. Suffice today, our archival building, erected in 1980, emerged structurally intact, though it sustained extensive cracks and other very visible reminders of the quake.

The contents of the building were strewn everywhere. Approximately half of our 1200 file boxes pitched forward onto the floor, spilling materials in all directions and, in most cases, breaking the boxes beyond repair.

Except for the books behind glass doors in the library, almost every shelved volume in the entire building ended up in one gigantic mountain of printed works, with many spines broken or ripped.

Although the display cases in the Historical Museum remained closed and intact, there was extensive breakage of anything made of glass or crystal. The huge monstrance used for Mary's Hour at the Los Angeles Coliseum was thrown across the room and damaged almost beyond recognition.

The contents of our vault were also hurled to the floor. It was three days before we could even gain access to the room. Practically all the wall hangings in the building were smashed, as was much of our statuary and other memorabilia.

The only item still in its proper place was a porcelain statue of Our Lady of the Angels which had been given to us in 1981 by the late Vicar General of the archdiocese, Msgr. Benjamin G. Hawkes.

Like every home and business in our area, the inside of the Archival Center was one gigantic shambles. Thirty-two years of collecting, sorting, arranging and cataloguing had been undone in less than a single minute. It was a bit disquieting, to say the least.

We were several days recovering from the emotional effects of the quake. Even now, there are people in the area who adamantly refuse to return to their homes or places of work. The local parks were flooded with people who camped out for several weeks, even during inclement weather. One needs to figure the psychological damage into the equation of recovery. Fifty-seven people, including a seminarian, were killed and that factor also complicated the healing process.

Through a cellular phone, I was able to call Cardinal Roger Mahony's residence and was told that he was already enroute to the disaster zone. He arrived about 5 o'clock in the afternoon, after personally visiting the damaged area from one end of the San Fernando Valley to the other.

The Cardinal is always at his best in times of crisis. His presence among our ruins was a badly-needed and much-appreciated dose of encouragement. He repeated Job's observation that "The Lord gives, the Lord takes away, blessed be the name of the Lord." We all needed that reminder.

A brief discussion on how we went about getting back into operation might be useful here.

The Archival Center was insured for earthquake under the blanket coverage for the archdiocese, which had $40 million of earthquake insurance, with a 20% deductible stipulation.

Even presuming that the archdiocese received a $36 million settlement, and I am told that figure is still being negotiated, there wasn't much likelihood that the Archival Center would receive much or any of it, when nine churches and as many schools had to be either totally replaced or extensively rebuilt.

So, early on, we decided to raise funds on our own to put us back in service. The Board for the Friends of the Archival Center gave us $6,000 over and above their already approved quarterly allocations and *Las Damas Archivistas* added another $1,000.

An appeal letter was sent to our membership and that resulted in gifts totaling $7,125, which is remarkable, considering that we only have 218 dues-paying members. Replacing broken glass, ordering new file boxes (which are now selling for $18 each), rebinding several dozen books, purchasing bungee cords for all our shelves, moving and remounting the file cabinets, securing plastic locks for wooden cabinets, acquiring, several dozen packages of "Quake Hold" adhesive, reframing broken pictures and employing a carpenter for four weeks consumed the entire $13,124 we had at our disposal.

But, on May 16th, 1994, four months after earthquake, we were fully operational, one month ahead of our contemplated schedule. And we did it without a dime's worth of ecclesial assistance, one more proof that the private sector in the American Church is alive and well.

A story is told about an earthquake striking while some American tourists were visiting a Tokyo museum. There were screams, shrieks, terrified pleas. Above the din a voice is heard shouting, "I'm from California! We stand in the doorway!" Then someone else calls out, "I'm from Illinois—where should I stand?"

Earthquakes come without warning and how a person reacts can and often does determine personal survival and the extent of physical damage. Everyone, especially those residing in sensitive areas should plan for the worst. Here are some suggestions that can easily be programmed into a person's memory bank:

Stay where you are. Most quake injuries occur as people enter or leave buildings. The greatest danger is from falling objects just outside exterior doorways and walls. If you're inside, stay inside and take the best available cover.

a) Get under a sturdy table or desk.
b) Stand or crouch in a strong doorway in a load-bearing wall, not a partition wall.
c) Brace yourself in an inside corner of the room.
d) If possible, shield your head with a coat, cushion, or blanket.

e) Stay away from windows, mirrors, or other glass that might shatter.

f) Avoid chandeliers and other heavy hanging objects that might fall.

g) Keep clear of bookcases, cabinets, and other pieces of heavy furniture that might topple or spill their contents.

h) Stay away from stoves, heating units, fireplaces and any area where bricks might fall from the chimney.

If you're outside, find shelter outdoors—unless you're lucky enough to be in an open space where nothing can fall on you.

Be sure to stay clear of power lines and poles, trees or branches, external stairs, building facade ornaments, chimneys or anything that might fall.

If you're downtown, hazards increase—especially in areas of high-rise buildings. Windows and building facades can shower the streets with deadly litter. Get under a strong doorway or crawl under a parked vehicle (the bigger, the better).

If you're in a high-rise building, don't use the elevators or stairs during the quake.

Stay in place for some minutes after the earthquake. Remember that aftershocks are commonplace. They will continue for some days—even months, but will start decreasing in intensity and length.

Most people do NOT die in earthquakes. Remember that it will take some days before a return to normal can be assured. Do not hesitate to call for assistance, but realize that public authorities will be overwhelmed for some time.

Communicating with the outside world, or getting help, may be difficult or impossible. You should be prepared to survive on your own for two weeks or more. Act thoughtfully and rationally. Use common sense and remind others to do so. Here are some general principles to follow:

Immediately afterward, assuming you're lucky enough not to be a casualty, you may have one or more immediate emergencies to deal with.

a) People around you may be injured.

b) Fires may break out and there may be no water to fight them.

c) You may be trapped in a building with unsafe elevators and stairwells.

PROCEDURE:

1. Put on shoes with heavy soles. Wear gloves.
2. Check for injured or trapped persons in your building and neighboring buildings. Mark known hazards like weakened structures.
3. Check for fires and gas leaks from ruptured lines or connections.
4. Open windows and doors for ventilation if you smell gas.

5. Turn off stove, heaters and other appliances.
6. Don't light a match or turn on any gas appliance until you're sure the gas lines haven't been ruptured.
7. If you smell gas or have other reason to think the lines have been damaged, turn off the gas as soon as possible. Don't turn the gas back on yourself; wait until your local utility confirms that it is safe and sends someone to turn on the gas and re-light the pilot lights.
8. If you have reason to believe the electrical lines have been broken or power is out, don't turn on electric switches. Unplug appliances. Don't attempt to shut off your house's electricity or even unplug appliances if you smell gas. *One spark could set off a fire.*
9. Extinguish fires. Before the quake, place fire extinguishers in strategic locations (including some outside) where they will be easily accessible after the quake.

   Before using a fire extinguisher, be sure you have a safe exit in case the fire gets out of control. Use the proper extinguisher for the type of fire:

   a) Class A for normal combustibles (wood, paper, cloth).
   b) Class B for flammable liquids and most electric fires.
   c) Class C for electric fires. In most cases you should shut off electricity before attempting to extinguish the fire.
   d) ABC fire extinguishers are good for all types of fires.
   e) Rakes and hoes also come in handy for breaking up small fires.
   f) A water-soaked blanket can also be useful in smothering a small blaze.

10. Assist injured people.

    Administer first aid or CPR if necessary. Hospitals and clinics will be overwhelmed, and only the worst emergency cases should be referred to them.

11. Avoid fallen power lines.

    Don't stand under power lines during or after the quake. Rescuing someone in contact with a live electrical line is very dangerous, and utility companies warn against attempting it.

OTHER RECOMMENDATIONS

1. Don't depend on the telephone. Keep all calls brief, even the most important ones.
2. Use the phone only to report extreme emergencies—like life-threatening injuries, major fires, or fallen power lines.
3. Be careful about water. Don't drink tap water or use toilets until you know the water and sewage lines are intact.

Contaminated water lines could spread epidemic.
Overflowing toilets will create a health hazard.

An archive is one of the places where contents are more important than the building which houses them, hence contents should be given priority over other considerations.

The clean-up procedures can be psychologically discouraging. There will be rubble everywhere. At the first opportunity, make a quick appraisal of what immediate steps should be taken to avoid further damage or risk to endangered materials. Move fast after the quake to stabilize, remove or otherwise protect exposed or damaged materials.

ACA

The Association of Certified Archivists was established on November 30, 1989 and I was among the first members of the Association of Diocesan Archivists to be certified.

Cardinal Roger M. Mahony

13
The Cardinal Archbishop

I have had a long and pleasant relationship with Roger Cardinal Mahony and I regret that his defamers, small in number but vociferous in expression, couldn't know him personally. He is a hard person to dislike, even when one disagrees with him, as I have on occasion. Like most effective leaders, he is often stubborn, but I can identify with that characteristic in my own demeanor. The cardinal is pragmatic on many issues and I have seen him change direction after listening to intelligent opposition, which recalls to mind what Justice Oliver Wendell Holmes once said: "Show me an open mind and I will show you the prime ingredient of greatness".

Cardinal's Biographer

As long ago as 1998, the Cardinal wrote to suggest that I have "an open discussion" with Doctor Michael Downey "about how one would go about locating all of the data and information that would be necessary to someone who would eventually" write his biography. He also asked if I thought "it would be advisable to send someone to CUA for a degree in ecclesial history". While he hoped that I would "be around for a few more major works," he stopped short of asking me to take on the task myself.

Clearly he had Dr. Michael Downey in mind for the task. He told me that "Michael is interested in seeing what type of biographical data and information might be available". Though he denied that Michael himself was "preparing to write my biography" he then recommended that I speak with Michael, which I did on several occasions.

Several years later, I wrote the following missive to His Eminence:

> Over the past years I have been greatly edified and impressed with the work that Michael Downey has done for you and the archdiocese. I feel it's imperative that you keep him aboard because the next few years are going to be challenging in many ways.

> Might I suggest that you consider giving him some public recognition. Perhaps a knighthood of Saint Gregory. (Maybe if he had that distinction he could revive their newsletter.) Or maybe the *Pro Ecclesia* medal.
>
> Loyal and faithful servant of the Church that he is, I am sure he would be indifferent to such recognition. On the other hand, it would be helpful for him to add this papal honor to his already impressive academic pedigree.

Whether it was *post hoc* or *propter hoc,* I know not, but Downey was included in the next list of Knights of St. Gregory.

Nothing more transpired until early in 2006 when the Cardinal had a meeting with Michael, me, and the Vicar General about the biography. On August 26th the Cardinal sent a memorandum to the Leadership Team and the auxiliary bishops, which read as follows:

> For some time now, people have been inquiring about at what point should some kind of biography be written about my life and ministry.
>
> Frankly, this issue is of no real concern to me personally. But since I am a public figure in the Church and our Archdiocese—for many years; some say too many years!!—it is inevitable that a biography needs to be written.
>
> I have consulted several people about this topic, and I have finally decided that Dr. Michael Downey will be the author of this biography. No one has worked more closely with me in the Archdiocese over these past critical years of the Synod, its preparation and its implementation. He knows my pastoral mind and my ecclesial outlook.
>
> Dr. Downey will begin research for the biography in the coming months, and it is anticipated that this project will go through several years. Obviously, this is not a fulltime project for Dr. Downey; he has other important commitments at the same time. I ask all of you to be of assistance to him in his research efforts over the coming months and years. He will probably be interested in interviewing some of you as well.
>
> We anticipate the biography coming out a year or two following my retirement, and it will be published by a reputable national publisher.
>
> Thanks for your assistance to Dr. Downey in any way that he requires for this project!

Several days later, I sent the following letter to the Cardinal.

> Thank you for the memorandum of August 26, 2006 about your "future biography." All things considered, I think you made a reasonable decision.
>
> Given Michael Downey's status as a lay employee, I would suggest you draw up a contract for this work that is over and above his present status as your theologian. Should the next administration want to distance itself from its predecessor, such a contract would guarantee Michael a fair recompense for his efforts. Also a contract will be an incentive for finishing his work.

Quite honestly, I was greatly relieved. I feel that Dr. Downey, a highly qualified theologian, will acquit himself of the task.

In the fall of 2005, I was asked to submit a draft of a talk the Cardinal was supposed to deliver at the re-dedication of Blessed Sacrament Cathedral at Sacramento:

> California has experienced most everything in recent years-riots, floods, droughts, fires, earthquakes and, now killer bees. Yet, the Golden

State is still the garden spot of old planet earth. One often recalls and affirms what Fray Junipero Serra said: "In California is my life and there, God willing, I hope to die."

California is truly a state of superlatives. Twelve percent of the nation's residents live in California, an area that boasts of 64,500 millionaires, 57% of them women! Well over 56% of the state's population own their own homes, and 90% have at least one car.

Despite the rape, mayhem, robbery and murder, California is still El Dorado to refugees from boredom, poverty, stagnation and despotism. A favored statistic, quoted for the benefit of easterners, is that Blue Canyon, California is the snowiest town in the country with a mean average of 243.2 inches.

However decadent it may appear to outsiders—weakened by unemployment and inflation, demoralized by crime, deluded by cultists, corrupted by pornographers, debased by junk bond dealers, decimated by psychopaths and pillaged by rioters—California remains a never-never land of riches, fame and freedom to millions around the world. Despite pockets of poverty, Californians are fabulously wealthy in other ways.

In a booster pamphlet issued in 1886 by the Illinois Association, one reads that "in this grand country, we have the tallest mountains, the biggest trees, the crookedest railroads, the driest rivers, the loveliest flowers, the smoothest ocean, the finest fruits, the softest breezes, the brightest skies and the most genial sunshine to be found anywhere else in the world."

California has yet another unique distinction in that it not only has the largest number of cathedrals of any other state, but those houses-of-worship are unquestionably among the most artistic, beautiful and distinctive of any in the nation. Especially is that true in San Jose, San Francisco, Los Angeles and Sacramento whose mother churches are truly outstanding expressions of a peoples' love and devotion to the saints, the Mother of the Savior and the Blessed Sacrament.

Today as we gather in our State's capitol to celebrate the re-dedication of what was once the largest religious structure west of the Mississippi, we need to recall a trinity of pioneers who made this cathedral a reality. We are awe-struck at what its talented architect, Bryan J. Clinch, was able to design and build in just thirty-six months, a period of time when money, building techniques and raw materials were in desperately short supply.

Clinch was indeed a rare personality. The Irish-educated scholar, architect and historian, remembered also for his spectacular Cathedral of St. Joseph in nearby San Jose, adroitly managed scores of laborers, mechanics and skilled artisans in their use of 900 barrels of Portland cement, thousands of locally made bricks, tons of iron, stone and timber in constructing this soaring structure. It's exhausting even to contemplate his accomplishments.

Equally impressive, was the diligence and ambition of Bishop Patrick Manogue who determined to build a Cathedral that would rival the state capital for domination of the local skyline. Occasionally bishops are accused of being "gold diggers." Pat Manogue was the only member in the

American hierarchy to have actually been a gold prospector in his early years. But when it came to paying for his cathedral he was close to penniless. He left it to God to defray the expense and somehow it worked.

There are many anecdotes about Patrick Manogue, none more amusing than his relationship with his predecessor who once chided him for neglecting to preface his signature with the cross customarily used by bishops when signing their names. Bishop Manogue is said to have replied that "he had long been of the opinion that one cross in a diocese was amply sufficient!"

The third person of our historical trinity was already a memory when this cathedral was erected. His name was Father Peter Augustine Anderson whose privilege it was to celebrate the first Mass in this now beautiful city which was described in his time as "one great cesspool of mud, garbage and dead animals," His imprint on this edifice is featured in a cartouche prominently portrayed as one enters this cathedral.

Historians tell us that the story of the Catholic Church began in Northern California with the advent of this Dominican priest, a native of Elizabeth, New Jersey. Shortly after his conversion to the Catholic Faith, Anderson became a candidate for the priesthood at Saint Rose's Priory.

He was ordained on April 5, 1840, and spent the early years of his ministry in Kentucky and Ohio. After working briefly in the missions of Canada, the young Dominican turned up in California where, according to his superior, he had journeyed for the purpose of bringing "spiritual assistance to those of our American Catholics who have already strayed from our congregation here or elsewhere to this country."

In August of 1850, Father Anthony Langlois notified the Catholics of Sacramento that he was sending Anderson here "to commence a religious establishment in your midst and so to have more opportunity to worship our God, to promote the good of holy principles and, particularly, for you to profit in spiritual and moral ways and, by so doing, to procure future salvation."

Father Anderson bore the distinction of being the proto priest of San Francisco to set out for the mining regions. He celebrated the initial public Mass in Sacramento on August 11th. The young friar, soon recognized as a very zealous and exemplary cleric, came highly recommended. One authority noted that there were few young priests who labored harder in the missions of this country than Father Anderson.

Surely no missionary ever entered upon his work under more adverse and discouraging conditions. Father Anderson managed, however, to obtain temporary quarters for a church and soon had a permanent edifice under construction at the corner of K and 7th streets. That, new place of worship was placed under the patronage of Saint Rose.

The *Sacramento Illustrated* noted, "During the memorable season of cholera, Father Anderson labored unceasingly. He visited the hospital several times daily, sought out the poor and afflicted in their uncomfortable tents, administered all the consolation and relief within his power and procured medical aid for such as had no one to care for them. Overcome and exhausted by excessive labors, he contracted typhoid fever and fell victim to his self-sacrificing charity and zeal." He died on November 27, 1850. Catholics and non-Catholics alike mourned the loss of this martyr of charity who had given his life in the service of the plague-stricken.

Four years after Anderson's death, Archbishop Joseph Sadoc Alemany had the remains of his confrere moved to the Dominican monastery in Benicia and buried beneath the altar of the old church. In 1859, the remains were transferred to the nearby cemetery.

Peter Augustine Anderson was the first martyr of charity among the priests who came to minister to the inhabitants of Gold Rush California. As such, he walks through history's pages in the distinguished company of Fray Junipero Serra and a host of other clerics who should not be forgotten.

Others more familiar with this magnificent cathedral than I will surely speak eloquently and at greater length about its architecture, artwork, beauty and restoration. May I say only that, as one knowledgeable about cathedral buildings myself, I salute and congratulate your bishop, his consultors, benefactors and staff on what has been accomplished here for the Mother Church of the Diocese of Sacramento. May the Lord bless you all!

Early in 2007, I was asked by a Roman curial official who didn't want to be identified, to submit a list of suggestions to whomever would be appointed the next archbishop of Los Angeles. Here is a direct transcript of my response:

A New Age for Archdiocese of Los Angeles

1) Proclaim the ministries of Catholic Charities as the "Supreme Priority" for the archdiocese;
2) Declare an archdiocesan "State of Emergency" for priestly vocations;
3) Enlist assistance of such previously untapped clerical and religious resources as the Franciscan Friars of Renewal and the Legionaries of Christ. Entrust a canonical parish to *Opus Dei*;
4) Triple the number of seminarians by reviewing and expanding the recruitment policies of the Department for Priestly Vocations. Reorganize the sacerdotal Personnel Board;
5) Explore the feasibility of acquiring the Legionaries of Christ to operate the seminary with an archdiocesan rector. Re-open the college seminary *quam primum*;
6) Inaugurate a year-long archdiocesan drive for return of alienated and/or fallen-away Catholics;
7) Establish an "Endowment Fund" for the Cathedral of the Our Lady of the Angels.

NEW
CATHOLIC
ENCYCLOPEDIA

SUPPLEMENT 2009

VOLUME 1
A-I

in association with

THE CATHOLIC UNIVERSITY OF AMERICA • WASHINTON, D.C.

Detroit • New York • San Francisco • New Haven, Conn • Waterville, Maine • London

8) Expand the scope of the speakers forum for the Catechetical Congress;
9) Print the weekly schedule of activities aired on EWTN in *The Tidings*;
10) Cancel the mandatory retirement program for priests, remove term limits on pastoral appointments and encourage able-bodied retirees to a limited return to ministry;

11) Cut all archdiocesan budgets by 10% for three consecutive years. Reduce staff at the Archdiocesan Catholic Center by 20% over three years. Install strict accountability on all parochial and ministerial entities;
12) Appoint regional bishops as pastors of parishes where they will reside;
13) Enlarge and update the diaconate program, appoint an "archdeacon" to serve as vicar and name a deacon to serve as personal secretary and director of ceremonies to the archbishop;
14) Examine and adopt measures to reverse declining enrollment in Catholic elementary schools. Open a dialogue with and provide assistance for home schoolers and establish a high school in Simi Valley.

Collapse of exhaustion after three years.

14

Archdiocese of Los Angeles

When I was a student at The Catholic University of America, I was influential in getting the then Auxilary Bishop of Los Angeles, Most Reverend Timothy Manning, to write the essay for *The Catholic Encyclopedia*. It was a superb essay to which I contributed considerable input. With the passage of forty years, I was asked to prepare a totally new article on the same subject which was to appear in the supplemental 2009 volume of the encyclopedia. Because of its relevance to my overall ministry, we are reproducing it in its entirety in this volume.

Historical commentators are quick to observe that almost everything in Southern California has been imported—plants, flowers, shrubs, trees, water and even religion!

More than three decades ago, the late Carey McWilliams pointed to the unprecedented influx of peoples—a factor that today accounts for the ethnic diversity of the onetime *Pueblo de Nuestra Señora de los Angeles.*

The Native Americans were the first to inhabit the area. And though they are mostly gone now, they left behind an indelible mark in such names as Cahuenga, Malibu, Mugu and Pacoima.

Then came the Catholic *pobladores* from Sonora who laid out the original *plaza* on a bluff above the river named by Fray Juan Crespi to honor Our Lady of the Angels. For a while after the war with Mexico and the discovery of gold, Los Angeles remained a small and insignificant town. But that was soon to change.

Statehood came, in 1850, and then, following the Civil War, the railroads reached out to touch Los Angeles, bringing newcomers from the south and midwest, many of them lured westward by the well-publicized sunshine.

The roots of the Bible were solidly transplanted by this great midwestern migration. Los Angeles remains predominantly Protestant, though the importance of the Catholic faith was attested in 1953, when the

Archbishop of Los Angeles became the first cardinal in the western United States.

Though the city is famous for its revivalists and cultists, they have probably drawn attention out of all proportion to their numbers. Studies indicate that the great majority of churchgoers belong to the traditional faiths.

The Chinese and Japanese arrived; French, Poles and German Jews also came and many of the beach areas became popular resort meccas for English tourists.

Early in this century, the Mexican population began rising again, this time forming the bulk of the migratory work force. The African Americans, who presently constitute 12.5% of the population, began their trek in 1900.

And the waves of immigration roll on. In the last decade, Vietnamese and Koreans, with their distinctive contributions, have flooded into Los Angeles to join dozens of other Asiatic groups, like the Samoans, more of whom live in Los Angeles than reside on the Island of American Samoa itself.

The people thronging to the area have generally been an adventurous and inventive lot. In Hollywood, for example, creative minds have entertained and informed the whole world, reflecting both America's manifold problems and its unique promise.

A major port city, the aircraft and electronics industries expanded to meet the challenges of World War II and then spun around to handle contemporary transportation and communication needs.

As it welcomed Pope John Paul II as the Vicar of Christ in 1987, this largest of the world's cities dedicated to Our Lady provided a haven for its perpetual transplants. It amazes, amuses and eventually absorbs. New arrivals are confronted with culture shock—the climate, the freeways, the lifestyles and the ethnic mix.

PUEBLO DE NUESTRA SEÑORA DE LOS ANGELES

The *Pueblo de Nuestra Señora de los Angeles* was established on September 4, 1781, within the parochial confines of San Gabriel Mission, with a contingent of eleven families, or forty-four people. Four square leagues of land, good for planting all kinds of grains and seeds, about three-fourths of a mile west of the river, on a ledge rising above the present Alameda Street, were set aside for the furthest extension in the presidial district of San Diego de Alcala.

Fray Junípero Serra first visited the *pueblo* on March 18, 1782, seven months after its foundation, enroute to San Gabriel. He referred to the town endearingly as *La Porciuncula*, though he did not describe it. His biographer relates how the inhabitants of those days worked in the fields, ate tortillas, beans and tamales and, for recreation, played cards.

Though Serra and his confreres harbored serious reservations about the expediency of establishing the *Pueblo de Nuestra Señora de los Angeles,* the foundation, like its sister metropolis to the north, San Francisco, bears that distinctively Seraphic imprint that can only be predicated of the earliest penetrators into this far-away Province of California.

Franciscan influence in Los Angeles reflects, at the local level, what the friars accomplished along the whole expanse of the Pacific Slope. Even Governor Pedro Fages, whose relationship with Serra was anything but cordial, admitted, in 1789, "that the rapid, pleasing, and interesting progress both in spiritual and temporal matters . . . are the glorious effect of the apostolic zeal, activity, and indefatigable labors of these missionaries."

That viewpoint has been generally sustained, even by the most hostile of observers. The openly antagonistic Frances Fuller Victor, for example, once remarked that "the spectacle of a small number of men, some of whom certainly were men of ability and scholarship, exiling themselves from their kind, to spend their lives in contact with a race whom it was impossible in a lifetime to bring anywhere near their level, excites our sympathy and commendation." The early Franciscan heritage has endured into the 21st century. Indeed, Fray Junípero Serra's biographer stated that "nowhere else does Serra have so conspicuous a location today" as he does in contemporary Los Angeles.

The handsomely sculptured bronze statue of the *Presidente,* now prominently enshrined in the Old Plaza area of the city, embodies one of the nation's most meaningful tributes to a religious founder. Fray Junípero is also remembered in the names of numerous streets, schools, plaques, buildings, institutions and even the national capital.

The Franciscan influence has been manifested rather consistently since the earliest days. One creditable author acknowledges that up to 1854, the only organization in Los Angeles upholding any standard of morality "whatever was the Roman Catholic church. It erected houses of worship, hospitals and schools; it was the pioneer in all good works." Little wonder that there is a renewed interest in the work that Serra and his band of Franciscan collaborators accomplished in Southern California, the more so when one recalls that Los Angeles today is second only to Mexico City in the number of inhabitants who carry the blood and speak the beautiful tongue of the old vice-royalty of New Spain.

A METROPOLITAN DISTRICT

The geographical derivation of the 8,762 square miles presently comprising the Archdiocese of Los Angeles (Archidioecesis Angelorum) can be traced to April 27, 1840, when Pope Gregory XVI created the parent jurisdiction from the already-established See of Sonora, naming Fray Francisco Garcia Diego y Moreno (1840-1846) the proto bishop.

Boundaries for the gigantic Diocese of Both Californias were the Colorado River in the east, the 42nd degree of north latitude (Oregon line), the Pacific Ocean in the west and south to all of Baja California. The title was officially changed to the Diocese of Monterey in 1849.

The subsequent transfer of sovereignty in California made a further delineation of boundaries imperative. On April 17, 1853, Bishop Joseph Sadoc Alemany (1850-1853) received word that the Sacred Congregation of Propaganda Fide had removed Peninsular California from its attachment to the Diocese of Monterey.

Several months later, on July 29, Pope Pius IX created a Metropolitan District at San Francisco. The southern parallel of the parish at San Jose was fixed as the demarcation between the new Archdiocese of San Francisco and the larger but suffragan Diocese of Monterey.

The Monterey jurisdiction, which encompassed all of Southern California, remained territorially intact for the next seven decades. On July 8, 1859, Bishop Thaddeus Amat (1853-1878) was authorized to move his episcopal seat to Los Angeles. At that time he was also permitted to add that city's name to the diocesan title.

During the subsequent years, there were a number of proposals for dividing the large and unwieldy Diocese of Monterey-Los Angeles. As early as 1866, Bishop Amat confided to a friend that he expected, "within a few years," to see another bishopric formed in the southland.

While no official action was taken by Amat, his successor, Bishop Francis Mora, (1878-1896) petitioned the Holy See several times for a reduction of his jurisdiction. The proposal was shelved temporarily, in 1894, when Mora was given a coadjutor in the person of Bishop George T. Montgomery (1896-1903).

Rumors of a division were revived after the death of Bishop Thomas J. Conaty (1903-1915) and were sustained by the long inter-regnum that ensued before the appointment of John J. Cantwell (1917-1947).

Early in 1922, Bishop Cantwell asked that the 90,000 square mile Diocese of Monterey-Los Angeles be dismembered, with twelve counties formed into a separate jurisdiction. Pope Pius XI acquiesced and, in June, created the new Diocese of Monterey-Fresno. The larger area, known as the Diocese of Los Angeles-San Diego, embraced the remaining southland counties and stretched to the Mexican border.

The penultimate alteration in the southland occurred on July 11, 1936, with the erection of a second Metropolitan District in California at Los Angeles. Simultaneously, the four southernmost counties were fashioned into the Diocese of San Diego. Included in the newly-formed Province of Los Angeles were the suffragan Sees of Monterey-Fresno, San Diego and Tucson.

In January of 1948, the Apostolic Delegate informed officials at Los Angeles that in order to avoid confusion with the older Archdiocese of *Puebla de Los Angeles* in Mexico, the southland's jurisdiction would henceforth be known officially as the Archdiocese of Los Angeles in California.

The archdiocese retained its geographical integrity from 1936 until June 18, 1976, when Pope Paul VI created a new diocese for Orange County. Remaining in the parent See were the counties of Los Angeles, Ventura and Santa Barbara.

The assertion made in 1903, that California's glory "lies not in the fact that her wilderness was conquered, nor that her priceless treasures were unearthed, but in the propagation and marvelous growth of religious faith" has lost none of its force, even with the passage of eight decades.

The Archdiocese of Los Angeles, largest of the state's twelve ecclesial divisions, encompasses an area of 8,762 square miles, or the totality of Los Angeles, Ventura and Santa Barbara counties. Ranking first among the nation's 183 juridic units, the archdiocese provides for the spiritual needs of 4,212,887 Catholics with 1,155 priests serving 287 parishes.

In order to facilitate its apostolic mandate of spreading the Gospel message, the educational system in the Archdiocese of Los Angeles currently enrolls 56,888 youngsters in 219 elementary schools, 30,604 teenagers in fifty secondary schools and 11,845 students in five colleges and universities.

The latest statistics indicate an annual enrollment of 270,000 public school youngsters in the various programs operated by the Office of Religious Education. Students ranging from kindergarten to twelfth grade are engaged in pedagogical pursuits in after-school, Saturday and Sunday sessions. Teacher-training courses are available throughout the archdiocese.

The extensive involvement of the Church in the active apostolate is exemplified by its network of thirteen general hospitals, which accommodated 1,820,256 patients in the most recent statistics. An additional seven special hospitals or sanitaria looked after the physical needs of numerous other persons.

While these and other statistics have been described as the "dry bones" of history, one can easily perceive that ecclesial accomplishments in the Archdiocese of Los Angeles indicate a vibrant and healthy Catholic populace, firmly dedicated to the furthering of Christian ideals.

LARGEST ECCLESIAL JURISDICTION IN THE U.S.A.

Since 1983, the Archdiocese of Los Angeles has been the largest ecclesial district in the United States. Interestingly enough, the runner-up to Los Angeles in California is the Diocese of Orange, which was only severed from its parent jurisdiction in 1976. The figures are based on those reported by the nation's thirty-five Latin and Eastern Rite archdioceses and 150 Latin and Eastern Rite dioceses as enumerated in the *Official Catholic Directory.*

Naturally, the Church's growth reflects the civil structure. The metropolitan area of Los Angeles continues to grow at a phenomenal rate. Its 34,000 square miles encompass an area larger in population than all the states except California, New York and Texas.

It has the largest Latino market, with 2.7% of the population of Latino heritage or origin, as well as the largest Asian Pacific Islander market, with 8.2% of the population of Asian heritage or origin.

There are 157 separate incorporated cities in the district, ranging in size from Los Angeles (3.3 million) to Vernon (ninety) people. It is first in manufacturing shipments, as compared to second-place Chicago. (The Archdiocese of Chicago was formerly the largest in the nation.) Upwards of a hundred million tourists come every year, many of them to shop in an area which is fourth in production of apparel after New York, California and Pennsylvania.

Ranking third in the manufacture of furniture, to cite another example, Los Angeles and its metropolitan area is a major market for imported cars.

And the area is not all highways either, but ranks just behind Washington and Oklahoma in the quantity of land devoted to agriculture.

Financially, the area has a firm base. It is the savings and loan capital of the United States, having eleven of the fifty largest such institutions headquartered here. Savings deposits total 104.4 billion, nearly twice that of second- ranked Chicago. For those who distrust American banks, there are 120 foreign banks located here.

In terms of gross national product, the metropolitan area of Los Angeles ranks tenth among the nations of the world. The most recent figures of the GNP place it at 275 billion, putting it ahead of Brazil, India, Mexico, Australia, Spain, the Netherlands and Switzerland.

In 1968, James Francis Cardinal McIntyre (1948-1970) predicted that "Los Angeles would become a world center with an orientation to the Pacific." His Eminence may not have been a prophet in the scriptural sense, but he was exceedingly shrewd at reading the signs of the times. His successor was no less astute. Timothy Cardinal Manning (1970-1985) likened Los Angeles to Ellis Island (in New York); a multi-cultural archdiocese, destined to take its rightful place as the flagship of the American Church.

When Pope John Paul II came to the archdiocese, in September of 1987, he found the Church experiencing what Archbishop Roger Mahony (1985 onwards) described as "a New Pentecost, a vigorous growth in faith and in diversity of peoples, a renewal of spirit and joy in our Lord Jesus Christ and in the tradition of Fray Junípero Serra".

REACHING TO THE FUTURE

Even those outside her fold must accord the Catholic Church a special "historical pre-eminence" in discussions about the earliest days of Los Angeles.

The "Catholic presence" in the area now comprising the City of Los Angeles actually pre-dates the city by a dozen years. The very name derives from the diary of Fray Juan Crespi, who introduced the Feast of the *Portiuncula* into California's vocabulary.

On January 17, 1837, just a year and a half after Los Angeles had been raised to the status of a city, the *ayuntamiento* or council passed, without a dissenting voice, a resolution declaring that "the Roman Catholic apostolic religion shall prevail throughout this jurisdiction."

While there is no evidence that this expressed but never enforced "establishment of religion" benefitted Catholics, it did provide adherents with a unique distinction in Western Americana's historical annals.

Plans were unveiled to open a Catholic school in the city in 1849 and two years later the institution opened its doors with twenty-six "scholars." Bishop Joseph Sadoc Alemany entrusted the administration of the school to the Picpus Fathers.

As late as 1853, Harris Newmark said that "nearly all the population was Catholic." Another creditable authority noted that "up to 1854, the only organization in Los Angeles upholding any standard of morality whatever was the Roman Catholic Church. It erected houses of worship, hospitals and schools, it was the pioneer of all good works."

And while it all changed following the onrush of the gold seekers, Los Angeles continued through the decades to be a unique haven for religious-minded peoples of all creeds.

In a survey of local history published in 1967, Christopher Rand observed that "there are probably more religions in Los Angeles than in the whole previous history of mankind." And it all started with the Catholic Church, in 1781.

RELIGIOUS PATRONAGE

On June 8, 2006, The Vatican Prefect of the Congregation for Divine Worship and Discipline of the Sacraments notified Catholics in California's southland that Our Lady of the Angels has been named principal patroness of the Archdiocese of Los Angeles, a decision approved by Pope Benedict XVI.

The earliest ecclesiastical patronage in California dates from January 4, 1843, when the first bishop, Francisco Garcia Diego y Moreno, placed his jurisdiction under the spiritual protection of Our Lady, Refuge of Sinners. When the diocese was divided in 1853, the Archbishop of San Francisco adopted another heavenly intercessor while the southland retained its earlier allegiance. On September 1, 1856, Pope Pius IX gave the Diocese of Monterey Vibiana as its patroness, a saint unearthed in the Roman catacombs a few years earlier.

The term "Los Angeles" had been a part of the episcopal title since 1859, but that appellation, a shortened form of *Nuestra Señora de los Angeles*, never figured in the original religious patronage of Southern California.

It was suggested that a transfer of patronage to Our Lady of the Angels would be highly appropriate for the Archdiocese of Los Angeles. Possibly the late Archbishop John J. Cantwell had that in mind when plans were drafted for a proposed cathedral by that name in the 1940s. That the title of the archdiocese had no connection with its patronage, however, is not without precedent in the United States where only four of the twenty-eight archdioceses identify title and patron.

Fray Juan Crespi recorded in his diary that late in the afternoon of July 31, 1769, the expeditionary force of Gaspar de Portola crossed an *arroyo* of muddy water and stopped a little further on in a wide clearing. He stated that the following day was set aside to celebrate the jubilee of Our Lady of the Angels de Porciuncula. The next morning on the vigil of the feast, the party continued its journey and came through a pass between two hills into a broad valley abounding in poplar and older trees. A beautiful brook crossed the valley and later turned around a hill to the south. After traveling another twenty miles, the Spaniards camped along a river which they fittingly named in honor of *Nuestra Señora de los Angeles de Porciuncula*, a title derived from the day's liturgical calendar.

According to canonical procedures, the patron of a place is the saint honored as the special protector of that locale. In the case of Los Angeles, this distinction was accorded to Our Lady of the Angels when the name given to the *Rio Porciuncula* was extended in its alternate form to the *pueblo* founded in the fall of 1781.

Since the feast of Our Lady of the Angels of the Porciuncula was not observed in the universal liturgical schema, the patronage of Mary under that title could not be applied to the *pueblo* as a formal ecclesiastical patron except by privilege and even then only after consultation with the clergy and laity of the place. In this, as in other similar cases, it has been the practice of the Holy See to bestow as the titular feastday that of Mary's Assumption into heaven. Hence as early as 1814, Fray Luis Gil of San Gabriel spoke of laying the cornerstone of the church at Los Angeles on the 15th of August on which day the *pueblo* celebrates its titular feast.

To rephrase it more succinctly, until recently religious patronage in the Archdiocese of Los Angeles had no connection with that of the City of Our Lady of the Angels, which proudly saluted its patroness each year on the 15th of August under her original title, *Nuestra Señora de los Angeles.*

The feastday for Our Lady of the Angels, which some years ago was moved to coincide with the anniversary of the city's establishment, will continue to be observed on September 4th.

FRANCISCO GARCIA DIEGO Y MORENO (1840-1846)

Francisco Garcia Diego y Moreno was born on September 17, 1785, at Lagos de Moreno, Mexico, the son of Francisco and Ana Maria (Moreno) Garcia Diego. Invested with the religious habit of the Order of Friars Minor at the College of Nuestra Señora de Guadalupe on November 26, 1801, Francisco was ordained a priest on November 14, 1808 by Bishop Prime Feliciano Marin de Porras of Linares.

Upon completion of his service as Novice Master for the Franciscan community at Zacatecas, Fray Francisco Garcia Diego was elected *Comisario-Prefecto* of the missions attached to the Apostolic College. In 1832, he led a contingency of friars to peninsular California and then north to Alta California, arriving at Santa Clara Mission where he labored for several years.

On April 27, 1840, Pope Gregory XVI erected the Diocese of Both Californias naming Fray Francisco Garcia Diego as the proto bishop of the new jurisdiction. The friar was ordained (consecrated) by the Right Reverend Antonio Maria de Jesus Campos on October 4, 1840 at the National Shrine of Our Lady of Guadalupe just outside Mexico's Distrito Federal.

Upon his return to Alta California, Bishop Garcia Diego took up residence at Santa Barbara Mission where he lived for the relatively few years of his episcopal tenure. Beyond opening a seminary at Santa Ines Mission, the prelate was frustrated in bringing his other objectives to completion because of the economic, political and religious challenges in the region.

The bishop succumbed on April 30, 1846, probably from tuberculosis. He is buried in a vault on the epistle side of the sanctuary at Santa Barbara Mission.

JOSEPH SADOC ALEMANY

Joseph Alemany was born July 13, 1814 at #9 Rambla del Paseo in the ancient town of Vich, Spain, the third youngster of Antonio Alamany and Micaela de los Santos Cunill. In 1830, Joseph Alemany (he preferred and always used the "e" rather than the "a") entered the Priory of Santo Domingo and, on September 23, 1831, took solemn vows as a member of the Order of Preachers (Dominicans) at which time he was given the name "Sadoc."

After philosophical studies at Tremp's Priory of San Jaime de Pillars and theological training at Gerona's Priory of Our Lady's Annuntiation, Joseph completed his sacerdotal preparations at Viterbo's Priory of Santa Maria dei Gradi. He was ordained to the priesthood by Bishop Gaspar Bernardo Pianetti on March 11, 1837, at Viterbo's Cathedral of San Lorenzo.

Following reception of a lectorate in theology and extensive courses in English at the Urban College of Propaganda Fide, Father Alemany was sent to the United States. Arriving on April 2, 1840, he was assigned to Saint Joseph's Priory in Somerset, Ohio.

Naturalized as an American citizen on April 15, 1841, Father Alemany served at Zanesville, Nashville and Memphis. He was elected Master of Novices in 1847 and, the following year, he was named Major Superior for Saint Joseph's Province in which capacity he attended the Seventh Provincial Council of Baltimore.

Appointed Bishop of Monterey on May 31, 1850 by Pope Pius IX, Alemany was consecrated (ordained) on June 30 in Rome's Church of San Carlos al Corso by Giacomo Cardinal Franzoni, assisted by Archbishop Giovanni Stefanelli and Patriarch Guiseppe Valerga.

Disembarking at San Francisco on December 6, 1850, the newly appointed Bishop of Monterey immediately journeyed to Santa Barbara, where he presented himself to the Vicar Capitular of the vacant jurisdiction, Fray Jose Maria Gonzalez Rubio. He was formally installed on January 28th. While in Santa Barbara, Alemany issued his first pastoral letter in which he exhorted Catholics in California to a greater "purity of morals" in the practice of their faith.

By the end of the following year, Alemany had established himself at Monterey where he designated the presidio Chapel of San Carlos Borromeo as his cathedral. On December 21, 1851, at Alemany's request, the Diocese of Monterey was separated from its attachment to the Metropolitan District of Mexico City. Alemany also took steps to establish a vicariate for peninsular California. He invoked a diocesan synod which was held in San Francisco on March 19-23, 1852.

While attending the First Plenary Council of Baltimore, Bishop Alemany initiated proceedings for the recovery of the Pious Fund of the Californias, a legal action that remained prominent in American juridical annals until its ultimate solution in 1967. On July 17, 1853, Alemany laid the cornerstone of Saint Mary's Cathedral in San Francisco.

On July 29, 1853, Pope Pius IX created the Metropolitan District of San Francisco with Alemany as its first archbishop, a distinction bestowed on only six other districts during the [longest pontifical rein in history.] On November 18, 1855, Alemany was invested with the sacred pallium by his suffragan, Bishop Thaddeus Amat, C.M., of Monterey.

Death claimed the prelate on April 14, 1888 in the city of Valencia, where he was endeavoring to re-establish his Order's ancient Province of Aragon. He was interred on the epistle side of the main altar in the chapel of Santo Domingo.

Alemany's remains were disinterred in January of 1965 and returned to San Francisco where, after services conducted in old Saint Mary's Cathedral, he was placed in a vault alongside his successors at Holy Cross Mausoleum in Colma.

THADDEUS AMAT Y BRUSI, C.M.

Thaddeus Amat, C.M., born December 321, 1811 at Barcelona, Spain, the son of Pedro and Martha (Brusi) Amat, was received into the Congregation of the Mission (Vincentians) on January 4, 1832. Ordained a priest on December 23, 1837 by Hyacinthe Louis de Quelen of Paris. Amat arrived in New Orleans on October 9, 1838. He served at posts in Perryville, Cape Girardeau and Saint Louis until 1847 when he became rector of Saint Charles Seminary in Philadelphia. He attended the Seventh Provincial Council of Baltimore.

Consecrated (ordained) Bishop of Monterey on March 12, 1854 by Giacomo Cardinal Franzoni in the chapel of Propaganda Fide, Rome, Amat arrived in California with the relics of Saint Vibiana, under whose patronage he erected a cathedral in 1876. He was installed at Monterey on November 25, 1855.

Amat issued his first pastoral letter in 1854 and authored a catechism on matrimony (1864) which was used widely throughout the United States. He moved to Southern California and had the name of the diocese changed to Monterey-Los Angeles in 1859. Amat attended the sessions of Vatican Council I and brought to an end the first phase of the settlement for the Pious Fund of the Californias (1875). Later, he engaged in a protracted canonical dispute with the Franciscans at Santa Barbara.

Bishop Amat died at Los Angeles on May 12, 1878 and was interred beneath the main altar in Saint Vibiana's Cathedral. In 1962, his remains were moved to the episcopal vault at Calvary Mausoleum, and then reinterred in the new Cathedral of Our Lady of the Angels in 2004.

BISHOP FRANCIS MORA

The fourth of the southland's bishops, Francis Mora, was born on November 25, 1827 in the 12,414 square mile Principality of Catalonia, in the northeastern corner of the Iberian peninsula.

Christened on the very day of his birth at Gurb, Francisco was enrolled on the parochial roster of the 5th century church of San Andres. He entered the Conciliar Seminary of San Joachim as a student for the bishopric of Vich. After several years there he was accepted as a divinity student by Bishop Thaddeus Amat, the newly consecrated Bishop of Monterey-Los Angeles.

Raised to the priesthood on March 19, 1856, his initial assignment was to the presidio chapel of San Carlos Borromeo at Monterey. Later he served at San Juan Bautista Mission and then became pastor of the parish of the Immaculate Heart of Mary in Pajaro Valleys, Watsonville. For a while he also functioned at San Luis Obispo Mission. Mora was called to Los Angeles and the pastorate of the old Plaza Church of Nuestra Señora de los Angeles in 1863, a position he held for the following fifteen years.

On July 25, 1866, Mora was named Vicar General for the Diocese of Monterey-Los Angeles and, when the health of Bishop Thadeus Amat began to decline, Mora was appointed Coadjutor bishop of the diocese. He was consecrated on August 3rd. He became the residential bishop of the 75,984 square mile Diocese of Monterey-Los Angeles on May 12, 1878.

During his episcopal tenure, Mora encouraged the formation of a Catholic newspaper, selected the sites of several cemeteries, combated the local activities of the American Protective Association and expanded diocesan services and outreach programs. There was modest expansion of educational services, establishment of several teaching communities of women and convocation of a synod.

After sustaining a carriage accident, Bishop Mora asked for and was given a coadjutor in the person of George Montgomery. With Montgomery's elevation, Mora handed over his crozier and returned to Spain where he lived for the final years of his life.

The bishop died on the thirty-second anniversary of his episcopal consecration in 1905. He was interred in the local cemetery at Sarria until 1962, when his remains were returned to Los Angeles. He is now entombed in the Cathedral of Our Lady of the Angels.

BISHOP GEORGE MONTGOMERY

When Bishop George Montgomery succeeded Bishop Francis Mora on June 10, 1896, anti-Catholic bigotry in the guise of the American Protective Association was rampant. The need for vigorous leadership to defend the Church was fully met in this able prelate.

Chancellor of the Archdiocese of San Francisco, he was consecrated April 8, 1894, shortly after Bishop Mora's request for a Coadjutor had been approved. Immediately he assumed almost complete administration of the Diocese of Monterey and Los Angeles for the ailing Bishop Mora.

This was the year when the A.P.A. was showing alarming power in the Los Angeles city elections. Bishop Montgomery acted promptly and decisively, organizing a branch of the Catholic Truth Society and instituting a series of popular lectures on Catholic doctrine. By the end of the century the wave of bigotry, had subsided.

When the precarious health of Bishop Mora compelled him to resign and he returned to his native Spain, Bishop Montgomery continued his vigorous program of establishing Catholic prestige in Southern California and at the same time providing for the spiritual needs of an expanding population.

He was the first native American bishop of the diocese. Born in Daviéss County, Kentucky, December 30, 1847, he was ordained to the priesthood by James Cardinal Gibbons, Archbishop of Baltimore on December 20, 1879.

On February 3, 1903, Bishop Montgomery left Los Angeles to become Coadjutor Archbishop of San Francisco. But his life was cut short by appendicitis, from which he died after a week's illness, January 10, 1907. He was mourned throughout the entire state, for he had proved himself not only a dynamic churchman, but also a great civic leader and an outstanding American.

During nearly nine years of residence in the southland, Bishop Montgomery achieved widespread respect through his numerous associations and activities not only for himself but for all Catholics. He was a fearless and convincing speaker.

An inscribed plaque to his memory was placed on the pulpit in the Cathedral of St. Vibiana. Bishop Montgomery High School in the South Bay area is named for him.

THOMAS J. CONATY

In his younger days, Thomas James Conaty, second Rector of the Catholic University of America, was described in terms as realistic as they were poetic: "We can easily imagine him a Peter waking up Europe to the crusades, but would find it hard to see in him the same Peter in a hermit's cell. God made him an active man, and in every agitation for the people's health he is the angel who, stronger than the rest, can best stir the waters".

Thomas James Conaty was born in Kilnaleck, County Cavan, Ireland, on August 1, 1847, the son of Patrick and Alice Lynch Conaty. Two years later the infant was brought to the United States by his parents who settled in Taunton, Massachusetts. The boy grew up in the Old Colony State and after attending the local public schools, he entered Montreal College on December 30, 1863, transferring four years later to Holy Cross in Worcester. Under the patronage of a cousin, Conaty returned to Montreal in 1869 and enrolled at the Grand Seminaire. He was ordained for the Diocese of Springfield on December 21, 1872, by the Most Reverend Ignatius Bourget.

The following spring Father Conaty was named curate at Saint John's Church in Worcester and in 1880, when the parochial boundaries were adjusted, Conaty was given charge of the newly erected parish of the Sacred Heart. That the years of his pastorate were filled with activities is understandable in view of his reputation as an "agitator who loves the work of the multitude." A school, rectory, convent, gymnasium and finally a church were built and, within a few years, the parish had no less than sixteen societies to coordinate its many-phased apostolate.

With the completion of his term in Worcester, Conaty was named Bishop of Monterey-Los Angeles in 1903. In California, Conaty became involved with a host of activities. He purchased a newspaper for the diocese, took an active interest in all manner of laity groups, was a pioneer in charitable and hospital works and educational expansion. He brought a number of Religious women to the diocese, worked closely with Saint Vincent College and even tried, unsuccessfully to build a cathedral.

Conaty interacted well with ethnic groups and was a close collaborator with movements to better the conditions of native Americans. A noted preacher, he was involved in ecumenical activities. He died at the seaside town of Coronado on September 18, 1915. He is now interred in the Cathedral of Our Lady of the Angels.

ARCHBISHOP JOHN J. CANTWELL

The first Archbishop of Los Angeles was a man of vision. Reading well the signs of potential and real growth for Southern California, he boldly proposed to the Holy Father the need for establishing a Metropolitan District for Los Angeles.

Though the people of a new era probably associate him mostly with the high school bearing his name, John J. Cantwell left his mark, and a prominent one at that, in the Catholic annals of California's southland. In fact, he was a pioneer whose stature contrasts favorably with the Golden State's great missionary founders. The prelate's accomplishments were as spiritually profitable to the faithful of his day as they are statistically phenomenal to those of a succeeding generation.

John Cantwell was one of seven California prelates from the Emerald Isle. Born in Limerick, he was baptized in Saint Michael's Church on December 7, 1874, the only one of Patrick and Ellen Cantwell's ten children not initiated into the Mystical Body at the ancestral city of Fethard. Sent at the age of six to the Patrician Monastery National School and later to the nearby Classical Academy, young Cantwell began early to prepare for the clerical life he was to share with three of his brothers in the archdiocese of San Francisco. From Fethard, John went to Sacred Heart College in Limerick near the home of his grandparents on George Street.

The future bishop entered Saint Patrick's College at Thurles, one of Ireland's renowned missionary seminaries in 1892, and spent the following seven years preparing for his ordination. He was raised to the priesthood on June 18, 1899, at the hands of Robert Browne, Bishop of Cloyne, in the 19th Century Cathedral of the Assumption.

Soon after his ordination, Father Cantwell arrived in San Francisco and served for the next five years at Saint Joseph's Church in Berkeley. An enthusiastic promoter of educational activities, he helped to organize the Newman Club at the University of California and taught classics at Saint Joseph's Presentation Convent. In 1905, he became secretary to Archbishop Patrick W. Riordan and nine years later was promoted to Vicar General under Archbishop Edward J. Hanna. He was named to the long vacant Diocese of Monterey-Los Angeles in 1917, after having refused an appointment to Salt Lake City some years earlier. The staggering problems facing the young bishop on his arrival in Los Angeles were manifold, but he took as his yardstick the sage advice of his longtime friend Father Peter C. Yorke:

Don't start by building a cathedral . . . . get the little ones to love Christ . . . . concentrate on Christian education of the youth and you will be a great success in the eyes of the Lord.

During an episcopate that stretched over three full decades, Cantwell saw his original diocese divided twice, first in 1922 when the Monterey-Fresno area was detached and again in 1936 when San Diego became a distinct ecclesiastical jurisdiction. In the latter year Los Angeles became a Metropolitan See thus making California the only state in the Union with two separate provinces.

By the time of his death on October 30, 1947, Archbishop Cantwell had developed a bustling, sprawling diocese of a few churches and schools into one of the major provinces in the nation.

As noted by his long-time friend and collaborator, the archbishop "was a worthy successor to the prelates who preceded him. He piloted the Church of Los Angeles from a frontier rim of the Christian world to the edge of greatness in the family of American jurisdictions." He is interred in the Cathedral of Our Lady of the Angels.

JAMES FRANCIS CARDINAL MCINTYRE

Fulton J. Sheen once credited the second Archbishop of Los Angeles with being the greatest spiritual inspiration of his life, "not because of what he told me about the priesthood, but because of the way he lived it."

James Francis Aloysius McIntyre was born on June 25, 1886 in mid-Manhattan, the son of James and Mary (Pelley) McIntyre. After the death of his mother in 1896, James Francis was reared by a cousin, Mrs. Robert F. Conley.

He spent several years in the employ of H. L. Horton and Company, an investment house on the New York Stock Exchange. Young McIntyre took night courses at New York City College and Columbia and, following the demise of his father in 1915, he entered the preparatory seminary for the Archdiocese of New York.

The next year he enrolled in Saint Joseph's Seminary at Dunwoodie where he spent five years until May 21, 1921, when he was advanced to the priesthood by Patrick Cardinal Hayes.

Immediately after ordination, Father McIntyre was appointed assistant to the pastor of Saint Gabriel's Church where he remained until September 1923, when he was named Vice Chancellor and liaison officer between Cardinal Hayes and the curial staff. He became Chancellor in 1934, and, on December 27th of that year was designated a Private Chamberlain by Pope Pius XI. Two years later, on November 12, 1936 he was promoted to the Domestic Prelacy.

After the arrival of Archbishop Francis J. Spellman in 1939, Msgr. McIntyre became a member of the Board of Consultors for the Archdiocese of

New York. On November 16, 1940, Pope Pius XII appointed him Auxiliary Bishop of New York. He was consecrated by Archbishop Spellman in Saint Patrick's Cathedral on January 8, 1941.

Bishop McIntyre was made Vicar General of the archdiocese on January 27, 1945 and, eighteen months later, on July 20, 1946, the Holy Father advanced the prelate to Coadjutor Archbishop of New York. On February 7, 1948, Archbishop McIntyre was transferred to Los Angeles.

Shortly after his installation at Los Angeles, Archbishop McIntyre set about to reorganize the archdiocesan curia, to erect a new chancery, and to refurbish Saint Vibiana's Cathedral—all of which he deemed necessary to the efficient management of a jurisdiction encompassing an area of 9,508 square miles with a steadily increasing Catholic population.

Pope Pius XII elevated Archbishop J. Francis A. McIntyre to the cardinalate, presenting him with the scarlet *galero* in Saint Peter's Basilica on January 12, 1953, as the twelfth American member of the Sacred College.

Undoubtedly Cardinal McIntyre's greatest contribution was his program for expanding Catholic educational facilities. In the first fifteen years of his tenure, Catholic schools were tripled from 141 to 347, an average of one a month.

In addition to serving a significant role in the Central Preparatory Commission for Vatican Council II, the cardinal attended all the sessions of the council and was active in its deliberations.

After his retirement, Cardinal McIntyre spent the final nine years of his life serving as a parish priest at Saint Basil's in mid-town Los Angeles. By the time of his demise, on July 16, 1979, he was the acknowledged "Elder Statesman of the American Hierarchy. He is interred in the Cathedral of Our Lady of the Angels.

TIMOTHY CARDINAL MANNING

Trained in the noble tradition of the Cantwell years, seasoned in the expansionary complexities of the McIntyre archiepiscopate and steeped in the spirit of Vatican Council II, Timothy Cardinal Manning has left an impressive imprint on the pilgrim Church of Our Lady of the Angels.

One of the four children of Cornelius and Margaret (Cronin) Manning, Timothy was born Nov. 14, 1909, at Ballingeary, County Cork, Ireland. In 1915, he enrolled at the local National School and seven years later advanced to the educational facilities operated at nearby Cork by the Christian Brothers.

His preparation for the priesthood began in 1923, at Mungret College, a secondary school staffed by the Society of Jesus for the foreign missions. The youthful clerical aspirant was attracted to California by an appeal on behalf of the Diocese of Los Angeles-San Diego. Leaving Ireland in October 1928, he traveled to Menlo Park where he joined the student body of St. Patrick's Seminary.

He was ordained to the priesthood by Bishop John J. Cantwell on June 16, 1934, in Saint Vibiana's Cathedral. His initial assignment was that of curate at Immaculate Conception Church in Los Angeles. The following year, Father Manning was sent to Rome for post-graduate studies at the

Pontifical Gregorian University, where he received the doctorate in Canon Law in 1938.

Upon his return to Southern California, Father Manning was named secretary to Archbishop Cantwell, a post he occupied for eight years. In 1943, he was made a papal chamberlain and, two years afterwards, was promoted by Pope Pius XII to the domestic prelacy.

On August 17, 1946, Msgr. Manning was appointed Titular Bishop of Lesvi and Auxiliary of Los Angeles. Episcopal orders were bestowed on October 15, by Bishop Joseph T. McGucken, then Apostolic Administrator for the Diocese of Monterey-Fresno. At the time and for a goodly while thereafter, Bishop Manning was the "Benjamin of the American Hierarchy."

With the appointment to Los Angeles in 1948 of Archbishop J. Francis A. McIntyre, Manning was named Chancellor. From 1953 to 1967 he also occupied the pastorate of Saint Gregory's, a parish on the western rim of downtown Los Angeles. On November 29, 1955 he became Vicar General of the archdiocese.

A popular speaker and writer, Bishop Manning published a chapter of his doctoral thesis dealing with Clerical Education in Major Seminaries, a fifty page treatise called *The Grey Ox* and the entry for the "Archdiocese of Los Angeles" in the New Catholic Encyclopedia.

A number of his sermons and addresses have appeared in various ecclesiastical journals in recent years. The bishop served the commonweal in several capacities during his tenure as Auxiliary of Los Angeles, including a fifteen year stint on the Los Angeles City Library Commission and a lengthy term as a director for El Pueblo de Los Angeles Commission.

Upon realignment of ecclesial boundaries in Central California. Bishop Manning was named to the newly-erected Diocese of Fresno on Oct. 24, 1967. His work in the eight counties of the San Joaquin Valley was described as "a servanthood of justice and reconciliation." In eighteen brief but intensely fruitful months, he created a diocesan housing commission, established four new parishes and five missions, approved formation of a priests' senate, authorized a task force to marshal resources for inner city and minority groups, shared the bitter anguish of the Delano labor dispute and visited each of the eighty parishes scattered through the 35,239 square mile jurisdiction.

Bishop Manning was recalled from Fresno to the scene of his earlier priestly labors on May 6, 1969 as Coadjutor to James Francis Cardinal McIntyre. Assigned to the titular See of Capri, Archbishop Manning was re-named Vicar General and given the pastorate of Saint Brendan's Church.

Upon the retirement of Cardinal McIntyre on January 21, 1970, Archbishop Manning became Chief Shepherd of the Church of Los Angeles. He received the *pallium*, symbolic of the metropolitan office, on June 17, 1970.

In addition to pursuing administrative and expansionary policies, Archbishop Manning established a priests' senate, an inter-parochial council and a clerical personnel board. He energetically supported a host of ecumenical involvements and warmly endorsed and participated in the *Cursillo* movement. He personally chaired the Commission for Liturgy, established a spirituality house and erected an Archival Center, to mention but a few of his many activities.

He made a solemn pilgrimage to Mexico City's National Shrine of Our Lady of Guadalupe, where it all began for California, there to thank the Mexican people for their role in bedrocking the faith along the Pacific Slope. It was also in 1971 that the Archbishop was elected proto-president of the newly-created California Catholic Conference.

In his concern for and identification with the archdiocesan founded and sponsored Lay Mission Helpers, Manning visited missionaries in South Africa, Rhodesia, Ghana, Kenya, Malawi and Uganda. It was while en-route to another segment of that far-flung apostolate early in 1973 that he received word that Pope Paul VI once again had honored the People of God at Los Angeles, by naming him to the College of Cardinals.

Though the Catholics of Orange county were given their own diocese in 1974, Los Angeles continued to expand and, by 1984, was acknowledged as the largest ecclesial jurisdiction in the United States. He died in Los Angeles on June 23, 1989, and is buried in the Priest's Plot at Calvary Cemetery.

ROGER CARDINAL MAHONY

Catholics in California's southland rejoiced when word reached them that one of their own was returning to be the fourth archbishop in 1985. Their new prelate was the fourth native of Los Angeles and the twenty-third Californian called to the episcopate.

Roger Michael Mahony's ecclesial pedigree is deeply imbedded in the area's heritage. His relationship to Timothy Cardinal Manning, for example, went back almost forty years. It was in the pages of *The Tidings* for October 18, 1946, that their kinship began. That issue, describing Manning's consecration as Auxiliary Bishop of Los Angeles, carries a picture of a ten-year-old Roger and his twin brother, Louis.

Thirteen years later, Bishop Manning conferred the minor orders of Lector and Porter on Mr. Mahony and, the following year, those of Acolyte and Exorcist. In 1967, when Bishop Manning was named to the Diocese of Fresno, young Father Mahony served as chief liaison between the new Ordinary and retiring Bishop Aloysius J. Willinger.

Roger Michael Mahony was born to Victor James and Loretta Marie (Baron) Mahony on February 27, 1936. His entire elementary training was acquired at St. Charles School in North Hollywood, where he fell under the pastoral tutelage of the late Msgr. Harry Meade.

In 1950, he entered Los Angeles College, the preparatory seminary for the Archdiocese of Los Angeles. He was among the initial enrollees at Mission Hill's Queen of Angels Seminary, in 1954. Upon completing his collegiate courses at St. John's Seminary, Camarillo, young Mahony asked for and received incardination as a clerical aspirant for the Diocese of Monterey-Fresno.

He received priestly ordination at the hands of the Most Reverend Aloysius Willinger on May 1, 1962. A few days later, he was assigned to a curacy at Saint John's Cathedral, Fresno. In the following fall, Bishop Willinger asked Father Mahony to take further studies at the National Catholic School of Social Service in Washington, D.C.

Soon after returning to Central California in 1964, Father Mahony was named diocesan Director for Catholic Charities and Social Service, an assignment he held for six years. In September, 1964, he became Administrator (and later Pastor) of Saint Genevieve's Parish, Fresno.

Among other positions occupied by the tireless priest during the late 1960s were executive director for both the Catholic Welfare Bureau and the Infant of Prague Adoption Service, as well as chaplain of the diocesan Saint Vincent de Paul Society. He also found time to teach during those years at Fresno State University and Coalinga College.

Long interested in the apostolate to Hispanic peoples, Father Roger Mahony served a term on the board of directors for the West Coast Office of the Bishops' Committee for the Spanish Speaking. He was also active as Secretary for the United States Catholic Bishops *Ad Hoc* Committee on Farm Labor.

There was time for civic responsibilities too. Father Mahony was affiliated with the Fresno County Economic Opportunities Commission, the Alcoholic Rehabilitation Committee, the United Crusade, the Community Worship, the Urban Coalition and the Fresno Redevelopment Agency.

It was recognition of those manifold duties that prompted the Junior Chamber of Commerce to proclaim Father Mahony "Young Man of the Year for 1967." It was also in that year that he was named Honorary Chaplain to His Holiness, Pope Paul VI.

In 1970, shortly after the transfer of the Most Reverend Hugh A Donohoe to Fresno, Msgr. Mahony was appointed diocesan chancellor, a position he continued to hold after his episcopal consecration on March 19, 1975, as titular Bishop of Tamascani. He became pastor of Saint John's Cathedral in 1973.

Bishop Mahony was transferred to Stockton as residential ordinary in 1980, and presided over the pastoral needs of that 10,023 square mile, six county diocese. Transferred to Southern California as Archbishop of Los Angeles on September 5, 1985 Mahony became a Cardinal Priest, June 28, 1991.

During Cardinal Mahony's tenure in Los Angeles, numerous new apostolates and ministries were launched, including formation of an *Ad Hoc* Womens Task Force (1985), launching of five pastoral regions with an auxiliary bishop in charge of each, the *Tercero Encuentro Hispano*, new Immigration Policies and Initiatives, establishment of the Catholic Education Foundation, organization of annual Cardinals Awards, publication of a Spanish language newspaper (*Vida Nueva),* inauguration of an annual appeal for poor parishes and schools (Together in Mission), formation of a Clergy Misconduct Oversight Board, acquisition of a central Archdiocesan Catholic Center, installation of Catholic Mortuaries at Archdiocesan Cemeteries and erection of the largest Cathedral in the United States (Our Lady of the Angels) to mention but a few.

The Archdiocese of Los Angeles welcomed Pope John Paul II in 1987 when the Holy Father paid the first papal visit ever to a California mission (San Fernando, Rey de España).

15
A Selection of Mostly Funeral Homilies

I am privileged to have had the final words for hundreds of pilgrims along the way to eternal life. Here are some for whom there is a typescript:

Kay Haley

(1919-1999)

One of the Zamorano Club's most colorful and supportive members returned her noble soul to the Lord on Christmas Day this last year. Katherine (Kay) Haley, 80, a fourth-generation daughter of Ventura County, succumbed at Rancho Mi Solar after a lengthy illness.

Following her marriage to Robert Haley in 1940, she and her husband settled on the Rancho Casitas, where they reared their four children. In addition to operating a working ranch, Kay was intensely interested in thoroughbred racing. The walls of her home were full of public service citations, including the prestigious Milton M. Teague award for Outstanding Volunteerism. She was named Woman of the Year in 1970 by the California Museum of Science and Industry.

Throughout her long and busy life, Kay was involved in charitable and political activities. She spearheaded the building of the Ventura County Museum of History and Art, and was a long-time fixture on the board of the Ventura Community Hospital, and, in both of those pursuits, Kay was a generous benefactor. Over the years she was active in the political campaigns of Congressman Robert Lagomarsino, Governors Earl Warren, Goodwin Knight, and George Deukjejian, and Governor and President Ronald Reagan.

Kay was likely the most knowledgeable bibliophile in Ventura County. In addition to expanding the western americana collection begun by her mother, Edith Hobson Hoffman, she amassed an incomparable collection of etchings by Ed Borein. Kay's interest in Borein was

In Celebration of Life

Sister M. Michael Doherty, I.H.M.
1902- 2000

an outgrowth of her many visits, as a youngster, to the artist's studio in Santa Barbara.

I got to know Kay in the late 1970s, while I was pastor at Mission San Buenaventura. Even then, Ventura's tireless dowager was driving the county's longest car, wearing the area's most exotic hairdos, and running up monumental telephone bills at Pacific Bell. Less widely known was her support of an endless list of needy causes, always with the caveat that "no one needs to know where this came from." She also hosted two gatherings of the Zamorano Club at her ranch on June 28, 1980 and June 20, 1987.

One of my favorite recollections about Kay, and a measure of her influence on the national level, dates back to the mid -1980s when the Serra Bicentennial Commission was trying to get a commemorative stamp issued for the famed Mallorcan friar. After unsuccessfully exhausting all the normal channels, I called Kay, whose mother had been one of Fray Junípero Serra's earliest supporters, and asked if she would serve on our commission. "Precisely what do you want," she responded. After expressing my frustration about the stamp, I wondered if she had any recommendations. "No problem," she said. "I'll call Judge William Clark (then Secretary of the Interior), and he'll take care of it," Clark approached President Ronald Reagan, long an admirer of Serra, and the president issued an override to the complicated process. The 44-cent commemorative stamp was issued in 1985. Later, when I called to thank her, Kay responded, "Well, it was easier than serving on your commission."

Sister Michael Doherty, I.H.M.

(1902-2000)

Seldom in the history of religious life has the Church in any area been so indebted to a single family as the Archdiocese of Los Angeles is to the children of Michael and Mary Ellen Doherty who gave five daughters and a son to its service.

Today, we come to bid adieu to the matriarch of that family, Sister Michael Doherty, who graced planet earth with her gracious presence for almost a hundred years.

To have known that great lady and to have been known by her is a blessing that we all will cherish until the day when we join her in eternal life.

The pedigree of Sister's accomplishments for her community and the Church in California is long and impressive, something of a roadmap of Catholic education in the Golden State.

She taught various times at Immaculate Heart of Mary and Blessed Sacrament in Hollywood, Saint Anthony and Saint Matthew in Long Beach and Immaculate Heart College. Her other major positions included Dean of the School of Education at Immaculate Heart College, Guidance Councilor at Bishop Amat High School, Principal of Saint Bernardine High School and Mission High School in San Luis Obispo and longtime Moderator for the Immaculate Heart Auxiliary.

Sister Michael wrote four major books and scores of learned articles in educational journals during the seventy-eight years she wore the habit of the California Institute of the Sisters of the Most Holy and Immaculate Heart of the Blessed Virgin Mary.

Sister Michael was old (or young) enough to remember the pioneers of the Immaculate Heart Sisters in California. As a little girl, she visited the old motherhouse in Pico Heights long before there was an Immaculate Heart College (1916).

That the college was eminently successful was due in great measure to Sister Michael's academic credentials and education accomplishments. She was the first Nun ever to receive a doctorate from the University of California at Berkeley in 1939.

Her 412 page dissertation, a copy of which we have in the Archival Center, was entitled "History of Catholic Secondary Education in California". The legendary historian, Herbert Eugene Bolton, was one of the official university readers. Over so many years, whenever I needed a quick fix for an educational date, Sister could roll it out of her mental computer.

Most of you remember Sister Michael in her later years., a gentle, friendly and motherly lady who epitomized what total dedication to a religious vocation was all about. But there was an earlier Sister Michael who was forceful, courageous and outspoken, characteristics associated with all the Church's great women religious pioneers and founders.

In one of my recent visits, she told me that I would be asked to preach her homily "at the proper time." I think the reason was that she had outlived the long litany of priests far more qualified that I for this task.

"Well," I responded, what do you want me to say?" Without the slightest hesitation, she said "Talk about the role of women in the Church. Tell the oldsters to be proud that they are women, remind the middle aged to rejoice in their motherhood or their religious calling and, finally, tell the young ones how happy and fulfilling is a vocation to sisterhood in the contemporary Church." "Oh, yes," she said, "and keep it short."

In endeavoring to fulfill that mandate, I would like to reflect ever so briefly on the role that women have and are playing among God's people.

A feature story in a recent issue of Time magazine referred to Los Angeles as the "Orient of the Western World" and, in that regard, I thought you might like to hear a Chinese version of the creation story:

> "Lord, I need a companion," said the first man on earth. So God took the beauty of a flower, and the song of a bird, the color of the rainbow, the laughter of the wave, the gentleness of the lamb, the cunning of the fox, the fickleness of the showers and the waywardness of the clouds and wove them into a female which He gave to man.

In spite of the occasionally anti-feminine strain in Catholicism, traced from St. Paul through Sts. Augustine and Thomas Aquinas, there has always been a rich treasure of womanhood in both the Jewish and

Christian traditions. Before Sarah was loyal, before Rebekah was wise, before Rachel was beloved of her husband, they were, first of all, women.

In the gospels, Elizabeth prophesied and women of Samaria and Canaan professed their faith; the woman at the temple gave all she had, two small coins, and the widow at Nairn mourned for her only son; Martha and Simon's mother-in-law prepared the meals, and the Magdalen wept for her sins. Each was a woman-some wives, some single women, some widows, and one divorced.

In the apostolic generation, Priscilla and her husband offered St. Paul the hospitality of their home; the charitable Dorcas made dresses and cloaks for those in need; and Phoebe was a deaconess "who gave great help to the apostles." Wife, widow and single they were, but their names are now immortalized in the book of life . . . . .

The Russian scholar, Nicholas Berdyaev, said that we are entering the "feminine age of history," an age he equated to be an "age of mercy." Maybe so, but I strongly suspect we entered the feminine age about the year that Sister Michael Doherty entered the convent in 1922.

Those who belittle the Catholic Church's attitude toward women really don't know much about the Church or her history. For most of this century, for example, there have been more Catholic female college presidents, hospital administrators, school principals and more women signing checks than is true even today in America's corporate world.

And for the chauvinist, who dared to criticize God for creating man before woman, remind him that one always makes a rough draft before the final masterpiece.

In Sister Michael's case, I think we could best characterize her by quoting that part of the Talmud which says:

God did not create
woman from man's head

that he should command her,
nor from his feet,
that she should be his slave,

but rather from his side,
that she should be near his heart.

The Doherty chapter in the religious annals of California is now closed. And what a glorious chapter it has been. Sisters Enda, Eileen, Benedict Joseph, Stanislaus Marie and now Michael all belong to the canon of history. May they continue, from their place in Heaven, to bless and pray for us as they have for so many years in the convents of the Golden State.

No prophet is recognized in his own neighborhood. I've always thought it strange that when there was a unique opportunity for greatness in the Immaculate Heart Sisters, in the 1960s, the shakers and doers didn't turn to Sister Michael Doherty. When I asked around for the reason, the common response was that she was too old! That was thirty-five years ago! Too bad because Sister Michael would have kept the community out of trouble.

James Trent

(1933-2001)

People are generally defined and remembered by what they did or tried to do while sojourning in this vale of tears known as planet earth.

Jim Trent was a loving husband, an attentive father, a loyal parishioner, a valued friend—in fact, he was role model in all those areas.

But, above and beyond those roles, he was a teacher par excellence. Just before he died, Jim received word that he had been selected as a "distinguished" professor at UCLA for this academic year.

Like all good teachers, Jim's primary concern in his chosen profession was his students. That concern stretched far beyond the classroom and into the very lives of the students. Their hopes became his and he was ever alert and concerned for their needs, aspirations, trials and disappointments. He was always ready to listen and to help. His daily routine began early, ended late and extended far into the weekends, evenings and even vacations. For every hour he labored in the classroom, he spent another three or four hours looking after those entrusted to his tutelage.

Students sensed that concern and reacted accordingly. They knew that even during his several illnesses, he was there to support them, sometimes from a hospital bed. He showed me some of the hundreds of letters from current and past students received during his cancer and heart ailments. They were clearly written from love, not from duty.

Jim was anything but an ivory-towered professor. Here at the Old Mission, for example, he established and trained our guides who, over subsequent years, have given innumerable hours of service to visitors, tourists and friends who came here to learn about our history.

We need to mention and thank Gretchen, his long-time and faithful life's companion. She it was who nurtured and looked after their two children, assisted him in his work and nursed him in his illnesses. If Jim was a distinguished professor, Gretchen was surely a "distinguished" wife.

Perhaps a more cautious ship's Captain would have trimmed the sails in these final, storm-tossed years. But not Jim. I am sure that he was pleased that he was able to turn his ship directly into the wind, through the choppiest of waters, with all the sails at full mast to the very end.

Today, we publicly acknowledge and proclaim our affection and admiration for this truly unique individual. Like the great council for which his family name was derived, Jim Trent will be remembered long after his mortal remains are carted off to the cemetery.

In a sense, teachers never die—they live on in their students. Vicariously, Jim's influence will be felt by future generations of UCLA students. How fortunate they and all of us are to have known him.

Richard Gilmour might have been thinking of Jim Trent when he said that:

> No nobler mission (exists) than that of a teacher, by office a leader, by talent an inventor, and by genius an originator and director of power . . . . The scholar belongs to neither race nor country. His home is the world; his pupil, man; and his reward, God. His mission is to know truth and fearlessly to proclaim it. He is not to take from the masses nor swim with the current. Like the general of an army, he must strike home fearlessly where ignorance or evil exist.

Sister Catherine Louise

(1917-2002)

I once jokingly referred to Catherine Louise and her two sisters as the unholy Trinity. There was always lots of hearty laughter and honest fun when the three arrived at Mission Hills for a visit. For 67 years, Sister Catherine Louise wore the distinctive badge of Saint Joseph.

On the very day of Sister Catherine Louise's demise, I read in the Los Angeles Times that one of the great Cedars of Lebanon had fallen in Israel. That was no mere coincidence. Sister Catherine Louise was one of her community's Cedars of Lebanon.

Customarily, eulogists for nuns rattle off the roadmap of their religious missions. Indeed, Sister Catherine Louise's curriculum vitae reads like an itinerary arranged by the Automobile Club of Southern California. She taught at such primary schools as Transfiguration, Holy Cross and Saint Vincent's and, for forty-three years, at Mary, Star of the Sea, Salpointe and Bishop Montgomery. Her humility kept her from mentioning that she was once a Fulbright scholar.

Then, in 1978, at an age when most reasonable people would anticipate retirement, she announced that she was becoming an archivist. I didn't dissuade her because I knew that whatever Sister put her mind to would be done well. And she didn't disappoint me for the next eighteen years.

As in her other pursuits, Sister's role as archivist was stellar in every way. What the Diocese of San Diego may have lacked in other areas was far out-balanced by its archival program. From a little, unheated, dark and dingy basement office in the old chancery, Sister's ministry blossomed forth into an updated, modern and respected operation second to none.

Shortly after we formed the Association of Catholic Diocesan Archivists, Sister Catherine Louise was elected treasurer, a position she occupied with distinction until her health began to fail. At the appropriate time, she stepped aside with enviable grace and dignity.

Though she lined up with the more conservative flank of her community, Sister Catherine Louise had a decidedly "post Vatican II" attitude about authority. She didn't wait for the pink slip—she was a natural-born navigator who knew where she was going and how best to get there.

Parenthetically, that attitude was and is present in all the great religious leaders. Sainthood is only rarely achieved by the meek and humble.

While she outspokenly deplored many of the modern innovations in her community, her love for the Sisters of Saint Joseph never diminished. In fact, she used them to her own advantage whenever possible. When she noticed for example, that some of the nuns were living in apartments, she conned her superiors into allowing her to follow their bad example. When I questioned her on that point, she laughingly said "what is good for the goose is good for the gander. And I am rather partial to ganders."

Several times I asked her when she was going to retire. Her answer was typical: "God will tell me when its time" and He did, in 1999 when she was visited by the big "C". But never, till the day she went home to the Lord, did Sister Catherine Louise become a shrinking violet. She firmly believed that Almighty God calls each of His people to take full charge of his or her early destinies.

People didn't just walk behind her—they were washed along in her wake. Generously endowed by God, Sister Catherine Louise could out-think, out-perform and out-maneuver most of her religious contemporaries, and those are qualities not easily understood or tolerated by those of us who are less endowed by God.

We all have lots of pleasant memories of this good woman. She was cut from the fabric that created the American Catholic school system, and only if and when her type comes back into ascendancy will the Church in the United States regain its singular position of excellence in the religious and secular education of its youngsters.

Many are the women of singular beauty, but Sister Catherine Louise has exceeded them all. May her community profit by her prayers and learn by her good example in the century that lies ahead.

Mary Helen Dawson

(1916-2002)

Mary Helen Dawson paid me the ultimate compliment many years ago when she said I was her "favorite Catholic". That distinction, in the years before ecumenism, was one I greatly cherished.

With all the fanfare associated with Glen's recent ninetieth birthday during these past few months, we may be inclined to overlook the fact that Mary Helen was also a person of some significance in the book world. For over thirty years, she presided over the miniature book department of Dawson's Book Shop. And, in that capacity, she dealt with hundreds of collectors in all corners of the world. No catalogue ever came forth from North Larchmont Boulevard without her *nihil obstat.*

She was in at ground zero on all the happenings in the field. A charter member of the Miniature Book Society, she it was who conferred the name of "conclave" on the gatherings which has met annually in a host of cities over the years since 1983.

Though few women knew as much about books as she did, Mary Helen, like her husband, Glen, remained a person of a single book and that

Mary Helen Dawson
February 20, 1916 - November 23, 2002

book was the Bible. It was her inspiration, her guide and her compass. Everything in life derived its meaning in Sacred Writ.

A measure of Mary Helen's long love affair with the Bible was the distinction she had of actually being mentioned, by association if not by name, in the Book of Proverbs where the role of the "Capable Wife" is defined. Here is what the inspired writer wrote about the woman whom we mourn today:

The Capable Wife (Proverbs 31:10-31)

10 How hard it is to find a capable wife! She is worth far more than jewels!

11 Her husband puts his confidence in her and he will never be poor.

12 As long as she lives, She does him good and never harm.

13 She keeps herself busy making wool and linen cloth.

14 She brings home food from out-of-the-way places, as merchant ships do.

15 She gets up before daylight to prepare food for her family and to tell her servant girls what to do.

16 She looks at land and buys it, and with money she has earned she plants a vineyard.

17 She is hard worker, strong and industrious.

18 She knows the value of everything she makes, and works late into the night.

19 She spins her own thread and weaves her own cloth.

20 She is generous to the poor and needy.

21 She doesn't worry when it snows, because her family has warm clothing.

22 She makes bedspreads and wears clothes of fine purple linen.

23 Her husband is well known, one of the leading citizens.

24 She makes clothes and belts, and sells them to merchants.

25 She is strong and respected and not afraid of the future.

26 She speaks with a gentle wisdom.

27 She is always busy and looks after her family needs.

28 Her children show their appreciation, and her husband praises her.

29 He says, "Many women are good wives, but you are the best of them all."

30 Charm is deceptive and beauty disappears, but a woman who honors the Lord should be praised.

31 Give her credit for all she does. She deserves the respect of everyone.

Rev. Patrick Sullivan

(1928-2003)

Good morning! Can you hear me? I had a funeral here last Friday. The microphone wasn't working and I complained to Sister Teresa, explaining that my first funeral in this chapel took place forty-three years ago and that the microphone wasn't working then either—or probably ever since.

She assured me that everything would be ready for Monday. "Why", I asked. And she told me that "the cardinal is coming." Thank you, Your Eminence!

Michelle Sullivan will deliver the eulogy after Mass and I will leave the telling of Father Pat's pedigree to her. I would only like to recall one event in that context.

Someone once asked Pat why he had never become a bishop. He responded that he had gotten off to a bad start with the then Auxiliary

IN LOVING MEMORY OF

Rev. Fr. Patrick H. Sullivan

September 15th 1928 - July 16th 2003

The Lord is my shepherd; I shall not want. He maketh me to lie down in green pastures; He leadeth me beside the still waters. He restoreth my soul; He leadeth me in the paths of righteousness for His name's sake. Yea, though I walk through the valley of the shadow of death, I will fear no evil; for Thou art with me; Thy rod and Thy staff they comfort me. Thou preparest a table before me in the presence of mine enemies; Thou anointest my head with oil; my cup runneth over. Surely goodness and mercy shall follow me all the days of my life; and I will dwell in the house of the Lord forever.
~HOLY CROSS MORTUARY~

Bishop Timothy Manning when he came to Saint John's Seminary in the early 1950s.

Manning asked Pat where he was born. "County Cook" he responded. "No, no," the bishop said. "You mean County Cork." To which Pat answered: "No, it was County Cook, I was born in Chicago."

Some years ago, Father Pat Sullivan and I made a day of recollection at a Benedictine monastery near San Diego. At one session, when the speaker ran out of subject matter, he suggested that everyone write down the one thing he would want if there were no tomorrow. As we left that night, the packet with the responses somehow got into my bag. Most of the responses were rather silly and unrelated to the spiritual life. But the one written by Pat was a quotation, in Latin, no less, of Psalm 27:

One thing I ask of the Lord: this I seek:
To dwell in the house of the Lord
all the days of my life,
That I may gaze on the loveliness of the Lord
and contemplate his temple.

We are here today to celebrate the granting of that request. What a wonderful occasion for Father Pat, his first day in the temple of the Lord.

As most of you know, Father Pat Sullivan didn't mince words and be disliked speaking about himself. He had a rather ingenious and effective way of directing attention away from his person. Though we had dinner together every other Sunday evening for almost fifty years, I never really got beyond stage one in knowing about his innermost being. That was just off-limits. He preferred to talk about theological matters and he was surely the most informed priest on that subject that I have ever known. And he spoke about it in terms that were simple and easy to understand. He read voraciously and I was the beneficiary of the dozens of journals to which he subscribed. A masterful and imaginative storyteller, he could have been a best selling fiction writer. Interestingly, however, he never wanted to do anything aside from his ministry.

With all his learning, his belief system was simple and uncomplicated. He faithfully said the daily breviary, recited the rosary, did his spiritual reading (especially the lives of the saints) and made his daily meditation. He was especially pleased when Cardinal Mahony allowed him to have a chapel in the rectory.

On the memorial card of his mother, who died just a few years ago, Pat enclosed a meditation which seems to have special meaning today.

On the wings of death and sorrow
God sends us new hope for tomorrow
And in His mercy and His grace
He gives us strength to bravely face
The lonely days that stretch ahead
And know our loved one is not dead
But only sleeping and out of our sight
And we'll meet in that land
Where there is no night.

Like most priests, Pat suffered during his ministry from a goodly share of unfilled dreams, broken promises, unkind and undeserved criticism, false accusations unattractive assignments, and on and on. His life helps us to understand what Nathaniel Howe meant when he said that "the way of this world is to praise dead saints and persecute living ones."

Now, of course, it no longer makes any difference. Keep in mind that there are three ascending levels of how one mourns: with tears—that's the lowest; with silent prayer—that's the higher. And with resolve—that's the highest. What consolation to know that our brother has reached the pinnacle of human existence. The Preface for the Mass we are offering today puts it so well: "Lord, for faithful who die, life does not end, but it is changed. With the destruction of our earthly bodies, an eternal dwelling place is ready and waiting."

Lying here now like a broken box of alabaster, the good odor of Pat's life penetrates our memories and fills this spiritual house of God which epitomizes the Church he served so faithfully for almost half a century.

May the angels lead you to paradise,
May the martyrs receive you
at your coming.

Catholic folklore is often as interesting as Catholic theology and, sometimes, equally accurate. In any event, Cardinal Manning liked to invoke Catholic folklore to the effect that on the day of a priest's death, a percentage of all the graces derived from the sacraments he dispensed, all the good works he inspired and all the fine example he gave redounds to his own spiritual benefit. And, if that be true, and I suspect it is, there was indeed a noble reward waiting for Father Pat Sullivan when he returned his soul to the Lord.

Of all the new and wonderful dimensions unleashed within the Church by Vatican Council II, none is more meaningful to me than the notion of joy which surrounds the time of death. Catholics are reminded that we are a resurrection people, a people that looks beyond the grave and into the bosom of Abraham. Our bodies will one day be united with our souls in the bliss of the afterlife.

When I was a kid learning the catechism in summer vacation school in rural Indiana, I recall vividly the final stanzas of the Apostles Creed. To me, even at that tender age, to believe in the "resurrection of the body" was something that greatly impressed me. The fact that we all one day would be re-united with our mortal bodies was indelibly imprinted on my soul.

While I was later impressed in dogmatic theology by all the traditional proofs from scripture, the fathers and the general teaching of the Church, I was even more moved by the fairly widespread notion of bodily resurrection in secular literature. A prime example would be the testimony of that greatest of all pioneer Americans, Benjamin Franklin, who was, I think, a deist. This is important because it reflects how imbedded this teaching is in the minds and hearts of the general public.

> Here lies the Body of Benjamin Franklin, printer, like the covering of an old book; its contents torn out, and stript of its lettering and guilding, food for worms. But the work shall not be lost. It will appear once more in a new and more beautiful edition, corrected and amended, by the author.

Winston Churchill planned his own funeral, a service that took place in Saint Paul's Cathedral in London. He included many of the great hymns of the church, using the eloquent Anglican liturgy. At Churchill's direction, a bugler positioned high in the dome of St. Paul's intoned after the benediction the sounds of "Taps," the universal signal that says the day is over. Then came a most dramatic turn. As Churchill had instructed, as soon as "Taps" had been played, another bugler, placed on the opposite side of the dome, played the notes of Reveille": "It's time to get up! It's time to get up! It's time to get up in the morning!"

That was Churchill's testimony that at the end of history, the last note will not be "Taps;" it will be "Reveille." What a consolation for us to know that our bones and those of Pat Sullivan will rise again on that day.

For myself and the many people that Father Sullivan served, especially at Saint Mary Magdalen Parish, the Feast of St. Bonaventure this year will always be associated with Father Pat Sullivan. For as you know, "the saints are remembered and celebrated not on their birth date, but on the date of their death."

Sister Miriam Joseph Larkin, C.S.J.

(1928-2003)

For those among us who find it hard to imagine that Sister Miriam Joseph Larkin's life has ended, I have good news: "It's not true!" And that's not just a wishful sentiment of a long-time friend. In the Preface for today's Liturgy, we are reminded that "for God's faithful people, life is changed, not ended." For "when the body of our earthly dwelling place lies in death, we gain an everlasting dwelling place in heaven."

There is abundant confirmation of this notion from all kinds of human sources. In Newsweek magazine, for example, not a journal known for its theological expertise, deaths are listed under the heading of "transition" and transitions they surely are because Christians look upon death as the beginning of a whole new plain of existence with God. Sister Miriam Joseph has died to this world, only to be born into a new existence where the frailties of this life are wiped away. No longer will she have to drag her frail human body around in a walker.

Today, hers is the refrain of the Johannine passage: "I have brought You honor upon earth, I have completed the task which You gave me to do. Now, Father, honor me with Your presence."

The Book of Sirach tells us that while the more illustrious of worldly figures occasionally leave behind "a name that is remembered to their praise . . . of others there is no memory, for it perished when they perished, and they are as though they had never lived." Such a fate, we are reliably told, is shared even by "stalwart people." And yet, that great book of Hebrew wisdom-literature softens that seemingly harsh statement with assurances that the illustrious persons are remembered in ways apart from their outward stature, public recognition or visible magnificence. They are buried in peace, but their name lives on and on. At gatherings, their wisdom is told and retold, and the assembly sings their praises. Surely Sister Miriam Joseph qualifies as an "illustrious" person.

This was the first Christmas that Sister Miriam Joseph didn't pull herself into her moving van and head to Mission Hills with a gift of her own making. Maybe I should have sensed that as an "omen" or maybe an "amen". We did talk by phone and she promised to come out after her hospital stay. Always she was concerned for others, never for herself.

But then, suddenly on January 11th, the last day of the Christmas season, she was called to be with her parents, her brother Pat, Cardinal Manning and the host of friends, students, and community members of earlier years. All of those people must have rejoiced when she rang the doorbell of heaven. The door was ajar. She didn't need any recommendations. Her life was itself a ticket for eternal life.

Little did Paul, Dotty and I imagine as we celebrated Thanksgiving Day here with Sister Miriam Joseph that in just six weeks we would be across the hallway bidding her adieu. God works in strange ways.

I am grateful, as we all are, that the end came abruptly, even though it deprived us of the opportunity for saying goodbye. When she explained the latest of her many surgeries, I told the Lord, in my own presumptuous way: "Lord, enough is enough. No more pain for this gracious lady." He appears to have heard me.

All of us feel a knot in our stomachs this evening. Surely her community members do. Her vocation was that of an earlier vintage. It was anchored to the notion of service. So dedicated was she that in the last year or so, she had to tape a wooden tongue depressor to one of her frozen-in-place fingers just so she could hit all the keys of the organ. Probably most of you didn't notice that.

If memory serves me correctly, she only got upset with me once. And it was a few years ago when I gently suggested that it might be time to retire. Her answer was pretty persuasive: "I will do that when the Vicar of Christ steps down." And then she reminded me of something that Pope John Paul told a reporter who rudely asked him about retirement: "Christ didn't come down from the cross."

Her pedigree was indeed impressive. She taught at all the levels of education, from college to kindergarten. At Cardinal Manning's behest, she began the Archdiocesan Liturgy Commission and remained at its helm for fifteen years. And that was long before bishops began naming women to policy-making roles.

We do no disservice to Sister's memory to mention that she loved gossip and always wanted to know what was going on. But, invariably, she looked beyond the crisis of the moment. She loved the Church and she personally felt pain when someone or something violated the fabric of faith.

As one who craves to know the background of persons and events, I was always stunned at how much this little lady knew about most everything. I once asked her about someone she had known a half-century earlier and, without hesitation, she rattled off that person's grade point average.

Perhaps one day, an enterprising young religious will string together the events in Sister Miriam Joseph's life. It could be published as the "Larkin Tapes" and I can guarantee you it would make for good reading. She probably touched more lives and influenced more decisions than a swarm of other more loquacious people. She moved quietly behind the scenes, in the pews of her chapel and on the backroads of Los Angeles. She turned up at all sorts of events, sat in a back seat and came away with a documentary report of what transpired.

I cannot let this opportunity pass without recalling how many times she interceded with Cardinal Manning on behalf of some errant priest. She was one of the first to practice "shuttle diplomacy" and, not infrequently, she was the last recourse at court for someone who needed, wanted or deserved special attention. She knew just which of the Cardinal's buttons to push and, invariably, she got her way. She "cared" when caring was a virtue. And, today, there's no one left to do things like that—and that makes the world, the nation and the archdiocese a poorer place.

The Russian scholar, Nicholas Berdyaev, said that we are entering the "feminine age of history," an age he equated with the "age of mercy." Maybe so, but I strongly suspect we entered the feminine age about the year the Sister Miriam Joseph entered the convent.

A feature story in a recent issue of a national magazine referred to Los Angeles as the "Orient of the Western World" and, in that regard, I thought you might like to hear a Chinese version of the creation story:

"Lord, I need a companion," said the first man on earth. So God took the beauty of a flower, and the song of a bird, the color of the rainbow, the laughter of the wave, the gentleness of the lamb, the cunning of the fox, the fickleness of the raindrop and the waywardness of the clouds and wove them into a female which He gave to man."

And that woman was Sister Miriam Joseph Larkin.

Ruth Hoffman

(1914-2003)

Catholics believe that at the time of death, "life is not ended, life is changed." And that's the context of today's tribute to Ruth Hoffman. For her, life begins all over, this time in the presence of the God whom she so faithfully served during so many years.

Throughout her long and productive life, Ruth Hoffman was many things to many people; a gifted pedagogue, a talented Sunday School teacher, an enthusiastic bibliophile and an optimistic spokesperson for many wonderful and worthwhile causes.

What a blessing she was to her daughters, her extended family and her host of friends. She was like an actress insofar as she could play any part but unlike the actress who only plays a role. Ruth was totally authentic—what you saw was what you got.

She was a woman of deep faith in the Lord. Once she asked her husband to print a copy of Benjamin Franklin's testimony for the next life: Here lies the Body of Benjamin Franklin, printer, like the covering of an old book, its contents torn out, and stript of its lettering and guilding, food for worms; But the work shall not be lost. It will appear once more in a new and more beautiful edition, corrected and amended, by the author. . . .

We do no injustice to the memory and genius of Richard Hoffman by observing that Ruth, his faithful wife for 55 years was, for much of that time, the "enabler" who made it physically possible for Richard to continue his work as one of the nation's premier letterpress printers long after illness stole away his ability to speak and much of his facility to work. She was there for him at every hour of the day or night as his voice, his critic, his nurse and his overall helpmate.

During the years that Richard printed the *Hola Volante* for the Zamorano Club I personally observed Ruth at Richard's side, stitching the pages, proofreading the galleys, slip-sheeting the leaves, tipping in the illustrations and the hundreds other chores that transform the blank page into an attractive and even artistic example of fine printing. And she did all those chores in a way that didn't compromise or lessen his own self-esteem.

Even into her ninetieth year, Ruth Hoffman remained the poster girl for the ideal Christian woman. And she didn't have to pretend because it flowed out of her innermost heart and soul as naturally as water plunges over a falls.

Socrates once said, "Ask not that you live long, but that you live well." Ruth did both—she lived long and she lived well. And throughout those many years she echoed Schopenhauer's dictum:

> I believe that when death closes our eyes we shall awaken to a light, of which our sunlight is but the shadow.

I rather think that on this occasion Ruth would like me to recall for you the beautiful reflection by N. MacLeod:

We picture death as coming to destroy; let us rather picture Christ coming to save,

We think of death as ending; let us rather think of life as beginning,

We think of losing; let us think of gaining,

We think of parting; let us think of meeting,

We think of going away; let us think of arriving,

And as the voice of death whispers "You must go from earth." let us hear the voice of Christ saying, " You are but coming to me."

On a card she once sent in return for some little gift, Ruth enclosed a meditation which seems to have a special meaning today:

On the wings of death and sorrow
God sends us new hope for tomorrow—
And in His mercy and His grace
He gives us strength to bravely face
The lonely days that stretch ahead
And know our loved one is not dead
But only sleeping and out of our sight
And we'll meet in that land
Where there is no night.

Funerals are really for the living. And in Ruth Hoffman's case, her life itself was the most perfect eulogy imaginable. Let me close with one more allusion to the final resurrection by telling you a short story:

Winston Churchill planned his own funeral, a service that took place in St. Paul's Cathedral in London. He included many of the great hymns of the church, using the eloquent Anglican liturgy. At Churchill's direction, a bugler positioned high in the dome of St. Paul's, intoned after the benediction the sounds of "Taps," the universal signal that says the day is over. But then came a most dramatic turn. As Churchill had instructed, as soon as "Taps" had been played, another bugler, placed on the opposite side of the dome, played the notes of "Reveille": "It's time to get up! Its' time to get up! It's time to get up in the morning!"

That was Churchill's testimony that at the end of history, the last note will not be "Taps;" it will be "Reveille. What a consolation for us to know that the bones of Ruth Hoffman shall rise again on that day.

Sister Ruth Kent, I.H.M

(1912-2004)

Before Our Lord's victory over death, the grave reigned supreme as the last and greatest enemy of humankind. But all that changed with Christ. For

In Loving Memory

Sister M. Ruth Kent, I.H.M.

Funeral Mass
Saturday, April 24, 2004 ~ 11:00 am
Mother of Good Counsel Church

Interment: Calvary Cemetery

Remember, O most gracious Virgin Mary,
that never was it known that anyone
who fled to your protection, implored your help,
or sought your intercession, was left unaided.
Inspired with this confidence, I fly to you,
o Virgin of virgins, my Mother.
To you I come, before you I stand,
sinful, and sorrowful.
O Mother of the Word Incarnate,
despise not my petitions, but
in your mercy, hear and answer me.
Amen.

Callanan Mortuary Directors

the believer, to be joined to Christ in death means that the merits of the Savior's death are communicated to each baptized person. Saint Thomas put it beautifully when he wrote that "Christ, by His Passion merited not alone for Himself, but he also merited salvation for all His followers".

The Fathers of Vatican Council II put the whole theology of dying in its further perspective by noting that "through Christ and in Christ, the riddles of sorrow and death grow meaningful." Hence it is and must be that for Christians, death is not extinguishing the light. It is putting out the lamp because the dawn has come.

What reluctance I had about preaching today was dissipated when I recalled that Sister Ruth attended my first Mass forty-five years ago at Saint Brendan's and, in the intervening time, she has never missed sending an anniversary card on April 30th. This will be the first year she will have missed.

When I first knew Sister Ruth, I couldn't comprehend how such a tiny woman could get so much accomplished in such a short time. Then I discovered that she was a member of the celebrated Kent family from the planet Krypton. Her cousin Clark Kent a hero of my youth, was known the world over as SUPERMAN. I fantasized how Sister Ruth would disappear into a telephone booth and then re-appear as SUPER WOMAN.

Who else could say so many prayers, accession so many books or visit so many sick people. Certainly no mere human.

I had the privilege of knowing her brother, Father Mark Kent. And, when I taught at Immaculate Heart College in the early 1960s Sister Corita was in her glory as one of the great pop artists of the day. All the Kents were cut out of the same cloth, hard workers, talented teachers and gifted innovators.

Though few of a later generation knew it, Sister Ruth had a distinguished academic pedigree. She acquired a graduate degree in library science from the University in Southern California when few Sisters were given that opportunity.

Sister Ruth's seventy-four year long ministry can be divided into four major segments. Though the term may sound secular, I would say that she had four careers, any one of which would have satisfied the normal person's quest for fulfillment.

The first career was her classroom period of twenty years in which she taught thousands of kids at no fewer than a dozen parochial schools, including an Indian School in Victoria, Canada. She was a natural-born educator who intuitively knew how to motivate students. Gently but persuasively, Sister Ruth expected and received the best in her youngsters. To have been one of her students was to bear the unmistakable imprint of a Catholic education.

Then in 1952 came the second career when Sister was appointed librarian at Immaculate Heart College, a position she held for nine years. I knew her first in that capacity. She was one of those few librarians who actually read the books she catalogued and accessioned.

Every one of the entries made in the card catalogue during those days bears a secret code identifying her association with the book. She was pleased that the library remains intact. It was purchased by former Mayor Richard Riordan and is in his private home in Brentwood.

For reasons beyond anyone's comprehension Sister's tenure at the library was terminated in 1961. Then in one of his more inspired moments, James Francis Cardinal McIntyre asked Sister Ruth to launch her third career by beginning the library for Saint John's College in Camarillo. From a small desk in the basement of the theologate, Sister assembled over a hundred thousand books into one of the most extensive and comprehensive liberal art collections of any college in California. In a report issued by WASC, her library was referred to as "a delight to behold and read," a rare compliment from a very snooty group of academicians.

When the seminary college was opened, Sister moved to lovely new quarters where her books became available to young seminarians, for whom Sister Ruth became a valued confidant, spiritual director and role model. She always had a moment to listen and advise. Many of our younger priests were strengthened and confirmed in their vocation because of her advice and good example.

Not infrequently, during those years Sister would call me and others. The conversation would go like this: "Good morning Father. You know I just came across a wonderful new book that you really should buy and

read." After promising to send the order blank, she would conclude with this observation: "Now Father, when you finish the book would you please send it to our library?" I would rejoinder with: "Well, Sister you do have a budget, don't you?" Oh yes she would say" but this month we are a wee bit over and the rector told me to quit purchasing books." That telephone diplomacy brought many fine and important books into the collection. How could anyone refuse Sister Ruth?

It was while at Camarillo, that Cardinal Mahony bestowed upon her the coveted honor of the Pro Ecclesia award from the Holy Father, a distinction given to only two religious woman in this archdiocese.

But there was to be a fourth career. After leaving Camarillo in 1990, Sister wondered how to remain active in the ministry. Having spent so many years with books she got the idea of "reading" some of those books to the people at Braille. There she became a fixture, maybe even a monument. She became God's voice in a dark world for many whose eyes no longer functioned. What a marvelous impression she made on so many of those good people. And she did much more than read—she counseled, listened and prayed, in an apostolate that lasted almost to the end.

When my own eyes were beginning to fail, I stopped at Braille one day to purchase a special magnifying glass they had in the gift shop. I walked in, spotted what I wanted and then tried to purchase it. The attendant said I would need my doctor's prescription. All my arguing had no effect. Finally as I turned to leave, I asked if Sister Ruth was still there. "Are you a friend of Sister Ruths? she asked. When I said "yes," she pulled out the magnifying glass wrapped it and even gave me a discount!

The conciliar Fathers of Vatican II taught that "man rebels against death because he bears in himself an eternal seed which can not be reduced to sheer matter." Yet, how unbecoming for the Christian to rebel against the thought of dying. Benjamin Franklin didn't fear death. He noted that:

> All people face what is inevitable. Why should death be feared? We begin to die as soon as we are born. Understandably, there may be a desire to postpone the transition-for ourselves and for our loved ones-but of what is there to be afraid? Our physical body is lent to us as a house in which we live. When that dwelling becomes unfit for the purpose for which it was intended, a kind and benevolent nature has provided a way to get rid of that shell. That way is death. Why should we be sad or rebellious? Death does bring changes and adjustments for those who are left behind. The warmth and association of former days are gone. The silence, the finality, the incommunicability disturb, but for our loved one who has triumphed, there should be rejoicing. Sorrow is centered on self.

And one of Franklin's contemporaries, John Adams, was equally positive when speaking of death. The story is told how a young man approached the former President on his eightieth birthday, asking: "Well how is John Quincy today? The old man, with a twinkle in his eye, replied: "John Quincy is very well, thank you." Then, tapping his shrunken chest, he went on to say "The house he lives in is weather- beaten and ram-shackled. The plumbing is bad and the lighting is poor and I dare say it will soon collapse. But, to answer your question, John Quincy is very well."

A friend of Sister Ruth summed her up in these words: She was like an old railroad watch, "full of good works."

Blessed Pope John Paul II

(1920-2005)

A goodly percentage of contemporary Catholics have known only Pope John Paul II. They cherish, as we all do, his visit to Los Angeles and San Fernando Mission in 1987. What a thrill it was to have had the Vicar of Christ with us—if only for four short hours.

We come not so much to mourn Pope John Paul II, as to celebrate his life as well as a papacy that broke all records. This humble Polish successor of Peter traveled more miles, visited more nations, greeted more people, canonized and beatified more saints, appointed more cardinals and bishops, convened more synods, wrote more books and encyclicals, made more doctrinal and moral pronouncements and prayed with more non-Catholics than any of his predecessors.

He also established diplomatic relations with over sixty countries, restored ties with former Soviet countries, published the first catechism since Trent, promulgated a new Code of Canon Law and the first ever Code of Canons for the Eastern Church, solidified Catholic-Jewish relations, and turned around Vatican finances. He liked to joke that he had also buried dozens of writers who predicted his demise.

Billy Graham once said of Pope John Paul II that he will "go down in history as the greatest of the modern Popes. He is the strong conscience of the whole Christian world." David Aikman, a former Time magazine correspondent and a widely known Evangelical Protestant, wrote that such a description didn't go far enough. He said:

> I am not a Roman Catholic, and I certainly share many of the Protestant reservations about some aspects of Catholic doctrine and some forms of Catholic devotionalism. Yet it is my view that Pope John Paul II, in his profound spiritual depth, his prayer life, his enormous intellectual universe, his compassion and sympathy for the oppressed, and above all his vision of how Christians collectively are supposed to live, is the greatest single Christian leader of the twentieth century. When he is gone, he may well be viewed, quite simply, as one of the most exemplary figures in all of Christian history.

Pope John Paul II may or may not be, as one recent book proclaims, the "Man of the Century." But there is no one who has spoken with a greater range and intensity on behalf of human dignity than this Pope.

One ecclesial wag rather unkindly said that hundreds of people on every continent may have nodded during his homilies, but they went to see him; they stayed to listen and they wanted to be there. What preacher in all history can make that claim?

If you think you can change the world by the power you wield, the books you write, the speeches you give, and the people who flock to see you, you might conclude that there is no greater world-changer than John Paul II.

John Kavanaugh wrote in *America* that

> The moral vision of John Paul II was far larger and more capacious than pronouncements on birth control and abortion. It had to do with the law of God, the dignity of persons and the sanctification of our lives. Sex and unborn babies obviously count in this arena. So also does our relationship to money, property, politics and poverty.
>
> His moral doctrine was about life and love and social justice. It was about following Christ, whether we are dealing with sex, money or power. It was about conscience, truth and admitting when we are wrong. It was about compassion and mercy when we fail. It was even about martyrdom and holiness.

If it is true, and I firmly believe it is, that the last century, proclaimed at its beginning as the "Christian century," became by its end the "century of genocide." It was a time of legalized and widely accepted abortion, birth control and euthanasia, all of which John Paul fought.

Historians of the future will write and speak copiously about this pontiff's accomplishments. But this much we can say with certainty: He will be remembered as "John Paul the Great" because he was the greatest man in the world, the greatest man in the worst century.

Regis Graden

(1934-2005)

There are printers and there are "fine" printers. Regis Graden was among that small but distinguished handful who qualified as a "fine printers". Ordinary or commercial printing is a trade, whereas "fine" printing is a vocation. In that vein, Regis stands tall among that exclusive clan of Ward Ritchie, Richard Hoffman and Grant Dahlstrong, all fine printers of the past and all members of the Zamorano Club.

It has been my pleasure to know Regis since I was first stationed at Queen of Angels Seminary in the 1960s. For a while he printed the bulletin for Saint Victor's parish in West Hollywood where I served as "weekend" priest for over a decade.

Upon my return to Mission Hills in 1981, Regis became official "Purveyor of Fine Printing" to the mission named for King Saint Ferdinand of Spain. Visiting his shop was always a memorable and rewarding experience. Truly, to him printing was a vocation and though for many years he functioned as a commercial printer, the quality of his work was always a step above the local competition.

Regis was thrilled when I first invited him to a meeting of the Zamorano Club and a talk by Earl Nation on April 3, 1991. He became a member later that year and thereafter he rarely missed a monthly meeting even when he had to travel from such faraway places as Washington, Oceanside and Chico.

Subsequently Regis printed the club's quarterly, *Hoja Volante,* for eleven years and the monthly announcements for most of that time, all of which were impeccably designed and executed. He produced several books for the Club, including Zamorano Choice II and Zamorano Club Biographies and Memorial Tributes 1956-1997. Dr. Edward Petko's A Tribute to the Work of Richard John Hoffman, was a prize winner and Regis oversaw every aspect of the production of that monumental bio-bibliography.

After much encouragement, Regis addressed the Club earlier this year. And his topic, not unexpectedly, was "fine printing" and how to identify such specimens which are anything but plentiful, even in a world of mass publications. Fittingly, the last of his books, a miniature on Blessed Teresa of Calcutta, was cited and applauded by the Rounce and Coffin Club in their 2005 Western Books Exhibition.

During the days of his commercial career, his business was known as Custom Printing. Later, when he was able to concentrate on "fine printing," his firm was identified by the moniker Nut Quad Press.

Like all great members of his profession, Regis was a natural-born and gifted teacher who loved to share his talents with others. Over the years, dozens of aspiring printers learned the basics of their trade at 416 North Maclay Street in San Fernando, including our own member, Dr. Andre Chavez.

A discerning collector himself, Regis had a small but discerning library of volumes mostly about the history of fine printing and outstanding practitioners of that art form. Not a few of his books had been printed by fine printers of earlier ages such as Daniel Berkeley Updike whose Book of Common Prayer was the capstone of his collection. Through the kindness of James Lorson, Regis was also able to acquire one of the rare shipping boxes manufactured especially for that book.

Regis liked to say that his blood type was "Van Son Negative" and indeed from his teenage years he became adept at distinguishing the components and characteristics of various inks and how they adhered to differing paper stocks. During his service in the Navy, he was the official printer aboard the USS Helena, the flagship for the Seventh Fleet.

Regis was a family man whose wife, two daughters and grandchildren were always uppermost in his thoughts. I asked him once what was the greatest day in his life and, unhesitantly, he answered: "the day I married Donna." She was more than a partner for life, Donna was his chief motivator, critic and help-mate.

Regis was a lifelong Christian. Christians of all persuasions live and die under the shadow the cross. Benjamin Franklin, a hero of Regis, was a Deist who believed very much in the resurrection. That's why I think that Franklin's epitaph could be used, with only a change in nomenclature, for the present occasion:

The body of Regis Graden, printer,
like the cover of an old book,
Its contents torn out and stripped
of its lettering and gilding, lies
Here, food for worms. Yet the work
itself shall not be a lost
For it will appear once more in a new
and more beautiful edition,
Corrected and amended by its Author.

Alphonse Antczak.

Alphonse Antczak

(1922-2006)

Occasionally, very occasionally, a person moves across center stage of old planet earth who epitomizes not one but all of the virtues associated with a true man of God. Over a long life I have known myriads of people, I have read about thousands of others and written about still more. But Al Antczak remains the only one I would pray to not for.

Most of you know something about Al's pedigree. There's much in it that's edifying for those of us who stay behind today.

If the editorship of The Tidings had been an elective office, Alphonse Antczak would easily have won the position when it became vacant in 1973. Born on August 3, 1922, to Frank and Adela (Garcia) Antczak, young Alphonse attended Assumption School in the Polish corridor of Detroit, an institution operated by the Felician Sisters.

Al's father, a native of Poznan, Poland, came to the United States via Ellis Island. His mother, displaced from her home in Central Mexico by revolutionary turmoil, walked across the Rio Grande with her parents, brothers and sisters. A cousin is today the town physician in Jesus Maria, their birthplace in Aguascalientes.

The future editor was brought to Los Angeles in 1931, settling in San Antonio de Padua Parish in Boyle Heights. His pastor was Msgr. Leroy Callahan who did exceptional work in the growing Mexican parishes of the eastside.

After graduation from Loyola High School, Al enrolled as an English major at Loyola University. There he became a protege of the legendary Father Vincent Lloyd-Russell. Al joined the staff of *The Loyolan* and served twice as editor of that college newspaper, before and after World War II.

In 1943, Al enlisted in the United States Army Air Corps, first as a cadet and subsequently as a radio operator. He was on detached service with the Coast Guard for a time to learn airborne LORAN, then a secret navigational system.

Upon his return to Loyola after the war, Al resumed writing for *The Loyolan*. Msgr. Thomas McCarthy, editor of *The Tidings*, was impressed by several of Al's articles about wartime experiences in India and China and offered him a position with the archdiocesan newspaper.

On the Monday after his graduation, Al was assigned to a desk at *The Tidings* which was then located at Jefferson and Figueroa Streets. From January of 1947, the imprint of Alphonse Antczak was felt on no fewer than 2,200 weekly issues of *The Tidings*.

During the ensuing forty-two years, Al witnessed and wrote about a host of topics touching upon the Archdiocese of Los Angeles, including the five great western migrations—European displaced persons (late 1940s), easterners (1950s), Cuban refugees (1959), Asian boat people (mid 1970s) and the Central Americans (1980s). He moved among these new peoples as friend, advocate and chronicler. In August 1973, Al Antczak became the 15th editor of *The Tidings*. During the next sixteen years, he continued and expanded the coverage of California's oldest Catholic newspaper. He served as editor longer than any other person in the paper's long history.

During the Antczak years, *The Tidings* won awards for reporting, editorials and layout. Among those citations, none pleased the editor more than that given for the paper's editorial support of farm workers at Rancho Sespe in Ventura County.

In those years, *The Tidings* operated in the black and continued to help subsidize such projects as the construction of the Education Building, the Catholic Charities headquarters and Santa Marta Hospital.

The personages interviewed by Al read like a Who's Who: They include John F. Kennedy, General Vernon Walters, President Ramon Magsaysay, King Hussein, Dr. Thomas Dooley, Josef Cardinal Mindszenty, Prime Minister Itzakh Rabin and Karol Cardinal Wojtyla (later Pope John Paul II).

Al has also served as a Los Angeles correspondent for the Catholic News Service and the US Information Agency. His stories for the latter were published in Eastern and Western Europe, Latin America, Asia and particularly Africa.

During those hectic times, Al and his wife, Helen, lived quietly in a modest home in the shadows of San Gabriel Mission. Among their eight PIMA children (Polish-Irish Mexican-American) are Sister Mary Catherine, Helen Sanchez, Margaret Antczak, Teresa White, Alphonse Jr., Thomas, John and Joseph.

Though he probably wrote more stories, edited more releases and covered more events than any of its employees in the 100 plus year history of *The Tidings*, Al was no ivory tower visionary. The paper in those days was laboriously printed by letterpress and involved weekly treks to the composition house in Compton. His manual typewriter qualifies for the Smithsonian Institution along with his antiquated car that rolled up over 400,000 miles before collapsing in a puddle of oil in the family driveway at San Gabriel.

During four archbishoprics, Alphonse Antczak was a primary witness and faithful chronicler for the life of the Church in Southern California. He verbalized his role as that of reporting the works of God's people living out their spiritual destiny in the 20th century. In 1989, after forty two years, Alphonse Antczak wrote the traditional "30" across his last editorial for *The Tidings*, to conclude a long and distinguished career in the public service of the Church.

There are many aspects in Al's life that are worthy of imitation by those of us still making our way along the roadway to eternal life. The one that stands out most prominent to me is this: No one ever had stronger viewpoints than Al Antczak on the current flash points in modern society. Yet never did he belittle opposing views, deride dissenting motives or impugn outlandish opinions. He was a true gentle man who respected others, however uninformed they may have been.

Another of Al's remarkable characteristics was that of being able to motivate and direct those who shared with him the ministry of the written word and he always did it in a kind but informative charm. He carried a large stick, but he rarely slammed it down.

You will recall that the four evangelists were the first to proclaim the "Glad Tidings" to an expectant world. Al was God's evangelist in the 20th century using *The Tidings* as his mouthpiece for bringing the good news to the Catholics of Southern California.

Eugene Donohue

(1920-2008)

The democracy of death has invaded our family environs to claim yet another soul for the Beatific Vision. While our hearts are understandably heavy, our emotions are happy and relieved that Eugene Francis Donohue has exchanged the imperfections of this life for the perfection of a life that is destined to last forever.

People are generally defined and remembered by what they did or tried to do while sojourning in this veil of tears known as planet earth. Over the past few days I have compiled a fairly extensive account of Eugene's eventful life.

Eugene Donohue, a well known podiatrist, was the loving husband of Genevieve, an attentive father of Julia and Rose, and a valued role model in those and other areas. Impressive as his lifespan surely was, I have a feeling that he wouldn't want me to dwell on the details. From what I have ascertained, he didn't esteem earthly accomplishments very highly.

And why not? Because a good life is its own eulogy. Those who knew him over his eighty-seven years could hardly hope to enhance his stature by a few feeble remarks.

Perhaps it would be enough to borrow the words of an ancient theologian who once was heard to say:

> Show me a man of integrity, a man with an open heart, a man of many friends and a man unafraid of death and I will show you another Solomon or maybe even another Moses.

Happily for Eugene and for all faithful Christians, the death of the human body has none of that tragedy so dreaded by those who walk only by worldly standards.

Because of his medical background, Eugene was a realist. He wasn't afraid of dying because he accepted death for what it truly is, a part of living. It was that way with the gentle Francis of Assisi who even praised the Lord "for the death of the body which no man escapes." Thereby we all affirm that earthly death has no power to bring harm to one found walking by God's holy will.

Oh, that's not to say that the believer in Christ has no anxiety about the afterlife. The recent Vatican Council pointed out that "it is in the face of death that the riddle of human existence grows most acute. Not only is man tormented by pain and by the advancing deterioration of his body, but even more so by a dread of perpetual extinction." Our overriding consolation is the promise of Christ that the best is yet to come.

In a letter to his mother, the twenty-three year old Aloysius Gonzaga wrote that he had contracted the deadly plague while ministering to the sick. It was a lovely letter, which says all there is to say about the Christian aspect of dying:

> Take care above all things, most honored lady, not to insult God's boundless loving kindness; you would certainly do this if you mourned as dead one living face to face with God, one whose prayers can bring you in your troubles more powerful aid than they ever could on earth. And our parting will not be for long; we shall see each other again in heaven; we shall be united with our Savior; there we shall praise him with heart and soul, sing of his mercies for ever, and enjoy eternal happiness.
>
> When he takes away what he once lent us, his purpose is to store our treasure elsewhere more safely and bestow on us those very blessings that we ourselves could most choose to have.
>
> I write all this with the one desire that you and all my family may consider my departure a joy and favor and that you especially speed with a mother's blessing my passage across the waters till I reach the shore to which all hopes belong. I write the more willingly because I have no clearer way of expressing the love and respect I owe you as your son.

Like Aloysius Gonzaga, who worked with those suffering from the plague, Eugene was interested in "healing." Let me just read for you what the conciliar fathers had to say about this matter.

> Although the mystery of death utterly beggars the imagination, the Church has been taught by divine revelation and firmly teaches that man has been created by God for a blissful purpose beyond the reach of earthly misery. In addition, that bodily death from which man would have been immune had he not sinned will be vanquished, according to the Christian faith, when man who was ruined by his own doing is restored to wholeness by an almighty and merciful Savior.
>
> For God has called man and still calls him so that with his entire being he might be joined with Him in an endless sharing of a divine life beyond all corruption. Christ won this victory when He freed man from death. Hence to every thoughtful person a solidly established faith provides the answer to his anxiety about what the future holds for him. At the same time faith gives him the power to be united in Christ with his loved ones who have already been snatched away by death; faith arouses the hope that they have found true life with God.

Whether a devoted husband for years, a father of two devoted daughters, brother to his two older siblings, Daniel and Rosemary or just a valued friend, Eugene always had time for a smile, a compliment or an encouraging word. He was an upbeat man in a downbeat world.

He was an outstanding Catholic whose presence tolerated no preferments or reservations. I am told that he had the remarkable ability of bestowing his total interest and concern on those with whom he spoke and worked. No matter how exalted or lowly, his friends and patients were kings of the mountain in Eugene's presence.

A while ago, someone once asked Eugene if it bothered him that the Lord leaned rather heavily on him in his final years. His unhesitating response was typical of the man: "Certainly not. He carried me for over eighty years and I can well afford to carry him for the rest of the journey." Then he added this footnote: "You know, the man who hasn't suffered hasn't really lived. I think the way a person suffers says a lot about his priorities." To that we can all say, "Amen."

I am sure that many of us envy Eugene's being able to have his interment in this beautiful mausoleum where he can be part of all the Masses offered each day.

And how meaningful it is that this event occurs on Saint Valentines Day, when all of us are reminded of the love which God has for all His people living and dead.

Today I suspect he rejoices in seeing all of you, his dear friends and family, gathering to wish him well as he enters eternal life.

It was obviously a Christian who wrote:

THINK of stepping ashore and finding it heaven;
of taking hold of a hand and finding it God's;
of breathing a new air and finding it celestial;
of feeling invigorated and finding it immortality;
of passing from storm and tempest to an unknown calm;
of awaking and finding you're home.

Clare Berger
St. John of God Hospital Chapel
July 6, 2002

I am not here today to eulogize Clare Berger. Her life was its own eulogy. She was among those thousands of unknown laity whose entire lives are spent in the service of the People of God. She was special only because she performed her duties in such a quiet and unassuming manner. If Heaven didn't already exist, the Lord would have had to create it for her.

Everywhere one looked during the Manning era, one sees Clare's imprint. One example would be the carefully typed card he kept in his pocket listing every appointment for the next month. Clare would update it daily when His Eminence took off his coat for his afternoon siesta.

Though probably not known by most priests of this archdiocese, Clare Berger surely knew every one of them. Like the Cardinal whom she served, she probably knew much more about the local clergy than she wanted to know. And her mouth was like a trapdoor from which only good things escaped.

Throughout her many years at the old chancery, Clare knew all the secrets and she knew how to keep them. Never once could even I trip her into revealing something that she knew was confidential. I knew I was on thin ice when she looked me in the eye and said: "Now, Father!"

In the days when electric typewriters were new, Clare used to get different people to take hers home on weekends so she could finish the Cardinal's letters. Those machines were heavy and I suggested to Msgr. Hawkes that it would be appropriate to provide Clare with a machine of her own. He did it and she eventually wore it out.

I can claim some credit for Clare going with the then Bishop Manning to Fresno. It came about this way: I asked the bishop if Clare was going with him and his response was: "Well, I would like that very much but I would never ask her to pick up and move from Los Angeles where she has lived so long." Then I asked Clare if she wanted to go to Fresno: "Yes, of course, but I am sure that the bishop has already made other plans." When I told that to Manning, he rejoiced, noting that "Now I will have a lot less to worry about in Fresno."

Only once did Clare write from Fresno and I sensed she wasn't all that pleased with the place. She didn't have to endure it very long. Manning liked to recall that when the Apostolic Delegate inquired as to whether he would be willing to return to Los Angeles as coadjutor, it took him all of twenty seconds to respond in the affirmative. The next morning, at 6 o'-clock, he telephoned Clare with these words: "Start packing, Clare, we're going home."

Clare rarely bragged but she liked to recall that Cardinal Manning was named to the Sacred College on her birthday in 1973. When we went to Rome for the investiture, Clare came along and enjoyed every one of the many liturgical services. I recall that we came back through Chicago and while we were claiming our bags at O'Hare Airport, Cardinal Cody approached me, wanting to know why I was in the Windy City. Clare was standing nearby and I introduced her to him. His response was very revealing and quite accurate: "We Cardinals are mostly what our secretaries make us to be." Surely that was true for Clare Berger.

Clare was always very protective of the Cardinal's correspondence and never would she allow his letters to be filed along with the others in the chancery. After he retired, she guarded several dozen huge boxes of letters as if they were the lost treasure of the Superstition Mountains. She never forgave me for "kidnapping" the materials and removing them to the archives after he retired. When I told the Cardinal what I was going to do. His response: "I never heard a word you said." Then he quoted our Lord's words to Judas: "What you must do, do quickly."

When I took her the book about Cardinal Manning, she didn't say anything for the longest time. She slowly paged through the tome, then smiled and said: "He would like it." That meant more to me than all the book reviews for only she knew him longer and better than I and she was satisfied.

When I heard that Clare Berger had given back her noble soul to the Lord, I went to the chapel, but I found it hard to pray for a woman of such spiritual accomplishments. It occurred to me that Clare wouldn't want much said about her person. So, in deference to that, might I just say a few words about the role of women in the Church of today.

A feature story in a recent issue of *Time* magazine referred to Los Angeles as the "Orient of the Western World" and, in that regard, I thought you might like to hear a Chinese version of the creation story:

"Lord, I need a companion," said the first man on earth. So God took the beauty of a flower, and the song of a bird, the color of the rainbow, the laughter of the wave, the gentleness of the lamb, the cunning of the fox, the fickleness of the raindrop and the waywardness of the clouds and wove them into a female which He gave to man.

In spite of the occasionally anti-feminine strain in Catholicism, traced from St. Paul through Sts. Augustine and Thomas Aquinas, there has always been a rich treasure of womanhood in both the Jewish and Christian traditions. Before Sarah was loyal, before Rebekah was wise, before Rachel was beloved of her husband, they were, first of all, women.

In the gospels, Elizabeth prophesied and women of Samaria and Canaan professed their faith; the woman at the temple gave all she had, two small coins, and the widow at Naim mourned for her only son; Martha and Simon's mother-in-law prepared the meals, and Magdalen wept for her sins. Each was a woman—some wives, some single women, some widows, and one divorced.

In the apostolic generation, Priscilla and her husband offered St. Paul the hospitality of their home; the charitable Dorcas made dresses and cloaks for those in need; and Phoebe was a deaconess "who gave great help to the apostles." Wife, widow and single they were, but their names are now immortalized in the book of life . . .

The Russian scholar, Nicholas Berdyaev, said that we are entering the "feminine age of history," an age he equated with the "age of mercy." Maybe so, but I strongly suspect we entered the feminine age about the year that Clare Berger was born.

Those who belittle the Catholic Church's attitude toward women really don't know much about the Church or her history. For most of the last century, for example, there have been more Catholic female college presidents, hospital administrators, school principals and more women signing checks than was true even in America's corporate world.

And for the chauvinist, who dared to criticize God for creating man before woman, remind him that one always makes a rough draft before the final masterpiece.

In Clare's case, I think we could best characterize her by quoting that part of the Talmud which says:

God did not create
woman from man's head,
that he should command her;
nor from his feet,
that she should be his slave;
but rather from his side,
that she should be near his heart.

Today, we bid adieu to one of the last major if unknown figures in the Manning era, a lady who graced planet earth with her presence for almost ninety-six years.

Over the years, I have known hundreds of people who have worked for the Church in one capacity or another. None is etched more deeply into my memory bank than Clare Berger. She epitomized what commitment to the Lord was all about. Like the saintly little lady from Assisi, whose name she bore, Clare served the Church in good times and in bad, asking only for the opportunity of proving her love for the Lord in a lifetime of selfless service.

Don't mourn for Clare. Rejoice with her that she has fought the good fight, she has finished the race and she has kept the faith. Now there awaits for her the reward reserved for those who love and serve the Lord in this life so as to be happy with Him in the next.

Homilies from the Past

For the most part, the talks, sermons and reflections in this book are those delivered since 2000, the year our first set of Memories appeared in print.

Looking back over the extant manuscripts of earlier reflections, I noticed that most of them had been predominantly "churchy", which seems logical.

Margaret Cassidy

August 30,1985

One of Peg Cassidy's favorite characters was Charley Brown and those of you who read the antics of this little creature can testify that he often utters statements of considerable relevance.

It may surprise some of you to know that there is a "Gospel according to Charley Brown." And its theology is pretty well stated too. I recall that in one episode, Charley says that "God leans heaviest on those he loves the most."

In Loving Memory of

ROSARIO A. CURLETTI

1913 - 1986

LET US PRAY

Father,
We entrust our loved one to your mercy. You loved her greatly in this life. Now that she is freed from all its cares, give her happiness and peace forever. The old order has passed away. Welcome her now into Paradise where there will be no more sorrow, no more weeping or pain, but only peace and joy with Jesus, Your Son, and the Holy Spirit for ever and ever.

Amen.

Welch-Ryce-Haider

"Trinity" Series
3116

© SUPERIOR
Printed in U.S.A.

If that be true, and I strongly suspect it is, Peg Cassidy was indeed a favored daughter of the Lord. We can all testify that she crowded into her last two and a half years enough purgatory for a dozen people.

And, flippant though she was, Peg never once wavered in her faith or lessened in her devotion to the God who allowed all that pain and suffering to occur. She saw it all within the framework of salvation.

It seems like I have known Peg forever. When I first met her, she worked in the front area of a printing shop on Western Avenue. When she heard that I was studying to be a priest, she blurted out that "the world wasn't ready for that." Then, when I left to go, she gave me $20 for textbooks I needed at school. From that moment onward, she never missed a birthday or Christmas. If I forgot to call her for a few months, she would be on the phone wanting to know why.

Outwardly tough and often grumpy, she had a heart far bigger than her tiny body. I quickly learned that beneath the seemingly irritable surface she was a remarkably good-natured and gentle person.

When I asked her some years ago to join *Las Damas Archivistas*, she shouted back, "no—no—no." She launched into a five-minute harangue outlining reasons why she didn't want any part of the organization. When she finished she asked for the dress pattern.

Peg Cassidy touched all our lives in different ways and we are here today because she is and always will be a treasured memory. We are all richer because the tail of her comet flashed across our horizons.

Rosario Curletti

3-31-1986

On March 25, 1986, in the bicentennial year of the mission she loved, on the feast of Our Lady for whom she was named and in the room where she was born, Rosario Andrea Curletti fell asleep in the Lord.

Those of us who stay behind must speak about and remember Rosario in the context of the God whom she served so long and so faithfully. Her life would have no meaning apart from her faith. There were three great loves in Rosario's life and they were grafted to and flowed from the promises made on the day of her baptism.

The first of those great loves was her family. Rosario was a direct descendant of Jose Francisco de Ortega, an esteemed friend and traveling companion of Fray Junípero Serra. Her family tree was adorned with some of the brightest lights of California.

Had there been a royal family here in Santa Barbara, the bluest of bloods would have flowed through Rosario's veins. Knowing her own rich genealogical heritage explains why she was always so generous with her time and talent when it came to helping native Americans trace their ancestry.

Rosario's second love was Fray Junípero Serra, the religious founder of California. She never tired of telling how the gray-robed friar traveled across her own *Rancho Punto de la Laguna* in the Santa Maria Valley.

It was to afford a suitable home for Serra's letters and related items that Rosario chaired the drive to build the Santa Barbara Mission Archive-Library. Her most cherished treasures were a tiny statue of San Antonio and a *retablito* of the *Mater Dolorosa* both of which had been given by Serra to Captain Ortega.

Rosario took an active part in the proceedings of the Serra Bicentennial Commission and, in July of 1984, she made the most fulfilling trek of her life—a pilgrimage to the birthplace of Serra in Petra de Mallorca.

Finally, there was the island of Santa Cruz, with its tiny Rosario chapel, perhaps the only house-of-worship in all of Christendom named for a living person. Each year, on the Feast of the Holy Cross, she would journey across the Santa Barbara Channel for a day's outing on the only parcel of California land that remains the way Serra knew it in the 1770s.

Incidentally, last year upon our return to the airbase at Camarillo, she almost off-handedly quipped to me: "Well, *padre*, that was my last trip to Santa Cruz. Next time I go to the real paradise."

There is little to say about Rosario beyond those three great loves that occupied her time. I would only say that her life itself was a homily, a living portrayal of the Gospel and how it unfolded throughout her lifespan.

I must interject here a footnote about something that occurred enroute to Mallorca. We had stopped at Barcelona and from there made our way to the beautiful mountaintop monastery of Our Lady of Montserrat, perhaps the most devotional of all the world's Marian shrines.

While waiting to depart, I wandered into a store, where I was immediately captivated by a full-sized, carved statue of Our Lady of Montserrat. I was staring at the lovely statue, imagining how handsome it would look in our church at San Fernando, when Rosario appeared, seemingly from nowhere.

"Would you like that statue for the Old Mission, *padre*?" she asked. I said "yes," but noted that there were two major obstacles to its purchase: It was much too expensive for a poor country priest and would prove very difficult to transport back to California. "Well, *padre*," she responded, "I can solve one of those problems, if you'll tackle the other." So she paid and I carried.

This morning, before leaving San Fernando, I lit a candle for Rosario before that statue of Our Lady of Montserrat. And, for the briefest moment, I could see her smiling down from heaven on the old priest.

Two weeks ago, this day, when last I visited her, Rosario was well enough to quip that General Telephone might have to file for bankruptcy when news of her demise got out. Then came a final warning: "I'll be keeping an eye on you *padre*, you'd better behave."

We'll all miss Rosario—her honesty, her candid remarks, her generosity, her amazingly accurate reading of the times. The mark she leaves on all of us who loved her is indelible. We are better people because we've known her—and that's about the highest compliment a person could ever have.

For the first time in seventy-three years, Rosario Andrea Curletti is speechless, her noble soul has returned to its Creator. We will soon inter the body she left behind, a mute reminder that one of God's favorite creatures has moved on to a better life. For Rosario and for all who sleep in Christ, life has not ended, life has changed.

I think I speak for Jean, Carey, Doyce and this whole church-full of people when I say: "We'll always remember you, Rosario. Goodbye dear friend. Say hello to Father Maynard, Harry Downie and all the others. Make ready for us, your friends, a place in heaven."

Carl Dentzel

August 26, 1980

One evening, about ten days ago, I stopped at the Huntington Memorial Hospital to see Carl. He was asleep, so I didn't bother him. But as I came out of his room, I met a somewhat elderly lady who, seeing my Roman collar, identified herself as a Catholic. I would like to share with you what she told me.

Seems as if a few days earlier, during the worst part of the heat wave, she was cleaning Carl's room and he asked if she would fetch him a tall

In Loving Memory of

MARIE W. HARRINGTON
PASSED AWAY
JUNE 13, 1986

O gentlest heart of Jesus, ever present in the Blessed Sacrament, ever consumed with burning love for the poor captive souls, have mercy on the soul of Thy departed servant. Be not severe in Thy judgment but let some drops of Thy Precious Blood fall upon the devouring flames, and do Thou O Merciful Saviour, send Thy Angels to conduct Thy departed servant to a place of refreshment, light and peace. Amen.

May the souls of all the faithful departed, through the mercy of God, rest in peace. Amen.

Merciful Jesus grant eternal rest.

glass of orange juice with lots of ice. When she returned to the room, he smiled and said: "Now, you must sit down and drink it, it's for you."

That's the Carl Dentzel I've known for these past twenty years—a considerate and sensitive man who never allowed wealth, position or even pain to distort his human values.

In his ministry, a priest runs across many kinds of people: Some there are who resemble wheelbarrows, effective only when pushed; a few are like canoes, they have to be paddled; others are similar to kites, needing always to be restrained; a percentage are reminiscient of trailers, towed along by others and then there are those who react like basketballs, bouncing in every direction.

Carl Dentzel was unlike any of these. Rather, he was something akin to a faithful old railroad watch, full of good works—his message clearly visible to all observers, his personality etched in pure gold and his tireless talents ticking away on behalf of others.

Today, the noble State of California, the grateful City of Los Angeles, the bereaved community of museum administrators, together with a host of family, friends and admirers, remember and enshrine Carl Dentzel as one who towered mightily over his contemporaries.

As most of you know, Carl was not a Catholic—at least by formal profession. Yet, interestingly enough, he knew more about the Church than most of its staunchest adherents.

He could recite more Latin than most priests, more liturgical chant than many religious and more ecclesial history than an army of professionals. His knowledge and collection of *santos* is among the finest in Western America.

Perhaps Carl's concept of God could best be described by the term"catholic," with a small "c." He saw divinity reflected in the hearts and souls of America's native races. He devoted his life and talents to preserving their heritage for others to see and admire. While the do-gooders talked about Indian rights, Carl did something and he did it many long years before such campaigns were popular.

That lifelong commitment necessarily spilled over into a dozen allied fields of interest, all of them related, in one way or another, to restoring the image and status of this nation's forgotten peoples. Carl was a practitioner par excellence of the Golden Rule.

And he approached the greatest and last of this world's challenges in the spirit of Leonardo da Vinci who wisely observed that "just as a well-filled day gives joy to sleep, so too does a well spent life give joy to death."

For all of us, the mystery of death is probably best explained in one of the ancient Prefaces for a Requiem Mass, where the priest chants aloud: "Lord, for Your faithful who die, life does not end, but it is changed; with the destruction of our earthly bodies, an eternal dwelling place is ready and waiting." To have known Carl Dentzel, to have been edified by his unashamed love for wife and family, to have witnessed the causes he championed, to have shared his friendship, to have listened as he extolled the pleasures of a fine book, to have been thrilled by his love for America's history and ideals, is to understand what Socrates had in mind when he said: "ask not that you live long, but that you live well."

This Carl most assuredly did.

Marie Walsh Harrington

(June 17, 1986)

Those of you who have known Marie Walsh Harrington in these her final epilogue years are perhaps unaware that the greatest chapters of her busy life were those of the 30s, 40s, 50s, 60s and 70s. She was an accomplished and published writer before some of us were born.

A native of Santa Monica, Marie was by profession a journalist. Her first book, written fifty-six years ago, occasioned a personal commendation from Eugenio Cardinal Pacelli who became Pope Pius XII in 1939!

To this day, her subsequent book on *The Mission Bells of California* remains the standard authority on a subject that continues to fascinate readers all over the world.

During years that stretched from the depression to the space age, Marie's byline appeared above a veritable litany of essays in magazines, journals and newspapers throughout the west. To this day, she remains the official biographer for the Hearst newspapers in Los Angeles.

Her latest and probably best book is about the man she married, a personal account of the life and career of Mark Raymond Harrington published just last year by the Great Basin Press.

Marie knew Mark for many years before they were married. She once told me that the first time she met him, she knew they would one day marry. I must have registered some surprise to that observation, because she quickly added: "Oh, I didn't tell him then, I just got in line." She became the fourth Mrs. Harrington in 1949.

There were many facets of Marie's life that were absolutely fascinating. One relates to her close relationship with Archbishop Francisco Orozco y Jimenez, the famed and fugitive Archbishop of Guadalajara, who spent several years of his exile during the Mexican persecutions hidden away in her home.

Marie's assistance to the archbishop and her concern for the plight of Mexicans persecuted by a hostile government was officially acknowledged by Pope Pius XI who awarded her the Pro Pontifice medal in 1933.

It's been my privilege to know Marie for well over thirty years. When Mark died in 1971, she called me to recite his rosary. Six years ago, when I learned that I would be returning to San Fernando, Marie came to see me at San Buenaventura mission.

There we began planning for the establishment of *Las Damas Archivistas*, a group of docents for the Archival Center, many of whom are here today as a final tribute to their founder and first president.

For many decades, this mission has been the focal point of Marie's life. In mid 1981, she presented San Fernando Mission with twenty-one Indian baskets that had belonged to her husband. They are on permanent display in one of the exhibition rooms.

At that time, she promised to leave her many personal notes, papers documents, books and mementos about San Fernando and the other missions to us and it is our intention to have them properly displayed as a lasting memorial to a woman whose name has become synonymous with the Old Mission.

Those of us who have worked with Marie will always recall her as a determined, forceful (one might even say stubborn) person, one who outlived many of her doctors and defied the rest. When she was told, about four years ago, that she had three months to live, she simply shrugged her shoulders and said: "We'll see about that."

And if anyone might be inclined to remember Marie as occasionally "cranky," he might recall that the same complaint was made about Therese of Lisieux, and she was later canonized a saint!

We must mention here her dear and loving family—John and Virginia—who could not have treated Marie more lovingly. The bond that existed between them and Marie is not broken by death, it is strengthened by eternal life.

Maynard Geiger, OFM

(May 13, 1977)

The Vatican Council reminds us that "when we look at the lives of those who have faithfully followed Christ, we are inspired with a new reason for seeking the city which is to come." Surely that is so today as we gather to pray over and bid farewell to an esteemed colleague and fellow levite, Father Maynard Geiger.

This good and gentle friar met his final challenge without fear for he anticipated "death as one of the last functions of the priesthood. It was his last Mass."

We are not here as judges. That's a prerogative we happily leave to God. Yet we do know that a person's life can be at least partially evaluated by the range of its interests, the skill of its performance and the measure of its fulfillment.

Though he was first, last and always a priest, and a good one at that, Maynard Geiger was other things too. By obedience, he was an archivist; by training he was an historian and by acclaim, he was a scholar.

His priestly specialty was that of breathing life into the dry old bones of earlier ages. Most of his attention since June 9, 1929, the day of his ordination, was given to studying, preparing and writing several shelves full of the finest historical works yet published in the field of Western Americana.

The patience for details, accuracy of expression and passion for truth that characterized his work needs no further elaboration. The publication of his bibliography, in 1971, is tribute enough to what a single priest accomplished in response to the scholarly mandate.

Like the great Junípero Serra, whose biographer he was and in whose footsteps he walked, Father Maynard Geiger was a tireless worker. With Edna Saint Vincent Millay he could say:

> My candle burns at both ends;
> It will not last the night;
> But, ah, my foes, and oh, my friends,
> It gives such a lovely light.

This humble friar accepted the Pauline exhortation about being all things to all men:

To clerical students, he was a fascinating and engaging professor;

To researchers, he was a helpful and accommodating archivist;

To scholars, he was a distinguished and recognized historian;

To attentive audiences, he was a sought-after and provocative lecturer;

To hostile protagonists, he was an ever-patient and polite apologist;

To thousands of visitors, he was the genial and cheerful host;

To those in the pews, he was an effective and moving preacher

And to his religious confreres, he was an affable and generous companion.

Great men need no eulogies. May we only say that spiritually, intellectually and every other way, the earthly sojourn of Maynard Geiger measures up most perfectly to Robert Louis Stevenson's definition of one who has achieved the maturity of manhood:

That man is a success

who has lived well, laughed often and loved much;

who has gained the respect of intelligent men and the love of children;

who has filled his niche and accomplished his task;

who leaves the world better than he found it

whether by an improved poppy, a perfect poem or a rescued soul;

who never lacked appreciation of earth's beauty or failed to express it;

who looked for the best in others and gave the best he had.

Something of the Franciscan Order will be interred with Maynard Geiger. It is our prayer that the example of his priestly zeal may become the seed that springs up anew for still other generations of service along *El Camino Real* for the Order of Friars Minor.

Sr. Miriam Ann Cunningham

(February 2, 1987)

During these past three years, those of us here at the Old Mission have had our lives enriched immensely by the presence of one who epitomized what the religious vocation is all about.

If we were to cast about for a definition of what it means to serve Christ as a Holy Cross Sister in the modern world, I rather suspect we could do no better than to point at the life of Sister Miriam Ann Cunningham.

She certainly needs no eulogy this evening. Most of you here have known her longer than I. Yet it's profitable to reflect on the good examples of others, especially if that example inspires us to upgrade our own demeanor as committed Christians.

I knew about Sister Miriam Ann and her interest in history long before I had the pleasure of meeting her personally. And when the wheels of Divine Providence made it possible for her to work with us in the archives, we eagerly welcomed her into our midst.

Perhaps I should mention a little about her work in the archives. She began the monumental task of indexing the correspondence on file between 1903 and 1947, a massive collection that numbers several hundred thousand letters. For each one of those letters, she made a brief digest, cut and ran off the stencils, and then filed four or five cards into one of thirty large drawers.

It was a challenging, often boring but terribly important task that will make it possible for researchers the world over to use and profit from our resources.

Scholars for generations to come will be able to know about the church's apostolate here in the west through her efforts.

Monsignor John Patrick Languille
(1925-1985)

O Lord, we implore your clemency on behalf of the soul of John Patrick your servant and priest. Grant him eternal fellowship with you, in whom he placed his faith and hope.

And I pledge to you this evening that this work will be continued and completed. When the published volume is ready for distribution in about two years, it will bear Sister Miriam Anne's name—a perpetual tribute to the industry of a truly remarkable religious.

All of us who have worked along side Sister these past years were impressed with her quiet, persevering dedication. She often remarked that her whole life in the classroom had been a preparation for this final and perhaps most important phase of her life.

Even when illness began to curtail her days, there was no complaint—except perhaps an occasional note of disappointment that she couldn't always meet her self-imposed allotment of cards in a given day.

There may be something very symbolic about the fact that Sister was brought to work every morning by Peter Buffo in what is known in automobile circles as "comet".

A comet comes into our presence, stays for a brief spell and then departs. But it leaves a brightness, an excitement, a renewal that reminds us of God's graces.

Sister Miriam Ann did that to our lives here at Mission Hills. She left a lasting impression of what it means to be a front liner for Christ.

She may have been locked away in a convent all her life. But her teachings will live on in her students, her writings will live on in her readers and her spirituality will live on in her community. In that sense she will never die.

We've come here today only to consign a worn-out body to the earth whence it came. Being Christians, though, we look beyond the grave and we see Sister Miriam Ann now residing in God's house—and that can only cause us to rejoice.

We thank the Lord for allowing us to have known Sister Miriam Ann as a person, to have enjoyed her as a friend, to have profited from her as a scholar and to have been enriched by her exemplary commitment as a Christian.

John Patrick Languille

1925-1985

John Patrick Languille, a priest whose lifeline was c-h-a-r-i-t-y, returned to his native Seattle—there to surrender his gentle soul to the Lord. A few years after his birth, Victor Languille and his infant son moved to Long Beach, California, where "Pat" entered Saint Matthew's school. It was under the watchful tutelage of Msgr. Bernard J. Dolan that "Pat" enrolled at Los Angeles College, preparatory seminary for the newly created Archdiocese of Los Angeles.

Ordained to the priesthood on May 7, 1949, Father Languille was assigned to Saint Andrew's parish in Pasadena, which at that time was shepherded by Bishop Joseph T. McGucken. From that relationship evolved a life-long friendship.

Early in 1950, Father Languille began his long association with the charitable works of the archdiocese. His first appointment was assistant director of the Catholic Welfare Bureau and then, the following year, his apostolate was broadened to include the Catholic Youth Organization.

During the ensuing decades, Father Languille found himself engaged in a host of activities related to the Church's outreach programs. These included the Neighborhood Youth Corps, several refugee projects, the commission on aging and, finally, Las Torres Corporation for seniors.

The Languille imprint was felt even more widely when he became director of the CYO (1958), the Catholic Welfare Bureau (1973) and the Saint Vincent de Paul Society (1974). One of the friends from USC noted amusingly that "Pat got more mileage from his ACSW degree than all his classmates combined." In his "spare time," Msgr. Languille was director of Mary's Hour, Moderator of the Catholic Alumni Club and Coordinator for the Cardinal's Christmas Parties, to mention but a few his "sideline" involvements.

He was fiercely proud of the Church's frontline identification with the poor. If he ever bragged, it was only to point out that he presided over the largest family service agency west of the Mississippi River!

Twice honored by the Holy See, Msgr. Languille remained a "street priest" in every sense. Besides keeping a firm hand on the pulse of the Los Angeles *barrios*, he was a respected member of the local French community. His command of Spanish and French was the envy of his priestly collaborators.

Since 1967, Msgr. Languille had been pastor of Our Lady of Loretto parish in downtown Los Angeles. Though several times offered other pastoral assignments, he opted to remain in the inner city "with the people I love the most."

"Pat" Languille was not alone a first class administrator of Catholic charities. He went several steps beyond and dedicated his life to eradicating the causes of poverty and need. His name was probably on every city administrator's Rolodex.

His sixty year "war on poverty" terminated in the city of his birth on September 23, 1985. The Catholics in California's southland can join in saying: 'Thank you Seattle for a fine priest, a loving pastor and a great exemplar!" Msgr. Languille lived close to death, having lost all his relatives at an early age. On his desk was a laminated copy of Alan Seeger's poem "I have a Rendezvous with Death:"

I have a rendezvous with Death
At some disputed barricade
When Spring comes round with rustling shade
And apple blossoms fill the air.
I have a rendezvous with Death
When Spring brings back blue days and fair.
It may be He shall take my hand
And lead me into His dark land
And close my eyes and quench my breath;
It may be I shall pass Him still.
I have a rendezvous with Death
On some scarred slope of battered hill,
When Spring comes round again this year
And the first meadow flowers appear.
God knows 'twere better to be deep
Pillowed in silk and scented down,
Where love throbs out in blissful sleep,
Pulse nigh to pulse and breath to breath
Where hushed awakenings are dear.
But I've a rendezvous with Death
At midnight in some flaming town
When Spring trips north again this year,
And I to my pledged word am true,
I shall not fail that rendezvous.

Homily preached by Msgr. Francis J. Weber,
Pastor, San Buenaventura Mission
October 3, 1978
For The Funeral Obsequies Of Pope John Paul I

Today, we rejoice in the glories of the resurrection. Almighty God has called to Himself not alone His vicar here on earth, but one who typifies what Saint Catherine of Siena meant when she referred to the Holy Father as "the sweet Christ of this earth."

In the short but eventful days that Albino Luciani governed the People of God as Pope John Paul I, the bark of Peter felt a new but steady hand on the tiller.

And then, with the suddenness of a giant wave breaking on the stern of a ship, this 263rd chapter in the Life of the Church was abruptly terminated. Once again the flock is bereft of its shepherd.

That beautifully contagious smile which the world so quickly came to know and love is forever frozen into the cold and impersonal annals of humankind.

God's plans for His people are not subject to committee hearings or public discussions. Often He finds it expedient to refocus world attention on the climatic part of Jesus's life—the pinnacle towards which everything led—Mount Calvary.

Death is the culmination of every life. Were it not so, there would be no point to living. With the death of Jesus, the world , began anew.

So must it be with all Christians, especially that one known as the Vicar of Christ. It is a lesson underscored by Albino Luciani himself when, in his younger days, he recalled the advice of Socrates: "Ask not that you live long, but that you live well."

Seizing and utilizing the opportunities of life, however long or short, is the only adequate response that one committed to the resurrection promise can maintain in the face of death's mystery.

This Pope John Paul did in a most remarkable fashion. He needed only thirty-four days to imprint onto the universal consciousness the beauty, happiness and contentment of a truly Christian lifestyle.

With him the role of a follower of Christ took on a whole new image. His life was a public demonstration of the joys of faith, the consolations of hope and the radiance of charity.

Leonardo da Vinci surely had the likes of John Paul in mind when he noted that "just as a well-filled day gives joy to sleep, so too does a well-spent life give joy to death. For one who uses life well, death seems spontaneous without the least pretense, to come not as the destruction, but as the fulfillment of life."

Historians will not remember John Paul for what he did, but for what he was—a kindly, open and radiant pastoral shepherd of souls who looked upon the Christian world as one gigantic parish.

After consigning the human remains of the Holy Father to the ground whence it came, we dispatch the cardinals back to their drawing boards in Michelangelo's Sistine Chapel with a commission to provide us with a new shepherd in the mould of John Paul.

The orphanhood that fell upon the Catholic world last Friday morning is only a transitory cross. Just a century ago, when the great Pio Nono was called to his eternal reward, one of the great pioneers of the California Church said: "Fear not. Peter will live in his successors; Peter will speak forever from his chair."

Jubilee Sermon
Noel Moholy
August 28, 1985

This city has great meaning to the evening's jubilarian. On the way over here I was thinking about another man whose path led through these environs. Herbert Hoover, who was married just down the street by Father Ramon Mestres, dearly loved Monterey.

Anyway, on his 80th birthday, Hoover's friends had a party for him and during the course of the after-dinner remarks, someone asked if he harbored any bitterness about the way he was cruelly criticized during and after his White House years.

"No," he said. "I have no rancor for anybody. But your question reminds me of an old fellow, about my time in life, who attended a prayer meeting at which the preacher spoke of brotherly love. When the preacher asked if there was anyone in the congregation who could honestly say that he did not have a single enemy, this old gentleman stood up and said 'Right here, parson. I don't have an enemy.' The preacher commended him on the exemplary life he must have led and then asked him to explain how he had achieved such a noble goal. The old man shouted back. 'I outlived the bastards!' "

Our jubilarian this evening was far more liberal than Hoover and that's why he waited until FDR entered the White House before taking his final vows in the Order of Friars Minor.

Father Noel Moholy really doesn't look his age until one reflects that he and social security began their public service the same year. Actually, 1935 was a banner year. The first Heisman trophy was awarded and the first Sugar Bowl game was played.

Folks nationwide eagerly awaited news of the year's biggest story, the kidnapping and murder of the Lindbergh baby. Six year old Shirley Temple dazzled audiences with her first full-length film. And sales of undershirts plummeted when Clark Gable appeared in public stripped to the waist.

The average farm family earned only $951 a year; less than a third of all the nation's households had a telephone; there were fewer than two million autos on the highways and a new Chevrolet cost a paltry $465.

Savings accounts earned 3% interest and the budget deficit was a mere two million dollars. It was the era of the penny postcard and even first class mail was only 3¢. Great dust storms eroded away America's bread basket.

That was the historical setting into which Father Noel Moholy launched his Franciscan apostolate. Those of us who have known him for all or part of the ensuing fifty years can easily enough sketch in the details of his ministry.

His career as God's *troubador* has had three phases: teaching, administering and postulating. That he has been remarkably successful in these pursuits is amply attested to by a generation of grateful students, by a still functioning Santa Barbara Mission and by a now venerable-ized Fray Junípero Serra.

We are not here this evening to eulogize Father Noel—that's a task which hopefully won't be necessary for a long while. What we are about is celebrating an adulthood of service to God's people.

Hundreds, even thousands of priests have walked along *El Camino Real* since 1769 and many have left behind footprints of notable achievements in California's spiritual and material realms. The imprint of this evening's honoree is deeply imbedded on the royal highway—not alone as an outstanding theologian, an innovative builder, an acclaimed preacher and public speaker or even a published historian. Father Noel goes beyond all of that. He is and always will be remembered for being an echo chamber for his and our hero, Fray Junípero Serra.

Father Noel's fifty years are forever couched within the framework of Serra and there his life takes on its distinctive coloration. For thirty-five years, he has carried the Serra banner with great dignity.

If today Serra is venerable, if today Serra is portrayed on the postage stamps of four nations, if today he is a household word to much of our nation, the major share of the human credit redounds upon the man we honor this evening.

Oh, others may crowd into the spotlight, others may share the benefits and others may gobble up the publicity, but let it be said for the record that for most of the years since 1950 Father Noel Moholy has walked the Serra trail alone.

In that often lonely and frustrating role, Father Noel has become as much a pathfinder as the man he seeks to have beatified. And that's why I am pleased to have a part in this ceremony which is extolling a man too long overlooked. His golden jubilee as a Franciscan is indeed a glorious occasion for the Order of Friars Minor. Would that his contagious Christian enthusiasm could be cloned as a model for the Friars of the future.

Sig Schlager Eulogy

1980

Many years ago, when I was a young priest, my first pastor told me that his favorite day was Thanksgiving. He often remarked that throughout his life, all good things occurred on that day.

Though he's been dead for well over three years, Msgr. John Devlin's fortunes have held for, on Thanksgiving Day of 1980, he welcomed his dearest friend Sig Schlager, to the threshold of heaven.

And on Thursday, I could almost hear the roaring laughter and smell the clouds of cigar smoke as those two noble characters embraced and wandered off into the shadows of eternity.

Those of us who knew Sig could use a lot of adjectives to describe him: stubborn, outspoken, autocratic, impulsive, determined, restless and inquisitive.

Those descriptive words are also predicated of the truly great personages in human annals. History testifies that those who leave their mark in the world are the ones who dare to buck the tide, to defy public opinion and to attempt the impossible.

By instinct Sig did them all. He never followed the rulebook. His mind was too imaginative and his energies too forceful.

He was surely hard to live with at times—but so were the saints. And when a person travels in that exalted company, he soon discovers how to fit all the jagged pieces of human nature into place.

A good life needs no eulogy. Sig Schlager's life was an open book—a book which any reviewer would immediately consign to the best seller's list.

The entertainment industry, in all its many forms, was part of Sig's very bloodstream. Probably no man better understood how that vast network operated. Certainly few shared his perspective into the intricacies of motion pictures, stage plays, technical productions, operatic portrayals, story composition and all their human components.

Providentially, for fifty-eight of his eighty-one years, Sig had Marian as his companion and helpmate. She it was who rounded off the rough edges.

Michael J. Weber—Last of the Mission Shelties.

When I once mentioned this to Sig, he simply winked and, in a voice only I could hear, said: "I chose the finest."

He came to the faith fairly late in life—but soon enough to share its comforts and to benefit from its graces. Like the Savior he served so faithfully, he bore in his body both the old and the new testaments.

It was a logical step for Sig to embrace Christianity because he always looked upon the Catholic faith as a gigantic stage on which people acted out the drama of life. His life was an integral part of the greatest story ever told.

Those of us who live as Christians see death for what it really is—the joyful returning of the faithful soul to the Lord who created it. We see those sentiments spoken in the Preface for the Mass of the Resurrection:

Lord, for Your faithful who die,
life does not end, but is changed;
With the destruction of our earthly bodies,
an eternal dwelling place is ready and waiting.

For us, who like Sig, bear the indelible imprint of Baptism, "the light that flickers out at midnight symbolizes not the end of an old day, but the promise of a new dawn."

It's always humanly hard to say goodbye, so perhaps we best say "until we meet again!"

16
Some Talks and Addresses

Over many years I have given zillions of talks and addresses. Here are some for which there still exists a text:

Local Heroes of Our Times
(December 13, 2001)
Thomas Aquinas College

In one of his exhortations, Pope John Paul II asked Catholics to honor their heroes, especially those many brave believers who have given their lives for the faith during the 20th century. Recently a book has been published listing their names.

And, while extolling the memory of those who have actually shed their blood, the Roman pontiff also suggests that we also honor those "dry martyrs" who have been willing to accept isolation, humiliation, rejection and social opprobrium for their beliefs.

Such great people as these were not surprised at encountering hostility in the world. On many occasions Jesus clearly warned His followers that they would face persecution. Indeed He extorted them to "rejoice and be glad," when they were so treated.

The Holy Father's call for heroes has long been echoed in the literary world. Samuel Johnson, for example, said: "Almost every man . . . will be found to have . . . some hero or other, living or dead, . . . whose character he endeavors to assume, and whose performances he labors to equal. When the original is well-chosen and judiciously copied, the imitator arrives at excellences which he could never have attained without direction . . .."

Thomas Carlyle taught that hero-worship is a natural human tendency. All people look for heroes because of inadequacies in their human nature. That people often tend to complete themselves vicariously is really not unreasonable. Social beings look to those whose lives and examples provide clues about life's questions. When such persons are identified, they become authentic heroes.

Hero-worship is so ingrained in the human psyche that failure to find one can result in the discovery of pseudo-heroes and that can and often does lead to disastrous consequences.

Pope John Paul reminds us that the Catholic Church has a treasury of admirable people where everyone can browse for heroes. In the Church heroes are called saints most of whom have never been formally canonized. By imitating the heroes of holiness, people can achieve ultimate completeness.

The church's heroes have withstood the scrutiny of modern technology. Contemporary holy people who will likely be canonized, such people as Fray Junípero Serra, Mother Teresa of Calcutta and Dorothy Day of New York, are among that growing group of heroes whose lives reflect uncompromising examples of virtue and greatness.

There are saints for every temperament. Eric Schekse observed that there is a saint suited to each person's situation. The tough guy in the mold of Jean Claude Van Damme can take the example of St. Ignatius Loyola, a nobleman and a soldier, who was transformed into a valiant "soldier" of Christ and His Church; the quiet, withdrawn type can imitate St. Simeon Stylites or any cloistered saint. For the wealthy, there are many saints of royalty, like St. Louis of France or St. Stephen of Hungary (forget Donald Trump and Ted Turner); the young woman caught in a web of sexuality and disrepute can turn to St. Margaret of Cortona; the intellectual, to St. Thomas Aquinas; the middle-class person, to St. Therese of Lisieux, For the sensualist seeking sanctity, there's St. Augustine and for the professional looking to practice holiness, there's St. Thomas More. The diplomat seeking a balance between two kingdoms can look to St. Catherine of Siena; and the poet to St. John of the Cross. There are patron saints—heroes for almost every calling, condition, and event in life.

The rejection of saints for veneration, a practice begun during Reformation times, has and will deprive people of their heroes and cause them to seek out pseudo heroes.

Thomas Carlyle, who was there at the beginning of the modern age, viewed heroes as a solution to modern society's evils. Authentic heroes could have helped society in the 19th century and they can help society today. A society that rejects its saints is spiritually doomed.

As long ago as 1910, George Wharton James, a Methodist minister and prominent historian, included Fray Junípero Serra in a book he wrote on the Heroes of California.

In response to the Holy Father's pleas for identifying and extolling local "heroes," we have erected here at Thomas Aquinas College a statue honoring our own Fray Junípero Serra, a person whose endurance in the pursuit of his faith commitment is worthy of emulation by those of us who walk in his footsteps.

Knights of St. Gregory the Great
October 28, 2003
Cardinal Manning House of Prayer

Pope Saint Gregory the Great, who guided the Church from 590 to 604 was the last of the Latin Fathers of the Church, a member of the Roman nobility and the son of a senator. He initially pursued a purely secular career, which eventually culminated in his appointment as perfect of Rome in 573. After the death of his father, he was drawn toward a strict ascetic life, renouncing worldly pursuits and converted his personal estate into a monastery. With his inheritance he founded six other monastic institutions in Sicily. He spent the next years in constant prayer. By 578 he was so esteemed in Rome that Benedict I made him a deacon and Pelagius II sent him as an ambassador to the Byzantine court at Constantinople in 579.

Returning to Rome in 585, Gregory served as abbot of his monastery until 590 and the death of Pelagius II. To his genuine horror, he was unanimously elected pope, struggling for months to avoid the terrible burden of the papacy because he desired to remain in his contemplative community. Despite protests to anyone who might listen, Gregory was consecrated on September 3, 590.

Once convinced that his place as pope was the will of God, Gregory proved an amazingly active and forceful pontiff, overcoming his often severe bouts of poor health. The work before him was truly daunting since Italy and Rome were in dire straits from plagues, famines, and the constant menace of war with the Lombards. As there was no central government, Gregory assumed the task of civil administration, reorganizing the territorial possessions of the Holy See—and using its financial assets to feed the starving and care for the sick.

While acknowledging the political supremacy of the Byzantine emperors, Gregory essentially ignored the presence of the exarch of Ravenna and personally negotiated peace with the Lombards. He also took steps to resist the increasing claims by the Patriarch of Constantinople to an equal status with the Bishop of Rome.

Beyond his temporal labors, Gregory also instituted a variety of reforms to the Church. The first monk elected pope, he favored monasteries and appointed monks to numerous posts in the papal government. He also wrote a guide to religious practices and promoted missionary activities, especially in England. A prolific writer, he authored the *Dialogues*, an account of the lives of early saints; homilies on the Gospel; over 850 letters and a work on the *Book of Job*.

He is given credit for launching the form of music called Gregorian chant and for making contributions to the Gregorian sacramentary. Soon after his death on March 12, 604, he was canonized by popular demand. He is honored as a Doctor of the Church.

But now, as Paul Harvey likes to say, "for the rest of the story" or the California connection. There were in all sixteen Gregorys who occupied the throne of Peter, though none ever measured up to the reputation of Gregory I, known in the annals as Gregory the Great.

Peoples of the Pacific Slope have long held the memory of Pope Gregory XVI in high esteem. He was the pontiff who created the Diocese of Both Californias, on April 30, 1840, and appointed the first bishop in the person of Fray Francisco Garcia Diego y Moreno.

Gregory XVI (1765-1846) was the first of the "modern" popes. Formerly a Camaldolese monk, he had occupied many positions in the curia prior to his election to the Chair of Peter, including that of Prefect for the Sacred Congregation of Propaganda Fide. His fifteen-year pontificate marked an important milestone in the effective exercise of papal authority.

The great revival of missionary activity, for example, dates from Gregory XVI who created seventy diocese and vicariates apostolic, including ten in the United States. The former Bartolomeo Cappellari was both an accomplished theologian and a skillful diplomat.

Among the Holy Father's many innovations was the establishment of the Order of Saint Gregory the Great in 1831, as a way of honoring people of unblemished character who had "promoted the interests of society, the Church and the Holy see." Because of his great admiration for Saint Gregory the Great, the pontiff named the new order for his illustrious predecessor and namesake.

There were no knights appointed for the United States in those earliest years after 1831, mostly because of the commonly held belief that it was improper (and possibly unconstitutional) for Catholics in this country to receive titles from the head of a sovereign government.

Recall that prior to the suppression of the Papal States, the popes were also temporal kings. (That, by the way, explains why there were no cardinals in the United States until 1875.)

Shortly after re-organizing the Order and making it more responsive to the needs of contemporary society, Pope Pius X issued a decree on February 7, 1905, extending to local bishops the prerogative of nominating candidates for the papal knighthood.

It was in 1919 that Bishop John J. Cantwell first responded to the Holy Father's invitation by proposing Joseph Scott as a Knight Commander of the Order of Saint Gregory. Cantwell bestowed the honor at a pontifical Mass offered at Saint Vibiana's Cathedral on Pentecost Sunday, May 15, 1921. The Bishop of Monterey-Los Angeles praised the recipient for "having interested himself during his entire career in all questions affecting the welfare of the people."

Three years later, the Order was again conferred on an outstanding Catholic layman, Isidore B. Dockweiler. Others cited in subsequent years were W. I. Moore (1935), P. H. O'Neil (1937) and Harry E. Johansing (1944). Though the record keeping has been less than perfect, it would appear that 202 men and women have been honored with the Order of Saint Gregory the Great in California's Southland since 1921.

Knights of Saint Lazarus (December 3, 2005) San Fernando Mission

I was asked to speak briefly this afternoon on this mission, the seventeenth of the historic foundations established along Californias *El Camino Real*. But I have for each of you a brochure that tells the story better than I could.

So I thought about our patron, Saint Lazarus, whose tomb I visited some years ago at Bethany, a small village just a few miles outside the city of Jerusalem.

Legend has it that he and his two sisters were childhood chums of Jesus. He knew the Lord as few others did and it occurred to me that Lazarus would have a lot to say about Christ. His testimony would surely be unique.

What we can only surmise from Lazarus, about Christ we can discover from the writings of other prominent people in the world even those who are not believers.

Here are some samples:

The highly-respected historian, George Bancroft, admitted that he stumbled across "the name of Jesus Christ written on the top of every page of modern history."

Another well-known scholar, H. G. Wells, confessed that taking "Christ seriously is to enter upon a strange and alarming life, to abandon habits, to control instincts and impulses, to achieve an incredible happiness."

Ralph Waldo Emerson said that the influence of Christ, "whose name is not so much written as ploughed into the history of the world," is "proof of the subtle virtue of this infusion. Jesus belonged to the race of prophets. He saw with open eyes the mystery of the soul. He is, I think, the only one in history who has appreciated the worth of man."

The usually-verbose Lord Byron, George Gordon, offered only the crisp observation that "if ever a man was God or the God-man, Jesus Christ was both."

The contemporary sociologist, Andrew Greeley, confided that he found Christ and His message "irrelevant to the problems of the modern world." But, he pointed out, Christ was "irrelevant to His own world, too; so irrelevant that it was necessary for Him to be murdered."

Napoleon Bonaparte, the French military genius, stated that "I know men; and I tell you that Jesus Christ was no mere man. Between Him and every other person in the world there is no possible term of comparison. Alexander, Caesar and Charlemagne founded empires based on force. But, Jesus Christ founded His empire upon love; and even at this hour millions would die for Him."

In the view of Joseph Ernest Renan, "all history is incomprehensible without Christ. He was the greatest religious genius that ever lived. His beauty is eternal, and His reign shall never end. Jesus is in every respect unique, and nothing can be compared with Him."

The timeless nature of the Christian message is reflected in the reply of William Ellery Channing: "The sages and heroes of history are receding from us, and history contrasts the record of their deeds into a narrower and narrower page. But time has no power over the name and deeds and words of Jesus Christ."

From San Francisco, or there abouts, Mark Hopkins wrote that "no revolution that has ever taken place in society can be compared to that which has been produced by the words of Jesus Christ."

Writing from England and claiming to be "no more a Christian than Pilate was," George Bernard Shaw said he was ready to admit that "I see no way out of the world's misery but the way which would have been found by His will."

Expressing wonderment that there was ever anyone who questioned the divinity of Christ, Tertullian replied that "they should have known He was God. His patience should have proved that to them."

For John Tracy Ellis, Christ represents "very clearly the Son of God and He's the only thing in life to me. I mean taking Him out of life would make life utterly senseless and I could see then why at times in great depression one might well commit suicide."

Giuseppe Garibaldi confided that his love and veneration was based on the fact that "Christ came into the world to deliver humanity from slavery, for which God had not created it."

That towering reformer, Martin Luther, wrote his answer in bold capital letters: "Anything that one imagines of God apart from Christ is only useless thinking and vain idolatry."

And so it seems that Jesus Christ, "the stone which the builders rejected," has become the "capstone" of the literary world.

That message, and more would have been echoed by our patron, Saint Lazarus.

California Mission Studies Association
(February 20, 2005)

I want to thank the CMSA for the Norman Neuerberg Award and I am especially honored to share this award with Doyce Nunis, my mentor for so many years.

Though Doyce and I were as close as anyone to Norman during his lifetime, neither of us profited from his demise. Though he had promised several times that certain of his historical and artistic holdings, including the Henry Chapman Ford painting of San Fernando Mission, would one day come back to the Old Mission, such never materialized.

So what I say today is motivated by genuine admiration, not gratitude. This is how I saw Norman for over forty years, with all his virtues and blemishes.

I first became acquainted with Norman in 1962 shortly after being appointed Professor of History at Queen of Angels Seminary in Mission Hills, California. Norman was spending his spare time compiling a card index file for the artifacts on exhibit at the adjoining mission named for Saint Ferdinand, King of Spain. Unfortunately, Father James Hanson, the director of the Old Mission, carelessly loaned the card file to a researcher who never returned it. Norman was legitimately displeased.

Even by then Norman already had a long relationship with the seventeenth missionary foundation established along California's *El Camino Real*. As a youngster, he befriended Edith Buckland Webb whose book on *Indian Life at the Old Missions of California* was regarded by the late Maynard Geiger as the finest book of its kind ever written, a distinction still valid after the passage of another half century. Parenthetically, in later years, Norman was instrumental in having Mrs. Webb's rich and extensive collection of books, manuscripts and assorted other treasures incorporated into the Santa Barbara Mission Archives.

Edith Webb was a superb mentor for her young friend who even then possessed a photographic memory. She recommended to Brother James Hart, the resident Oblate caretaker at the old mission, that Norman be allowed to conduct tours on Saturdays. For many years, Norman would ride out to Mission Hills on the big red cars and spend most of an enjoyable day meeting tourists from all over the world as they arrived to examine and hear about San Fernando Mission.

When his academic career took Norm to Europe and other places, he retained his interest and fascination in the California missions, especially San Fernando. Forty years later, when he formally retired from his position as professor at Cal State University Dominguez Hills, Norman devoted almost all his waking hours to studying and re-doing the art work in several of the California missions, most notably San Juan Capistrano. In addition to writing extensively on the subject, he also traveled to the peninsular California missions and those established by the Franciscans in Central Mexico. He took thousands of photographs and slides all of which are now housed at the Santa Barbara Mission Archives.

In the years after I returned to San Fernando in 1981, Norman came at least once a week for lengthy discussions and projects, one of which involved decorating the Serra chapel which we located in two rooms at the eastern end of the mission triangle. On other occasions, he worked on various artistic embellishments in the *convento*, with special attention to the Governor's Room. He always left the walls more beautifully and authentically decorated—and he always found an historical precedent for whatever challenge he tackled.

No one among his contemporaries knew as much about the missions and their architecture than Norman. One scholar dubbed him "Rex" because he appeared to be a reincarnation of Rexford Newcomb. He could identify any photograph—which mission it was, when it was taken and often by whom. I never recall catching him in a factual error. His phenomenal, almost encyclopedic memory bank was never exhausted or compromised.

Gentle man that he was, Norman had a ferocious temper. He never forgave me for installing chandeliers in the *convento* despite the fact that their design and components were entirely appropriate, except for electricity.

His dislike for the chandeliers stemmed from their source, Carl's Jr. Restaurants. He left instructions with my assistant, Kevin Feeney, to call him immediately if ever I died suddenly. "We have to get Weber's follies out of the *convento* before anyone knows." He probably wasn't pleased that I outlived him.

Norman accompanied our pilgrimage to Europe in 1975 for the beatification of Fray Junípero Serra. On the isle of Mallorca, he became our tour guide to everyone's delight. He and Father Noel Moholy, the postulator for the Serra cause, forged a lasting friendship.

Norman was an unabashed purist. When we were reconstructing San Fernando Mission after the Northridge earthquake, he was omnipresent with a raft of suggestions that the FEMA people wouldn't consider. Their guidelines mandated that the 1.9 million dollar restoration of the mission was to be exactly the way that the mission existed on the day prior to the earthquake. On numerous occasions when they circumvented Norman's plans, he would launch a campaign to the local newspaper, radio and television, even sending letters to the Cardinal—most of which ended up on my desk for explanation. It wasn't a very pleasant interlude, but totally in keeping with Norman's uncompromising mindset.

It would not be out of place to classify Norman as an eccentric. He apparently never owned a suit and for an artist, he was totally oblivious to color coordination. His socks and shoes rarely matched and like his good friend, Father Maynard Geiger, Norman always looked as if he had gotten out of bed with all his clothes on. Dry cleaning was not a term in his vocabulary.

He would drive his car until it collapsed of old age or mechanical neglect. Though he was hardly a poor man, he never used air conditioning in his car or home. It was an expense he couldn't justify. He was the only person I ever knew who used a teabag several times.

In some ways these were the characteristics that gave Norman so much charm. What you saw was what he was. No pretenses, no false pride and no exaggerated self esteem. He was a Dickensonian character—unique and self contained.

I wouldn't say that Norman was cheap. Maybe "frugal" would better describe him. He liked to trade, but rarely gave; if ever we dined out it was at the Sizzler and he preferred being a guest to acting as a host. When once I suggested that we go to the Odyssey Restaurant, he graciously demurred—for reasons more amusing than convincing.

And now that we are some years away from his departure from old planet earth, perhaps I can explain how I was instrumental in getting Norman into heaven. Though he knew more about the Catholic Church than 90% of Catholics, Norman always avoided a formal declaration despite many suggestions and invitations. I suspect that like many people, he hadn't planned on dying, at least so suddenly.

Following his being taken to Kaiser Hollywood Hospital, Norman couldn't speak. In fact he never emerged from his coma. At his bedside, I took his hand in mine and suggested we communicate by hand signals—one for "yes," two for "no." I asked him several questions: Norman, do you know who I am, do you love God? Do you want to die a Catholic? Would you like me to give you the sacraments and are you sorry for any sins you may have committed. After he responded "yes" to all my questions, I baptized, confirmed and anointed Norman and then gave him the apostolic blessing.

He died a few moments later—a Catholic in good standing. I strongly suspect that Fray Junípero Serra was pleased.

Christmas Appreciation Dinner
December 4, 2005
Thomas Aquinas College

Heavenly Father,

Each year during this holy season, we, the faculty, alumni, friends and benefactors of Thomas Aquinas College gather to honor the birthday of Your Son, Jesus.

We do this in recognition that love is the strongest force in the world—stronger than hate, stronger than evil, stronger than death and that the blessed life which began in Bethlehem two thousand years ago is the image and brightness of eternal love.

And so we pray this evening that once the song of the angels is stilled, when the star in the sky is gone, when the kings and princes have returned home, when the shepherds are back with their flocks, that the real work of Christmas will begin—

To find the lost,
to heal the broken,
to feed the hungry,
to rebuild the nations,
to bring peace among brothers and sisters,
to make music in the heart!

Finally, We ask you to bless our food this evening—and to accept our gratitude for your bounty.

California and the Catholic Church
(August 1, 2005)

California has experienced everything in recent years—riots, floods, droughts, fires, earthquakes and, even killer bees. Yet, the Golden State is still the garden spot of old planet earth. One often recalls and affirms what Blessed Junípero Serra said: "In California is my life and there, God willing, I hope to die."

California is truly a state of superlatives. Twelve percent of the nation's residents live in California, an area that boasts of 64,500 millionaires, 57% of them women! Well over 56% of the state's population own their own homes, and 90% have their own car.

However decadent it may appear to outsiders—weakened by unemployment and inflation, demoralized by crime, deluded by cultists, corrupted by pornographers, debased by junk bond dealers, decimated by psychopaths and pillaged by rioters—California remains a never-never land of riches, fame and freedom to millions around the world. Despite pockets of poverty, Californians are fabulously wealthy in other ways.

In a booster pamphlet issued in 1886 by the Illinois Association, one reads that "in this grand country, we have the tallest mountains, the biggest trees, the crookedest railroads, the driest rivers, the loveliest flowers, the smoothest ocean, the finest fruits, the softest breezes, the brightest skies and the most genial sunshine to be found anywhere else in North America."

Realistically, Los Angeles is the most interesting metropolis in all God's creation. In altitude, it ranges from 5,049 feet in Tujunga (which is higher than all but a few mountains east of the Mississippi) to below sea level at Terminal Island.

There has always been a strange loyalty to the rhythmic flow of life in Southern California. Perhaps that was best expressed by a youngster who, when asked where she came from, answered, "I was born in Los Angeles at the age of six."

Admittedly, the city has come a long way since Westbrook Pegler proposed that Los Angeles "be declared incompetent and placed in charge of a guardian." Today, the most commonly used adjective describing Los Angeles is "big." Los Angeles County, for example, stretches over 4,083 square miles or a geographical area larger than Rhode Island and Delaware combined.

Despite what one might hear to the contrary, Los Angeles is a religious city. There are seventy columns of listings in the yellow pages under "churches." Los Angeles has become overwhelmingly Catholic with ninety-eight parishes in the city and four million plus Catholics in the archdiocese.

Some of the legends are true - Los Angeles is the divorce capital of America, with one couple getting divorced for each one married (three times the national average). And Los Angeles is the bankruptcy capital—about 40,000 a year. The city is also the bank-robbery capital of America. Not a single day has gone by since October 4, 1979, without a bank or savings and loan being knocked over.

The "Catholic presence" in the area now comprising the City of Los Angeles actually pre-dates the city by a dozen years. The very name derives from the diary of Fray Juan Crespi, who introduced the Feast of the *Portiuncula* into California's vocabulary.

And it was a group of Catholics, most of them predominantly Negro in racial strain, who effected the actual foundation of *E1 Pueblo de Nuestra Señora de los Angeles*, in the fall of 1781.

Los Angeles continued for some years to be a "Catholic" enclave, with most of its inhabitants worshipping, at least sporadically, at the Old Plaza Church. Oh, that's not to say that the *pueblo* was, by any means, a virtuous city. Unfortunately, the Catholic Church has always been blessed (or cursed) with more than its share of renegades.

On January 17, 1837, just a year and a half after Los Angeles had been raised to the status of a city, the *ayuntamiento* or council passed, without a dissenting voice, a resolution declaring that "the Roman Catholic apostolic religion shall prevail throughout this jurisdiction."

While there is no evidence that this expressed but never enforced "establishment of religion" benefitted Catholics, it did provide adherents with a unique distinction in Western Americana's historical annals.

As late as 1853, Harris Newmark said that "nearly all the population was Catholic." Another creditable authority noted that "up to 1854, the only organization in Los Angeles upholding any standard of morality whatever was the Roman Catholic Church. It erected houses of worship, hospitals and schools; it was the pioneer of all good works."

And while it all changed following the onrush of the gold seekers, Los Angeles continued through the decades to be a unique haven for religious-minded peoples of all creeds.

In a survey of local history published in 1967, Christopher Rand observed that "there are probably more religions in Los Angeles than in the whole previous history of mankind." And it all started with the Catholic Church, in 1781.

Sr. Mary Jean Meier
(March 19, 2005)
Los Angeles Marriott Hotel

As I was walking toward the lobby this evening, someone asked me to confirm or deny that Sister Mary Jean Meier would soon celebrate her eightieth birthday. Knowing how women, especially nuns, are extremely reluctant to speak about their age, I sidestepped the question. But I can confide to you that she is the only one here tonight who personally knew Bishop Amat.

There really isn't much one can add to the public persona of Sister Mary Jean. Surely she has been and continues to be the most visible of the women religious in the Archdiocese of Los Angeles. We have thousands of nuns, hundreds of priests, a plethora of bishops but only one Sister Mary Jean.

Her office at the ACC is directly above that of the Cardinal who probably gets some of his best ideas by osmosis from above.

Her vital statistics are printed for all to see, I can only add that she has known more people; influenced more churchmen; participated in more programs; attended and organized more events; and moved around the archdiocese more rapidly and quietly than anyone half her age. And she appears to have thrived on it.

But there's more. Sister Mary Jean has organized more pilgrimages, written more acknowledgements, traveled more miles, spearheaded more galas, acquired more papal blessings, drafted more letters, raised more money, cultivated more friends, known more celebrities and been involved in more training programs than anyone else.

Such stats don't put others down, they raise her higher. Some years ago, when Sister celebrated her golden jubilee in religious life, Cardinal Mahony told me that he wished he could have her cloned five times, once for each of our regional areas.

Busy as she is, Sister Mary Jean always has a kind word, an infectious smile and an encouraging note for others. She makes time for everyone, even when the pressure is greatest.

Of all her virtues, and there are many, none surpasses her patience with old country priests and I consider that a powerful incentive for imitation.

One of our clerical wags once referred to Sister Mary Jean as "Sister Mary Money Bags." Understandably she didn't like that title because it only describes one aspect, and a small one at that, of this grand lady's activity as she moves among the three counties of this archdiocese as an ambassador of good will.

Historians frequently get hung up with statistics but, in that vein, Sister Mary Jean Meier stands alone in this city and archdiocese dedicated to Our Lady of the Angels. She is unique in every aspect of that term. She is being honored tonight as a person of the year, but I would suggest that she easily qualifies as the person of the century for the local church.

A Note of Hope
Thomas Aquinas College 35th Anniversary
(September 30, 2006)
Beverley Wilshire Hotel

We conclude this evening on a note of hope and we do that in an era plagued with global terrorism, widespread disdain for organized religion and horrendous scandals within the family of God's people.

While having only minimal credentials as an historian and even less as a prophet, I do see glimmers of better days for the mud splattered Catholic Church in the years ahead.

In the providence of· Almighty God, three movements have come on the scene which are destined to re-invigorate the Church as part of Christ's assurance of being with His followers until the end of time.

The FIRST is *Opus Dei* and such religious innovations as the Franciscan Friars of the Renewal which are rekindling the wonderful missionary and educational outreach of the Jesuits, Franciscan and Dominicans of earlier centuries;

The SECOND is the emergence of lay leaders who, by word and example, are quietly but forcefully telling the world about Christ in the 21st century. (This evening's speaker is among that handful of influential and outspoken individuals, a man whose recent essay in the pages of the Los Angeles Times confronted its editors for daring to lecture the Holy Father;)

FINALLY is the small Catholic College movement of which Thomas Aquinas was and is a pioneer and which is effectively preparing clergy, religious and lay leaders for the next generation.

You good people here tonight are in the front line of this future because it is your treasure, support and prayers that are helping this trinity of events come alive.

As bystanders for these birthpangs of a new Catholic thrust into modem society, we can identify with old Simeon who, we are told, waited patiently long years for that marvelous day when the infant Jesus was presented in the temple.

Perhaps we can close our gathering by praying Simeon's *Nunc Dimiuis*

> Lord, now you let your servant go in peace;
> your word has been fulfilled:
> my own eyes have seen the salvation
> which you have prepared in the sight of every people;
> a light to reveal you to the nations
> and the glory of your people Israel.

The Dawson Eighty
(October 24, 2007)
Pasadena Faculty Club

Many of you journeyed to the Getty Museum earlier this year for the visit of the Sinai Icons. So successful was that exhibit that the very term "Icon" has taken on a wholly new and expanded meaning in the world of culture.

This evening I would like to apply that term to the man of the hour. Surely he is an Icon in the book trade. Enter "books" on the Internet and the name *Glen Dawson* still flashes all across the screen, though he has been retired for over a decade.

I am not here to canonize Glen or even beatify him, though I could probably make a good case for either of those distinctions. Nor am I here to eulogize him or dominate the program. Others need to be heard, let me just relate one anecdote about Glen.

It revolves about an ancient lady known in bookish circles of earlier times as K. Gregory. She sold books out of her apartment in New York City to select collectors. Her phone number was unlisted and she had no interest whatever in expanding her base of customers.

Glen Dawson

Once while visiting the Big Apple, I heard that she had some miniature books. After tracking her address through a 1930 telephone directory at the New York Public Library, I journeyed to her condo and asked, on the intercom, if I could come for a visit.

Her companion answered and told me, in no uncertain terms, that Miss Gregory did not receive strangers, wanted no additional customers and was totally unavailable.

Sensing that the companion might be a Catholic, I told her that I was a priest. Would that help? "No", she replied, "not even if you were a monsignor." How about the fact that I was a book collector?

that I was president of the Miniature Book Society? After a pause, Miss Gregory sent word that she had never heard of that organization. Even when I invoked the name of the Zamorano Club, there was no recognition.

Finally in one last and desperate attempt, I mentioned being a friend of Glen Dawson. Without hesitation, the reply came back: "Miss Gregory will see you." I went up to her seventh floor suite and was able to acquire the last of the miniature books held by this remarkable lady who was then in her late 90s.

I have dropped Glen's name in other parts of the book world. Once, on London's Cecil Court, a dealer accepted my personal check only because I alluded to my friendship with Glen Dawson.

Now, relating Glen to this evening's celebration, we are here to celebrate the publication of a new bibliography. How appropriate it is that its compilers have chosen to name it after a man who has probably purchased, sold and/or published books to more people and libraries along the Pacific Slope than any other single individual.

Glen epitomizes what is best about California and the books written on the subject. Few local historians know more about the Golden State than this man who has climbed its most challenging mountains and published its most gifted writers. I remember once overhearing him enlightening a customer with the observation that "it snows more in the mountains of California than it does at the North Pole." Talking with Glen has always been a learning experience.

As one familiar with all the literature written about California, Glen liked to startle people with such outlandish statements as the one from Richard Henry Dana's *Two Years Before the Mast*: "This is a beautiful country, a perfect climate with every natural advantage; but the people, are lazy, ignorant, irreligious, priest-ridden, lawless, vicious and not much more than half civilized."

I think it was Glen who once told me that "it is a good thing to read books, and need not be a bad thing to write about them but, in any case, it is a pious thing to collect them"

Another Dawsonian comment, which the drive-by media attributes to Earl Schenck Meiers, stated that "if you bring into a room two statesmen, very likely you will have a war; two churchmen and you will have schism; two businessman and you will have a merger or a panic; two murderers and you will have a crime. But bring into the same room two people who work and live with books and the walls will ring with camaraderie."

While one could go on all evening recalling Glen Dawson the bookman, I prefer here to remember Glen as a friend. John Steven McGroarty, California's fabled poet laureate, once described a friend "as one who writes the faults of his brothers in the sands for the winds to obscure and obliterate, and who engraves their virtues on the tablets of love and memory." Glen has done that religiously for over ninety-five years.

I am grateful to the Lord for many blessings in my long life, but none more than being a friend and admirer of Glen Dawson who remains the "doyen" of bookmen along California's *El Camino Real.*

Together in Mission
(February, 2008)
San Fernando Mission

The beginning of the Lenten Season is an appropriate time to launch our annual *Together in Mission* appeal.

As you will recall, each worship community is expected to raise 10% of its annual income for this appeal which helps to keep 35 parishes and 48 schools operational in the three county archdiocese. The goal of San Fernando Mission this year is $7,286.

Should there be an excess of funds generated in a given place, that amount may be retained for local use. Last year we were able to retain here in Mission Hills a modest overage.

Part of this overall process, which is being repeated in all of our parishes, is the registration of each of our families, which we will do here in a few moments.

Another part of the process is the showing of a film by the Cardinal with his homily on the needs of the archdiocese. Because we don't have the machinery needed, we will have to forego that part which I will try to explain on his behalf.

In the Beatitudes, Saint Luke emphasizes how Christ befriends the poor, the suffering and the outcast. He welcomes them; He blesses them and He gives them hope. Christ emphasizes to His followers the importance of caring for the poor, the suffering and the outcast. And that this is not an option, but a mandate. It provides one of the many examples of Christ's concern for the less fortunate among us. Christ, the One in whose footsteps we are called to walk, healed the sick, fed the hungry and defended the oppressed. He never missed an opportunity to reach out to those in need.

We are asked to do as Jesus did; to make caring for the less fortunate a priority in our lives. When we see media coverage of natural disasters like a tsunami, a hurricane or a flood, the plight of the people effected touches us deeply and we provide amazing levels of financial support to help them recover.

It is more difficult to focus on the poor who are among us all the time. Their circumstances rarely receive significant media coverage. We might even tend to be so put off by their circumstances that we look away when we see them on the street. We make excuses for not supporting them saying that they should get jobs or the government will take care of them.

But, the reality is that we should offer effective support to many thousands of disadvantaged people right here in our own archdiocese.

This campaign provides an opportunity to provide funding for ministry, education and services in the parishes and schools that will receive financial support from *Together in Mission* this year.

I will be gently reminding you over the next few weeks about the need to join in this campaign. Please be informed that every cent of your pledge goes directly and only to the goals of helping the parishes and schools mentioned.

Together In Mission
2007 Appeal
San Fernando Mission

Once each year, Catholics of California's Southland are asked to look beyond their own parish to the larger Church in what is known as the Archdiocese of Los Angeles.

Even though we live in the most prosperous country of the world, there are those among us who do not share many of the gifts that we take for granted.

Together in Mission is a unique fund raising campaign. The Roman Catholic Archdiocese of Los Angeles is the only one in the United States that dedicates its entire Annual Appeal to assist parishes and schools that cannot survive economically without outside financial support.

The people of all of our 290 parishes, including those that are subsidized, are asked, once a year, to make a significant financial commitment to this important cause.

In 2007, 35 parishes and 48 schools will receive funding through Together in Mission. These funds help to maintain a meaningful Catholic presence in some of the most impoverished areas of Los Angeles, Santa Barbara and Ventura Counties.

The Good News can thus be proclaimed where God's grace, healing, and hope are, perhaps, most desperately needed.

The Annual Appeal, Together in Mission, provides an opportunity to share our financial gifts in order to help provide Catholic education, ministry and services through the parishes and schools that are assisted by the campaign.

Another reason to support this campaign is born of the fact that we are not a congregational church. All parishioners should hear and understand this fact. Every time that we say the Creed, we reaffirm the fact that we are members of the "one, holy, Catholic and apostolic Church".

Our part in this annual appeal is $7,286. We do hope that everyone will participate in this campaign. Every penny is meaningful.

We are saying that every parish and every parishioner is responsible not only for his or her parish but also for the well being of the Church throughout the Archdiocese and throughout the world.

Since we are one community of believers, members of all parish communities throughout the Archdiocese of Los Angeles, including those that are receiving subsidies, are asked to give to *Together in Mission.*

17
Miscellaneous Correspondence

A while ago someone, perhaps in a moment of charitable abandonment, told me that I had "diarrhea of the pen". Okay, I agree, though I don't think there is anything intrinsically wrong about that. Actually my postal and FAX interventions are fairly rare. Often I have wished that I had been more outspoken. Anyway, here are a **couple** of my observations over the past decade.

In May of 2003, at the suggestion of Sister Marilyn Vollmer, I wrote a memo about a meeting of a panel dealing with the Synod held at the Cathedral: I had some experience, having been one of the few to have attended the previous Synod forty years earlier:

Here are some observations I was asked me to make about the sessions of the Synod:

> I was deeply impressed by the competency of those attending the gathering. With no exceptions among those I interviewed, the members were obviously among the doers and thinkers of their parishes. They were polite, alert, committed and open-minded. Their selection was well orchestrated.
>
> Father Robert Schreiter, C.Pp.S. was a bit of a disappointment. I sat next to and spoke with him at dinner. He was far more adept at conversing than he was at speaking. His carefully crafted address really said nothing new. I am sure you'll notice that when you study the printed version. He didn't effectively challenge his listeners. He spoke well and enunciated carefully, but made no lasting impression. His was an opportunity lost. He resembled the typical clerical bureaucrat from the NCCB who desperately needs a five-year dose of parochial experience.
>
> The "observers" were impressive and I spoke with every one of them. They appeared interested and pleased to be with us. I suspect they were edified by our openness and willingness to share our dreams for the future. Likely they took home a refreshing and more positive experience of their Catholic neighbors. It was wise to invite them.

Interestingly, most had stories to relate about pedophilia among their own ranks, it is a bit refreshing to know that this problem is not solely a Catholic scourge.

I would question how representative the members were. For example, there was not a single recipient of the cardinal's award, a significant donor to the cathedral fund (or Together in Mission) or a winner of any medal, etc. Maybe they are too young. But, where were those who keep the engines of the archdiocese running? Admittedly, such people are generally more affluent, but keep in mind that they make this archdiocese work. Those who put their treasure where their hearts are were conspicuous by their absence.

The number of "older" clergy didn't appear very numerous either. Why? They are often overlooked but, without them, this program cannot work. The cardinal stressed the need for priests, but he keeps accepting their resignations (often earlier than 75) with little encouragement to stay on. I believe we have far too many retired priests. They need to be challenged to remain—maybe in a different capacity. Retirement is a luxury the church can ill afford at this moment in our pilgrimage.

Along those lines, I spoke with one prospective seminarian. I forget his name (he was the mitre bearer for the liturgy). I discovered that he was already open to a priestly vocation and was getting spiritual counseling. I gave him my card if he ever wanted to talk.

The food and surroundings were superb. From what I could determine, the participants were happy to be there and wanted very much to be part of the church's future. It will be important not to let them flounder in a sea of inactivity after this whole scenario is over. We have identified a valuable resource for the future.

The proposal about "the possibility of women's ordination" is a red flag to Rome. Why go that route? It is forbidden in the guidelines to even speak about it. I also believe that discussing the norms for denying Holy Communion to certain individuals is beyond the competency of the synod. Again, why wander into those murky waters?

One thing needs some further attention—the question of a diocese for Santa Barbara. If that goes through, I would strongly recommend that the new jurisdiction be Santa Barbara—San Luis Obispo. Maybe Bishop Ryan should be brought into that discussion. Santa Barbara alone would have difficulty functioning as a viable entity.

Implementation will be a vital step in the fall. That is terribly important. In earlier gatherings, we called people to service and then abandoned them. That procedure is unfair, wasteful and demoralizing. Let's not repeat that mistake.

As one of two or three who was present at the last synod, forty-years ago, I was pleased to see how the Church is reacting to the changing world, probably because of a force beyond us all. It's been fun for me to write about the past, but even more satisfying to know that there will be a future for someone else to write about—down the way.

In 2004, I wrote to thank the cardinal for attending a meeting of our Confraternity of Catholic Clergy. He had obviously been wrongly informed by one of his loquacious and ill-informed auxiliaries about the group. His answer was most gracious:

> Thank you very much for your recent note, and I was delighted to spend time with members of the Confraternity of Catholic Clergy.
>
> I was very impressed with the deep spirituality and sense of discipleship with the Lord Jesus as shared by the members that afternoon. Setting aside time for a holy hour is so important for all of us, and I was truly impressed with the spirit of prayer that prevailed.
>
> The evening came to a delightful conclusion with dinner at the Dresden Restaurant, thus helping to deepen even more those fraternal bonds among us . . . .
>
> That was surely a fascinating letter from Father X, and I was quite humbled with his assessment and evaluation. I am not really certain what should be done with his opinion piece, and as you might imagine, I would be the very last one to offer suggestions about its publication. No doubt you and he could pursue that avenue if you felt that there would be some advantage.

On another occasion I wrote Archbishop George Niederauer of San Francisco to congratulate him on his recent transfer from Salt Lake City:

> A belated welcome back to the Golden State and "Baghdad by the Bay".
>
> Once when I told Bishop Ward about a rumor that he was going to Oklahoma, he responded: "I would rather be an altar boy in Los Angeles than Archbishop of Oklahoma City." Maybe you can quietly hold out in the wings until the southland opens up!
>
> Seriously, I pray that your ministry in San Francisco will be bountiful. You will walk in the footsteps of Joseph Sadoc Alemany, Patrick W. Riordan and Edward J. Hanna, the giants of an earlier age.
>
> May you wear the mitre and carry the crozier as gracefully and successively as they did.

When Archbishop William Levada was named to a pivotal Roman position, I reminded him of his past service on the Serra Bicentennial Commission:

> Do you remember back to the days of 1983-1984 when we were all members of the Serra Bicentennial Commission? One of our accomplishments resulted in the issuance of a United States commemorative stamp for Fray Junipero Serra, thanks to the close relationship of Catherine Haley with President Reagan.
>
> Twenty years later much has changed. Noel Moholy, Bishop Shubsda and Kaye Haley have now joined Serra and there remains only the final challenge of having Blessed Junipero canonized.
>
> Father Noel was replaced by Father John Vaughan, a former Minister General of the OFMs. We all expected that his influence in Rome would be advantageous to the cause. Unhappily, because he has suffered a major stroke, he has been unable to do much for the cause. The burden has

fallen on Brother Timothy Arthur who, unfortunately, has no standing in Rome.

As the most influential American cleric ever to serve in Rome, I am appealing for your assistance at the Congregation for the Cause of Saints. A phone call or maybe a visit with Msgr. Robert Sarno may be all it takes to get the cause back on course, and surely you can imagine the effect that such an action would have on vocations in California and other places.

From what I can gather, all the preliminary work on the remaining miracle is progressing through the Archdiocese of Denver where the purported cure took place. Maybe all that is needed is a little jog by someone like yourself who can bring Serra's name to the head of the long list of worthy candidates.

Years ago, the late Father Maynard Geiger told me that I would live to see Serra canonized. But my time is fast running out and it would be a shame to see Maynard's prediction unfulfilled.

Back to Niederauer, on January 31, 2007, I wrote as follows:

You surely have more to do than respond to old country priests, but I do feel that the American bishops are not doing enough to inform our political leaders about basic moral and even doctrinal issues.

An example would be speaker Nancy Pelosi who lives in your jurisdiction. She appears to be a practicing Catholic who is in a pivotal position to influence her confreres.

Might you suggest to her and others the wisdom of establishing in the House (and Senate) a "Catholic Caucus" which would meet monthly on issues facing Catholics in the country.

There are 155 Catholic members of Congress, many of them ignorant of the basic teachings of the Church.

There could be a forty-minute monthly lecture on such subjects as abortion, partial birth and stem cell research by recognized and orthodox Catholic theologians. A committee of bishops might occasionally meet with members of the Caucus.

In response to a letter from Father Melvin A. Jurisich, O.F.M., Provincial Master of the Order of Friars for California, I wrote a blunt letter spelling out my disappointment with the progress (or non progress) of the Serra Cause:

Thank you so much for your letter. I was disappointed about the Denver case. However, that whole scenario could have been avoided had the vice-postulator sought competent judicial advice.

I would suggest that you have Father Chinnici carefully check out the factual and historical aspects of any future case. And obviously you need a better canonical adviser. An effective lawyer would have never submitted a case that wouldn't stand critical scrutinizing.

> And between the two of us, I believe that the present Vice Postulator is physically unable to handle the cause. While understanding why his Roman connection made him the logical candidate for the position, I think that his subsequent health problems call for a new vice postulator. I say that as a friend of John's since our days together on Detroit Street in the 1940s.
>
> Although a Franciscan would be the ideal candidate, I believe the new regulations allow for even a layman in that position. I only wish Brother Timothy Arthur were twenty years younger. He is a wonderful man, totally dedicated to Serra.
>
> I am glad you are planning some additional activities. It's important that the Franciscans appear interested in the cause even though I sense few really are.
>
> Thank you for allowing me to "vent" on this important matter. If and when Serra is canonized, it may well be in spite of his confreres rather than because of them.

Finally, a letter to Justin Cardinal Rigali who had recently been named to the Roman Congregation for the appointment of Bishops:

> Last Sunday I saw an hour-long interview with Archbishop Charles Chaput of Denver. It confirmed what I had read and heard about this good man in recent years.
>
> While I am sure that you have far better sources than this old country priest, maybe you can at least put this suggestion in the hopper marked "Future Archbishop of Los Angeles."
>
> Though I am not generally inclined to the notion of "religious" bishops, for a lot of reasons, here is one giant exception!
>
> This man's age, track record, theological acumen and sound spiritual life fit perfectly into what I and many others have been praying for in recent times.
>
> He would, I am sure, attempt to rejuvenate our seminary system, uplift clerical morale, elevate our public image and restore credibility of the ordinary as spiritual father of the local church.
>
> Finally, to make this transition easier for *him*, his predecessor and our Catholic community, I would further suggest that he be named "coadjutor" soon so he can have time to adjust to and learn about the needs of this the largest Catholic enclave in the country.
>
> Please do not bother to acknowledge this intervention.

Oh, there were others. I never pursued a matter after once having expressed myself. I felt an obligation to inform, but none to usurp the role of those in authority.

Pilgrimage to

France, Switzerland, and Rome

An Archdiocesan Pilgrimage
Switzerland, France and Rome
Including

BEATIFICATION OF MOTHER TERESA

and Mass with

CARDINAL MAHONY
in his Titular Church

Spiritual Guide
Reverend Monsignor Francis Weber

October 9th – 20th, 2003

For information call:

Sister Mary Jean Meier, R.S.M. (213) 637-7520

18
Pilgrimages

My only pilgrimage in the last decade was as chaplain with Sr. Mary Jean Meier's archdiocesan trek to Switzerland, France and Rome in October of 2003. Each day we began with a novena to Fray Junípero Serra.

Most of the twenty-five seasoned travelers set out for Europe on October 9th from LAX. The whole group reconnoitered at the airport in Lyon, from which we set out for the tiny village of Ars, the parish of Saint John Vianney.

The official journal for the pilgrimage recorded that "each day Monsignor Weber's homily included not only a delightful story, but also a specific suggestion for us to ponder and carry with us through the day". Daily Mass at the basilica of Ars was a joyful event, using as I did the

Beatification of Mother Teresa in Saint Peter's Square.

chalice actually belonging to John Vianney. Besides a lot of prayer, we toured the little town, its several museums and the shrine where the Cure's heart is enthroned.

Then on to Taize, a gathering place for the world's youth. From there we went to Cluny and Paray-le-Monial where we visited the Visitation Convent and venerated the shrine of Saint Margaret Mary.

Lyon is located at the point where the Rhone River merges with the Saone, gateway to the Alps. There I visited a small church housing the remains of the venerable Pauline Jaricot. From the 10th century Basilique Notre Dame de Fourviere we were able to get a panoramic view of Lyon.

Then on to Annecy, a beautiful town in the northern French Alps, a village dating from the Neolithic era. Our quarters in Annecy were situated on the edge of a nine mile long lake. Following Mass we took time to visit the shrines of Saints Francis de Sales and Jane de Chantal.

Leaving the beautiful lakes, we set out for Rome by air where we lodged in the Hotel Pamphili. A bus took us to the tomb of St. Peter with Roger Cardinal Mahony. In the bascilica we were photographed at the place marked off for our cathedral on the floor. Next day we did the usual touring of the Eternal City and a superb private tour of the Sistine Chapel.

One afternoon we gathered at the cardinal's titular church of Santi Quattro Coronati for Mass in one of the oldest shrines of Christianity. The Augustinian Sisters hosted us to a small reception.

Our reservations for the beatification of Mother Teresa were given away by the Holy Father himself (to the homeless) which meant that most of our pilgrims watched the ceremonies on the hotel television! Two miniature books eventually were motivated by the pilgrimage and each tells its own story fairly accurately.

Blessed Teresa of Calcutta

Two persons I have personally met have been beatified by the Catholic Church—Pope John XXIII and Mother Teresa of Calcutta. By the grace of God, I was able to be present when that distinction was given to Mother Teresa on October 19, 2003 in the Vatican's Piazza de San Pietro.

Of the several times Mother Teresa visited Los Angeles, I recall greeting her at a luncheon given in her honor by the Ladies of Charity and again when she visited the Chancery Office on West Ninth Street in the summer of 1990.

On both of those occasions, I recall thinking that she was one remarkable and dedicated person. She appeared to be single-minded and rather oblivious to anyone or anything unrelated to her immediate objectives, truly great people are like that. Rarely if ever are they distracted by the mundanities of everyday life.

This most celebrated woman of the twentieth century was born in Skopje, now in Macedonia, on August 26, 1910. At the age of seventeen, "Agnes" heard her call to the service of the Church at the Shrine of Our Lady of Latnice.

PREFETTURA DELLA CASA PONTIFICIA

CAPPELLA PAPALE
presieduta da Sua Santità
GIOVANNI PAOLO II
per la Beatificazione di
MADRE TERESA DI CALCUTTA

domenica 19 ottobre 2003
Piazza San Pietro ore 10

Ingresso: dalle ore 7,30

187238

In 1928, she entered the Sisters of Our lady of Loretto in Ireland and shortly thereafter was sent to Darjeeling, India, where she pronounced her vows on May 25, 1931 as "Teresa." She went to Calcutta for a teaching assignment at Saint Mary's High School, later becoming headmistress. In 1948 she became an Indian citizen and thereafter was referred to as "the First Lady of India."

In that same year, Sister Teresa received permission from the Vatican to work among the poorest people teaching hygiene, manners, faith, math and reading. Within a few years, twenty-eight women had joined her Missionaries of Charity to look after lepers, homeless and those dying in the streets.

Her work rapidly spread to the far corners of the earth and, in 1960, she was interviewed by Malcolm Muggeridge for BBC. That program, coupled with his biography, *Something Beautiful for God*, made her world famous.

In 1971, Mother Teresa was awarded the first John XXIII Prize for Peace and a decade later the Nobel Prize for Peace. In her acceptance speech, she asked that the usual banquet funds be used to feed the poor. She utilized the prize money to build a center for those afflicted with leprosy.

Though internationally famous, she always considered herself simply as "a pencil in God's hands." When her health began to fail, she resigned as superior of the sisters and died on September 5, 1997.

Today over 4,500 Sisters of Charity, active and contemplative of eighty nationalities operate 710 houses in 132 countries where they staff shelters for the homeless, malnutrition centers, home for rehabilitation, hostels for unwed mothers, hospitals, mobile clinics, feeding centers, relief stations, schools for the poor and havens for street people and those suffering from Aids.

Blessed Teresa, however, always made it clear that there is no need for any of us to travel across the globe to follow Jesus. "Stay where you are in your own Calcutta. Find the sick, the suffering, the lonely, right there where you are—in your own homes and in your own families, in your workplaces and schools."

On another occasion, Blessed Mother Teresa said: "In the Eucharist, I see Christ in the appearance of the bread. In the slums, I see Christ in the poor. Sometimes we meet Jesus rejected and covered in filth in the gutter. Sometimes we find Jesus stuffed into a drain, or moaning with pain from sores or rotting with gangrene, or even screaming from the agony of a broken back. The most distressing disguise calls for even more love from us."

Finally

Among the most treasured moments in my long life occurred on October 17, 2003 when I was able to see and venerate one of Christendom's oldest and most revered relics, the Veil of Veronica, which is housed in the Tribune of Saint Veronica in Saint Peter's Basilica.

According to the historian Eusebius in his commentary on the Legend of Abgar and remarks contained in the apocryphal work *Mors Pilati*, several authentic portraits of Jesus Christ were made at various times during His lifetime.

The oldest and most authenticated of these images has been known to Romans for centuries as the *Vera Icon* or Veil of Veronica, a term used by Giraldus Cambrensis in his *Speculum Ecclesiae*. So highly was this image held in Roman esteem, that a Mass celebrating it was composed and inserted into at least one of the early Augsburg Missals.

There is no reference in Scripture to a woman offering her veil to Christ during His Sacred Passion. But it is highly plausible that there was such a compassionate soul among those who followed Christ on His way to Mount Calvary. The incident itself is undoubtedly worthy of some credibility, since it has found its expression since very early times in the Christian devotion of the Stations of the Cross.

Apparently the holy woman in question, known in pious legend only as Veronica, found her way to Rome, where she presented her *Vera Icon* to Pope Clement I (1046-1047). There was a great devotion to it in the Middle Ages.

The veil, ostensibly bearing the image of the suffering Jesus miraculously pressed into it, was venerated in several places until the pontificate of Pope John VII who had it enclosed in an ornate reliquary.

During the ensuing centuries, the Holy See has exhibited particular solicitude for this precious relic. It has been reserved to the Holy Father's own chapel, Saint Peter's Basilica, where it was formerly exposed briefly during Holy Week for veneration by the faithful.

While there is a fairly substantial literature on Veronica's veil, it is important to point out that the spiritual value of any relic is directly proportional to the devotion it inspires in those who venerate it. Apart from its spiritual significance, the relic is merely a historical curiosity. It may or may not be of archaeological value to the museums of the world.

My long attempts to see the Veil of Veronica began in September of 1996, when I asked Roger Cardinal Mahony to write one of his counterparts in Rome, Virgilio Noe, then Archpriest of Saint Peter's Basilica for permission to see the holy relic, a privilege that I knew had rarely been granted in recent years. Noe diplomatically demurred.

Knowing that I would be again accompanying a group of pilgrims to the Eternal City for the beatification of Mother Theresa in 2003, I contacted a friend in Rome, Archbishop Francesco Marchisano, who had recently succeeded Noe as Archpriest of the Basilica. The archbishop asked me to meet him at his office in the Vatican Canonica on the morning of October 17th.

Following the formalities of greetings, the archbishop instructed his vicar, along with the papal sacristan and Antonio Grimaldi, who heads the "fabrica" of San Pietro, and two other Vatican attendants to accompany me to the Tribune of Saint Veronica. There we entered a tiny area with a stone stairwell, probably designed by Michaelangelo himself.

Extending from the ceiling of the circular stairwell is a tightly-knit rope, which assists climbers as they mount the narrow steps hewn out of the stone casing. After what seemed like eternity of tiny stairs, we emerged into a foyer that opens onto a small balcony from which the Veil of Veronica was exhibited for centuries during Holy Week.

One of the attendants, who carried five gigantic keys in a cloth purse, consulted a well worn booklet on which was written the code for opening the vault housing the reliquary.

Each of the keys had its own distinctive length, size and design. They were carefully fitted into the locks in the prescribed succession. Once in place some of the keys were turned left to right and the others right to left in a manner that would surely confuse even the most experienced locksmith.

Only when all the complimentary movements were in the proper sequence did I hear a "click" indicating that the tumblers had fallen into place. With that the attendant opened the metallic door, revealing three large reliquaries, one for a piece of the sacred lance, another for a substantial segment of the true cross and the final one for the Veil of Veronica.

The veil itself, about the size of a large altar card, is housed in a glass case behind a damask curtain. When the curtain was parted, the relic became visible. I had always heard that the veil had faded over the centuries, but that is not true for there is a very discernible image on the cloth. The poor lighting made it impossible to see many details, but the image is quite apparent.

The glass and metallic reliquary itself appears to date from the 15th century. In the Basilica's *tesoro* or treasury, is an ancient frame used for the relic in earlier times.

In Volume V of the 1917 edition of *The Catholic Encyclopedia* is a notation stating that "none but an ecclesiastic of very high rank is allowed to examine" the Veil of Veronica! For that and other reasons, I will always remain grateful to the Lord that such a privilege should come to little Frankie Weber of Valley Mills, Indiana.

19

Questions & Answers

Q. What do you think of Global Warming?

A. If you believe that much of the global warming hype is one gigantic hoax, as do I, then it is reasonable to feel a little irritated by the newspapers, television and radio campaigns to portray this issue in such extreme terminology.

Apart from the evidence, which certainly does indicate that the world is in one of its normal warming cycles, I worry that proponents of global warming have almost totally denied the Lord a place in the overall context.

For those who believe that the earth (and everything else in nature) is part of God's creation, would be so presumptuous as to think that man could seriously interfere, much less destroy or damage what God has wrought.

Of course, people must properly use God's creation in a responsible manner - that's basic good common sense. But even if people were to do otherwise, I cannot imagine that such actions would endanger what God has set in place. There is a hierarchy of existence and little man is at the bottom of creation's totem pole.

Pope Benedict XVI has warned that "any solutions to global warming must be based on firm evidence and not on dubious ideology." He suggested, in his message for World Peace Day in 2008, that "fears over man-made emissions melting the ice caps and causing a wave of unprecedented disasters were nothing more than scare-mongering."

While some concerns may be valid, the "world needs to care for the environment but not to the point where the welfare of animals and plants are given a higher priority than that of mankind."

Hence no less a person than the Holy Father believes that the case against global warming is over-hyped. "Fluctuations in the earth's temperatures are normal and can often be caused by waves of heat generated by the sun."

While not subscribing to the claptrap about global warming, which appears to be part of God's cycle of existence, I do feel strongly that as stewards of creation, people are obliged to behave like the "good stewards" mentioned in Holy Scripture. To do otherwise would indicate a selfishness unbecoming our Christian calling.

Q. How do you view the Church in Los Angeles?

A. Sorrowfully I have to admit that the Church of today, (2010) is greatly diminished in numbers and influence in Southern California. About a fifth of today's Catholics attend Sunday Mass, a scenario familiar in many other areas of the nation. Perhaps we are entering what the late Cardinal Manning described as the "post Christian era" in the United States.

Q. What do you think about "altar girls"?

A. Shortly after the bishops in this country were allowed to have girls as altar servers (which many pastors had already implemented) a young lady approached me asking that she be allowed to join our League of Altar Servers. I put the question to each of our eighteen servers and to a person they all objected. The candidate kept appealing until I put the following notice in our weekly bulletin.

> A number of people have expressed concern over the recent reports in the religious and secular press over the permission given by the Vatican for girls and women to be allowed to serve at the altar during Mass. The origin of this is an interpretation of the Code of Canon Law which is permissive, rather than prescriptive in character, and to be applied where the circumstances seem to require it (as in the case of Extraordinary Ministers of the Eucharist.) There is no question of any ministry being exercised as of right. At the Old Mission we will continue to recruit servers from among boys respecting and observing the provision made in the permission by the Pope "that it will always be very appropriate to follow the noble tradition of having boys serve at the altar which has led to a reassuring development of priestly vocations. The obligation to support such groups of altar boys continues."

In my opinion, service of the Lord at the altar is one of the most effective means of encouraging priestly vocations. Might I quote a letter from Father Dennis Kleinmann, the pastor of Saint Mary's in Alexandria, Virginia:

The altar server functions entirely in support of the priest and is, therefore, most closely identified with him. All others who serve at Mass, such as cantors, lectors, ushers, and extraordinary ministers of Holy Communion, are directed toward service to the people. The connection to the priest and what he does at the altar breeds a natural attraction to the priestly role. Yet the Church has always clearly taught and has recently affirmed in absolute terms that Christ intended priestly Ordination only for men. For with Christ, as priests consecrate His Body and Blood, they give themselves as Bridegrooms to their Bride, the Church. Any young person directly assisting a priest at Mass is implicitly but surely invited to identify with the priest and so encouraged to aspire to a necessarily masculine priesthood.

I cannot in good conscience even take the chance of putting our daughters in a situation that leads to false hopes and unreasonable aspirations regarding the ordained priesthood. I must add that this is not a theoretical problem but an occurrence that I have encountered in my time as a priest.

For the same reasons as explained above, a strong fraternity of altar boys in close association with the priest is indispensable in inviting young men to meaningful consideration of a priestly vocation. If girls were allowed to serve, the connection of server and priest will necessarily diminish, and with it a chance for young men to hear and respond to God's call.

Thus the connection of priest and altar boy has always been a vital part of the life of the Church. In 1994, while allowing girls to serve, the Vatican stated the following:

> *The Holy See wishes to recall that it will always be very appropriate to follow the noble tradition of having boys serve at the altar. As is well known, this has also led to a reassuring development of priestly vocations.*

John Paul II in 2004 accordingly encouraged priests to show a special concern for altar boys, saying that they "represent a kind of 'garden' of priestly vocations" and that their service at the altar can be "a valuable experience of Christian education and become a kind of pre-seminary" (*Letter to Priests for Holy Thursday, 2004*).

Further, in these days where there are reports on increased loss of opportunities for boys to be formed in male virtues, the tradition of altar boys provides a healthy masculine identity and formative fraternal activity. Our program here at St. Mary's is thriving with well over 110 young men serving in the liturgies.

Q. Are there statistics about pedophilia by priests?

A. Someone once observed that there are lies, damn lies and statistics. The government publishes *The Statistical Abstract* each year to officially recognize the need for examining statistics and what they indicate or validate.

Virtues of Catholic Leadership

L - Loyalty to Church and commonweal

E - Equality with employees and associates

G - Gratitude to God and nation

A - Attitude about goals and principles

T - Temperance in food and drink

U - Usefulness to family and parish

S - Simplicity in lifestyle and demeanor

San Fernando Mission
April 12, 2000

Jubilee Prayer for 2000

***B**lessed are you, Father, who, in your infinite love, gave us your only-begotten Son. He became our companion on life's path and gave new meaning to our history, the journey we make together in toil and suffering, in faithfulness and love.*

***B**y your grace, O Father, may the Jubilee Year be a time of deep conversion and of joyful return to you. May it be a time of reconciliation between people, and of peace restored among nations, a time when swords are beaten into ploughshares and the clash of arms gives way to songs of peace. Father, grant that we may live this Jubilee Year docile to the voice of spirit, faithful to the way of Christ.*

***F**ather, by the power of Spirit, strengthen the Church's commitment to the new evangelization and guide our steps along the pathways of the world.*

***T**o you, Almighty Father, be praise and honour and glory now and for ever. Amen!*

Anyway, along comes Sam Miller a prominent Cleveland Jewish businessman, who recently complained that "the press is vindictive and trying to totally denigrate in every way, the Catholic Church in this country."

"They have blamed the disease of pedophilia on the Catholic Church, which is as irresponsible as blaming adultery on the institution of marriage. Let me give you some figures that you as Catholics should know and remember. For example 12% of the 300 Protestant clergy surveyed admitted to sexual intercourse with a parishioner; 38% acknowledged other inappropriate sexual contact in a study by the United Methodist Church; 41.8% of clergywomen reported unwanted sexual behavior; 17% of laywomen have been sexually harassed. Meanwhile, 1.7% of the Catholic clergy have been found guilty of pedophilia while 10% of the Protestant ministers have been found guilty of pedophilia. This is not just a Catholic problem."

Q. What personal observations do you have about the Chancery Archives?

A. In my humble but biased opinion, the Archives for the Archdiocese of Los Angeles are the best organized of their kind in the United States. The credit for that goes to the foresight of James Francis Cardinal McIntyre who authorized, encouraged and supported the archives from their formal opening on July 8, 1963. Both of the Cardinal's two successors have followed his good example. It was Msgr. Benjamin Hawkes who convinced the board members of the Dan Murphy Foundation to provide our building, the first of its kind ever erected by the Catholic Church in the United States, at San Fernando Mission in 1980. And another Vicar General, Msgr. Terance Fleming, secured the entire basement area of what is now Bishop Alemany High School in 1996 for additional space.

I have been Archivist since 1962, the longest tenure ever held by anyone in the American Catholic Church. It's been a wonderful lifetime, hard work and lots of fun.

Q. What do you think of the CCD Congress?

A. Not much. During the time I was director of the *Borromeo Guild*, I attended the Congress annually where we staffed a booth. The Congress is unlike any similar gathering in the USA or maybe in the world. It is the largest, has the greatest attendance and reflects the greatest diversity of speakers on religious topics. In its present format, it is mostly the genius of Sister Edith Pendergast who directs every aspect of the gathering. The Congress provides a forum for a wide ambit of divergent speakers, some of them with openly unorthodox viewpoints. The next Archbishop of Los Angeles should be told, in no uncertain terms, to get a better handle on the speakers and their presentations. Interestingly, it is the one of the few organization in the archdiocese with no oversight as to finances. It is a magnificent forum for propagating the faith, but it could be even better.

Q. Why is the papacy so slow to react?

A. It's not. Here's one example referred to by John Allen in his superb book, *All The Pope's Men*:

> John Paul II is today numbered among the strongest antideath penalty campaigners in the world. During his January 1999 trip to St. Louis, his personal plea to Missouri's then-governor Mel Carnahan saved the life of convicted murderer Darrell Mease. The Vatican's diplomatic corps around the world is under instruction to deliver papal requests for clemency every time an execution is scheduled. Various Catholic organizations, such as the San't Egidio Community, are leaders in grassroots activism against the death penalty, and this activity is blessed and celebrated form the Apostolic Palace. Yet just over one hundred years ago, popes not only supported capital punishment, they practiced it. In Rome's Museum of Criminology, one can still see the official twelve-foot tall papal guillotine, last used in 1868, just before the fall of the Papal States. More than a hundred people were beheaded by papal edict on the guillotine, introduced in Rome by Napoleon. As is well-known, Catholic catechisms presented the death penalty as not merely acceptable, but indeed obligatory, well into the post-Vatican IT period. Indeed, a provision for capital punishment remained part of the fundamental law of the Vatican City-State until Paul VI declared it null

Class of 1959 celebrates its golden anniversary Mass in the Serra Chapel at San Fernando Mission.

in 1969. It was not actually removed from the books until February 2001. The theological, liturgical and political nexus surrounding capital punishment developed in the Catholic church over centuries, yet it needed only one determined papacy to dissolve. Rapid movement on seemingly intractable issues is, therefore, possible.

Over the years, I have been often asked about my personal views concerning various happenings in the curial government of Los Angeles, often by reporters who needed to meet deadlines.

I have always been quite reluctant to express myself. I have never felt any compulsion to "go outside the system". Had the Lord wanted my humble viewpoints made public, He would surely have called me to a higher position than that of humble archivist.

20
Golden Sacerdotal Jubilee

Old age has many perks. In particular, I can now boast of a personal knowledge of the institutional Catholic Church in Southern California for a full century! That's indeed a coveted position for an historian. I have always been enamored by older people, for a lot of reasons. Not only are they advanced in wisdom, age and grace, but their personal recall of past events is usually greater than for the happenings of more recent times.

Class of 1959 celebrates its Golden Jubilee at San Fernando Mission.

When I was a youngster in Los Angeles, I actively cultivated the acquaintance of oldsters in our Los Angeles neighborhood who were generally fond of recalling their life experience; then as a youthful priest, I befriended older clergymen and people whose knowledge stretched back as far as sixty years; as a young pastor at San Buenaventura Mission, I spent many hours listening to and asking questions of seniors who remembered events back to the early 20th century. Finally as a thirty-two year columnist for *The Tidings*, I enjoyed interviewing senior clergy and aging laity about their first-hand impressions of earlier decades. What this all means is that my own institutional memory of the Church in the southland dates back over a century. Truly I am an endangered species!

If memory serves me accurately, the first priest I recall who celebrated his fiftieth sacerdotal anniversary was Father James Cody, CM. (1876-1952) who served as professor of physics and chemistry at Los Angeles College Minor Seminary from 1927 until his demise. Father Cody's Golden Jubilee was held at Saint Vincent's Church in Los Angeles well over half a century ago.

Since longevity has not been a characteristic in the Weber heritage, I gave minimal or no thought to the possibility of achieving that distinction myself. All of a sudden, April 30, 2009 was approaching and little old "Frankie" from Valley Mills, Indiana, was on the threshold of being among the elder clergymen of Los Angeles, a goal I never envisioned or much desired. Surely this would not have been likely without the medical and pharmaceutical advances of recent times, together with a host of talented physicians like my dear friend Richard Doyle. Oh yes, . . . and the patience of Almighty God!

When we were in the seminary, our class elected John Rohde to be our "arch" deacon or class representative, a position he occupied with great efficiency until his premature demise in 1995 while serving as pastor of St. Vibiana's Cathedral. One day while visiting his grave, in the adjoining San Fernando Mission Cemetery, John's mantel seemed to fall on to me, at least as far as arranging for a class celebration of our jubilee on April 30, 2009. With that in mind, I sent out the following letter on May 29, 2008:

> I have been exploring options with the seminary class of 1959 for a celebration next year on or about April 30th.
>
> As of now, we are thinking about gathering here at San Fernando Mission on April 30th for a Mass and dinner at the Odyssey Restaurant.
>
> Traveling to some exotic place might be well, but I don't sense any sentiment for that at our advanced age.
>
> Please let me know if you would like to join in this simple, but meaningful gathering. There's a nice motel nearby for anyone wishing to spend the night.

Originally, I had intended to include only the Class of Saint John's Seminary for 1959. Classmate Michael Killeen wisely suggested that the invitation be extended to include all the priests in the archdiocese ordained in 1959. That included:

Old Country Priest observes Golden Jubilee on Santa Cruz Island.

St. John's Seminary Class of 1959

Harry Freiermuth
41 Tharp Avenue
Watsonville, CA 95076
(831) 724-4460

Michael Killeen
1835 Larkvane Rd.
Rowland Heights, CA 91748-2501
(626) 964-3629

Thomas Peacha
Holy Trinity Church
3722 Boyce Avenue
Los Angeles, CA 90039-1810
(323) 664-4723 / 562-594-0726

Thomas Weible
Saint Peter Church
11 Prince Street
Provincetown, MA 02657
(580) 487-0095

John Mihan
635 South Hobart Blvd.
Los Angeles, CA 90005
(213) 738-0830

Alfonso Scott
St. Cyprian
4714 Clark Avenue
Long Beach, CA 90815
(562) 494-1745

Francis Weber
15151 San Fernando Mission Blvd.
Mission Hills, CA 91345
(818) 365-1501

Other Priests Ordained for Los Angeles, 1959

Francis Cassidy
Immaculate Conception Parish
740 S. Shamrock Avenue
Monrovia, CA 91016

John J. Daly
Church of the Holy Trinity
3722 Boyce Avenue
Los Angeles, CA 90039-1810
(310) 338-7445

Sean Flanagan
Saint Bartholomew Parish
252 Granada Avenue
Long Beach, CA
(562) 438-3826

John Foley
Holy Redeemer Parish
2411 Montrose Avenue
Montrose, CA 91020
(818) 299-2008

Kevin Larkin
St. Francis de Sales Parish
13360 Valleyheart Drive
Sherman Oaks, CA

William O'Keeffe
Our Lady of Refuge Parish
5195 Stearns Street
Long Beach, CA 90815
(562) 498-6641

Jeremiah O'Neill
St. Thomas More Parish
2510 S. Fremont Avenue
Alhambra, CA 91803
(626) 284-8333

Cornelius Phelan
Saint Basil Parish
637 South Kingsley Drive
Los Angeles, CA 90005
(213) 381-6191

Las Damas Archivistas *at San Fernando Mission for the Golden Jubilee of the Old Country Priest.*

I also invited the cardinal to join us for the celebration and dinner—but he had previously committed himself to a meeting of the National Federation of Priests Councils. He said our group would be invited to the 2009 Chrism Mass at the Cathedral as "vested concelebrants" and there would be a dinner for us around Labor Day at his residence. I asked Charleen Bennett and Martha McGrath to provide appropriate music in the Serra Chapel for the April 30th celebration.

We read out the names of our fallen brethren after paying a personal visit to John Rohde's grave:

John Thom	July 23, 1965
Tito Bongay	December 29, 1973
Warren Tierney	March 24, 1988
Vincent Haggin	February 14, 1990
John Rohde	May 1, 1995
Floyd Stromberg	December 22, 2007

The *Daily News* printed a photograph of the thirteen concelebrants. Remarkably, all the jubilarians were ambulatory.

Celebrations

There were several proposals for publicly commemorating my own jubilee, both social and liturgical. In 1984, my twenty-fifth anniversary, also observed at San Fernando Mission, elicited no special events and my personal preferences would have been the same a quarter century later. After much discussion, it was decided that a public reception would be held in Cantwell Hall from 2 o'clock until 5 o'clock on May 3rd. There was no need for a special liturgical observance since two Masses were already scheduled on that morning, one at 9 o'clock and the other at 10:30.

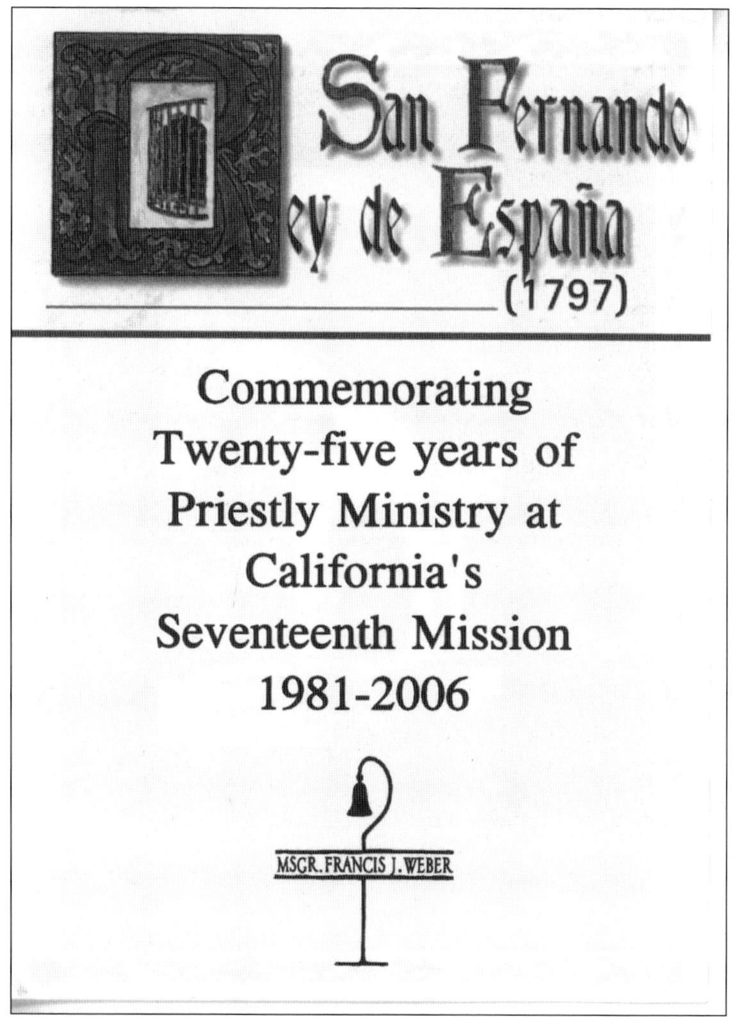

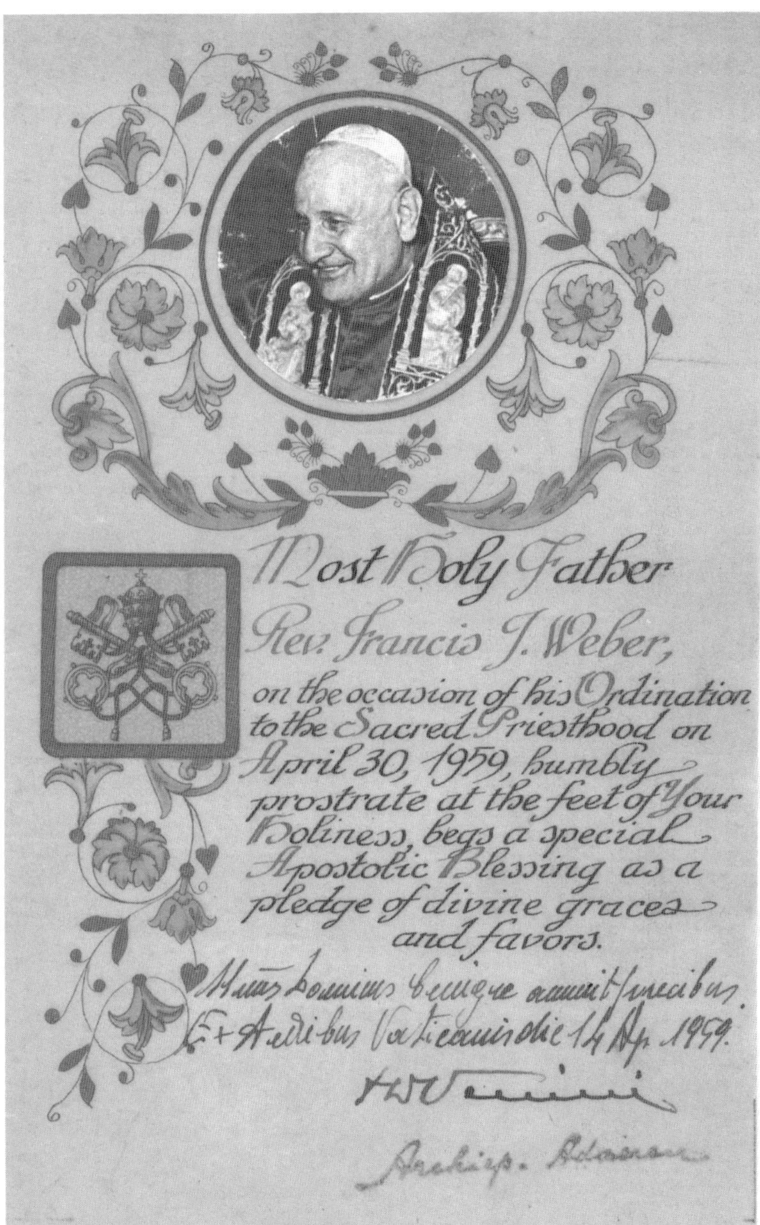

Most Holy Father

Rev. Francis J. Weber, on the occasion of his Ordination to the Sacred Priesthood on April 30, 1959, humbly prostrate at the feet of Your Holiness, begs a special Apostolic Blessing as a pledge of divine graces and favors.

Ex Aedibus Vaticanis die 14 Ap. 1959.

I sent out the following letter on March 20th:

> If the Lord preserves me here on planet Earth until April 30th, it will have been a half—century since I was ordained a priest! Imagine that—fifty years of ministry along California's *El Camino Real!*

Mary Alice Castagna and her jubilarian brother in 2009.

A lot of water has flowed down the Los Angeles River since James Francis Cardinal McIntyre conferred Holy Orders on this unworthy Hoosier in Saint Vibiana's venerable cathedral on the feast of Saint Catherine of Siena in 1959.

Pope John XXIII was the Roman Pontiff, Dwight D. Eisenhower was President, Edmund G. Brown was Governor, Norris Poulson was Mayor and Thomas F. Fogarty was Pastor of Saint Brendan's Parish five decades ago.

Since we already have two Masses scheduled for Sunday, May 3rd, it was decided that the occasion would be commemorated on that day by an informal reception in Cantwell Hall at San Fernando Mission from 2 o'clock until 5 pm.

I know many are otherwise busy and possibly a long distance away, but I would appreciate a remembrance in your prayers on that occasion.

While no personal gifts are expected, a donation to the Endowment Fund for San Fernando Mission would be greatly appreciated by this Old Country Priest.

The homily on the following Sunday, preached in the presence of my sister, Mary Alice Castagna, was thus:

Observing my fiftieth year as a Catholic priest is an occasion for gratitude that I have been around long enough to see how God allows His world to develop and change.

When I was a young clerical aspirant at Saint John's Seminary, Adolfo Camarillo, then in his nineties, came one day to address the students. He gave us much to think about. One observation stands out above the others. Here is a direct quote:

> Once, when I was a youngster, my daddy took us to Los Angeles in an oxcart. It took four days to make the journey. Last week, in recognition of my giving land on which to build an air base, they

Memories of an Old Country Priest

Msgr. Francis J. Weber

flew me by jet to Los Angeles in four minutes! Can you imagine! From four days to four minutes in a single lifetime! You young men will live to see interplanetary travel. God continues to share His wonders with us.

Recently I reflected on some of the many things that have occurred in my own lifetime. I came along before television, before penicillin, before polio shots, frozen foods, Xerox, plastic, contact lenses, Frisbees, heart transplants and the pill! My generation was born prior to radar, credit cards, split atoms, laser beams and ballpoint pens; before pantyhose, dishwashers, clothes dryers, electric blankets, air conditioners, drip-dry clothes and before man walked on the moon.

In those times closets were for clothes, not for "coming out of." Bunnies were small rabbits and not Volkswagens, Soda fountains adorned every drug-store.

We predated gay rights, computer dating, dual careers and commuter marriages. We came before day-care centers, group therapy and nursing homes. We had never heard of FM radio, tape decks, electric typewriters, artificial hearts, word processors, yogurt and guys wearing earrings. For us, time sharing meant togetherness, not condos; a "chip" meant a piece of wood; hardware meant hard-ware and software wasn't even a word.

His Holiness Benedict XVI
cordially imparts the
Apostolic Blessing to
Msgr. Francis J. Weber
and invokes an abundance of divine graces,
on the occasion of his Golden Sacerdotal Jubilee,
El Camino Real,
1959 - 2009.

In Pre World War II, "Made in Japan" meant junk and the term "making out" referred to how you did on an exam. Pizzas, fast foods and instant coffee were unheard of. There were no malls, ATMs or cell phones.

We came on the scene when there were dime stores where people bought things for five and ten cents; ice cream cones sold for a nickel; for a dime you could ride a subway, bus or streetcar, make a phone call,

This reversible
stole was given to
Fr. Francis J. Weber
by Betty Rooney
for his ordination
in 1959. It was
once worn by
Pope Pius XII

This chalice was
manufactured by the
Gordan Jewelrey
Company of New
York in 1887 and
presented to Father
Francis J. Weber by
Msgr. Thomas F.
Fogarty (1903-1966)
in 1959.

MSGR. F. WEBER

MSGR. FRANCIS J. WEBER

Thomas Cassidy, the "Voice of the Hollywood Bowl".

Stan Chambers of KTLA.

buy a Pepsi, or enough stamps to mail one letter and two postcards. You could purchase a new Chevy coupe for $600 and gasoline was eleven cents a gallon.

In our day, cigarette smoking was fashionable only for men, GRASS was mowed, COKE was a cold drink, POT was a vessel you cooked in, and CRACK was something you didn't step on. ROCK MUSIC was a Grandma's Lullaby and AIDS were helpers in the principal's office.

When I was ordained, fifty years ago, all liturgical services in the Roman Catholic Church were conducted in LATIN, Fridays and other days on the liturgical calendar were MEATLESS, no Masses were offered on vigils of Sundays and Holy Days. There were no permanent deacons or extraordinary ministers, nor any Masses offered facing the people, except in the Eternal City.

We made do with what we had. Occasionally we were surprised and maybe confused, but we enjoyed it when the Lord pulled aside the curtain. And, thanks be to God, we became survivors! May we rest in peace!

The reception in Cantwell Hall went quite well, with over 450 people attending. *Las Damas Archivistas* provided a wonderful culinary presentation, and my nephew, Tom Castagna, took a host of pictures. Given as a keepsake for that occasion was a folder with some personal reflections.

Miniature Book

In addition to a colorful memorial card, I commissioned a miniature book to be printed by Pat Reagh and bound by Mariana Blau, which told about "Old Melchisidek," an ancient mountain revered by many native Americans. Tipped into that little book was a commemorative United States postage stamp, issued for the Golden Jubilee of Devil's Tower National Monument.

The text of the twelve-page miniature book is here reproduced for the edification of readers:

There's a very high mountain known to the Shoshone Indians as Melchisidek, a picturesque elevation which has served for centuries as a landmark for the natives. When returning from some distant place, their hearts were overjoyed at seeing that shapely old mound of earth which reminded them that home was near-at-hand.

In wintertime, partially concealed by snow and fog, only its towering pinnacle assured the Shoshones of old M's presence. Early each spring, the snows melt, the fog blows away, the greenery returns and the historic mountain stands out once again—alone, majestic and supreme!

There has always been something supernaturally fascinating about M. Even today the freshness of its mountain air bestows new life on those who scale its peaks, restores vital signs to the abusers of nature, nourishes

Vicar General Msgr. Royale Vadakin.

with its flora and fauna, joins together forever those who exchange their pledges of love and, ultimately, hides from sight the earthly remains of those who fall asleep.

Presenting a formidable obstacle to physical endurance and human ingenuity, the statistics of its height are frequently misjudged by the careless, the steepness of its cliffs underestimated by the ignorant and the difficulties of its assent minimized by the unconcerned. The path of its trails is overlooked by the inattentive and the challenge of reaching its pinnacle belittled by the cowardly.

Yet, because it is high and strong and many years old, the presence of ancient M. conveys a clear message to sinners and saints, provides a haven, for the living and the dead and offers shelter for the ill and handicapped. The very sight of the mountain motivates the young and the old, while giving solace to the hunted and beleaguered.

Even when socked-in by layers of fog, the venerable mountain serves as a refuge for homeless creatures, sustains the life of plants and trees and exerts influence over the forces of nature. It makes food available to the hungry and deprived, while rejuvenating the weary and the travel-worn.

In 2009, as they have for centuries, the Shoshones steal away to the shadowy recesses of old M to reveal the secrets of their troubled souls, share the burdens of sorrowful experiences and heal the wounds of earlier battles. Its lofty grandeur helps dispel the doubts of weakened hearts, as it rekindles confidence for future conquests.

Those few chosen to identify personally with the mountain spend long years orientating their lives to the things of God, adjusting their pace to

Golden Jubilee Luncheon.

the service of His people and learning to explain the secrets of nature. They discipline themselves to observing His law, as they acquaint themselves with humankind's innermost needs.

The mountain is, of course, the priest of God. M refers to the Shoshones, the priest is Jesus Christ.

> For the priesthood, it is wintertime now. The mountain is shrouded in fog and covered with snow. Only the pinnacle is visible. Pray God that we may live until spring, when the fog of doubt will blow away, the snow of confusion will melt and the richness of the priesthood once more will flower forth as Christ lived it as Christ meant it to be—alone (in its human dignity), majestic (in its divine functions) and supreme (in its sacramental efficacy).

We kept open the "octave" of the celebration which included breakfasts lunches and/or dinners at Saint Victor's Parish in West Hollywood (my first assignment), the Archdiocesan Catholic Center (where I have been on staff for 47 years), Sister Disciples of the Divine Master (Los Angeles) and several private dinners. It was surely not a successful "Jenny Craig" octave. In the midst of it all I went out to Santa Cruz Island on May 2nd for our annual trek which included Mass, a gala outdoor barbeque and a beautiful cake with my logo spelled out in colorful and caloric sugar.

Memory Book

Someone suggested that I keep a *Memory Book* of the events surrounding the jubilee. It turned out to be a splendid idea and the book itself has been entrusted to the Archival Center for safekeeping.

The initial entry in the book is devoted to the thirteen of us who gathered in the Serra Chapel at San Fernando Mission on the actual day of the anniversary, April 30th, for a con-celebrated Mass. A photo of the group appeared in the May 16th *Daily News*. Each participant signed the *Memory Book.*

Those who attended the anniversary reception on May 3rd came next, with each one affixing his or her signature to the book. Then came copies of the "memberships" in a half dozen pious groups, along with a copy of my sermon at the two Masses celebrated earlier that day.

The events listed were meals and other gatherings, each one signed by attendants. The photo section featured thirty-eight notables including Thomas Cassidy (KFAC), Stan Chambers, (KTLA), Msgr. Royale Vadakin (Vicar General), Gary Strong (UCLA Librarian), Bob Sullivan (San Diego), Joe Ryan (San Luis Obispo), Leo Mathos (Tulare), and my beloved sister, Mary Alice Castagna who played a prominent place in all the festivities.

Surely the most treasured inscription in the book was that signed by Roger Cardinal Mahony who wrote:

> Monsignor Francis Weber has served the Church of California with an extraordinary depth of knowledge, wisdom, and the expertise to chronicle

Through the intervention of Kevin Feeney, the United States Postal service marked the golden priestly jubilee with a special 44¢ commemorative stamp.

Sister Mary Jean Meier.
(1925–2010)

> our history in a manner which keeps alive the spirit of Jesus Christ in these lands for generations to come. Without his scholarship and leadership I fear that our past decades and centuries would remain a blur of partial memories. Instead, Msgr. Frank has traced the hand of God through various epics of evangelization in this hallowed portion of the Lord's Vineyard.
>
> I am deeply grateful for our friendship which began at Los Angeles College in the 1950s and continues forward to this very day. Ad Multos Annos!

Included in the *Memory Book* is an "Epilogue" which summarizes the event.

> Almost 450 people gathered here at San Fernando Mission on May 3, 2009, to honor the Old Country Priest upon his golden priestly anniversary, including two people who were with me at my first Solemn High Mass at Saint Brendan Church in Los Angeles.
>
> In the interest of total disclosure, I am writing to tell you about the financial blessings that accrued to the Old Mission on the occasion of my fiftieth priestly anniversary.
>
> When I was ordained, associate priests received a monthly stipend of $75 and pastors $100. (In other words I could have expected a **lifetime** income of $45,000.) While that wasn't much, we managed to get along quite well with that modest amount.
>
> Of course, in subsequent years, the stipend was increased but, even today, priests are meagerly compensated. I'm not complaining, but just telling you the facts.
>
> **When my jubilee was planned, I said that no personal gifts were expected. However, I did pledge that offerings to the San Fernando Mission Endowment Fund would be gratefully accepted.**
>
> Never for a moment did I anticipate such a response. A total of $55,545 was sent to the Old Country Priest by friends in the local area, other parts along *El Camino Real*, and even from far away bastions around the country at large—a lifetime payment in a single month!
>
> **I want you to know that my original pledge has been observed to the penny**. Kevin has opened an account which will pay an annual amount to San Fernando Mission *per omnia saecula saeculorum*.
>
> **Many thanks and God's blessings!**

Those who participated in various aspects of my golden priestly jubilee will remain in my prayers until the Lord summons the Old Country Priest from planet earth.

On June 17th, *Las Damas Archivistas* gathered at the local Soup Plantation for a luncheon and, in mid-July, my sister, Mary Alice Castagna, had a number of relatives and friends to dinner at her home in Monterey.

To paraphrase Pere Lacordaire, "What a wonderful life it's been—o priest of Jesus Christ!"

21
Retirement

When I was ordained, a half-century ago, "retirement" among Catholic clergymen was not a familiar term or even a remote possibility. Priests were ordained "forever" and generally stayed at their posts until carted off to the local bone-yard. Even in those fairly rare cases when a priest was no longer physically able to function, the archbishop would appoint an administrator to the parish in question while the canonical pastor remained in place.

That all began to change in the 1980s when regulations were put into place for mandatory retirement. If I remember correctly, a priest could ask for retirement at seventy and was required to retire at seventy-five.

By late 1995, after thirty-three years as archivist, it seemed that I should allow the cardinal the option of selecting a new archivist. I had been on the job for over three decades and I told him that "I would be willing to step aside," noting that I didn't want to stay a single instant longer than "suited his pleasure". He very kindly responded that he was "absolutely delighted with all that you do as our archivist. It is my fond hope that you will retain that position for at least two years following my own retirement in the year 2011!"

My fortieth anniversary as archivist was mentioned in *The Tidings*.

> On Dec. 28, Msgr. Francis J. Weber will mark his 40th year as archivist for the Archdiocese of Los Angeles. Appointed by Cardinal James Francis McIntyre, Msgr. Weber oversaw the construction of a two-story annex at the former archdiocesan headquarters on Ninth Street in downtown Los Angeles that was completed and blessed by Cardinal McIntyre in 1963. In 1981, the archives were moved to their present quarters in a newly erected building on the grounds adjacent to the San Fernando Mission in Mission Hills. Additional storage space was acquired in 1995 in the nearby basement of Alemany High School, where the Cathedral Archives were also located in 2002. The extensively-organized and carefully-preserved archival collections include materials gathered by proto bishop Fray Francisco Garcia Diego y Moreno in 1842.

On January 3rd, 2003, The cardinal wrote the Old Country Priest the following letter:

> I am so grateful to you for the forty years that you have served as Archivist for the Archdiocese of Los Angeles.
>
> I doubt that this record has ever been matched anywhere in the country, and it surely will not be matched here in the Archdiocese in the future. Your leadership in the field of archival expertise is unparalleled, and you have helped so many other Archdioceses and Dioceses to see the great importance of good archives and sound archival policy and methodology. You have truly been a great gift to us!
>
> Thanking you again for all that you do for the good of the Archdiocese and for the Church, and with kindest personal regard.

Later that very month, another letter arrived "from headquarters."

> I understand that congratulations are in order tomorrow for a very auspicious occasion—your 70th birthday!
>
> Even though you have given yourself the title of "The Old Country Priest," I must remind you that you must plan for many years in the future. We can't let go of you until you have finished a complete narrative of the Archdiocese. That will be many years in the future.
>
> Your celebration of a significant milestone provides an opportunity for me once again to thank you for your many years of selfless ministry, and for the loyalty and support you have given to me and the Archdiocese. You know that I am grateful.

Over the ensuing years the cardinal reiterated his views. On August 21, 2007, I wrote him about the matter thusly:

> Several times in recent years you have suggested that I stay on until your own retirement I am willing to do that, if you are still of that mind and if my health allows.
>
> However, since I work mostly with the leadership team and Marge Graf you might want to ask if my remaining would be acceptable to them.
>
> There is little likelihood that San Fernando Mission will have Sunday or weekly Masses when I leave and, for that reason also, I would like to continue looking after the 500 or 600 people, who attend Mass here.
>
> Kevin Feeney, who was hired to eventually take my place, would be amenable to my staying for a while longer.
>
> Since I am not a "canonical pastor", the rules for retirement are not so definitive.

By return mail, the cardinal had this to say:

> Thank you very much for your kind letter of August 21, 2007, and I was so delighted that you would be willing to remain on as the Archdiocesan Archivist through my own term of office as Archbishop.

Your work for the good of the Archdiocese reached a new height during the sexual misconduct scandal because you had the archives so well organized that we were able to go back many decades into the history of the Archdiocese to locate essential documents and files. I shudder to think what would have happened had we not had an archival system so well developed and advanced.

You are correct that it might be difficult to find someone to celebrate the Masses at the Mission after your retirement, and therefore, I am very open to the plan which you have suggested.

Kevin Feeney is a very fine person who has been ably trained by you in this field, and I would anticipate a seamless transition when the time comes.

Then on December 5, 2007, another letter arrived, telling me:

Having consulted with Bishop Gerald Wilkerson and Monsignor Gabriel Gonzales, I believe that it would be extremely fitting that you remain beyond the June 30, 2008 date. Consequently, I am hereby dispensing you from the norm regarding the term for administrators here in the Archdiocese, and I wish to extend your appointment until I retire from the Archdiocese.

You have been a superb administrator and Archivist at San Fernando Mission Parish, and both you and that parish community have worked so well together. There is certainly no need to interrupt the pastoral stability and continuity which you have established so well.

On my birthday, a month later, the cardinal again wrote:

I understand that next Tuesday, January 22, is a red-letter day as you reach your 75th birthday.

Felicitations and warm congratulations as you celebrate that anniversary. However, good friend and unsurpassed Archivist, remember that you have permission to celebrate that day, and then I count on you to keep going—doing what you have done so admirably these 40+ years.

Have a wonderful day, Frank, and know that you will be very specially in my thoughts and prayers on Tuesday.

Thinking that I should inform the good people hereabouts, I sent the following letter out on February 2, 2008.

I am told that a favorite topic of conversation (gossip) here at the Old Mission is my "retirement". The archdiocese does indeed have a policy that priests must retire at 75 and that milestone passed for me on January 22nd of the current year.

Some months ago the Cardinal mentioned this to me, asking if I would be willing to stay on until his own retirement in three years. Not having any special plans for retirement, I agreed.

All of which explains a letter received in December, which reads:

I am hereby dispensing you from the norm regarding the term for administrators here in the Archdiocese, and I wish to extend your appointment until I retire.

Now, of course, this whole arrangement depends on the Lord's will. Maybe you good people could pray that my health will hold out for a while longer.

Interestingly there were several letters and verbal reactions. Patti and Charlene Flores wrote to say:

When we moved back to California, our search for that same reverence at Mass brought both of us much frustration and sadness. We actually live in Chatsworth, quite close to St. John Eudes Church, and my daughter attends St. Euphrasia Catholic School, so we have of course attended Masses at both, as well as numerous other churches in the area. I know I can't comment or criticize on what I feel is lacking in other churches, but I will say that when we "tried" mass at your mission, we felt like we had finally found our "home", and we now travel across the valley to attend. Occasionally we are forced to travel out-of-town or our Sunday schedule requires that we attend a Saturday night Mass, which means we can't attend at the Mission. On those occasions we truly miss your Mass. I know from chatting briefly with other "regulars" at your masses, that many, many folks travel quite long distances to attend your Masses for similar reasons.

What this is all leading to is . . . THANK YOU FOR NOT RETIRING! Before you left for your surgery, you mentioned that you had been thinking about it. My heart skipped a beat and at the same time my daughter grasped my hand tightly. I'll admit my gratitude is very selfish, and that you most certainly deserve to retire after so many years of dedicated service to our Church, but your delays in making that final decision are very much appreciated!!!

We pray every night for your quick and complete recovery, and hope you are well and mobile enough to truly enjoy a wonderful Thanksgiving holiday!

Take care, and may God bless you abundantly!

Another voice came to the fore when Andrea and Jake Kostyzak wrote on one of their pinkies:

The "old priest" cannot be replaced!!! He is one of a kind and terrific!!

There were others, a lot of them. But since I am not yet a candidate for sainthood, we can leave them to a later time.

One final related item emerged from a letter written by Del Acevedo to *The Tidings* about "Flags in Church."

At last I do not feel like a rat deserting a sinking ship each time I have changed parishes because the pastor does not display the American flag except maybe on national holidays. Thank you, Jerry Mazenko, for your letter (March 23). We're so lucky to live in a country that allow us to worship as we choose, so I feel that displaying our flag is the least we can do.

I finally found a church, San Fernando Mission, where the American flag is displayed along with the Vatican flag and the petitions always include a prayer for our men and women serving all over the world. Msgr. Francis Weber is a delight to have him celebrate Mass; I wish I had heard of him sooner. The drive is a bit farther but well worth the extra miles.

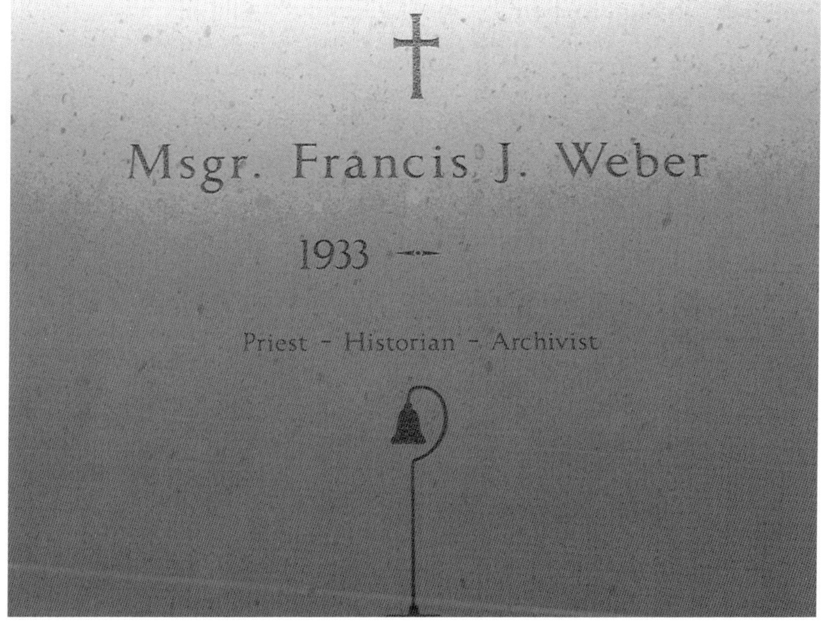

Permanent Earthly Residence at Cathedral of Our Lady of the Angels.

22
Finale

There will be no more *"Memories"* from The Old Country Priest. That's a promise.

As I approach the culmination of my earthly sojourn, I would like to invoke the words and sentiments which a fellow traveler along California's *El Camino Real* uttered a century ago:

A little more tired at close of day;
A little less anxious to have my way:
A little less ready to scold and blame;
A little more care for another's name;
A broader view and a saner mind;
A little more love for all mankind;
A little more charity in all my views;
A little less thirst for the daily news;
A little more leisure to sit and dream;
A little more real the things unseen-
And so I am moving a-down the way
That leads to the gates of a better day.

Appendix I

CONFERRING
the
DOCTOR OF HUMANE LETTERS DEGREE
upon
MSGR. FRANCIS J. WEBER
APRIL 30, 2010

"Those of us who live
and move among books
are probably among the
happiest of earthly creatures
for we are more apt than others
to learn their lessons and
live by their tenets."

This appendix reproduces the text of the commendation given by Dr. John Wallace at the conferral of the honorary doctorate at Azusa Pacific College on April 30, 2010.

AUTHOR and theologian Frederick Buechner reminds us that a vocation is a calling, "the work a person is called to by God." Where some are called to be historians, others are called to be essayists. Where some are called to be authors, others are called to be editors. Where some are called to be researchers, others are called to be archivists. Where some are called to be librarians, others are called to be bibliographers. Where some are called to be collectors of books, others are called to build collections for others. In the case of Msgr. Francis J. Weber, he has been called to wear all of these hats. Indeed, he has served his many vocations not only with distinction but also with an inclusive, welcoming generosity.

Azusa Pacific University has been the beneficiary of Msgr. Weber's many vocations and his largess in terms of gifts to the university's special collections.

Without cost to the university he has kept current the "Msgr. Francis J. Weber Collection" of rare books, fine printings, and monographs, including his considerable writings. In addition, he donated his impressive collection of "Presidential Signatures" from George Washington to George W. Bush to the university. One of the highlights of the collection is a presidential pardon signed by Abraham Lincoln. Recently he gifted APU with his personal copy of Francisco Palou's 1787 biography of Junípero Serra, a foundational book for the study of California history. For the past thirty-five years, Msgr. Weber has provided encouragement and support for the development of APU's rare book and manuscript collections in ways that define the role of servant leader.

Msgr. Weber recently celebrated his Golden Jubilee, fifty years as a priest. Among his many accomplishments, he has enjoyed a distinguished career as archivist for the Archdiocese of Los Angeles, now located at Mission San Fernando Rey de España. His archive is frequently cited as a model of organization and accessibility to researchers. He took on a second endeavor that lasted for almost thirty years, during which time he wrote a weekly historical column in the Catholic newspaper, *The Tidings*. It was a labor of love that turned out to be very successful in making history more appealing to the wider, general audience. Later, the articles were collected and published in eleven anthologies. Somewhere in all

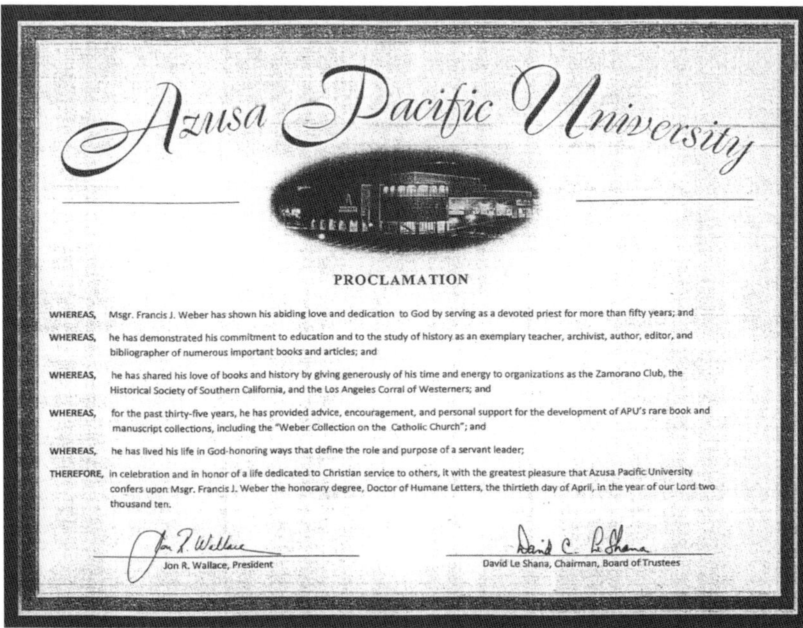

Azusa Pacific University

PROCLAMATION

WHEREAS, Msgr. Francis J. Weber has shown his abiding love and dedication to God by serving as a devoted priest for more than fifty years; and

WHEREAS, he has demonstrated his commitment to education and to the study of history as an exemplary teacher, archivist, author, editor, and bibliographer of numerous important books and articles; and

WHEREAS, he has shared his love of books and history by giving generously of his time and energy to organizations as the Zamorano Club, the Historical Society of Southern California, and the Los Angeles Corral of Westerners; and

WHEREAS, for the past thirty-five years, he has provided advice, encouragement, and personal support for the development of APU's rare book and manuscript collections, including the "Weber Collection on the Catholic Church"; and

WHEREAS, he has lived his life in God-honoring ways that define the role and purpose of a servant leader;

THEREFORE, in celebration and in honor of a life dedicated to Christian service to others, it with the greatest pleasure that Azusa Pacific University confers upon Msgr. Francis J. Weber the honorary degree, Doctor of Humane Letters, the thirtieth day of April, in the year of our Lord two thousand ten.

Jon R. Wallace, President

David Le Shana, Chairman, Board of Trustees

of this, he found time to teach at several local colleges, and to write, edit, and compile an impressive number of books, articles, essays, and bibliographies on California history. Students of California's religious and ecclesiastical history, for example, would do well to start their research by considering the vast array of works by Msgr. Weber.

The Weber Collection at Azusa Pacific University includes the writings of four distinguished Catholic historians: Msgr. John Tracy Ellis, Msgr. Weber's mentor at the Catholic University of America; Peter Guilday; Thomas T. McAvoy, C.S.C.; and Msgr. Francis J. Weber. The collection also includes many valuable journals and reference works as *The Catholic Historical Review, The Catholic University of America Studies in American Church History, The Illinois Catholic Historical Review, La Cruz, Annales de l'Association de la propagation de la foi, United States Catholic Historical Society Monograph Series, The Catholic University of America Canon Law Studies, and Records of the American Catholic Historical Society of Philadelphia*, among others. Standing alone these scholarly volumes are a welcome addition to the university's holdings, but there is more.

In 1961 Msgr. Weber set out a plan to do a series of publications on California Catholic history. He has faithfully carried out his plan over the past four decades, producing several basic documentary reference works; eight ecclesial biographies from Francisco Garcia Diego y Moreno to Timothy Cardinal Manning; twenty-two volumes documenting the history of California missions, from Mission San Diego de Alcala to Mission San Francisco de Solano; three documentary histories of California's asistencias, presidio chapels, and estancias; an *Encyclopedia of California's Catholic Heritage*; a history of the Archdiocese of Los Angeles; numerous ancillary monographs and bibliographies; and two autobiographical volumes, *Some Historical Reflections* and *Memories of an Old Country Priest*. It is the infusion of his own scholarly labors that makes the Weber Collection such an enduring treasure.

Msgr. Weber also writes and collects miniature books. I am told he has produced more miniature books that carry his name and imprint than any other individual. APU is fortunate to have a fine collection of his miniatures. His personal collection of miniature books, incidentally, was so extensive and impressive that it is now housed in the Huntington Library. In addition, as a lover of books and history, he has given generously of his time and expertise to organizations like the Zamorano Club, the Historical Society of Southern California, and the Los Angeles Corral of Westerners, where he has served on the boards and in positions of administrative leadership. The welcome of his presence has strengthened and energized these important historical and bibliophilic organizations.

Finally, it should be noted that while it may be true that "no man is an island," it is also true that one person can make a difference—a difference with life-changing consequences for years and years to come. Msgr. Weber, devoted priest, proficient historian, exemplary archivist, insatiable bibliographer, and consummate bookman, has made such a difference for this university, for this president, and for the faculty and students.

THEREFORE, by the power vested in me by the State of California and by the Trustees of Azusa Pacific University, I hereby confer upon Msgr. Francis J. Weber the degree Doctor of Humane Letters.

Congratulations!

Jon R. Wallace President

Azusa Pacific University

Fifty copies of this keepsake
were produced for
Msgr. Francis J. Weber,
family and friends
to commemorate
April 30, 2010.
The Parker Press ••••• North Hollywood
www.theparkerpress.com

Appendix II

The following essay appeared in *THE TIDINGS* for May 28, 2010.
CALIFORNIA'S CATHOLIC HERITAGE
A New Chapter Begins for Southland

The Church in California's southland has come full circle. The first bishop was Mexican-born and soon the leadership will be passing to a new prelate who also originates from that great republic to the south.

Though already launched toward its tricentennial, there is still something fresh and exciting about the one-time *Pueblo de Nuestra Señora de los Angeles.* The story of its progress, from Hispanic colonial foundation to international center for learning, art and commerce is as much a work of imagination as it is of history.

Historians and others maintain that more than any other major city, Los Angeles has achieved its unique place in human annals because a handful of pioneers—from the Kings of Spain to the barons of land, rail and industry—dreamt and decreed that it would be so, and because thousands of others, working people from Sonora and Indiana, Shanghai and Odessa, bought and built accordingly.

Los Angeles is not perched aside the confluence of major waterways or along a vital commercial route; it is not blessed with a great natural harbor or outstanding physical location; neither was it built atop some ancient center of human habitation or upon a pre-existing religious cult. About all the city ever had and continues to have is an unequalled place in human imagination. But, that's what really counts when all the chips are down.

If New York is identified on bumper stickers as the "Big Apple," and Chicago as "gangsters gulch," then Los Angeles must surely be the city of the giant dream, the grand illusion and the hard reality.

Unimpressed by its own past and certainly not intimidated by that of its sister cities, *El Pueblo de Nuestra Señora de los Angeles* is a place where everyone is entitled to a second, even a third chance.

Coajutor Archbishop Jose H. Gomez.

On January 17, 1837, just a year and a half after Los Angeles had been raised to the status of a city, the *ayuntamiento* or council passed, without a dissenting voice, a resolution declaring that "the Roman Catholic apostolic religion shall prevail throughout this jurisdiction."

While there is no evidence that this expressed but never enforced "establishment of religion" benefitted Catholics, it did provide adherents with a unique distinction in Western Americana's historical annals.

For some years Los Angeles continued to be a "Catholic" enclave, with most of its inhabitants worshipping, at least sporadically, at the Old Plaza Church. Oh, that's not to say that the *pueblo* was, by any means, a virtuous city. Unfortunately, the Catholic Church has always been blessed (or cursed) with more than its share of renegades.

Angelenos have never measured the cost nor considered the contradictions of their accomplishments. Their quest for water, to cite an outstanding example, is a monumental feat of human ingenuity and skill.

Or, again, when pressing demands of new immigrants and the financial interests of aggressive developers converged in postwar Los Angeles, the San Fernando and San Gabriel valleys blossomed forth with suburban housing tracts that defied demographers around the globe.

Probably no community in all of recorded history managed to house so many of its working-class and middle-income people so well, while continuing to provide them with amenities usually associated only with the wealthy. For the thousands who continue to pour into the area annually, Los Angeles is the community that invented itself. It remains the city of exceptions and exceptional "dreamers."

And why not? After all, was it not the "Dreamers of God" who began it all for *El Pueblo de Nuestra Señora de los Angeles?*

Before long, Archbishop Jose Gomez will become a fully-integrated Angeleno. Maybe he will eventually tell his friends about the youngster who was brought to the west in 1902 for his health. He wrote his mother and told her to tell his friends that: "I have died and gone to heaven." The letter was postmarked "Los Angeles"

Msgr. Francis J. Weber

Appendix III

Chronological list of books written, edited, translated, compiled and / or published by Msgr. Francis J. Weber., 2001–2011

156 (2001) *Books, Books, Books,*

157 (2001) *A Remarkable Legacy*

158 (2003) *A Tradition of Outreach*

159 (2003) *A Legacy of Healing*

160 (2003) *Requiescant in Pace*

161 (2004) *Unity in Diversity*

162 (2004) *Cathedral of Our Lady of Angels*

163 (2005) *The California Missions*

164 (2006) *A History of the Archdiocese of Los Angeles*

165 (2006) *Una Historia de la Arquidiocesis de Los Angeles y sus jurisdicciones Presursoras en el sur de California*

166 (2007) *Catholic Heroes in Southern California*

167 (2007) *San Fernando, Rey de España Mission*

168 (2008) *Blessed Fray Junípero Serra*

169 (2011) *More Memories of An Old Country Priest.*

Appendix IV

Chronological list of Miniature Books, written, edited, translated, compiled and / or published by Msgr. Francis J. Weber, 2000–2009

112. (2000) *Our Lady of the Angels*

113. (2000) *The First Mass in California*

114. (2003) *The Bayeux Tapestry*

115. (2004) *The Veil of Veronica*

116. (2004) *Blessed Teresa of Calcutta*

117. (2005) *The Ronald Reagan Presidential Library*

118. (2005) *John Paul the Great, a Eulogy*

119. (2006) *Bob Hope Memorial Garden*

120. (2007) *Hershey*

121. (2007) *Toward Equality in Our Schools: Mendez vs. Westminster*

122. (2009) *Space Needle*

123. (2009) *A Memoir 1959–2009*

124. (2009) *Air Force One*

125. (2009) *Cesar Chavez*

126. (2009) *Benjamin Franklin*

UNITED STATES OF AMERICA
UNITED STATES OF AMERICA
AIR FORCE ONE
December 28, 2005

Index

Page numbers in italic type refer to pages that contain photographs or illustrations. The abbreviation FW indicates references to the author, Msgr. Francis Weber. Unfortunately, titles of clergymen and religious were omitted in the preparation of this Index.